D1334377

Past and Present Publications

General Editor: PAUL SLACK, *Exeter College, Oxford*

Past and Present Publications comprise books similar in character to the articles in the journal *Past and Present*. Whether the volumes in the series are collections of essays – some previously published, others new studies – or monographs, they encompass a wide variety of scholarly and original works primarily concerned with social, economic and cultural changes, and their causes and consequences. They will appeal to both specialists and non-specialists and will endeavour to communicate the results of historical and allied research in readable and lively form. This new series continues and expands in its aims the volumes previously published elsewhere.

For a list of titles in Past and Present Publications, see end of book.

Past and Present Publications

Rituals of Royalty

Rituals of Royalty

Power and Ceremonial in Traditional Societies

edited by

DAVID CANNADINE

and

SIMON PRICE

The right of the
University of Cambridge
to print and sell
all manner of books
was granted by
Henry VIII in 1534.
The University has printed
and published continuously
since 1584.

CAMBRIDGE UNIVERSITY PRESS

Cambridge
London   New York   New Rochelle
Melbourne   Sydney

Published by the Press Syndicate of the University of Cambridge
The Pitt Building, Trumpington Street, Cambridge CB2 1RP
32 East 57th Street, New York, NY 10022, USA
10 Stamford Road, Oakleigh, Melbourne 3166, Australia

First published 1987

Printed in Great Britain at the University Press, Cambridge

British Library cataloguing in publication data

Rituals of royalty: power and ceremonial
in traditional societies. – (Past and present publications)
1. Rites and ceremonies – History
2. Kings and rulers
I. Cannadine, David. II. Price, Simon
III. Series
394'.4'09   GN473

Library of Congress cataloguing in publication data

Rituals of royalty.
(Past and present publications)
Includes index.
Contents: Usurpation, conquest, and ceremonial/
Amélie Kuhrt – From noble funerals to divine cult/
Simon Price – The construction of court ritual/
Averil Cameron – [etc.]
1. Rites and rulers – Cross-cultural studies.
2. Kings and rulers – Cross-cultural studies.
3. Power (Social sciences) – Cross-cultural studies.
I. Cannadine, David, 1950–   . II. Price, S. R. F.
GT5010.R56 1987   390'.22   86–29881

ISBN 0 521 33513 2

CE

Contents

Illustrations

Contributors

MAURICE BLOCH is Professor of Anthropology at the London School of Economics. His most recent book is *From Blessing to Violence* (1986). He is pursuing research on Madagascar and on Japan.

RICHARD BURGHART is Lecturer in Asian Anthropology at the School of Oriental and African Studies, London. He has recently edited *Hinduism in Great Britain: the Perpetuation of Religion in an Alien Cultural Milieu* and with Audrey Cantlie has edited *Indian Religion*. He is working on an historical study of the formation of the modern state in Nepal.

AVERIL CAMERON is Professor of Ancient History at King's College, London. Her most recent book is *Procopius* (1985) and in 1986 she gave the Sather Classical Lectures at Berkeley, to be published as *Christianity and the Rhetoric of Empire*.

DAVID CANNADINE is a Fellow of Christ's College, Cambridge and a University Lecturer in History. He is the author of *Lords and Landlords: The Aristocracy and the Towns 1774–1967* (1980), editor of *Patricians, Power and Politics in Nineteenth Century Towns* (1982), and co-editor of *Exploring the Urban Past: Essays in Urban History by H. J. Dyos* (1982).

MICHELLE GILBERT is a Mellon Fellow at the University of Pennsylvania. She took her Ph.D. in anthropology at the School of Oriental and African Studies, University of London in 1981. She did research on ritual and politics in the Akan Kingdom of Akuapem, Ghana in 1976–8.

AMÉLIE KUHRT is a Lecturer in History at University College, London. She has written a number of articles on Babylonian history in the Old Persian and Hellenistic periods, and co-edited a book on women in antiquity. She is currently preparing an introduction to the history of the ancient Near East before Alexander, and a source-book on the Old Persian empire.

DAVID McMULLEN is a University Lecturer in Chinese Studies at Cambridge and a Fellow of St John's College. He is pursuing research into the academic institutions of the T'ang dynasty (AD 608–906) in China.

JANET L. NELSON is a Lecturer in History at King's College, London. She has published *Politics and Ritual in the Early Middle Ages* (1986) and is currently working on a political study of Charles the Bald.

SIMON PRICE is Fellow and Tutor in Ancient History at Lady Margaret Hall, Oxford. The author of *Rituals and Power: the Roman Imperial Cult in Asia Minor* (1984), he is now co-authoring a book on Roman religion.

Acknowledgements

This book has grown out of our common interest in royal rituals, ancient and modern. Today's heads of state mark their 'rites of passage' with splendid ceremonial, from Reagan's inaugural to Andropov's funeral. Such spectacles continue to be a prominent part of modern political systems, of varied ideological hue, but their precise significance remains unclear. Although the societies studied in this book are far from our contemporary world in space and time, we share a conviction that these essays address a problem of abiding importance – the relation between power and ceremonial.

We should like to thank the contributors for their forebearance during the time that this book has been in the making, and also for their co-operation in reworking successive drafts of their chapters at our request.

DNC
September 1985   SRFP

Introduction: divine rites of kings

DAVID CANNADINE

> And what have kings, that privates have not too,
> Save ceremony, save general ceremony?
> And what art thou, thou idol ceremony?
> What kind of god art thou, that suffer'st more
> Of mortal griefs than do thy worshippers?
> What are thy rents? what are thy comings in?
> O ceremony, show me but thy worth!
> What is thy soul of adoration?
> Art thou aught else but place, degree and form,
> Creating awe and fear in other men?
>
> *Henry V*, Act IV, Scene i.

> Our theories tell us that the ceremonies of public life are merely the trappings of power. But it may be that such contentions are no less misleading about our own society than they are about classical Bali. Perhaps our own rituals are far more than drapery; perhaps they too play an altogether different and more substantial role in political affairs.
>
> Quentin Skinner, 'The World as a Stage', *New York Review of Books*, 16 April 1981, p. 37.

Power is like the wind: we cannot see it, but we feel its force. Ceremonial is like the snow: an insubstantial pageant, soon melted into thin air. The invisible and the ephemeral are, by definition, not the easiest of subjects for scholars to study. But this conceals, more than it indicates, their real importance. Many political historians – from the left and right, concerned with ruling élites or with mass movements – construe their subject rather narrowly, as the archival sources directly dictate both the topics they treat and the questions they ask. For them, the structure of politics is accepted as axiomatic, and the theatre of power is ignored as irrelevant.[1] But while

[1] For examples from the right and the left, see: L. B. Namier, *The Structure of Politics at the Accession of George III* (London, 2nd edn, 1957); *idem*, *England in the Age of the American Revolution* (2nd edn, London, 1961); E. P. Thompson, *The Making of the English Working Class* (Harmondsworth, 1968). Unlike Namier, Thompson's later work has become much more concerned with both the

1

the fortuitous survival of documents may guarantee future immortality, it is no necessary indication of real historical significance. Much that has been of greatest importance in the past lacks adequate archival evidence, and some of the most significant historical happenings have been over in the twinkling of an eye. It is often difficult to discern the underlying contours of an alien age; but that is no reason for refusing to look for them. It may not be easy to rekindle the glow of certain past events; but that is no justification for failing to try.

THE SCHOLARLY STUDY OF POWER AND POMP

Indeed, scholars from other disciplines and from other historical traditions have often argued for a much broader conception of political action, not as the decontextualised analysis of high or of low politics, but as the study of power in society, and as a system of social relations. For many sociologists, politics is not confined to the doings of those in authority and the responses of those who are subordinate, but is treated more widely, as the varied means whereby hierarchies of dominance and deference are created, maintained and overturned. Viewed in this light, the study of power is not limited to asking questions about who governs and how they govern, but involves an investigation of how it is that important issues and options are kept *off* the agenda of public discourse altogether.[2] In particular, some sociologists are concerned with the ways in which ruling élites try to make alternative and subversive modes of thought seem off-limits and even unthinkable, and seek to present what is in fact only one *particular* way of ordering and organising society as authoritative and God-given.[3] Not surprisingly, then, the power of ceremonial and the ceremonials of power have been major areas of interests for sociologists studying the workings of advanced industrial societies.[4]

structure and the theatre of politics: see E. P. Thompson, *Whigs and Hunters: The Origins of the Black Act* (London, 1975); *idem*, 'Eighteenth-century English society: class struggle without class?', *Social History*, iii (1978).

[2] R. Dahl, *Who Governs? Democracy and Power in an American City* (London, 1961); P. Bachrach and M. Baratz, *Power and Poverty: Theory and Practice* (New York, 1970); S. Lukes, *Power: A Radical View* (London, 1974), esp. pp. 16–27.

[3] S. Lukes, 'Political Ritual and Social Integration', in S. Lukes, *Essays in Social Theory* (London, 1977).

[4] The literature on this subject is vast, and much of it is cited and discussed by Lukes in 'Political Ritual' (see n. 3). But see in particular: E. Shils and M. Young, 'The

Likewise, many anthropologists entertain a notion of politics which is not restricted to the 'great' texts of political theory, or to the letters and infighting of public figures, or to the copious volumes of government publications, or to the interminable *longueurs* of parliamentary debates, but which encompasses instead a much wider spectrum of human activity. For them, political action and political rhetoric include: such artifacts as buildings and city planning, painting and sculpture, flags and costumes; such beliefs as those concerning the divine, magical and sacred properties of kingship; and such events as feasts and festivals, carnivals and ceremonies.[5] And this in turn leads to even more fundamental questions, about the ways in which notions of cosmic order and transcendental hierarchy are deployed and transmitted by ruling élites as a means of ordering their own terrestrial realms and of sustaining their own earthly dominance. For such scholars, the rituals of rulers, the 'symbolics of power', are not mere incidental ephemera, but are central to the structure and working of any society.[6] Indeed, Clifford Geertz has recently developed this argument to its most eloquently articulated extreme by suggesting that in pre-modern Bali, pomp was not in the service of power, but power was in the service of pomp.[7]

How have historians responded to these pioneering approaches from other disciplines? On the negative side, there are a variety of

Meaning of the Coronation', *Sociological Review*, new ser., i (1953); N. Birnbaum, 'Monarchies and Sociologists: a reply to Professor Shils and Mr Young', *Sociological Review*, new ser., iii (1955); J. G. Blumler, J. R. Brown, A. J. Ewbank and T. J. Nossiter, 'Attitudes to the Monarchy: Their Structure and Development during a Ceremonial Occasion', *Political Studies*, xix (1971); R. Rose and D. Kavanagh, 'The Monarchy in Contemporary British Culture', *Comparative Politics*, viii (1976); R. Bellah, 'Civil Religion in America', in R. Bellah, *Beyond Belief: Essays on Religion in a Post-Traditional World* (Los Angeles, 1970); R. Bocock, *Ritual in Industrial Society* (London, 1974); R. L. Grimes, *Symbol and Conquest: Public Ritual and Drama in Santa Fe, New Mexico* (Ithaca, N.Y., 1976); D. Chaney, 'A Symbolic Mirror of Ourselves: Civic Ritual in a Mass Society', *Media, Culture and Society*, v (1983).

5 Again, the bibliography is now enormous, but the following works offer an incisive way in: R. Firth, *Symbols, Public and Private* (London, 1973); V. Turner, *Dramas, Fields and Metaphors; Symbolic Action in Human Society* (London, 1974); G. Feeley-Harnick, 'Issues in Divine Kingship', *Annual Review of Anthropology*, xiv (1984).

6 C. Geertz, 'Centers, Kings and Charisma: Reflections on the Symbolics of Power', in J. Ben-David and T. N. Clark (eds.), *Culture and Its Creators: Essays in Honor of E. Shils* (Chicago and London, 1977).

7 *Idem, Negara: The Theater-State in Nineteenth-Century Bali* (Princeton, 1980), esp. pp. 13, 136.

problems inherent in such treatment of power and pageantry, which they can hardly fail to notice. Some of these studies find it very difficult to deal with time and change: they take a ceremonial which never alters, in a society which is entirely static, with the result that the end product can seem both rigid and over-schematised. Some become so preoccupied with the symbolism of the ritual events themselves that they lose all sense of social context and of historical perspective, and so produce what is little more than ceremonial antiquarianism. Some make the context so full, the description so 'thick', that the pageantry itself almost disappears beneath the mass of detail, the study then becomes virtually a potted account of an entire society, and the original purpose gets rather forgotten.[8] And some are so concerned to recover intuitive layers of personal and subjective meaning that the layers seem to fold inwards in a literary confection, rather than outwards to what historians would recognise as a rigorous scholarly argument.[9]

On the other hand, such approaches have produced some quite outstanding work, have generated a considerable body of theory and ideas, and have lead to the formulation of a broad range of questions highly pertinent to the study of political history conceived in its broadest sense. Some of these, which are primarily sociological in inspiration, centre around the functional relationship between power and ceremonial. Is spectacle the handmaid of power, is it the other way round, or is it something altogether more complex and subtle? Are ceremonial occasions consensual examples of 'collective effervescence', or conflictual instances of 'the mobilisation of bias'? Do such pageants reinforce community, or hierarchy, or both? A second set of questions, more indebted to anthropology, concerns the links between ceremonial events and systems of belief. What is the relation between the earthly order, the heavenly order, and splendour and spectacle? Is the king an exemplary centre or not? Is he a god, or isn't he, and if he is, then how, if at all, does ceremonial bring this about? Taken together, these questions possess a twofold significance: they make the notion of power essentially problematic; and they treat the subject of ceremonial as fundamental and important.

---

[8] For the notion of 'thick' description, see: *idem*, 'Thick Description: Towards an Interpretive Theory of Culture', in *idem*, *The Interpretation of Cultures* (London, 1975), pp. 7, 14.

[9] E. Leach, 'A Poetics of Power', *The New Republic*, 4 April 1981, pp. 30–3.

Not surprisingly, many historians have been influenced by this work in other disciplines, and have in their turn come to treat power broadly, and to take pageantry seriously. Recent work on the emperor cult in Asia Minor suggests that it was a major strand in the web of power which formed the fabric of Roman society.[10] The exact significance of Charlemagne's coronation in AD 800 remains one of the longest-running debates in early medieval history.[11] Ever since Kantorowicz first investigated the idea of 'the king's two bodies', historians have been forced to take seriously the almost Frazerian fact that kingship is often both a political and mystical phenomenon, and that kings are frequently both human and divine.[12] For the early modern period, the pageantry of politics and the politics of pageantry have been extensively studied: in Tudor and Stuart England, in the great courts of western Europe, and in the republics and city states of Renaissance Italy.[13] And for the very modern era, interest is almost as great: the Hanoverian monarchy and the French Revolution; the British in India from the time of the Mutiny; the proliferation of royal, republican and civic spectacles in late nineteenth-century Europe; and the more recent rites of rulers and personality cults in Communist Russia, Nazi Germany and Fascist Italy.[14]

[10] S. R. F. Price, *Rituals and Power: The Roman Imperial Cult in Asia Minor* (Cambridge, 1984).

[11] R. E. Sullivan (ed.), *The Coronation of Charlemagne: What Did It Signify?* (Cambridge, Mass., 1959); R. Folz, *The Coronation of Charlemagne, 25 December 800* (London, 1974).

[12] E. Kantorowicz, *The King's Two Bodies: A Study in Medieval Political Thought* (Princeton, 1957). For a recent attempt to apply this approach to a later period, see: M. Axton, *The Queen's Two Bodies: Drama and the Elizabethan Succession* (London, 1977).

[13] Here, too, the literature has greatly increased in recent years. For three of the latest and most important works, see: S. Hanley, *The Lit de Justice of the Kings of France* (Princeton, 1983); E. Muir, *Civic Ritual in Renaissance Venice* (Princeton, 1981); R. Strong, *Art and Power: Renaissance Festivals, 1450–1650* (Woodbridge, 1984). For a recent symposium which also contains much of value on this subject, see: S. Wilentz (ed.), *Rites of Power: Symbolism, Ritual and Politics Since the Middle Ages* (Philadelphia, 1985).

[14] Again, it is only possible to cite a limited number of recent examples: P. Fritz, 'The Trade in Death: The Royal Funerals in England, 1685–1830', *Eighteenth-Century Studies*, xv (1982); L. Colley, 'The Apotheosis of George III: Loyalty, Royalty and the British Nation, 1760–1820', *Past and Present*, no. 102 (1984); M.-L. Biver, *Fêtes révolutionnaires à Paris* (Paris, 1979); G. L. Mosse, *The Nationalization of the Masses: Political Symbolism and Mass Movements in Germany from the Napoleonic Wars through the Third Reich* (New York, 1975); D. N. Cannadine, 'The Transformation of Civic Ritual in Modern Britain: The Colchester Oyster Feast' *Past and Present*, no. 94 (1982); E. Hammerton and

For these historians – and the list could be very much extended –
spectacle and pageantry are neither the exercise of power nor the
practice of politics by other, subsidiary, transient and cosmetic
means: on the contrary, they are seen as an integral part of power
and politics themselves. The authors in question may not be fully
conversant with the most recondite works of sociological theory or
with the latest anthropological studies of African kinship, but at the
very least, they are seeking to confront the two basic questions
thrown up by those disciplines: what is the relationship between
power and pomp? What is the connection between divine and
terrestrial order? But in addition, they seek to answer these
questions in a specifically *historical* way. They have a strong sense
of the *particularities* of their societies: of the exact historical
circumstances which they are hoping to understand and to analyse.
They have a strong sense of the *dynamics* of human societies: of
growth and development, change and decay, evolution and revolution. And they want to explain *how things worked*: not just in
terms which contemporaries could understand then, but also in
terms which we can understand now. In short, these historical
studies are both unambiguously established in their time and place,
and are also looking outwards rather than inwards in their scholarly
orientation.

As these individual examples suggest, theatre-states do not
necessarily have to boast a royal box: oligarchies and dictatorships,
democracies and republics, may be as much concerned with spectacle and splendour as monarchical regimes. But it is the rituals of
royalty which have been the most enduring, and which even today
offer the most ostentatious corroboration for the view that there is
more to political life than elections and party management. Even in
the United States, monarchs are still presented as clad in regal
robes, sitting on a throne, and with a crown on their head – as a
glance at the cartoons published in such a sophisticated journal as

D. N. Cannadine, 'Conflict and Consensus on a Ceremonial Occasion: The
Diamond Jubilee in Cambridge in 1897', *Historical Journal*, xxiv (1981); P. Mel-
ograni, 'The Cult of the Duce in Mussolini's Italy', *Journal of Contemporary
History*, xi (1976); R. C. Tucker, 'The Rise of Stalin's Personality Cult',
American Historical Review, lxxxiv (1979); C. Lane, *The Rites of Rulers: Ritual
in Industrial Society – The Soviet Case* (Cambridge, 1981); N. Tumarkin, *Lenin
Lives! The Lenin Cult in Soviet Russia* (London, 1983); P. Ziegler, *Crown and
People* (London, 1978). For another symposium containing much relevant
material, see: E. J. Hobsbawm and T. Ranger (eds.), *The Invention of Tradition*
(Cambridge, 1983).

the *New Yorker* amply demonstrates.[15] And the recent wedding of the Prince of Wales and Lady Diana Spencer, with its blanket television coverage and its global audience of hundreds of millions, provided the most convincing illustration yet of the view that 'all the world's a stage'. As Walter Bagehot put it over a century ago, 'a princely marriage is the brilliant edition of a universal fact, and, as such, it rivets mankind'.[16] In this case it most certainly, and emphatically, did. Kings may no longer rule by divine right; but the divine rites of kings continue to beguile and to enchant – and to require explanation and analysis. And if this is so for the present, then how much more true is it of the past?

THE SCOPE AND SUBSTANCE OF THIS BOOK

The essays gathered here – all specially written by experts in their field, and none of them published before – seek to advance our understanding of power and ceremonial in royal regimes by considering those areas of human activity outside the scope of most professional historians, whose interests are overwhelmingly concentrated in Europe since the sixteenth century. Accordingly, they are devoted to the pre-industrial and the pre-modern world, to what might loosely but not inaccurately be called traditional society. The subjects covered range from the Babylon of the first millennium BC to late eighteenth-century Nepal, from imperial Rome to nineteenth-century Madagascar, and from eighth-century China to modern Ghana. And the disciplines represented here are almost as diverse: one Byzantinist, one Sinologist, one medieval historian, two ancient historians, and three anthropologists. Taken together, these essays offer a broad-ranging and interdisciplinary study of royal power and royal ceremonial in societies which are far removed from our own in time and space, yet which are in some ways much closer to us than we might suppose.

In her study of ancient Babylon, Amélie Kuhrt looks at royal power and royal ceremonial during the first half of the first millennium BC, with special reference to the New Year Festival, in which the king ostentatiously appeared in the capital city. Here she

---

[15] It is also, perhaps, significant that the number of such cartoons has increased markedly during the Presidency of Ronald Reagan.

[16] W. Bagehot, *The English Constitution* (London, 1963 edn, ed. R. H. S. Crossman), p. 85.

contrasts the great instability of the regime – undermined from within by coups and usurpations, and assailed from without by successive waves of invaders – with the consensual ceremonial centred on the monarch, which stressed the stability of the state, the legitimacy of the king, and the parallels between the celestial and the earthly hierarchies. Indeed, as she suggests, the need for tradition and for order, as met by ceremonials such as these, actually *increased* as the stability of the state became ever more uncertain. In a sense, therefore, these ceremonials took on a life of their own: they were related to, yet separated from, the actual ups and downs of royal dynastic politics. Such was their autonomous identity that when Cyrus invaded Babylon from Persia in 539 BC, and effectively brought its independence to an end, he not only continued the rites of the native rulers, but also appropriated some of them for the Persian monarchy itself. The armies of Persia may have vanquished the Babylonians; but the rituals of Babylon conquered the Persians.

Simon Price also takes a long span of time, by investigating imperial funerals from the death of the first Roman Emperor, Augustus, in AD 14, to that of the first Christian Emperor, Constantine, in AD 337. Here we see an entire, extended ceremonial cycle evolving, flourishing, and abruptly decaying. With their republican traditions, many Roman citizens found it genuinely difficult to venerate their emperors as gods, and one of the ways in which they got round this problem was to grant them divine status in death rather less unambiguously than they were prepared to grant them divine status in life. Accordingly, imperial funerals were not just the last rites of the empire's greatest men, but were also, in the majority of cases, the occasion on which they finally and unambiguously joined the gods. As Price clearly demonstrates, this ceremonial developed partly from the format of noble funerals, partly from the traditional ascensions of Romulus and Hercules, and partly from the more recent precedent of the divine honours granted to Julius Caesar. Initially, it was the senate which had the power to grant or to withhold such divine recognition; but as the emperor's power grew, this became more of a formality; and the ceremonials themselves became increasingly grandiose. But all this was rather abruptly ended when Constantine espoused Christianity: pagan apotheosis was no longer possible, and the meaning and the ceremonial of imperial funerals were drastically modified.

In her chapter on Byzantium, Averil Cameron explores the Roman legacy of kingship in the eastern Mediterranean, by looking at the *Book of Ceremonies*, compiled by the Emperor Constantine VII Porphyrogenitus, who reigned from AD 913 to AD 957. What, she asks, does this work tell us about the history and function of Byzantine court ritual? And what, in turn, does this show us about the nature of Byzantine politics and society? As she sees it, Byzantium underwent a major period of crisis and change between the seventh and the ninth centuries AD, after which the administration was largely reconstructed, and the emperor reasserted his power over it. Yet here, as in Babylon, the political order remained inherently unstable, as emperors were made and toppled with great speed. Accordingly, the circumstances in which the *Book of Ceremonies* were written were as complex as were the purposes which the ritual was intended to fill. As a handbook, it served as a manual of pomp, which codified past practice, specified exact performance, and sought to promote ceremonial aggrandisement. But the rituals and festivals thus prescribed were even more complex in their meaning and function: a representation of the cosmic order, a picture of secular stability in a time of strife, a reinforcement of the official hierarchy, a legitimation of a relatively *parvenu* dynasty, and a display of ecclesiastical and imperial amity after the traumas of the Iconoclastic controversy. In short, the *Book of Ceremonies* was one of the *new* ways in which the imperial office was being consolidated: but in essentially *traditional* terms.

Janet Nelson's chapter considers the other legacy of Roman rule, namely the evolution of western monarchy, as illustrated in the anointing and coronation rituals of the Merovingian and Carolingian kings in the eighth and ninth centuries. Her concern is to decide whether these ceremonials depict a Frankish kingship gradually subordinated to ecclesiastical dominion, or an autonomous sense of community, power and hierarchy on the part of the Frankish people and kings. She concludes emphatically that secular power was more significant than religious, and that it was the Frankish aristocracy, rather than the popes or their bishops, which made and unmade kings. The election, recognition and coronation were fundamentally secular occasions, at which the officiating clergy provided reassurance and benediction, but little more. And this view is further corroborated by evidence of non-sacred spectacles such as feasting and hunting. In all cases, the real setting for the

Frankish king, as shown by the royal ceremonial, was in the perspective of the Frankish community, neither elevated in majesty above his people, nor cowed into submission by the church. Indeed, it was the abiding strength, of the Frankish monarchy, administration and community, which probably explains why their rituals of royalty were less well developed than those of the more grandiose but less secure Saxon monarchs to the east.

By contrast, the T'ang period in China, from AD 618 to AD 906, saw an extensive flowering of ceremonial on the part of the ruling dynasty. Three separate codes of Confucian court ritual were drawn up (of which one, the K'ai-yuan code of AD 732, is extensively analysed here); elaborate buildings were constructed, such as the Hall of Light in AD 688; and there was a veritable army of ritual scholars and ritual bureaucrats so numerous that, at first sight, David McMullen suggests that T'ang China might indeed seem to be the precursor of Geertzian Bali. But, he argues, this was not in fact the case. The Confucian system of beliefs and cere- monial was only one among several, even for the emperors; the bureaucrats who administered it were part of a much larger government machine which had many other functions, arguably more important; and in any case, the meaning and significance of these T'ang rituals changed considerably over time. At the begin- ning, their prime importance was essentially cosmic, to show that ritual was an integral part of the universe, with heaven and earth bound together, by ceremonial and in the person of the emperor. But by the late eighth century, after the dynasty had been weak- ened by rebellion, the social and moral functions of the ceremonial became more important. Instead of being a picture of cosmic hierarchy, the rituals were increasingly seen as a reinforcement to earthly order: a means for controlling man's potential for socially disruptive behaviour.

In the late eighteenth- and early nineteenth-century Nepal, as Richard Burghart explains, the kingdom was expanding rather than under threat, and this partly influenced the forms and the meaning of its royal rituals. Much ceremonial centred on the giving and receiving of gifts, which in turn reveal much about the power and the person of the Nepalese king. As a monarch who gave gifts to his subjects, the King of Nepal reaffirmed his superiority and auton- omy as the pre-eminent person in the kingdom, subject to no one, and ruler of all. But as the man who also enjoyed the exclusive right to give gifts to the gods, the king also demonstrated his dependence on the celestial hierarchy for his earthly power, and his need for divine protection. Sometimes, as Burghart shows, kings made gifts to the gods in the hope of obtaining divine support and assistance in war and other expansionist ventures. Here, as so often in traditional societies, the essence of majesty (and the essence of power?) was the monarch's participation in two separate hierarchies: the earthly and the cosmic. In one guise, the king of Nepal was a divine actor in an earthly realm; but in another, he was a mortal figure in a cosmic hierarchy.

Maurice Bloch, in his essay on nineteenth-century Madagascar, considers this question of the king's two bodies from a slightly different standpoint. His concern is to try to show precisely how it was that a transcendent order could actually be made to beguile and enchant, to captivate and to impress, here on earth. How did it actually happen? He answers this question by looking at the ceremonial of the royal bath, which was simultaneously an expression of cosmic order, of royal authority, and of national corporateness. This account then forms the basis for an extended critique of Clifford Geertz's analysis of Bali. In the first place, Bloch argues that Geertz's pictures of a theatre state fails to explain *why* it was that ritual and ceremonial had the ideological and emotive power which he credits it with possessing. Splendour, Block suggests, is not *of itself* an adequate explanation. What really mattered was the fact that, at least in Madagascar, the grand royal ceremonials were themselves developments and extensions of ordinary, widespread, commonplace rituals, and it was this which gave royal display its compelling force. But in addition, he argues that Geertz does not explain how in practice these royal spectacles were actually devised. They did not just happen: so where did they come from? Logically, and chronologically, Bloch argues, they came after the local ceremonials. In short, he suggests it is the *construction* of the rituals, rather than the rituals themselves, which not only describes how they came about, but also explains how they could and did compel.

In the final essay, Michelle Gilbert investigates how, in the 1970s, monarchs were made in the kingdom of Akuapem in Ghana. Her concern here is not so much with the broader context of state and government power, but with the way in which ritual transformed ordinary mortals into monarchs, and so made them both magical and powerful in ways which they had not been before. And this requires an investigation of the symbolic objects involved, and the systems of belief which they in turn articulate. As she demonstrates, the repository of ancestral legitimation and the reservoir of kingly power in Akuapem are the black stools, which are recognisably the equivalent of royal thrones in western society. A man may be elected to be monarch, but it is the relatively private act of enstoolment which actually transforms an ordinary mortal into a person possessed of kingly properties and power. Only after this private ceremonial is there a more public installation. Power, in other words, is not intrinsic to a person as a human individual, but only to the monarch as the holder of an office. And that power is obtained by contact with the stool, for the simple reason that that is where the citizens of the kingdom believe royal power to reside.

THE GENERAL SIGNIFICANCE OF THESE STUDIES

Although we have done our best to ensure that all these essays address the same central subject, none of them has been pushed into a rigid or pre-ordained framework at editorial request. The treatment of the topic and the argument advanced have in every case been determined by the nature and limitations of the evidence available, and by the interests and expertise of the author. But even so, when read as a whole, these essays show a real unity of approach to the study of power and ritual. Political structure and political action are analysed and understood in a broad rather than a narrow perspective. And pomp and pageantry, spectacle and splendour, are treated as an integral part of the political process and the structure of power. As such, all these essays are exercises in extending our conceptions of political history, and in raising our ceremonial consciousnesses. But to what end? To say of pomp and pageantry that there has always been a great deal of it about, and here are some more examples, albeit from unusually exotic locations, is not of itself particularly significant. Considering the amount of material already published on the subject, there is hardly a need to provide *more* case-studies, merely for the sake of it. What, taken as individual pieces, do these essays tell us? And what, taking them together, are the broader insights which they reveal?

One obvious answer is to throw these questions back in the face of those who pose them. Whatever the claims to the contrary, the fact remains that all history, all anthropology, all sociology, is ultimately a case-study of something; just as, more precisely, all political history consists of case-studies in power, however defined. Accordingly, one of the justifications of these contributions, each unambiguously established in their own time and place, is to show the many ways in which the circumstances of pomp may differ. The countries described in this volume range from tiny kingdoms with a population of less than 100,000 to the vast Chinese Empire with more than 50 million inhabitants. Here are stable states with ordered and efficient bureaucracies, and here are polities riven by strife, conspiracy, treason, rebellion and invasion. Here are powerful kings, with ceremonial profiles that are sometimes high and sometimes low, and here are vulnerable monarchs in circumstances equally diverse. Here are courtly rituals which are unknown to or unobserved by the majority of the population, and here are ceremonials in which almost the whole nation actively participates.

Such diversity of ceremonial and political experience enjoins caution in making any easy generalisations about power and pomp. Indeed, as several of these essays further show, there is no necessary agreement, even among the experts, as to what exactly the evidence adds up to. Simon Price is partly concerned to criticise those Roman historians who have dismissed the imperial cult, its ceremonial and its beliefs, as being nothing more than a charade. Janet Nelson's essay deliberately takes issue with Walter Ullmann's interpretation of Frankish kingship, as being both subordinate to the church while exalted among the people. It is, she suggests, misleading on both accounts. Averil Cameron tries to bring together the two conventionally opposed views of the Byzantine past: the one that nothing ever changed, and that the whole civilization was by definition rigid and moribund; the other that it was much more dynamic and adaptive than is often supposed. And Maurice Bloch, in his study of the Madagascan kings' royal bath ritual, takes issue, not only with Clifford Geertz's study of Bali, but also with other scholars working in his own field.

What broader insights do these case-studies suggest if they are taken together as a whole? Most obviously, they are a real antidote to the parochialism of our civilisation, its history and its historians. The ceremonials described here are as far removed from the planes, the searchlights and the loudspeakers of Nuremberg, as they are from the carefully stage-managed television spectaculars of the modern British monarchy. The societies in which they took place were less rich, less egalitarian, less literate and less sophisticated than are those of the contemporary West. Communications were much worse, the mass media in most cases was unknown, and the expectations of life were a great deal lower. Yet on their own terms, these ceremonials seem to have fulfilled their functions as effectively as do the high-tech spectacles in advanced societies today. But in addition, many of these traditional displays of pageantry endured with much greater tenacity than more recent displays in modern Europe. The funeral cults of Roman Emperors lasted for three hundred years; the modern ceremonial associated with the British monarchy is not yet a century old; the cult of Lenin is even less venerable; and the Nuremberg Rallies lasted barely a decade. In ceremonial as in so much else, the rate of change seems to have speeded up.

Taken together, these essays also reveal the varied approaches to the same subject by those who might loosely be called historians (who have contributed the first five pieces), and by the anthropologists (who have contributed the remainder). Each of the historical essays takes a long span of time (in most cases several centuries); they are concerned with the ways in which ceremonial evolves and develops, changes and decays; and they try to relate this very carefully to what might be conventionally understood as the politics and formal structure of society. The anthropologists, on the other hand, take a shorter span of time (in no case more than one hundred years); the ceremonial tends to be accepted as unchanging; the structures of power are rather lightly sketched in; and their interests are more tightly focussed on what, precisely, the ceremonial meant and accomplished. At the risk of excessive simplification, the historians are interested in the working of ceremonial *in* society, whereas the anthropologists are more concerned with the working of society *through* ceremonial. The historians ask about structures of power, whereas the anthropologists ask about structures of meaning. The historians want to know how the ceremonial image and the stability of the state relate to each other, whereas the anthropologists want to know how a society constructs a transcendent symbolic idiom, and how human beings are transformed into divine kings.

Of course, these differences of approach and interest should not be over-emphasised. For what also emerges emphatically from these essays is the real degree to which each author has, regardless of background, been influenced by the theories generated and the questions posed by the sociologists and the anthropologists. In every essay which follows, the ceremonials studied are shown to display some real degree of 'collective effervescence', but also considerable evidence for the 'mobilisation of bias'. All of the pageants, in some way or other, seem to confirm consensus, to disguise conflict, and to support both hierarchy and community.[17] No matter which country is taken, its royal ritual centres on the secular and sacred identities of the king, and on his role as an exemplary centre, linking the earthly and celestial hierarchies. Without exception, the spectacles analysed carry a heavy payload of different meanings and different functions.

As such, the broader conclusions to be drawn from these case-studies seem clear: the relationship between pomp and power is much more complex and varied than any simple formulation might suggest; the whole notion of power as a narrow, separate and discreet category seems inappropriate and unsatisfactory; and the idea that splendour and spectacle is but superficial and cosmetic window-dressing appears equally ill-conceived. But it hardly seems adequate to leave the matter there. It is reassuring to know that the questions which the sociologists and anthropologists have asked are indeed worth posing; but do these case-studies not throw up some new questions of their own? It is comforting to learn that the material presented here partially validates most of the theories at present on offer; but does it not make it possible to generate some new theory in turn? If conventional notions of power seem to be unsatisfactory, what if anything may better be put in their place? In short: what future lines of further inquiry do these essays suggest?

The best place to begin is with Maurice Bloch's chapter, which poses two linked questions that seem well worth pondering. Why exactly is it that ceremonies impress? And what are the building bricks from which they are actually constructed? Indeed, for Bloch, to answer the second question is also to answer the first: it is not just the fact that royal ceremonials are usually constructed out of materials already available; it is also that this very fact provides the explanation as to why they captivate. That is his case for Madagascar, and there is a considerable amount of evidence scattered in

---

[17] For a brief discussion of the limitations to this approach, see Hammerton and Cannadine, 'Conflict and Consensus' (see n. 14), pp. 142–6.

the other essays in this volume which supports this view. In Babylon, the grand and kingly spectacles in the capital city were similar to those held elsewhere and on a smaller scale. In Rome, the last rites of the emperors were partly modelled on the older tradition of noble funerals. In the Frankish kingdom, the notion of anointing was derived from the Bible, and assemblies were an intrinsic part of local government. And in Ghana, the royal stools were clearly a more grandoise version of something more widespread and familiar. Indeed, it was Walter Bagehot himself who precisely anticipated Bloch's case in the phrase already quoted: 'a princely marriage is the brilliant edition of a universal fact, and, as such, it rivets mankind'.

But of course, there are difficulties with this approach when it is applied more broadly. Even in the case of Madagascar, the dominion of the Merina kings was never total, so that not everyone was assimilated in the ceremonial of the royal bath, and those who were had already been drawn into the Merina structure of power, whereas those who were not had not.[18] It may be possible to explain the construction and appeal of this one ceremonial in terms of other rituals which are logically and chronologically prior, but that still leaves the problem of explaining these anterior events. Otherwise it seems as if one ceremonial is simply being explained in terms of another. Many of the other countries discussed in this book were too big for the central spectacle to be replicated, state-wide, as was the case in Madagascar, which means they cannot have functioned in precisely the same way as the royal bath. Once again, there is the question of specific circumstances: Bloch's approach does not explain why it is that some princely weddings rivet attention more widely and compulsively than others. And, for the very modern period, it seems much more likely that the ceremonials are invented in the centre, and are then transmitted outwards (as in the case of the Investiture of the Prince of Wales, or Royal Jubilees), rather than the other way round.

Nevertheless, Bloch's approach focusses attention very precisely on the central issue addressed in this book, namely the relation between power and ceremonial, and the way in which each of these notions is conceived. And this in turn suggests two more questions which should, perhaps, be asked. How exactly, and if at all, does

18 M. Bloch, 'Tombs and Statues', in S. C. Humphreys and H. King (eds.), *Mortality and Immortality: The Anthropology and Archaeology of Death* (New York, 1981).

ceremonial convert systems of belief about celestial hierarchies into statements of fact about earthly hierarchies?[19] Or, to ask this the other way round, how exactly, if at all, does ceremonial convert statements of fact about power on earth into statements of belief about power in heaven? Indeed, this line of inquiry may usefully be pursued further. *If* it is the case, as is strongly suggested by the evidence displayed here, that pomp is of itself a visible form of power, then *precisely what form of power is it*? As these essays show, the answer to that question, as with the two which precede it, may vary, depending on the type of society and the type of ceremonial being considered. But regardless of these diversities, it seems clear that this is the right question to be asking: partly because, in empirical terms, it arises naturally out of the evidence; and partly because, in conceptual terms, it immediately serves to take ceremonial seriously, to make the notion of power problematic, and yet also to keep open the options as to how power might be more precisely defined.

It does not seem fruitful, in this introduction, to push these conceptual considerations any further. But these collected essays also suggest another set of questions, this time more empirical, which it might be useful to identify. One abiding problem for historians, anxious to do justice to the uniqueness of their particular society and subject, is that they need a comparative dimension to help them get a sense of what is typical and what is odd about the culture they want to study. Many of the most interesting and important questions about the past can only be formulated from an essentially comparative perspective, and the case-studies in this book provide just such a viewpoint for students of power and ceremonial, whatever the particular context they may be dealing with. And as such, they suggest a variety of questions. Why, for instance, do some societies and some centuries seem to need more ceremonial than others?[20] Why does spectacle sometimes accom-

---

[19] Cf. P. Wheatley, *The Pivot of the Four Quarters* (Edinburgh, 1971), pp. 477–8, where the author notes, concerning town plans and buildings in ancient China, that they 'projected images of cosmic order on to the plane of human experience, where they could provide a framework for social action'. But how, precisely, they actually did so, remains elusive.

[20] Compare, for example, the television spectaculars of the House of Windsor today with the 'Bicycling' monarchies of Scandinavia and the Low Countries. For an earlier example of a royal regime which deliberately kept a low ceremonial profile, see: T. F. Ruiz, 'Une royauté sans sacre: la monarchie castillane du bas moyen age', *Annales ESC*, xxxix (1984).

pany royal (and national) power, and sometimes go with royal (and national) weakness? Why does pomp sometimes go with stable government, and why is it sometimes an antidote to chaos and disorder? Why does some pageantry take root and 'work', and some dwindle and die? Why are some rituals deliberately and stridently contemporary in their technology, while others self-consciously cultivate anachronism? What is the connection between the overthrow of royalty and the overthrow of rituals? How does pomp appear to the alienated or dispossessed?[21]

There is a further historical perspective which needs consideration in the light of these essays. The danger of using words like 'power' and 'ceremonial', unavoidable though they may be, is that it implies that they are constant and unchanging notions. Yet of course, this is not so. As societies become more complex, then the distribution and the nature of power, and the functioning and substance of ceremonial, must and do change and develop. To put this in more appropriate terms, this means that the ceremonial and the divine kings of a primitive, Frazerian society were in many ways very different from the ceremonial and the dignified kings of a modern, Bagehotian, society. In many traditional societies, coronation ceremonies made a man into a king and into a god, who thereby linked the earthly and heavenly hierarchies. But in Britain in 1953, very few people believed that making a woman a queen meant making her a goddess, or that the coronation somehow connected the terrestrial and the cosmic order. Kings who are divine, kings who rule by divine right, and kings who are dignified, are very different things, in very different societies, wielding very different kings of power, and legitimated by very different kinds of ceremonial. Perhaps that is a point which deserves more attention than it usually receives.

CONCLUSION

Anyone interested in public affairs today knows that the subject encompasses an astonishing variety of human behaviour and activity. And the notion of contemporary politics (defined by

[21] For a brilliant discussion of public regicide (as distinct from private assassination) as the denial of kingly inviolability, with special reference to Charles I and Louis XVI, see M. Walzer, *Regicide and Revolution: Speeches at the Trial of Louis XVI* (Cambridge, 1973).

activity) is both broader and more problematic than the notion of past politics (defined by archives). Yet for any society, in any age, the study of politics ultimately comes down to one elemental question: how are people persuaded to acquiesce in a polity where the distribution of power is manifestly unequal and unjust, as it invariably is? There are many ways in which this question may be addressed, depending on the disciplinary route by which it is approached, the evidence that is available, and the manner in which the subject is conceptualised. What these essays try to show is that no approach which defines power narrowly and ignores spectacle and pageantry can possibly claim to be comprehensive. Politics and ceremonial are not separate subjects, the one serious, the other superficial. Ritual is not the mask of force, but is itself a type of power.

'The failure of the twentieth-century democracies', Keynes once wrote, 'is in part attributable to their failure to invest the state with ceremonial.'[22] Politicians may be forgiven for occasionally conceiving power so narrowly; but students of society would be unwise to repeat their mistake. Of course, it is no easier to make the invisible palpable than it is to make the ephemeral permanent. But if the workings of any society are to be fully unravelled, then the barriers dividing the study of power from the study of pomp need to be broken down. As these essays make plain, different disciplines approach this endeavour in different ways; different societies need different treatment; and at best, the results are often incomplete, speculative and open to disagreement. But even so, it is only by such means that we can begin to probe more deeply into those structures of power and structures of meaning without which no society – past or present, traditional or modern – can ever properly be understood. These essays are offered as a tentative step in that direction.[23]

[22] J. M. Keynes, 'Art and the State', *The Listener*, 26 August 1936.
[23] I am most grateful to my co-editor, Simon Price, for his very considerable help with this introduction, and also to Prof. L. J. Colley and to Ms L. Nixon.

1. Usurpation, conquest and ceremonial: from Babylon to Persia

AMÉLIE KUHRT

How many miles to Babylon?
Three score and ten!
Can I get there by candle light?
Yes, and back again!
'I wish one could,' the learned gentleman said with a sigh. 'Can't you?'
asked Jane. 'Babylon has fallen,' he answered with a sigh. 'You know it
was once a great and beautiful city, and the centre of learning and Art, and
now it is only ruins, and so covered up with earth that people are not even
agreed as to where it once stood.'

E. Nesbit, The Story of the Amulet (London, 1906)

The disappearance of Babylon, repeatedly forecast by Hebrew
prophets, has meant that the popular image conjured up by its
name is largely that bequeathed us by one of its bitterest enemies,
the Jews. It is, contrary to the more informed view of Nesbit's
'learned gentleman', that of a rich, vainglorious, idolatrous, super-
stitious, cruel and corrupt society, which was eventually totally
obliterated as a result of divine vengeance through the earthly
agency of the Persian empire.[1] To the people of classical antiquity
its history and culture were only scantily known because of its
remoteness from the Mediterranean world, and once it had been
incorporated into the Parthian empire (in the second century BC),
its name assumed for them an alien and exotic aura: it had been
built and ruled by a fierce, heroic queen, Semiramis; it was
associated with the mysterious and often suspect science of
astrology practised by 'Chaldaeans'; and it contained one of the
wonders of the ancient world, the Hanging Gardens.[2]

As a result of the development of archaeological exploration and
decipherment of ancient languages early in the nineteenth century,

---

[1] E.g. Jeremiah, ch. L, vv.1–3.
[2] A. Kuhrt, 'Assyrian and Babylonian Traditions in Classical Authors: a Critical
Synthesis', in H. Nissen and J. Renger (eds.), *Mesopotamien und seine Nachbarn*
25. Recontre Internationale Assyriologique, 2 vols. (Berlin, 1982), ii, pp. 539–53.

it has become possible to study the history of Babylonia and Assyria to the north from records written in the local languages and script and to assess its long-lived and complex civilisation within its own cultural framework. What has emerged from this is a very different and far more interesting picture; for example, Babylon was a city of virtually no importance until around 1800 BC, although the written record reaches back to the end of the fourth millennium BC (see below, pp. 23–30). Nor did it ever suffer any sudden destruction by either Persian or Greek conquest. Undoubtedly, Babylonian civilisation underwent enormous transformations over its remarkably long and eventful period of existence of more than three thousand years; but major elements of its traditional culture, in literature, scribal practice, religion and ritual, were studiously preserved. Rather than visualising this preservation of traditions as reflecting a tenacious and rigid adherence to obsolete practices in the teeth of the inexorable forward march of history, it is more fruitful to see it as demonstrating the vitality and intellectual scope of Babylonian culture when confronted with the fact of political upheaval and military conquest by peoples whose languages and habits of thought were entirely alien.

In order to demonstrate both the continuity and elasticity of these traditions, I have chosen to focus on the conquest of Babylon by the Persians, and particularly on a set of ritual acts centring on the king (see below pp. 30–48), and to examine both how these rituals were manipulated by the conquerors and how respect for them was demanded by the conquered (see below pp. 48–52). Before doing this a few words on the emergence of the Persian empire will be necessary.

Cyrus of Persia, founder of the Old Persian (Achaemenid) Empire (*c*.550–531 BC), began life as a client-king of a neighbouring Iranian peoples, the Medes, whose territory stretched from the Halys (central Turkey) to the Iranian plateau.[3] The political structure of the Median state is poorly known[4] but it seems likely that it resembled a tribal confederacy.[5]

---

[3] Herodotus, *Histories* i. 95–130.
[4] R. N. Frye, *The Heritage of Persia* (London, 1962), pp. 68–78; *idem.*, *The History of Ancient Iran* Handbuch der Altertumswissenschaft III.7 (Munich, 1984), pp. 66–70; J. M. Cook, *The Persian Empire* (London, 1983), ch.1.
[5] P. R. Helm, 'Herodotus' *Mêdikos Logos* and Median History' *Iran* xix (1981), pp. 85–90; H.W.A.M. Sancisi-Weerdenburg, 'What about the Median Empire?', in A. Kuhrt and H.W.A.M. Sancisi-Weerdenburg (eds.), *Achaemenid History III: Method and Theory* (forthcoming).

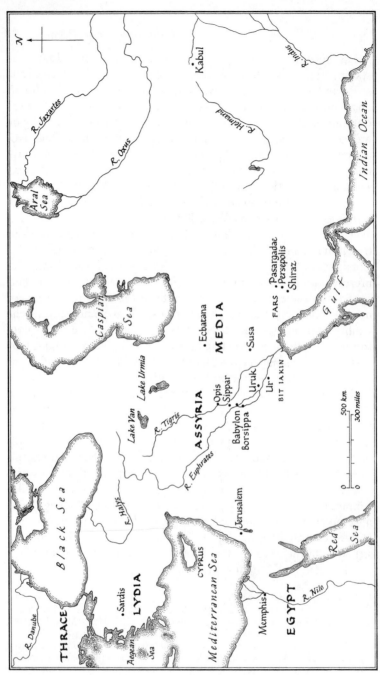

1 The ancient Near East.

By comparison with the highly evolved and sophisticated political systems of the Near Eastern states to the west (Babylonia, Egypt and Lydia) it represented an underdeveloped state;[6] the tribal origins of the Old Persian dynasty, too, continued to be reflected in later royal inscriptions at a time when this vertical relationship had declined in importance as the empire evolved.[7] In 550 Cyrus successfully attacked his Median overlord and inherited the territories that had been under his sway.[8] Possibly in the 540s[9] Lydia was conquered, extending Persian control to the Aegean coast, and in 539 Babylonia, which controlled the largest, most powerful and wealthiest empire extending to the Egyptian frontier (see Fig. 1), was incorporated into Cyrus' realm. His immediate successors added Egypt, North India and Thrace to the empire which now formed a political entity larger and more stable than any known in the world up to this point.

This process of rapid expansion had important repercussions on the development of the emergent Persian state.[10] One Greek author, who lived between 430 and 354 BC, and wrote a moralising, philosophical novel on Cyrus' life (the *Cyropaedia* of Xenophon), saw the most important change reflected in the articulation of Persian kingship. He defined the conquest of Babylonia as the central and culminating achievement of Cyrus' activities, which resulted in the latter conceiving 'a desire to establish himself as he thought became a king'.[11] It is this interaction which will be examined more closely below (see pp. 52–5).

BABYLONIAN HISTORY

The region usually referred to as Babylonia (an anachronism until the sixteenth century BC) constitutes the area of South Iraq

---

6 An observation made several times in Herodotus, for example *Histories* i. 89.
7 cf. R. Kent, *Old Persian: Grammar, Texts, Lexicon* (New Haven, Conn., 1953), pt II *passim*; Frye, *Heritage* (see n.4), pp. 51–2.
8 A. K. Grayson, *Assyrian and Babylonian Chronicles* Texts from Cuneiform Sources V (Locust Valley, N.Y., 1975), no. 7, col. ii, lines 1–4 (henceforth abbr. *ABC*).
9 *ABC* no. 7, col. ii, lines 15–17 and the additional comment on p. 282; J. Cargill, 'The Nabonidus Chronicle and the Fall of Lydia: Consensus with Feet of Clay', *American Journal of Ancient History* ii/2 (1977), pp. 97–116.
10 This is the central thesis of the important study by M. Dandamayev, *Persien unter den ersten Achämeniden* transl. (Wiesbaden, 1976).
11 Xenophon, *Cyropaedia* vii.5.37.

approximately from just north of Baghdad to the Gulf. Its history is one of the longest attested, stretching back to before 3000 BC. For the first one and a half millennia of this period the typical political pattern of the region was one of city-states each including smaller village settlements and dominating the surrounding countryside with its grazing land, fields and stretches of river or canal that provided essential irrigation. Each city was walled for protection from the frequent conflicts with neighbouring states and also contained temples, in particular that of the patron deity of the city. The temples controlled extensive estates and functioned as important resource centres, not only organising the kind of ceremonies usually associated with religious institutions, that is, festivals, day-to-day care of the gods, burials, but also performing some legal, social and economic functions such as oath-taking, care of orphans, providing employment for the poor, provision of capital for mercantile enterprises, and loans of corn to small farmers at low rates in times of shortage. In order to carry out these varied activities the temple also became a centre for training scribes and a repository of scribal learning.[12]

In many of these activities the temple complemented and co-operated with the activities of the palace, i.e., the household of the city-ruler. The ruler led his city in war and protected it against incursions from enemies, he took responsibility for repairing and/or constructing temples for the gods, especially the patron-god of his own city, as well as providing them at times with gifts of land, personnel and shares of war-booty; he came also to play an important part in establishing laws, was one of the main organisers of trading activities and dug canals to provide water for his subjects. His relationship to the patron deity of the city appears initially to have varied somewhat from place to place, a fact perhaps given expression in the differing titles borne by the rulers of the various states.[13] But in spite of continuous inter-state conflicts the cities of Babylonia shared a common language, literary traditions, scribal

---

12 J. N. Postgate, 'The Role of the Temple in the Mesopotamian Secular Community', in P. J. Ucko, R. Tringham and G. W. Dimbleby (eds.), *Man, Settlement and Urbanism* (London, 1972), pp. 811–25.

13 D. O. Edzard, 'Die frühdynastische Zeit', in J. Bottéro, E. Cassin and J. Vercoutter (eds.), *Die Altorientalischen Reiche I* Fischer Weltgeschichte, vol. 2 (Frankfurt-am-Main, 1965), pp., 73–7; *idem*, 'Herrscher', *Reallexikon der Assyriologie und vorderasiatischen Archäologie* (Berlin, 1975), iv, pp. 335–8 (henceforth abbr. *RLA*).

2334–2154	Dynasty of Agade founded by Saragon

1792–1750	Hammurabi of Babylon
1595	End of the First Dynasty of Babylon
?–1157	Kassite Period
1126–1105	Nebuchadnezzar I

	BABYLONIA	ASSYRIA	
979–*c*.770	17 kings (many uncertain lengths of reign;	Shalmaneser III	858–824
	5 with names not known)	Shamshi-Adad V	823–811
		Adad-nirari III	810–783
c. 770	Eriba-Marduk		
c. 760–748	Nabu-šuma-iškun		
747–734	Nabu-naṣir ┌──────	Tiglath-Pileser III	744–727
733–729	3 kings ┘		
728–727	←		
726–722	Shalmaneser V		726–722
721–710	Marduk-apla-iddina II ┌──────	Sargon II	721–705
709–705	← ┘		
704–703	← ────────────┐	Sennacherib	704–681
703–689	6 kings: Sennacherib's appointees and		
	Babylonian rebels ┘		
688–681	←		
680–669	Esarhaddon		680–669
668–667	← ──────	Assurbanipal	668–627
667–648	Šamas-šuma-ukin (Assurbanipal's brother)		
647–627	Kandalanu (Assyrian appointee)		
626–625	No king	END OF ASSYRIAN	
625–605	Nabopolassar	EMPIRE	*c*.610
604–562	Nebuchadnezzar II		
561–560	Amel-Marduk		
559–556	Neriglissar		
556	Labashi-Marduk	PERSIA	
555–539	Nabonidus ┌──────	Cyrus	before 550–530
538–530	← ┘		

(538: Cambyses, co-regent for one
year with his father)

530–522	Cambyses	530–522
522	Bardiya (= Smerdis)	522
521–486	Darius I	521–486
485–465	Xerxes	485–465
464–331	6 Persian kings	464–331
330–323	Alexander III of Macedon	330–323

HELLENISTIC PERIOD

2 Chronological table.

practices and art-forms and certainly came to share a common religion. The individual city-gods were by the late third millennium related to each other as family-members of a coherent pantheon. From c.2400 on there were attempts by individual city-rulers to include other city-states in their domain. The most spectacularly successful of these was Sargon of Agade (c.2340) who was able to establish control over extensive areas beyond the Babylonian region as well as the old city-states within it. His conquests were maintained and even extended by his descendants which resulted in a transformation of the earlier political pattern: garrisons were placed in frontier areas, local city-rulers were removed and replaced by officials from Agade and a number of important cultic offices given to members of the Agade royal family.[14]

The legacy of Sargon's dynasty was that for the next 5–600 years a number of different cities attempted (with varying success) to impose an overall control on the other city-states. Such successes as were gained did not usually last long, but one important outcome was that at the beginning of the eighteenth century BC the city of Babylon, which had been virtually unknown earlier, entered the arena of inter-city rivalry as a serious competitor for hegemony under its king, Hammurabi. By the end of his reign Hammurabi had established control over the other cities of the region and dominated areas to the north and north-west. Under his successors these conquests shrank rapidly and by 1595 his dynasty had vanished, Babylon had been destroyed in a Hittite raid and the cult-statue of its patron-god, Marduk, held 'in captivity' by a hostile kingdom.[15] But in spite of the apparently ephemeral character of Hammurabi's achievements his reign had two very important consequences: first, Babylon had become a major city after which eventually the whole country was named and its role as capital of the region remained unchanged until the Hellenistic period (after about 300 BC); secondly, with the greater political significance of Babylon, its local god, Marduk, also emerged as an increasingly important figure of the pantheon.

The vacuum left by the demise of this 'First Dynasty of Babylon' was filled by the kings of a people called Kassites, whose original

---

[14] W. W. Hallo and W. K. Simpson, *The Ancient Near East: A History* (New York, 1971), pp. 54–68; W. W. Hallo and J. J. A. van Dijk, *The Exaltation of Inanna* Yale Near Eastern Researchers 3 (New Haven, 1968).
[15] Hallo and Simpson, *The Ancient Near East* (see n.14), pp. 105–8.

homeland has still not been identified.[16] Sources for the next two hundred years are extremely sparse and not too full after that for some time. But some important changes are nevertheless observable. Babylonia from now on was a territorial state and not a collection of city-states competing with each other for political supremacy.[17] Although for almost five hundred years Babylonia was ruled by this 'foreign' dynasty who introduced some alien deities, the latter never played an important role nor did they usurp the function of the traditional pantheon.[18] Babylon, in fact, became the capital of the state and the statue of Marduk was restored; old religious centres such as Uruk, Isin and Ur had their temples repaired, extended and beautified. Moreover, at some point in or just after the Kassite period, the so-called 'Babylonian epic of creation' (*Enūma eliš*), was composed.[19] It is a poetic celebration of Marduk's rise to supreme power in the pantheon and was later recited during the Babylonian New Year Festival (to which we shall return later).

During the Kassite period it seems, there was a decrease in the level of urbanisation.[20] There were also two further changes in the pattern of population in the region. One is the appearance of large numbers of Aramaean tribal settlements especially in the East Tigris area and on tracts of land between the older cities; these appear never to have evolved beyond a basic village economy, tribally organised and they thus formed a distinctive and politically unassimilable element within the country. Secondly, the settlements of Chaldaean tribes formed another element of the population dominating particularly the southern areas of the country.

16 J. A. Brinkman, 'Kassiten', *RLA*, v, pp. 464–5.
17 J. A. Brinkman, 'The Monarchy in the Time of the Kassite Dynasty', in P. Garelli (ed.), *Le Palàis et la Royauté* 19. Recontre Internationale Assyriologique (Paris, 1974), pp. 395–408.
18 J. A. Brinkman, 'Kassiten', *RLA*, v, pp. 471–2.
19 For a date of composition in the Kassite period see T. Jacobsen, *The Treasures of Darkness: a History of Mesopotamian Religion* (New Haven, 1976), pp. 189–90; for a date in the reign of Nebuchadnezzar I (1126–1105 BC) see W. G. Lambert, 'The Reign of Nebuchadnezzar I: A Turning Point in the History of Ancient Mesopotamian Religion', in W. S. MacCullough (ed.), *The Seed of Wisdom: Essays in Honor of T. G. Meek* (Toronto, 1964), pp. 3–13. A translation of the epic in English can be found in A. Heidel, *The Babylonian Genesis* (Chicago, 1942) and in J. B. Pritchard (ed.), *Ancient Near Eastern Texts Relating to the Old Testament* 3rd edn (Princeton N.J., 1969), pp. 60–72 and 501–3 (henceforth abbr. *ANET*[3]).
20 J. A. Brinkman, 'Kassiten', *RLA*, v, p. 469.

These, too, were tribally organised but formed larger and more powerful units than the Aramaeans, they appear to have been markedly wealthy as a result of trade and had fortified 'capitals'.[21] These groups lived in tension both with each other and with the old-established, urban inhabitants of the region. The long-established Babylonian cities such as Uruk, Ur, Borsippa, Sippar, Nippur and Babylon, with their temple and civic institutions, were surrounded by these tribal groups. All these traditional centres laid claim to or were acknowledged to enjoy a special privileged status known as *kidinnūtu*, which came to mean 'protection' (the term was derived from a divine emblem, the *kidinnu*) and citizens enjoying this status were called the *ṣabe kidinni* (people of the *kidinnu*). It is not completely certain what their specific prerogatives were, but exemption from certain military and labour obligations and other dues in kind appear to have constituted some of them.[22]

Discontinuity in the royal dynasties is typical of the post-Kassite period in Babylonia: only for very limited spans of time can one trace a father–son succession, usurpation and periods of anarchy occurred fairly frequently, but at the end of the ninth century BC a serious disturbance within the royal succession was caused by Babylonia's relations with her increasingly powerful northern neighbour, the neo-Assyrian empire,[23] whose culture, language and religion shared a number of features with those of Babylonia.

The history of Assyro-Babylonian relations is a long and complex one which centred initially on frontier disputes. A treaty had been arrived at between the two states in the reign of Shalmaneser III (858–824) to regulate this, including an obligation to support the accession to the throne of the legally appointed successor.[24] This

---

[21] For a discussion of both the Aramaean and Chaldaean settlements in Babylonia see J. A. Brinkman, *A Political History of Postkassite Babylonia 1158–722 BC* (Rome, 1968), pp. 260–85 (henceforth abbr. *PKB*); *idem*, Review of M. Dietrich, *Die Aramäer Südbabyloniens in der Sargonidenzeit (700–648)* (Neukirchen-Vluyn, 1970), in *Orientalia* new series xlvi (1977), pp. 304–25.

[22] W. F. Leemans, '*Kidinnu*: un symbole de droit divin babylonien', in M. David, B. A. van Groningen, E. M. Meijers (eds.), *Symbolae ad Ius et Historiam Antiquitatis Pertinentes Julio Christiano van Oven dedicatae* (Leiden, 1946), pp. 36–70 (abbr. *Symbolae van Oven*); I. M. Diakonoff, 'A Babylonian political pamphlet from about 700 B.C.', in H. G. Güterbock and T. Jacobsen (eds.), *Studies in Honor of Benno Landsberger on his Seventyfifth Birthday, April 21, 1965* Assyriological Studies 16 (Chicago, 1965), pp. 343ff.

[23] J. Oates, *Babylon* (London, 1979), pp. 110–11.

[24] *ABC* no. 21, col. iii, lines 22–32; for discussion see *PKB*, pp. 192–218 and A. K. Grayson, 'Chronicles and the Akitu Festival', in A. Finet (ed.), *Actes de la XVIIe*

led to a massive military intervention by Assyria at the end of the ninth century with the result that complete chaos ensued in Babylonian dynastic affairs and parts of Northern Babylonia were, temporarily, virtually annexed to Assyria and ruled directly by the Assyrian king. This event set the tone for behaviour by Assyrian conquerors in relation to the region. The destabilisation suffered by Babylonia as a result of these actions was not resolved for about two hundred years: after the initial destructive Assyrian intervention and partial control, a Chaldaean ruler came to the throne around 770 (Eriba-Marduk) and the following years were marked by turmoil; in 732 a major civil war involving Chaldaean tribal leaders developed which was only ended by Tiglath-Pileser III of Assyria establishing himself as king of Babylonia, in which he was followed by his son Shalmaneser V. Shalmaneser V's reign ended in revolt within Assyria bringing to the throne, after struggles, a man not in line of succession, Sargon II. At this point Babylonia was lost again to Assyrian control and a descendant of Eriba-Marduk, Marduk-apla-iddina II of Bīt Iakin (extreme south of Babylonia) ruled as king for twelve years, before being defeated by Sargon II who assumed the role of rightful king of Babylonia on Tiglath-pileser III's pattern. Sargon's successor, Sennacherib, attempted to control Babylonia through personal appointees, but his marked lack of success resulted in his eventual devastation of the city of Babylon and destruction of the statue of Marduk in 689. His son, Esarhaddon, though proclaiming himself the restorer of Babylon, in fact ruled the area as an adjunct of Assyria and it was only in the reign of Assurbanipal, his successor, that the cult of Marduk was reintroduced.[25]

By 630 Assyria had entered on a long civil war related to the royal succession and this in 627 led to the ultimately successful emergence of a local Babylonian leader, Nabopolassar who by about 610 BC had, with the help of the Medes in the mountains north-east of

Recontre Assyriologique Bruxelles, 30 Juin-4 Juillet, 1969 (Ham-sur-Heure, 1970), p. 165 and n.8.
[25] For a detailed discussion of this complex period see for the earlier period down to 722 BC, *PKB*, pp. 218–45; for the later period to 627 BC, J. A. Brinkman, 'Babylonia under the Assyrian Empire, 745–627 BC', in M. T. Larsen (ed.), *Power and Propaganda: a Symposium on Ancient Empires* Mesopotamia 7 (Copenhagen, 1979), pp. 223–50; for Esarhaddon's rule of Babylonia see B. Landsberger, *Brief eines Bischofs von Esagila an König Asarhaddon* Mededelingen der Koninklijke Akadamie van Weteschapen, afdeeling letterkunde, Nieuwe reeds 28/VI (Amsterdam, 1965).

Babylonia, destroyed Assyria and brought its former territories under his control. This marks the birth of the neo-Babylonian empire, which, but for the shift in the location of political power to Babylon and a deliberate emphasis on Babylonian traditions, was structurally very similar to the Assyrian empire it replaced. The succession passed smoothly to Nabopolassar's son, Nebuchadnezzar II, but his grandson, Amel-Marduk, ruled only briefly before being deposed by his uncle Neriglissar, whose own son failed to succeed him effectively: he was eliminated in a palace coup which brought to the throne Nabonidus, a mature man of obscure origins, who ruled successfully for seventeen years before being defeated in 539 by Cyrus of Persia.

THE KING AS THE GUARANTOR OF THE DIVINE ORDER

The centrality of kingship to society in Babylonia from the earliest period on is striking: the king protected his subjects from devastation by war, guaranteed their access to water supplies either by keeping enemies at bay or by digging canals thus helping to ensure agricultural success, and made it possible for the temples to carry out their important rituals ensuring divine protection for the state by keeping them repaired and donating land and resources. The notion that kingship was a prerequisite for civilised existence is found in texts from the early second millennium; for example in the Sumerian King List[26] the institution is represented as already existing before the flood; the 'elements of culture' listed in the myth of 'Enki and Inanna'[27] include kingship and related concepts such as royal insignia, the sceptre, the throne of kingship; in the introduction to the myth of Etana it is stated that order for mankind was established only by placing kingship over it.[28] Civilised existence was conceived to represent a god-given and divinely established order and the king acted as its guardian against chaos which was unleashed by the uncontrolled, anarchic powers of demons (wild animals, enemy attacks, destructive natural phenomena,

---

[26] T. Jacobsen, *The Sumerian King List*, Assyriological Studies 11 (Chicago, 1939), col. i, lines 1–39.

[27] S. N. Kramer, *The Sumerians, their History, Culture and Character* (Chicago, 1963), p. 116.

[28] Translation: *ANET*[3], pp. 114–18 and p. 517; cf. E. Reiner, 'Die akkadische Literatur', in W. Röllig (ed.), *Altorientalische Literaturen* Neues Handbuch der Literaturwissenschaft vol. 1 (Wiesbaden, 1978), p. 168.

disease).[29] An interesting reflection of this contrast is that while gods were conceived anthropomorphically, organised in families, and had a socio-political structure like human society, demons lacked such definition.[30]

Some of these concepts were given specific expression in the poem concerning the elevation of Marduk, city-god of Babylon, to absolute power over the other gods (*Enūma eliš*). This recounts the threat to the stable and peaceful existence of the gods posed by an army of fearful monsters led by the female personification of the sea, Ti'amat. Marduk is selected to become the supreme king of the gods and invested with all requisite power by the assembly of the gods and goes forth to defeat the demonic army. After he has killed Ti'amat he creates the world out of her body, assigning everything to its place, that is establishing order. Moreover he creates mankind to act as servants for the gods thus freeing a group of low-ranking gods, the Annunaki, from compulsory service. In gratitude the Annunaki build Marduk the city of Babylon as a 'sanctuary'.

An important corollary to Marduk's rise to supreme power in the Babylonian pantheon was the greatly increased importance acquired by the New Year Festival of Babylon (*zagmukku/akītu*). Many cities, not only in Babylonia (e.g. in Assyria and at Mari), celebrated a festival of similar name (*akītu*).[31] But it was the festival at Babylon that had become by the end of the second millennium the most important one requiring the participation of the gods of other Babylonian cities who gathered to reaffirm Marduk's supremacy. The festival included recitations of the poem *Enūma eliš* and, for a full performance, demanded the active participation of the reigning king who may, it has been suggested, have ritually enacted the battle to the death between Marduk and Ti'amat.[32] In fact what had been in origin merely a civic festival was transformed into an event of national significance in which not only Marduk's supreme power and world creation but also the king's position and the order for which he was responsible were confirmed and celebrated.

[29] See generally E. Cassin, *La Splendeur Divine: introduction à l'étude de la mentalité mesopotamienne* Civilisations et Sociétés 8 (Paris, 1968), esp. ch.4.

[30] See, for example, T. Jacobsen, *The Treasures of Darkness* (see n.19), pp. 12–13.

[31] A. Falkenstein, 'akiti-Fest und akiti-Festhaus' in R. von Kienle *et al.* (eds.), *Festschrift Johannes Friedrich zum 65. Geburtstag* (Heidelberg, 1959), pp. 147–82.

[32] W. G. Lambert, 'The Conflict in the Akītu House', *Iraq* xxv (1963), pp. 189–90.

Reconstructing the Babylonian *akītu* in full is problematical as the longest preserved text is incomplete.[33] Further, as it dates from the Hellenistic period (that is, after Alexander), one cannot be absolutely sure that the New Year Festival described at the time was completely identical with the one practised in Babylon during the first half of the first millennium BC. However, given the occasional references to the festival in royal inscriptions of Sargon II, Assurbanipal, Nebuchadnezzar II, Neriglissar and Nabonidus[34] it would appear to have resembled it closely. The various rites and ceremonies forming part of the festival reflect the long and complex evolution it had undergone; particularly interesting among these are the ones which involved the king and the 'citizens'.

The festival took place from the first to the twelfth of Nisan, first month of the Babylonian calendar (March-April) and focussed mostly on the temple Esagila in Babylon, the huge sanctuary of Marduk, which also contained chapels for the other Babylonian gods. The main officiant was the 'chief priest' (*šešgallu*) of Esagila and the first seven days were taken up with what may be called preparatory activity largely internal to the temple and not involving the citizen-body directly. A prayer was offered to Marduk on the second day by the chief priest ending with the words:

> Have pity on your city Babylon.
> Turn your face upon your temple
> Maintain the freedom of the privileged citizens
> (*ṣābe kidinni*) of Babylon.

---

[33] The main text was published by F. Thureau-Dangin, *Rituels Accadiens* (Paris, 1921), pp. 127–54; an English translation of the text is in *ANET*³, pp. 331–4. For the problems involved in reconstructing the festival see R. Labat, *Le caractère religieux de la royauté assyro-babylonienne* (Paris, 1939), pp. 165–6; cf. for a brief discussion J. A. Black, 'The New Year Ceremonies in Ancient Babylon: "Taking Bel by the Hand" and a Cultic Picnic', *Religion* xi (1981), pp. 39–59.

[34] Sargon II: D. D. Luckenbill, *Ancient Records of Assyria and Babylonia* 2 vols. (Chicago, 1926–7), ii, para. 38 (henceforth abbr. *ARAB*); Assurbanipal: M. Streck, *Assurbanipal und die letzten assyrischen Könige bis zum Untergang Ninivehs* Vorderasiatische Bibliothek 7 (Leipzig, 1916), p. 149 and 150, line 32f.; p. 301, line 12; p. 271 and 272, line 19; p. 299 and 300 line 33f. (henceforth abbr. *VAB* 7); Nebuchadnezzar II: S. Langdon, *Die Neubabylonischen Königsinschriften* Vorderasiatische Bibliothek 4 (Leipzig, 1912), no. 14, col. i, line 48; Nbk. no. 15, col. iv, lines 1–13; col. viii, line 23; no. 19, Acol. iii, lines 47–53; Acol. v, lines 31–3; (henceforth abbr. *VAB* 4); Neriglissar: *VAB* 4, Ngl no. 1, col. i, lines 33–40; Nabonidus: *VAB* 4, Nbn no. 2, col. ii. line 30; Nbn no. 6, col. ii, line 50; Nbn no. 8, col. ix, lines 3–10 and lines 42–3.

On day four the king set out by boat along the processional canal for Borsippa, near Babylon, to fetch Nabû (often described as the son of Marduk) for the festival. In the evening of the same day the chief priest 'offered' a complete recitation of *Enūma eliš* to Marduk while the crown of Anu (the sky-god) and the throne of Enlil (god of the air), both of whom were displaced by Marduk in the poem, were veiled.

The fifth day saw the return of the king escorting the Nabû statue. As Nabû disembarked, food from Marduk's table was placed before him while the king, after washing his hands, was escorted to the temple for one of the most interesting rituals of the festival. He entered the temple alone and was met by the chief priest emerging from Marduk's shrine, who divested him of his sceptre, ring, mace and crown (in other words, the royal insignia) and placed them out of sight in the shrine. When the chief priest re-emerged he struck the king across the face, led him in to Marduk and forced him to kneel before the god's statue by pulling his ears. The king then made a negative confession:

> I have not sinned, lord of the lands,
> I have not been negligent of your godhead,
> I have not destroyed Babylon,
> I have not ordered her to be dispersed
> I have not made Esagila tremble
> I have not struck the privileged citizens
> > [*ṣābe kidinni*] in the face
> I have not humiliated them.
> I have paid attention to Babylon,
> I have not destroyed her walls.

After this the king left the god's presence while the chief priest gave him the god's reply: 'He will destroy your enemies, defeat your adversaries.' The king was then reinvested with the regalia, but the ritual was not yet complete. He was struck again on the cheek by the chief priest, the purpose this time being to obtain an omen: if the king's tears flowed Marduk was favourably disposed, if they failed to flow Marduk would make the foes of the king rise up and thus cause his downfall. The day's ceremonies were completed after sunset with the sacrifice of a white bull by the king and the chief priest who together addressed a prayer to the planet Mercury, called the 'star of Marduk'.

3 A procession passing through the Ishtar Gate at Babylon.

The following day was marked by the arrival of the divine statues from other cities in Babylonia and the festival neared its climax.

On day eight, participation in the festival apparently became more general. The chief priest offered water to Marduk and then sprinkled it, thus blessed, over the king and people, who must be presumed to have gathered in the courtyard. After the pouring of a libation, the king 'took Bel ("the Lord" = Marduk) by the hand' and led him out into the court where he was enthroned under a canopy. After this he was led to the 'shrine of destinies' where the statues of the other gods were gathered. These formally acknowledged Marduk's supreme authority by abasing themselves. Marduk then pronounced the 'destinies for eternal days', that is general ones, and destinies specifically for the king.

The ninth day began with the doors of the shrine being thrown open and the chief priest calling out: 'Go forth, Bel! O king, go forth! Go forth, our lady (i.e. Ṣarpanitum, Marduk's consort); the king awaits you.' With this cry the most colourful and public phase of the festival was inaugurated, as the procession, led by the splendid statue of Marduk, his consort and the king (again leading the god by the hand) together with all the other gods bedecked in their golden garments, set out along the brilliantly decorated and handsomely paved processional way in full view of the populace.

This was also the opportunity for the king to display his wealth and achievements in war: his troops took part, prisoners of war from campaigns were led in procession, tribute and exotic booty were displayed before the citizens. Some of these items were later presented to the temples as gifts.[35] The privileged citizens perhaps also took part in the procession following the divine emblem (*kidinnu*) from which they symbolically derived their prerogatives and to which status reference was made several times in the course of the ceremonies.[36]

The procession eventually embarked on boats and sailed beyond the city to a landing-stage whence a pine-tree planted avenue led to the festival house.[37] The statues of the gods were ceremoniously installed here and a banquet held. What happened after this and on day ten is unfortunately not known, although it is possible that a

[35] The clearest description of this is given by Esarhaddon in a Nineveh text but it is almost certainly also applicable to the Babylonian festival, see R. Borger, *Die Inschriften Asarhaddons, Königs von Assyrien* Archiv für Orientforschung Beiheft 9 (Graz, 1956), p. 64, vi, lines 58–61 (henceforth abbr. *Asarh.*); for dedication of booty to gods by Nabonidus cf. *VAB* 4, *Nbn* 8, col. ix, lines 3–41.

[36] W. F. Leemans, *Symbolae van Oven* (see n.22), p. 56.

[37] See for this P.-R. Berger, 'Das Neujahrsfest nach den Königsinschriften des ausgehenden babylonischen Reiches', in A. Finet (ed.), *Actes de la XVIIe Rencontre Assyriologique Bruxelles 30 Juin-4 Juillet 1969* (Ham-sur Heure, 1970), p. 157.

4 Coloured glazed brick-relief of the dragon associated with the god Marduk from the Ishtar Gate in Babylon built by Nebuchadnezzar II (604–562 BC). The public procession in which the king led the god Marduk out of his temple (Esagila) during the New Year Festival passed along the brilliantly decorated processional street and through this gate.

'sacred marriage' took place here.[38] The gods and procession returned to Esagila on day eleven, a final assembly took place in the shrine of destinies and the gods were given presents, the 'destinies of the land' were fixed and another banquet took place. On day twelve the festival ended with the return home of the gods. (At what point the hypothetical king's ritual re-enactment of Marduk's battle with Ti'amat might have taken place is not known, although the imperfect knowledge of the details of the festival after day six allow plenty of room.)

In origin the *akītu*, like *akītu*-festivals of other cities, presumably served as a spring harvest-festival (barley, the staple crop of South

---

[38] Problems of defining this ritual act are discussed by J. Renger, 'Heilige Hochzeit', in *RLA* (Berlin, 1975), iv, pp. 251–9; what is known of such a ritual in relation to the Babylonian *akītu*-festival is discussed by A. Falkenstein, 'akiti-Fest und akiti-Festhaus', in R. Kienle *et al.* (eds.), *Festschrift Johannes Friedrich zum 65. Geburtstag* (Heidelberg, 1959), pp. 162–3.

Iraq being harvested in the spring) and marked both the successful completion of the old year and the beginning of the new one.[39] But due to the importance of Babylon as capital and its god as head of the pantheon its celebration had a much wider significance. This is reflected in the emphasis on the supremacy of Marduk over the other gods expressed by the recitation of *Enūma eliš*, and the gathering of the gods from other cities in an assembly to acknowledge this and confirm him as their king who had freed or would free them from the forces of chaos and establish the world-order. A further aspect of this is the pronunciation of the 'destinies' by Marduk, which echoes his activity after his victory over Ti'amat, one of whose creatures had blasphemously worn the 'tablet of destinies' which Marduk wore himself after killing him. The banquet of the gods, too, could recall the banquet to which Marduk invited the gods after the Annunaki had built Esagila and Babylon for him.

An important aspect of the festival is its emphasis both on Babylon itself (temples, walls, rites) and on its inhabitants, particularly that privileged group called the *ṣābe kidinni*. The former is presumably in part related to the initially local character of the festival, although given Babylon's important position this must have developed to express a more general concern about the king's duty as a major initiator of building programmes particularly of the walls protecting cities, and of the temples which provided the gods with homes, as well as the main provider of resources, manpower and land to enable the temple-staff to carry out the daily divine services. This is, of course, what mankind was created to do in *Enūma eliš* – without this service the gods would withdraw their protection leaving mankind open to disasters and with no hope of survival. The king thus carried the responsibility for providing all the essentials for the divine order to be maintained.

But just as the society of the gods was stratified with a king, an assembly of older gods and groups of servant gods, so human society also consisted of persons of differentiated status. The king, himself, of course, stood at its head as Marduk did in the pantheon, but certain citizens, like the Annunaki after Marduk's creation of

[39] There is some debate as to whether the *akītu*-festival was the last or the first act of the year, see D. J. Wiseman, *Chronicles of Chaldaean Kings (626–556 B.C.) in the British Museum* (London, 1961), p. 27; *PKB*, p. 241, n.1547; A. K. Grayson, 'Chronicles and the Akitu Festival' (see n.24), p. 170, n.3.

man, had been freed from compulsory labour and dues. These are the *ṣābe kidinni*, the 'privileged citizens' who were superior to those groups of the population who did not enjoy the same exempt status, but on whose labour the continued existence of society depended. The plea for the maintenance of this system of privilege appeared early in the festival, forming the closing lines of the chief priest's prayer to Marduk early in the morning of the second day. It was there clearly expressed as a demand made to the god himself.

The king's ritual humiliation and confession on day five was closely related to this: stripped of his regalia, struck in the face and forced painfully to his knees, he not only confirmed that he had not damaged or destroyed Babylon or its population but included a specific statement that he had not struck the privileged citizens in the face or otherwise humiliated them (presumably by imposing on them tasks violating their status). In other words he had carried out his duty to maintain the social order as laid down by Marduk. Only after this accounting of his acts to the god's satisfaction was the king reinstated, and allowed to continue in office with Marduk's active support. He was, however, warned about the precariousness of his position: this must be, at least partly, the significance of the second blow administered to the king after the resumption of his regalia; kingship was a loan from the gods, not a permanent gift, and would become forfeit should its holder sin against the established order.[40] The king was thus under an obligation to Marduk to defend his creation against all threats which included maintaining the prerogatives of those of his subjects who were under his divine protection. Possibly the 'sacred marriage' ceremony, which was connected, in some instances, with the investiture of kings, gave the final seal of approval to the king's continued reign.[41]

A final important element of the festival was its public character; it probably involved almost everyone within the city and its immediate environs. All levels of the temple staff, many of whom were, of course, citizens, must have been involved in providing for the various rituals, preparing the food to be offered to all the visiting gods, supplying the two banquets, ensuring that the gods' garments were clean and in good repair, as well as the processional

---

[40] For a discussion of the concept of the divine bestowal of the 'royal splendour' (Akk. *melammu*) as a loan from the gods, see E. Cassin, *La Splendeur divine* (see n.29), pp. 77–8.

[41] This, of course, depends on the vexed question of what the 'sacred/divine marriage' meant precisely in this context cf. Renger, 'Heilige Hochzeit' (see n.38).

chariots and boats, to mention just some of the enormous activity that must perforce have taken place. One would presume that the gods from other cities (even if fetched by people from Babylon) must have been escorted by at least some of their own regular retinues. Thus the festival drew together more groups than just those people living in or close to Babylon. Who the 'people' were on whom, together with the king, water was sprinkled on day eight is unknown as they are not more closely defined, and this part of the festival is in any case restored from another text.[42] But if correct, it suggests some kind of blessing on a more general group than just the king and temple staff. Central to the festival was the procession. Spectators watching would have seen the king accompanying the chief god of the pantheon heading the train of the other gods, accompanied by musicians and singers, the armed forces, the booty of war and the privileged citizens following the emblem symbolising their status which had just been reaffirmed.

Further, the festival was a holiday, an occasion for feasting with many of the ingredients perhaps directly provided by the king through the banquets prepared for the gods. There is a reference in a contract to what would appear to be the dividing up of food between two priests that had been laid before a divine statue as a meal; the date and place makes it likely that this would have been the New Year Festival.[43] The fête-like atmosphere is particularly well illustrated by a passage from the late version of the Gilgamesh epic. When the hero Gilgamesh reaches the distant land where Ut-Napishtim (the Babylonian Noah) lives, the latter tells him in detail the story of the great flood. After the building of the Ark was finished, Ut-Napishtim held a feast to celebrate:

> I slaughtered oxen for [the people]
> Daily I butchered sheep.
> Beer, [...] sesame and date-wine
> The work[men drank] like river-water and
> they feasted as (on) the days of the *akītu*.[44]

[42] F. Thureau-Dangin, *Rituels Accadiens* (Paris, 1921), AO 6459, lines 22–3 (pp. 90 and 95).

[43] A. Ungnad, *Vorderasiatische Schriftdenkmäler* (Leipzig, 1907), iv, no. 89 (henceforth abbr. *VS* 4); translation in M. San Nicolò and A. Ungnad, *Neubabylonische Rechts- und Verwaltungsurkunden* (Leipzig, 1935), no. 316.

[44] Gilgamesh Epic, Neo-Assyrian version Tablet xi, lines 70–4; for translations in English see *ANET*³, pp. 72–99 and 503–7; A. Heidel, *The Gilgamesh Epic and Old Testament Parallels*, 2nd edn (Chicago, 1949).

One might assume then that certainly at the point where the festival moved into its 'public' phase, normal activities were suspended, people were free to watch the grand procession come and return, and feasted on meat and drink provided by the establishments for which they worked or within their families. People from other cities were present and news exchanged. The occasion helped to reaffirm their corporate identity, the social fabric and the prosperity of the country.

RITUALS IN CONTEXT

The Babylonian New Year Festival encapsulated perfectly the important notions connected with the maintenance of the status quo; yet the period at which one sees it becoming prominent is one of extreme and lengthy instability in the kingship.[45] Although a certain measure of peace and prosperity was established eventually by Nabopolassar and Nebuchadnezzar II, they failed to establish a dynastic succession and the throne was usurped twice in the ten years after Nebuchadnezzar II's death. It seems almost as though precisely because of this uncertainty the emphasis on traditional 'order' and its re-establishment increased. Virtually all the concepts expressed by the king's ritual confession were utilised by invaders and usurpers in their inscriptions, and formulated in a variety of ways.

Typical of Assyrian kings intervening in Babylonia in the ninth and eighth centuries was their statement that they had performed sacrifices in the sanctuaries of the Babylonian cities, but had punished the Aramaean tribes and exacted tribute from the Chaldaeans.[46] Related to this, but not limited to the Assyrian kings, was the declaration of the respect that they had shown the *kidinnūtu* status of Babylonian cities and their re-establishment of it. Confirmation of this status sometimes included land-donations made to the citizens.[47]

---

[45] Approximately 44 kings ruled Babylonia between 979 and 539 BC, which gives an average length of only ten years rule per king; in fact, several ruled longer while a number ruled less than a year and in some cases the names of kings and lengths of rule are not known at all (*see* chronological table, Fig.2).

[46] Shalmaneser III: *ARAB* vol.i, para. 624; Shamshi-Aded V: *ABC* no. 21, col. iv, lines 9–13; Tiglath-pileser III: *ARAB* vol.i, para. 788; Saragon II: *ARAB* vol.ii, paras. 35–7.

[47] Marduk-apla-iddina II: L. Messerschmidt and A. Ungnad, *Vorder-asiatiasche Schriftdenkmäler* (Leipzig, 1907), i, no. 37, col. iii, lines 10–15, 23–5, 31–2

'Gathering the dispersed/abducted peoples' (sc. deportees) and repatriating them is another common motif (harking back to Hammurabi) which emphasised the re-establishment of social and political order and norms.[48] Associated with this act was the repatriation of divine images to their former cult-centres: Sargon II restored gods taken to the Sealand (home of Marduk-apla-iddina II) to their sanctuaries in Babylonian cities;[49] Assurbanipal reintroduced the statue of Marduk and his cultic paraphernalia to Babylon from Assyria and returned the statue of Nanna and Uṣur-amatsu to Uruk from Elam;[50] Nabopolassar returned gods from Uruk to Elam;[51] Nebuchadnezzar II restored Ishtar of Uruk and Ishtar of Susa;[52] Neriglissar partly restored Annunitum of Sippar;[53] Nabonidus returned the statue of Sin of Harran to its home from Babylon.[54]

That the royal claimant should have been chosen by Marduk was an important feature related to the supremacy of Marduk as king of the Babylonian pantheon, god of its capital city and thus of the whole of Babylonia.[55] A topos that could serve to explain the reason for Marduk's sometimes surprising choice was that Marduk had become angry with Babylon because of the misrule of the

(henceforth abbr. *VSI*) (for a translation of the text into Dutch see W. F. Leemans, 'Marduk-apal-iddina II, zijn tijd en zijn geslacht', *Jaarbericht van het Vooraziatische-Egyptisch Genootschap 'Ex Oriente Lux'* Deel iii/9–10 (1944–8), pp. 444–8); Sargon II: *ARAB* vol.ii, para. 40; para. 78; para. 99; para. 102; Esarhadon: *Asarh.*, para. 11, cf.para. 2, col. ii, line 33 (Bab. Texte, ep.37); Assurbanipal: *VAB* 7, 226 and 227, 488 and 489; R. F. Harper, *Assyrian and Babylonian Letters belonging to the Kouyunjik Collection of the British Museum I–XIV*, (London, Chicago, 1892–1914), no. 301, obv. line 16 (henceforth abbr. *ABL*); Nabonidus: C. J. Gadd, L. Legrain and S. Smith, *Ur Excavation Texts I: Royal Inscriptions* (London, 1928), no. 187 (henceforth abbr. *UET I*).

48 Adad-nirari III: *ABC* no. 21, col. iv, line 19; Marduk-apla-iddina: *VS* I no. 37, col. i, lines 32–3; col. ii, lines 28–30; C. J. Gadd, 'Inscribed Barrel Cylinder of Marduk-apla-iddina II', *Iraq* xv (1953), p. 124, line 15; Sargon II: *ARAB* vol. ii, para. 40; Esarhaddon: *Asarh.* p. 25, ep. 37.

49 *ARAB* vol. ii, para. 40

50 Marduk: *ABC* no. 1, col. iv, lines 34–6; no. 15, lines 4–5; *ARAB* vol. ii, para. 957; Nanna and Uṣur-amatsu: *ABL* no. 1007; *ABL* no. 518; *ARAB* vol. ii, paras. 919–20 cf. para. 926.

51 *ABC* no. 2, lines 16–17.   52 *VAB* 4. Nbn 8, col. iii, lines 30–42.

53 *VAB* 4. Nbn 8, col. iv, lines 14–33.

54 *VAB* 4. Nbn 8, col. x; C. J. Gadd, 'The Harran Inscriptions of Nabonidus', *Anatolian Studies* viii (1958), pp. 35–92: H₂A/B col. iii, lines 21–8.

55 Marduk-apla-iddina II: *VS* I, no. 37, col. i, Gadd *Iraq* xv (1953), p. 124, line 12; Sargon II: *ARAB* vol. ii, para. 31; Esarhaddon: *Asarh.*, p. 16, Bab. ep. 10–11; Nabopolassar: *VAB* 4, Nbp. no. 4, lines 8–21; Nabonidus: *VAB* 4, Nbn 8, col. v, lines 8–10.

5 Boundary stone (*kudurru*) of Marduk-apla-iddina II (721–710 BC) recording a gift of land made by the king to an official. The text describes the chaotic state of the country before Marduk-apla-iddina's reign and how he was chosen by the god Marduk to re-establish order. The king is shown on the left wearing a pointed cap with a long ribbon; the person facing him is probably the recipient of the land-gift. Across the top of this stone are altars symbolising gods who acted as the divine guarantors of the document; on the right is shown the dragon and spade of Marduk.

preceding king. Marduk is represented as abandoning Babylon in anger, thus creating by his absence the requisite situation of complete chaos which it would be the task of his next more suitable candidate to reverse. The mythical formulation of this can be found in the Epic of Erra which begins with Marduk leaving Babylon in order to find artisans and materials to make his robes, leaving the field clear for Erra, god of strife and war and by extension the social turmoil and plague that are their inevitable outcome.[56] The horrors of his rule are ended only through Marduk's return. The theme of Marduk's anger with misrule and subsequent choice of a more fit ruler were certainly used by Marduk-apla-iddina II and Esarhad-don[57] and are implied in texts of Saragon II and Nabonidus.[58]

An account of the ceremonial entry into Babylon by a foreign king is a feature less often described in preserved texts. The only one extant is that of Sargon II who was invited into the city by its inhabitants, entered amid great rejoicing, re-dug a canal for the divine procession and then performed the New Year Festival in Babylon.[59] It seems, however, likely that Shalmaneser III acted similarly after helping his ally, the Babylonian king, to put down a revolt.[60] Although the two instances are different – Sargon II defeated a reigning king (Marduk-apla-iddina II) and Shalmaneser III aided the reigning king to overcome a threat to his authority – the essentials of the situation were conceptually the same: both kings removed challenges to the correct order of Babylonian life, a rebellion in the earlier case and a Chaldaean tribal leader who had wrested the rule of Babylonia from the Assyrian kings.

Because of the political turmoil in the first half of the first millennium BC in Babylonia 'anyone' could become a king: Marduk would choose and decide whether a claimant was worthy or not and the personal success of a king in keeping his throne was proof of divine approval. In such a fluid situation it was particularly

---

[56] L. Cagni, *The Poem of Erra* Sources from the Ancient Near East vol. i, fascicle 3 (Malibu, 1977).

[57] Marduk-apla-iddina II: *VS* I, no. 37, col. i, line 18; Gadd, *Iraq* xv (1953), p. 124, lines 8–9; Esarhaddon: *Asarh.*, pp. 13ff. Bab. ep. 5–9. The theme of Marduk's divine wrath resulting in foreign oppression (in this instance, by the Assyrians) and his choice of a 'nobody' to become king and put matters in order is also used in a recently found and published cylinder of Nabopolassar from Babylon (A Babylon 11, cols. i, 7–ii, 5); cf. Farouk N. H. al-Rawi, 'Nabopolassar's Restoration Work on Imgur-Enlil at Babylon', *Iraq* xlvii (1985), pp. 1–9.

[58] Sargon II: *ARAB* vol. ii, para. 31; Nabonidus: *VAB* 4, Nbn 8, col. iv, lines 40–1.

[59] *ARAB* vol.ii, paras. 35–6; para. 38.   [60] *ARAB* vol. i, para. 624.

valuable to emulate conspicuously successful predecessors in order to demonstrate to gods and people that one's acts were precisely like those of a king who had found approval on an earlier occasion. It also, of course, reinforced the claim of any one ruler to have successfully defended or restored the traditional order in keeping with divine 'plans'.[61] It served to create, in the absence of dynastic legitimacy, a line of kings basing their claims to authority on the fact that they had been chosen to continue and bring to completion the beneficial acts initiated by a series of divinely approved earlier kings.

This aspect is particularly well illustrated by the inscriptions of Nabonidus who was elevated to the throne as the result of the bloody coup, involving the murder of the under-age son of his predecessor, Neriglissar, who himself had forcibly removed his nephew Amel-Marduk, the young son of the great Nebuchadnezzar II, from the kingship (see above p. 30). The very fact that the two young men were unsuccessful in succeeding their fathers constituted proof that their accession to the throne was against the will of the gods and that they had disregarded the wise dispositions of their divinely approved (that is, successful) fathers. In contrast to them Nabonidus describes himself in the following terms:

I am the real executor of the wills of Nebuchadnezzar and Neriglissar, my royal predecessors! Their armies are entrusted to me. I shall not treat carelessly their orders and I am [anxious] to please them (that is, conform to their plans).[62]

The Babylonian *akītu* festival of course most pointedly and concretely expressed all the concepts just discussed including an emphasis on the personal performance and accountability of the king and the precariousness of his position (see above p. 38). Unfortunately it is not often mentioned directly in royal inscriptions, the exceptions being possibly Shalmaneser III (no more than a reference),[63] Sargon II, Assurbanipal's accounts of his re-establishment of the Marduk cult in Babylon, Nebuchadnezzar II, Neriglissar and Nabonidus (see above p. 41). There were clearly

---

[61] Akk. *uṣurtu*, see A. L. Oppenheim, *Ancient Mesopotamia: portrait of a dead civilization* (Chicago, 1964), p. 204.

[62] *VAB* 4, Nbn 8, col. v, lines 14–24. The translation is that of A. L. Oppenheim in *ANET*[3], p. 309

[63] The reference to Tiglath-pileser III's celebrations of the festival is contained in the calendrical 'Eponym chronicle', see E. Ebeling, 'Eponymen', in *RLA* ii (Berlin, 1938), p. 431, C[b]1, lines 45–6.

long periods during which the festival was not celebrated. This could be because of major political and military disturbances, for example in the reign of Nabu-šuma-iškun (*c.* 760–748), possibly due to serious internal disruptions, and during the revolt of Šamas-šuma-ukin (652–648);[64] and throughout the massive fighting and devastation in Babylonia resulting from Nabopolassar's claim to kingship in Babylonia (626) which was, in fact, a rebellion against the Assyrians.[65] Another reason for non-performance of the festival was the absence of the Marduk statue – it was destroyed by Sennacherib in the course of his devastation of Babylon in 689 and the statue was not restored until Assurbanipal's first regnal year so that the festival can only have been performed again after a long gap for the first time in 667.[66] Finally it was impossible to carry out a full celebration of the festival if the king was absent on campaign as was the case with Nabonidus who was continuously campaigning in North-West Arabia between (probably) 551 and 542,[67] although a curtailed ceremony was possible.[68] By contrast Nebuchadnezzar II appears to have made every effort to return from campaigning in order to participate in this event.[69]

However, the non-celebration of the festival never affected the recognition of a king as legitimate ruler as was once thought;[70] indeed Esarhaddon who did nothing to restore the cult so ruthlessly ended by his father appears to have enjoyed rather a good press among certain groups in Babylonia.[71] Inasmuch as the *akītu*

[64] *ABC* no. 15, line 22, cf. *PKB*, pp. 225–6; *ABC* no. 16, lines 17–23.

[65] *ABC* no. 16, lines 24–7.

[66] *ABC* no. 14, lines 31–7.

[67] H. Tadmor, 'The Inscriptions of Nabuna'id: Historical Arrangement', in H. G. Güterbock and T. Jacobsen (eds.), *Studies in Honor of Benno Landsberger on his seventy-fifth birthday, April 21, 1965*, Assyriological Studies 16 (Chicago, 1965), pp. 351–63.

[68] *ABC* no. 7, col. ii, lines 7–8; for an analogous situation in the Assyrian empire where the king's garment was sent as a substitute for his physical presence see *ABL* no. 667.

[69] E. N. von Voigtlander, *A Survey of Neo-Babylonian History* (diss. Ann Arbor, 1963), pp. 92–3.

[70] For the old notion see S. Smith, 'Sennacherib and Esarhaddon', *Cambridge Ancient History* (Cambridge, 1925), iii, p. 62; pp. 68ff.; B. Meissner, *Babylonien und Assyrien* (Heidelberg, 1920), i, p. 64. For rejections of this view (with earlier bibliography) see A. K. Grayson, 'Chronicles and the Akitu Festival' in A. Finet (ed.), *Actes de la XVIIe rencontre Assyriologique, Bruxelles 30 juin-4 juillet 1969* (Ham-sur-Heure 1970), pp. 163–70; A. Kuhrt and S. Sherwin-White, 'Xerxes' Destruction of Babylonian Temples', in H.W.A.M. Sancisi-Weerdenburg and A. Kuhrt (eds.), *Achaemenid History II: the Greek Sources* (Leiden, in press).

[71] *ABC* p. 30.

symbolised the correct order of things, both on the socio-political and transcendental plane it served a crucial function. Thus a number of chronicles focus their attention on the performance (or not) of the *akītu* and record instances of lengthy interruptions of it from the end of the second millennium on; one chronicle, in fact, is almost exclusively concerned with collecting instances of such interruptions.[72] Because of the extreme political insecurity it would seem that this festival above all represented a gauge for assessing the well-being of the country.

In the first half of the first millennium BC instability in the overall rule of the country almost became the norm and those persons laying claim to the Babylonian throne such as Assyrian conquerors, Chaldaean arrivistes, and people raised to kingship as the result of coups or rebellions, used what seems to have become a standard range of symbolic images to demonstrate their acceptability as rulers in the eyes of the gods and subjects. They were called to the kingship by Marduk, the supreme god, often because he had been angered by the preceding king's misrule. The predecessor having been proved to be unfit by the victor's success, the new king was invited into Babylon and other cities spontaneously by the citizen-body whose special privileges derived from divine protection which he, by contrast to the defeated ruler, respected. His aim and duty was to re-establish the order as it was deemed to have existed earlier and as Marduk himself had created it for gods and men at the beginning of time. A concrete act that expressed this was to return deported peoples to their original homes, reinstate them in their traditional positions and repatriate divine statues in their traditional sanctuaries. Such acts could be accompanied by land-grants to resettled citizens, the rebuilding and beautifying of temples, provision for regular or increased offerings to the gods, and civic building works (walls, canals). This was presented as continuing and bringing to fruition the work of earlier rulers who had clearly enjoyed divine support but whose plans, which were so much in keeping with the divine purpose, had been interrupted and aborted by unworthy successors. The ceremony which most clearly expressed the achievement of these aims and the fulfilment of these duties was the New Year Festival in Babylon praising the divine patron of the city, king of the gods, and providing public proof of

---

[72] The so-called 'Akitu Chronicle' = *ABC* no. 16.

6 King Assurbanipal of Assyria (668–627 BC) shown as temple-builder; probably from Babylon. He is depicted wearing the Assyrian crown and carrying a basket of earth on his head for the construction of the temple. Building, especially of temples, was a standard activity of pious rulers; the representation of the king with a basket is part of a very long tradition reaching back to the middle of the third millennium BC.

the ruler's success in making the country ever more prosperous and in keeping the destructive forces of chaos at bay.

CYRUS' CONQUEST OF BABYLON

From what has been said it will be clear that in spite of the fact that Cyrus of Persia represented a new linguistic, cultural and political element, occupation of the Babylonian throne by a foreign conqueror need not provide an ideological impasse to the Babylonians, on condition that the new king pledged himself to and showed himself active in maintaining the traditional order. This is clearly demonstrated by the fact that though Cyrus' conquest of Babylonia was not the smooth take-over which it is frequently presented as, but was the result of a bloody battle,[73] the three texts that provide a virtually contemporary account of this event all emphasise the lack of disruption caused by it. Two of these texts are clearly propaganda statements composed after the event and in Cyrus' interest, but the third – a chronicle belonging to a series remarkable for its unbiased, sober recording of facts[74] – supports their evidence. Taking all three together one can see very clearly how the ideological and symbolic repertoire was drawn on.

In 539, a battle was fought at Opis, east of the Tigris (see Fig. 1), in which Cyrus was eventually victorious; that it was probably a hard-won victory is indicated by the fact that it ended in a massacre of the population of the city and extensive looting. As a result of this Sippar, just to the north of Babylon, submitted, followed by the surrender of Nabonidus and his army. Cyrus did not proceed immediately to Babylon but sent a detachment of the army under one of his provincial governors ahead to invest the city and prepare for his formal reception as the new king. Although the evidence is lacking, it is possible that at this point an invitation to enter Babylon was extended to Cyrus by the citizens. Some kind of formal ceremonial entry is indicated by the fact that what should probably be translated as aromatic branches strewed the path along which the conqueror entered[75] and one would imagine the scene was similar to the reception offered to Alexander by Babylon in

---

[73] *ABC* no. 7, col. iii, lines 12–14.   [74] See *ABC*, pp. 8–10.

[75] Understanding of the Akkadian terms *ha-ri-ni-e* is disputed; *Chicago Assyrian Dictionary* vol. 6: Ḫ (Chicago, 1956), p. 102 and *ANET*[3], p. 306, n. 13 translate it 'branches'.

331:[76] on that occasion the conqueror was met by a procession of citizens and the Babylonian governor accompanied by musicians and was led into the city along flower-strewn paths. Both Cyrus and, over 200 years later, Alexander were modelling their behaviour on that practised by Assyrian invaders two and three hundred years earlier. The end to bloodshed and the maintenance of civic order were announced to the citizens: the chronicle reports that Cyrus 'spoke well-being' to the city (identical in Mesopotamian usage with a formal greeting), none of the rites in the temples were interrupted and arrangements for continuing the administration of the country were made.

Cyrus seems to have begun almost immediately to order building work on temples and city-walls in Babylon and other parts of Babylonia.[77] Again one can compare with this Alexander's activities as reported by the Greek historian Arrian: on entry into Babylon Alexander ordered all the temples of the city to be restored;[78] and yet again these actions become understandable as part of the traditional duties of a Babylonian king carried out by earlier Assyrian conquerors as well as by native rulers and usurpers. To commemorate this important act a foundation inscription in the form of a clay cylinder was composed, and it is to this document that we owe our quite detailed knowledge of how fully Cyrus' assumption of the kingship was integrated into Babylonian ideology.[79] The literary style of the text as well as its content is very close to Mesopotamian inscriptions especially those of Assurbanipal relating to Babylon,[80] and it makes use of virtually all the

---

[76] Especially as described by Q. Curtius Rufus, *Historiae* v, 1. 19–23; cf. also Arrian, *Anabasis* iii.16. A possible reference to Alexander's ceremonial entry may be contained in BM 36761 rev. 11–14, cf. D. J. Wiseman *Nebuchadnezzar and Babylon* (Oxford 1985; The Schweich Lectures of the British Academy 1983), pp. 116–21.

[77] Ur: *UET I*, nos. 194 and 307; Uruk: F. H. Weissbach, *Keilinschriften der Achämeniden* Vorderasiatische Bibliothek 3 (Leipzig, 1911), pp. xi and 8–9, no. Ib; J. Jordan, *Erster vorläufiger Bericht über die von der Notgemeinschaft der Deutschen Wissenschaft in Uruk-Warka unternommenen Ausgrabungen* (Berlin, 1930), no. 31.

[78] Arrian, *Anabasis* iii.16.

[79] An English translation of the Cyrus Cylinder is in *ANET³*, pp. 315–16; transliteration, translation and discussion of text including the newly joined fragment from Yale is in P.-R. Berger, 'Der Kyros-Zylinder mit dem Zusatzfragment BIN II no. 32', *Zeitschrift für Assyriologie* xliv (1975), pp. 192–234.

[80] J. Harmatta, 'The Literary Patterns of the Babylonian Edict of Cyrus', *Acta Antique Scientiae Academicae Hungaricae* xix (1971), pp. 217–23; C. Walker, 'A New Fragment of the Cyrus Cylinder' *Iran* x (1972), pp. 158–9; P.-R. Berger,

7 The famous clay foundation cylinder of Cyrus of Persia (*c*. 550–530 BC); it comes from Babylon where it served to commemorate his work on the Esagila temple. Like Marduk-apla-iddina II, Cyrus began the description of his accession to the throne of Babylon by describing the awful state into which Babylon had fallen under his predecessor; as a result of this, Marduk left Babylon in anger and searched for a more worthy man to rule his people.

symbolic elements already discussed. It starts with a long description of Marduk's wrath with Babylon because of the misrule of its king to the point where Marduk abandons the city and the dreadful suffering which the inhabitants have to undergo as a result. Although it is not clearly stated, the implication of the text is that they have lost their privileged status (*kidinnūtu*). Meanwhile Marduk roams the world seeking a suitable king until his gaze alights on Cyrus of Persia whom he leads, like a friend, into Babylon where he is received with joy. Cyrus guarantees the peace of the country and releases the citizens from their unjust burdens. He returns to their homes the divine images gathered in Babylon together with the people and personnel associated with them; cult-offerings are restored and increased and civic building projects in Babylon are completed or elaborated.

This last activity is, of course, a continuing of the works of

'Der Kyros-Zylinder' (see n. 79); A. Kuhrt, 'The Cyrus Cylinder and Achaemenid Imperial Policy', *Journal for the Study of the Old Testament* xxv (1983), pp. 83–97; R. J. van der Spek, 'Cyrus de Pers in Assyrische perspectief', *Tijdschrift voor Geschiedenis* xcvi (1983), pp. 1–27.

predecessors and this is made plain at the end of the cylinder, where Cyrus' completion of a quay-wall in Babylon begun by an earlier king is mentioned. The final lines of the text contain a reference to Cyrus' finding of an inscription by Assurbanipal 'a king who preceded me' which he, probably (text broken), replaced reverently in the foundations next to his own, thus carefully connecting himself with an earlier successful ruler. The same sentiment is quite unmistakably expressed in the other text relating to Cyrus' conquest. This is a poem vilifying Nabonidus' reign in detail which ends with a positive hymn of jubilation to Cyrus:[81] Cyrus is described as instantly setting to work to complete the walls of Babylon in which undertaking the Babylonians willingly join in order to execute '[the original plan] of Nebuchadnezzar'. Though the text is restored, in the light of the evidence from the cylinder this must be the import of the passage and it demonstrates how Cyrus was incorporated into the list of royal continuators of the divine will.

Whether Cyrus actually celebrated the New Year Festival in Babylon is unfortunately not clear. A broken passage in the chronicle at the beginning of Cyrus' first year contains a reference to Cambyses, Cyrus' son, enacting a ritual involving Nabû on 4. Nisan. This is generally interpreted as a reference to the *akītu* festival and connected with the fact that during Cyrus' first regnal year in Babylonia, Cambyses actually functioned as king of Babylon with Cyrus as a kind of overlord.[82] This might mean that Cambyses would have been the appropriate person to perform this ritual. In fact the identification of the ceremony is very uncertain, particularly given the partial preservation of the text. All one can venture is that it *may* concern the installation of Cambyses as king of Babylonia,[83] perhaps in *connection* with a celebration of the *akītu* festival. This is, of course, speculative, but given the fact that Cyrus made use of all the other royal ceremonial in regular use for over three hundred years it is not unlikely. Only scant evidence for continued celebration of the festival exists during the Persian

---

[81] Text published by S. Smith, *Babylonian Historical Texts Relating to the Capture and Downfall of Babylon* (London, 1924), pp. 27–97; translation only in *ANET*³, pp. 312–15.

[82] A. L. Oppenheim, 'A New Cambyses Incident', in J. Gluck (ed.), *A Survey of Persian Art from Prehistoric Times to the Present: volume xv, New Studies 1960–1973 in Memoriam Arthur Upham Pope* (London, New York, 1974), pp. 3497–502.

[83] For the difficulties of identifying the ceremony as the *akītu*-festival see A. Kuhrt and S. Sherwin-White, 'Xerxes' Destruction of Babylonian Temples' (see n. 70).

period,[84] but as it was still peformed in the Hellenistic period (reign of Seleucus III in 224 BC)[85] and as it has now been shown that Xerxes did not remove the cult-statue of Marduk from Babylon which would automatically have terminated the festival,[86] the cumulative evidence points to continuity in this important cere-monial act throughout the period of Persian domination of Baby-lonia and, indeed, beyond.

BABYLONIAN AND PERSIAN INTERACTION

One aspect still requiring consideration is what the Persian context might have been into which this elaborate ceremonial was received and how it might actually have shaped Persian kingship. How far was Xenophon correct in seeing Cyrus' conquest of Babylon as the crucial formative influence on its development? Given the scanty evidence from Persia itself this is impossible to answer with any certainty. There are however some curious similarities between the procession described in *Cyropaedia* viii 3–4, which was the immedi-ate result of Cyrus' decision to behave 'as he thought became a king', and some aspects of the Babylonian New Year Festival. Apart from its location in Babylon (significant in itself) the account describes an elaborate procession involving divine chariots and sacrificial animals followed by the specially robed king; a holocaust of bulls in honour of 'Zeus' recalls the bull sacrifice made by the king on the evening of day five (see above p. 33); the display of military strength and a banquet also figure and Cyrus is said to have ordered the festival to be performed regularly and for ever. This was also the occasion on which the socio-political relationships and future social patterns were supposedly established. If, as some have thought, the Xenophon passage is based on a Persian ritual procession he himself witnessed,[87] some elements of the Babylon-ian festival may have helped to shape what became an important

---

84 Reign of Darius I: *VS* 4, no. 89, cf. E. Unger, *Babylon, die heilige Stadt nach der Beschreibung der Babylonier* (Berlin, 1931), p. 150, n. 1; rebel-king in time of Xerxes' reign: F. M. T. de Liagre Böhl, 'Die babylonischen Prätendenten zur Zeit Xerxes', *Bibliotheca Orientalis* xix (1962), pp. 110–14.

85 *ABC* no. 13b.

86 A. Kuhrt and S. Sherwin-White, 'Xerxes' Destruction' of Babylonian Temples' (see n. 70).

87 M. Boyce, *A History of Zoroastrianism vol. II: Under the Achaemenians* Handbuch der Orientalistik 1. Abt. 8. vol. 1. Abschnitt, issue 2, part 2A (Leiden, 1982), p. 214.

8 Seal impression of the so-called 'Late Assyrian Royal Seal'. The device on these royal seals shows a royal hero overcoming a lion, symbolising the king as the guardian of order versus chaos.

Persian ceremony which regularly reaffirmed the king's central and superior position as well as confirming the social order.

Other elements of Xenophon's description, such as the chariot-racing competitions, are nowhere attested as forming part of the *akītu*. This, and the gifts made by the king after the 'games', have been regarded by some scholars as reflecting a specific Iranian contribution to the formulation of Old Persian kingship.[88] A further suggestion is that the Persian New Year Festival may have been substantially similar to that practised in India, which centred on the king as hero ritually overcoming a dragon who had imprisoned rain, water and women, that is all the life-giving, productive forces, and thus liberating them.[89] Although *totally* hypothetical (there is no actual evidence that a New Year Festival was ever celebrated in the Old Persian Period),[90] the suggestion is not without its attractions. The king as the constant warrior in defence of 'order-truth' (*arta*) against 'chaos-falsehood' (*drauga*) is the leitmotif of many Old Persian royal inscriptions. It may be precisely this aspect of the king that is symbolically expressed in the pictorial motif found so frequently at Persepolis of the royal hero struggling with a mythical beast.[91] The Persian king's concern with

[88] See, for example, H.W.A.M. Sancisi-Weerdenburg, *Yaunā en Persai: Grieken en Perzen in een ander Perspectief* (Groningen, 1980), pp. 203–6.

[89] P. Briant, 'Forces productives, dépendance rurale et idéologies réligieuses dans l'empire achéménide', in *idem, Rois, tributs et paysans* (Paris, 1982), pp. 431–73 at 445–446.

[90] See C. Nylander, 'Ritual Persepolis – a critical discussion', *Lecture delivered at the VIth Congress of Iranian Art and Archaeology, Oxford 1972*; and *idem*, 'Al-Biruni and Persepolis', *Acta Iranica I* (Leiden, 1974), pp. 137–50.

[91] M. C. Root, *The King and Kingship in Achaemenid Art: Essays on the Creation of an Iconography of Empire* Acta Iranica 3rd ser., vol. ix (Leiden, 1979), pp. 303–8; Boyce, *History of Zoroastrianism* (see n. 87), p. 105.

9 The royal hero struggling with a lion, from the Persian palace complex at Persepolis. The imagery picks up that used in the late Assyrian period.

provision of water and the creation of agricultural fertility is expressed most strikingly in the creation of *paradeisoi* – estates of well-watered, prosperous land forming in some places virtual oases.[92]

If this correctly characterises some of the fundamental features of Old Persian kingship, then it is possible to see it as a complex amalgam of differently derived elements. Some were basically Iranian mythological concepts given concrete expression and ritually articulated by an adaptation of the Babylonian New Year Festival. The latter's emphasis on the maintenance and defence of the world-order through the defeat of chaotic forces provided a perfect ceremonial counterpart to the former, despite the fact that these were differently formulated and had developed within a totally distinct cultural, geographical and historical milieu. Thus, Babylonian cultural identity was not forced to succumb to, or driven underground by the Persian (or indeed later Greek) conquest; rather it demanded and obtained recognition, support and the active participation of the conquerors and enriched their own ideological repertoire.[93]

---

[92] For discussion of this and a complete list of *paradeisoi*, see Briant, 'Forces productives' (n. 89), pp. 451–6 and n. 109.

[93] For a discussion of possible ultimate influence of the Babylonian New Year Festival on the Great Dionysia in fifth-century BC Athens, see M. C. Root, 'The Parthenon Frieze and the Apadana Reliefs at Persepolis: Reassessing a Programatic Relationship', *American Journal of Archaeology* lxxxix (1985), p. 115 and n. 50.

2. From noble funerals to divine cult: the consecration of Roman Emperors

SIMON PRICE

It is normal Roman practice to deify emperors who die leaving behind children to succeed them. The name they give to this ceremony is apotheosis ... The body of the dead emperor is buried with a very expensive funeral in the normal human way. But then they make a wax model of him [and place it on a pyre which is ignited]. Then from the very top storey [of the pyre] an eagle is released, as if from a battlement, and soars up into the sky with the flames; the Romans believe it takes the soul of the emperor from earth to heaven. After that he is worshipped with the rest of the gods.[1]

The apotheosis of Roman emperors offers a key to understanding the power of the emperors in their capital. Historians have generally neglected the subject, sometimes on the grounds that it was anyway just a charade. Robert Graves in *I, Claudius* encapsulated the modern, cynical attitude:

The joke was that on the night before the funeral [of Augustus] Livia had concealed an eagle in a cage at the top of the pyre, which was to be opened as soon as the pyre was lit by someone secretly pulling a string from below. The eagle would then fly up and was intended to be taken for Augustus' spirit. Unfortunately

---

I am very grateful for thoughtful guidance from Mary Beard, Lucia Nixon, John North and Bert Smith.

[1] Herodian iv.2. E. Beurlier, *Essai sur le culte rendu aux empereurs romains* (Paris, 1890) remains the only general study of the ceremonial and includes a list of the *divi*. The most interesting contribution is still E. Bickermann, 'Der römische Kaiserapotheose', *Archiv für Religionswissenschaft*, xxvii (1929), pp. 1–31 (= A. Wlosok (ed.), *Römischer Kaiserkult* (Darmstadt, 1978), pp. 82–121). Subsequent research is summed up by J.-C. Richard, 'Recherches sur certains aspects du culte impérial: les funérailles des empereurs romains aux deux premiers siècles de notre ère', in H. Temporini and W. Haase (eds.), *Aufstieg und Niedergang der römischen Welt* (Berlin and New York, 1972–), ii.16.2, pp. 1121–34, repeated almost verbatim in *Klio*, lxii (1980), pp. 461–71. Note also W. Weber, *Princeps* (Stuttgart and Berlin, 1936), i, pp. 75–101 on Augustus' funeral, and the information scattered throughout F. Taeger, *Charisma*, 2 vols. (Stuttgart, 1957–60), ii. Recent bibliography is listed in *Aufstieg und Niedergang* ii.16.2, pp. 865–8.

the miracle had not come off. The cage door refused to open. Instead of saying nothing and letting the eagle burn, the officer who was in charge clambered up the pyre and opened the cage door with his hands. Livia had to say that the eagle had been thus released at her orders, as a symbolic act.[2]

Scholars who regard the ritual as humbug have not unnaturally excluded it from their accounts of the period, but their attitude is anachronistic. The quotation at the head of this chapter forms part of a lengthy excursus on imperial apotheosis by a contemporary Greek historian; the outsider looking at the strange Roman ceremony treated it with complete seriousness. I propose to examine the ceremony of imperial funerals from that of Augustus, the first emperor, in AD 14, through to the burial of the first Christian emperor, Constantine, in AD 337. Thirty-six of the sixty emperors in this period and twenty-seven members of their families were apotheosised and received the title of *divus* ('divine').

The ceremony was an important part of the symbolism that defined the imperial house and rooted its power in Roman tradition. In the Republican period (traditionally 510–27 BC) the state was governed by the senate and people of Rome, though in the last two generations of the Republic the uncontrolled struggle for prestige within the senatorial aristocracy created certain temporary 'victors' who dominated the state: Sulla, Pompey, Caesar. From the chaos of the civil wars that followed the assassination of Caesar there emerged one undisputed victor, Augustus. Modern scholars have produced two very different pictures of the position held by Augustus and his successors. Some have stressed the constitutional powers of the emperor: his accession was formally counted from the time that the senate and people granted him specific powers and as emperor he held from time to time the traditional consular magistracy. Others have argued that these 'Republican' powers were unimportant against the reality of autocracy: even the best of emperors could issue edicts or execute people at will.

The ceremony of apotheosis poses problems for both these views of the emperor. On the one hand, raising the emperor's soul to heaven and worshipping him with the rest of the gods fits uneasily with the 'constitutional' view, while on the other, the fact that apotheosis was dependent on a senatorial decree hardly fits the 'autocratic' view. I want to argue that the ceremony of apotheosis

[2] *I, Claudius* ((London, 1934) Penguin edn, 1953), p. 164.

was deliberately ambivalent between these two (modern) attitudes to the emperor. The novel supremacy of one man in a state that prized its traditions was intolerable if expressed bluntly. So imperial funerals were in part identical with the funerals of distinguished Roman nobles, but they were also in part entirely new in their elevation of the emperor to heaven and in the consequent establishment of formal divine cult – temple and priests – to him. The ceremony thus evoked two traditional and acceptable models: Roman nobles and the cult of the gods. Evocation of divine cult enabled the emperor to transcend the position of a mere noble without shattering the Republican structures of the state.

After some further preliminary remarks on sources, the chapter will fall into five main sections. Taking the funeral of Pertinax as the focus I want to present briefly the overall shape of imperial funerals (pp. 59–61). They drew upon two quite different traditions, noble funerals (pp. 62–70), and the apparatus of divine cults (pp. 71–82). The ceremony also needs to be placed in a broader political context – the behaviour expected of the living emperor and the role of the senate (pp. 82–91). So far the picture is synchronic, but the institution of apotheosis and its context underwent important changes over the three hundred years of the empire, only to be transformed in the Christian period (pp. 91–103).

The sources for this study are numerous and diverse. The three central texts are the lengthy accounts by Cassius Dio of the funerals of Augustus (AD 14) and Pertinax (AD 193) and by Herodian of Septimius Severus' funeral (AD 211), part of which opened this chapter. Dio as a senator was well informed on the procedures of apotheosis; indeed he had himself participated at the apotheosis of Pertinax. Though a Greek by origin and writing in Greek, Dio offers the perspective of an insider. Herodian, by contrast, offers his Greek readers, as we have seen, an ethnographic excursus on the peculiarities of an alien custom. Other literary sources, especially historians and poets, offer much illumination on details and on general attitudes to apotheosis. Inscriptions record the official formulae and procedures both for imperial funerals and for the funerals of members of the imperial family. Coins provide evidence for the fact of apotheosis and also depict the funeral pyre, the eagle and the temple. Finally, there is the architecture of the actual monuments, some of which are still familiar landmarks in Rome: Hadrian's mausoleum, the Castel Sant'Angelo, or the

temple of Antonius Pius and Faustina, which became the church of
S. Lorenzo in Miranda and still overlooks the Forum.

AN IMPERIAL FUNERAL

Imperial funerals followed a standard pattern, starting in the
Roman Forum and moving in solemn procession to the Campus
Martius, a mile to the north-west. The funeral of Pertinax recorded
by the eyewitness Dio will serve as an illustration of the procedure.

In the Roman Forum a wooden platform was constructed right
by the marble rostra, upon which was set a shrine, without walls,
but surrounded by columns, cunningly wrought of both ivory and
gold. In it there was placed a bier of the same materials,
surrounded by heads of both land and sea animals and adorned
with coverlets of purple and gold. Upon this rested an effigy of
Pertinax in wax, laid out in triumphal garb; and a handsome boy
was keeping the flies away from it with peacock feathers, as
though it were really a person sleeping. While the body lay there
in state, Severus as well as we senators and our wives
approached, wearing mourning; the women sat in the porticoes
and we men in the open air. After this there moved past, first,
statues of all the famous Romans of old, then choruses of boys
and men, singing a dirge-like hymn to Pertinax; there followed
all the subject nations, represented by bronze figures attired in
native dress, and the guilds of the City itself – those of the lictors,
the scribes, the heralds, and all the rest. Then came images of
other men who had been distinguished for some exploit, invention or pursuit. Behind them were the cavalry and infantry in
armour, the racehorses, and all the funeral offerings that the
emperor and we [sc. senators] and our wives, the distinguished
knights, and communities and the corporations of the City had
sent. Following them came an altar gilded all over and adorned
with ivory and gems of India. When these had passed by, Severus
mounted the rostra and read a eulogy of Pertinax. We shouted
our approval many times in the course of his address, now
praising and now lamenting Pertinax, but our shouts were
loudest when he concluded. Finally, when the bier was about to
be moved, we all lamented and wept together.

The high priests and the magistrates, both those then in office
and those appointed for the following year, brought the bier

	AUGUSTUS	PERTINAX	'SEPTIMIUS SEVERUS'
	Senate in mourning; will read	temple, prayers and images	body buried
			image outside palace seven days; senators and wives in attendance; 'died'
Forum	body and image carried by magistrates. other images. parade of images: ancestors, relatives, Romans, subjects	image in shrine. senators and wives mourn	image to forum; stands for élite
		famous Romans subjects, guilds. chorus. funeral offerings	hymn
	funeral oration (double)	(single)	
Procession	through triumphal arch	magistrates and priests move bier	
	senators, knights, and wives praetorian guard	knights carry it	
Campus Martius		funeral offerings to pyre	funeral offerings
	decursio. decorations to pyre	decursio	decursio
			parade of images of Romans, generals, emperors
	pyre lit: centurion [eagle] statutory mourning. witness and s.c. priests and temple. image banned in funerary processions. birthday celebrated	consuls eagle	heir eagle worship with rest of gods
	(Cassius Dio lvi. 34–46)	(Dio lxxv. 4–5)	(Herodian iv.2)

10 The three stage structure of the three best attested imperial funerals.

down from the platform and gave it to certain knights to carry. Now all the rest of us walked in front of the bier, some beating our breasts and others playing a dirge upon the flute, but the emperor followed behind all the rest; and in this manner we reached the Campus Martius.

There a pyre had been built in the form of a tower with three storeys and adorned with ivory and gold as well as a number of statues, while on its very summit was placed a gilded chariot that Pertinax used to drive. Inside the pyre the funeral offerings were cast and the bier was placed in it, and then Severus and the relatives of Pertinax kissed the effigy. The emperor then ascended a platform, while we senators, apart from the magistrates, took our places on wooden stands in order to view the events both safely and conveniently. The magistrates and the equestrian order, dressed as appropriate to their status, and also the cavalry and infantry, passed in and out around the pyre performing intricate evolutions, both those of peace and those of war. Then at last the consuls set fire to the structure, and when this was done, an eagle flew aloft from it. Thus was Pertinax made immortal.[3]

The context of this ceremony was very irregular. Pertinax had been assassinated some months earlier and his successor had himself been overthrown by Septimius Severus, who was eager to establish a link back to the legitimate (and lamented) Pertinax. One might imagine that the peculiar political context of the funeral implies that the ceremony itself was aberrant. In fact the opposite is probably the case. Severus employed standard procedures in order to insinuate an atmosphere of normality. The other two extensive accounts of imperial funerals follow the same basic pattern, as the table shows. Some of the differences are due to the selection of different details by the sources, others reflect changes in the procedure, to which we shall return (see pp. 91–103). The striking point is the similarity between the three accounts. The funeral and apotheosis of an emperor was a firmly established institution; we need now to see what generated and continued to lend resonance to the ceremonial.

---

[3] Dio lxxv. 4.2 – 5.5 (Loeb translation adapted). I use the Loeb book numbers for Dio.

THE NOBLE TRADITION

The long tradition of noble funerals in Rome provided the overall structure for imperial funerals, but many old elements were modified and the structure as a whole came to bear a decreasing resemblance to the funerals of the nobility. Though evidence for these funerals in the imperial period is disappointingly scanty, it is adequate for the late Republic; in particular we have a lengthy description by the Greek historian Polybius of a typical noble funeral in his own day, the mid second century BC (vi. 53–4).[4] There is also from the early empire good evidence, partly inscriptional and partly from literary sources, for the funerals of members of the imperial family who did not receive apotheosis. These funerals are important for two reasons. The five funerals of Augustus' heirs who died at various points in his reign provided partial models for Augustus' own funeral.[5] They also illuminate for us the possible adaptations of the old tradition without the extra complication of divinisation.

Mourning the deceased was basic to the traditional funeral ceremony. Polybius reports that the whole populace gathered in the forum; when the facts of the dead man's career were recalled to their minds and brought before their eyes, their sympathies were so deeply engaged that the loss seemed not to be confined to the mourners but to be a public one which affected the whole people (vi.53.5). Grief at an imperial death was even more strongly displayed. At the death in AD 19 of Germanicus, Tiberius' heir, 'the populace stoned temples and upset altars of the gods; people threw their household deities into the streets and exposed their new-born children', while at the death of the emperor Otho (AD 69) some of his soldiers committed suicide at the pyre.[6] Life was

---

[4] For additional material see: Ch. Daremberg, E. Saglio (eds.), *Dictionnaire des antiquités* (Paris, 1877–1912), *s.v. funus*; F. Vollmer, 'De funere publico Romanorum', *Jahrbücher für classische Philologie* supp. new ser., xix (1892–3), pp. 319–64; H. Blümner, *Die römischen Privataltertümer*, 3rd edn (Munich, 1911), pp. 482–502; S. Weinstock, *Divus Julius* (Oxford, 1971), pp. 346–55; J. M. C. Toynbee, *Death and Burial in the Roman World* (London, 1971), pp. 43–64; W. Kierdorf, *Laudatio funebris* (Meisenheim am Glan, 1980),

[5] Cf. Dio liv.28.5 on Agrippa's funeral.

[6] Suetonius, *Gaius* 5 (H. S. Versnel, 'Destruction, *Devotio* and Despair in a Situation of Anomy: the Mourning for Germanicus in Triple Perspective', *Perennitas. Studi in Onore di Angelo Brelich* (Rome, n.d.), pp. 541–618, defends this account and elaborates upon it most interestingly). Tacitus, *Histories*, ii.49.

hardly worth living any more. Or at the very least, there was a hiatus in the order of things and those that were left had been diminished. At the first meeting of the senate after the death of Augustus the senators all marked their loss by (temporary) reduction of their status. Ordinary senators wore equestrian dress, magistrates wore senatorial dress without the purple-bordered toga; the consuls sat on the benches of the lower magistrates. This was customary when a great disaster befell the state.[7]

At a noble funeral the formal regulations for mourning affected only the immediate kin of the deceased. This was very different with imperial funerals. A *iustitium* was declared, that is a general cessation of all legal and other public business in Rome. The *iustitium* was an old tradition, employed at a time of civic crisis; it was first used at the death of an individual for Sulla in 70 BC and became standard at the death of an emperor or an important member of the imperial family. Thus at the announcement of the death (in southern Turkey) of Gaius Caesar, one of Augustus' heirs, the town of Pisa, taking its lead from Rome, closed all temples, baths and pubs, and enjoined fasting until the ashes were returned to Rome and buried.[8]

The regulations for mourning dress now affected not only the immediate kin. Thus Herodian (iv.2.3) reports that when Septimius Severus died the whole senate and women of distinction (presumably the wives or daughters of senators) sat on either side of the imperial corpse (actually an image); the men wore black cloaks and the women white, the conventional mourning colours for the two sexes. So too at Pisa everyone was to change their clothes until the funeral of another of Augustus' heirs, Lucius Caesar, and at the anniversary of his death the magistrates were to sacrifice to his spirit in sombre-coloured togas.[9] After Augustus' funeral, mourning was required by decree of the senate, for men for a few days, but for women for a whole year. The women in question are presumably not all Roman women, but the senatorial women such as later participated at the mourning of Septimius Severus. Even so the senatorial decree is very striking. The

---

[7] Dio lvi.31.2–3. Cf. xl.46.1; Tacitus, *Annals* iv.8.2, Dio lxxiii.21.3. According to John Lydus, *De mensibus* iv.29 magistrates renounced their official dress during the *Parentalia*, the festival in memory of the dead.

[8] L. Vidman, 'Inferiae und iustitium', *Klio*, liii (1971), pp. 209–212; *Inscriptiones latinae selectae*, ed. H. Dessau, 3 vols. (Berlin, 1892–1916), 140.7–24 (Pisa).

[9] *Insc. lat. sel.* (see n. 8), 139.16–22.

conventional period of mourning of a woman for her husband or father is now expected for the emperor.[10] The death of an emperor who was *pater patriae*, father of his country, redefined the boundaries of kinship.

If we turn to the funeral proper, permission for funerals at public expense was given, by the senate, in the second century BC, but became more common in the following century. The funeral of Sulla was particularly notable. In the imperial period, attention was naturally focussed on the imperial family, but public funerals of those in imperial favour did continue. A seemingly traditional name, *funus censorium*, was often used for imperial funerals, though it is first attested for Augustus and its precise significance is obscure. It might allude to the grand funeral of a *censor*, a highly respected office which Augustus had himself held, or it may just be the equivalent of a 'public funeral', originally authorised by the *censor*. In either case, a *funus censorium* was granted as a special favour to people not members of the imperial house, thus emphasising the real or alleged traditionalism of the imperial funeral.[11]

The display of the body in the Forum was also traditional. Polybius notes that the body of the deceased 'is carried with every kind of honour into the Forum to the so-called Rostra, sometimes in an upright position, so as to be conspicuous, or else, more rarely, recumbent' (vi.53.1). Thus the display of the savaged clothes and body of Caesar in the Forum was all the more shocking, allowing Antony to exploit the feelings of the crowd: 'If you have tears, prepare to shed them now. You all do know this mantle. I remember the first time ever Caesar put it on . . . '[12] In some cases the body itself was not available for display because the person had died far from Rome and in the early empire cremation at the place of death was regular. The convention was for an image to be used in the funeral ceremony in place of the body.[13] Similarly an effigy was necessary in the belated funeral of Pertinax.

The next stage in the funeral was the display of the masks of distinguished ancestors. The masks were worn by those of the right

---

[10] Dio lvi.43.1. Cf. Vollmer, 'De funere publico', p. 340 n. 5, Dionysius of Halicarnassus v.48.4, Ovid, *Calendar* i.35–6 and *Fontes Iuris Romani Antejustiniani*, eds. S. Riccobono *et al.*, 3 vols. (Florence, 1940–3), ii, pp. 535–6.

[11] Tacitus, *Annals* iv.15, vi.27, *Histories* iv.47. On the term see H. Temporini, *Die Frauen am Hofe Trajans* (Berlin and New York, 1978), p. 195 n. 69.

[12] Shakespeare, *Julius Caesar* Act iii, scene ii, drawing on the ancient sources.

[13] Tacitus, *Annals* iii.5. See further pp. 96–7.

build, who were dressed in the clothing appropriate to the rank of the ancestors; they rode in chariots with all the insignia of the deceased to the Rostra in the Forum where they sat in a row on chairs of ivory. The same procedure was followed for imperial funerals, except that the definition of ancestors was greatly extended. When Drusus, Tiberius' son, died, the procession of people carrying busts (which seem to have replaced masks by this time) started with Aeneas, the founder of the Julian family to which he belonged, and continued with all the kings of Alba, founded by Aeneas, and then Romulus, the founder of Rome, and so on.[14] Other noble families in the late Republic had been discovering ancestors (including ones from Troy), but Augustus was particularly successful at incorporating the great figures of early Rome into his genealogy and thus at laying claim to the whole of Roman history. The usefulness of this increased as the actual families of later emperors became less illustrious. The funeral of Pertinax, who was of undistinguished birth, was able to include a parade both of the images of all the famous Romans of old and also of two other categories not possible at the funeral of a mere noble: the subject nations of the empire and the guilds of the city of Rome.

When this parade was over it was time for the funeral oration, which was traditionally delivered by a close relative, or at a public funeral by a magistrate appointed by the senate. For example, the eminent senator Verginius Rufus, who died in AD 97, received the honour of an oration by 'the consul Cornelius Tacitus, a most eloquent orator, and his tribute put the crowning touch to Verginius' good fortune'. The speech-making was immensely important; when Tiberius rather curiously refused to allow his (adopted) son Germanicus a public funeral, praise of his memory was one aspect of the ceremony which was missed.[15] At the funeral of an emperor the speech would naturally be delivered by his son and heir, but the public and private aspects of the occasion were separated. Thus at Augustus' funeral, Drusus, his grandson, made a speech from the Rostra of the Orators, where the effigy of Augustus had been

14 Polybius vi.53.6–10. Tacitus, *Annals* iv.9. Busts were sometimes used in place of masks (Toynbee, *Death and Burial*, p. 48), but impersonation of the dead by an actor was also traditional (Suetonius, *Vespasian*, 19.2; cf. Plautus, *Amphitryo* 458, Diodorus Siculus xxxi.25). For Augustus' genealogy see e.g. Ovid, *Calendar* iv.19–60 and in general T. P. Wiseman, 'Legendary Genealogies in Late-Republican Rome', *Greece and Rome*, new ser., xxi (1974), pp. 153–64.
15 Pliny, *Epistvlae* ii.1.6. Tacitus, *Annals* iii.5 (and cf. iii.76).

11 Funeral procession. Marble relief from Amiternum, fifty miles north-east of Rome, depicting a funeral procession. The deceased, lying on his funerary couch, is carried on a bier, preceded by hired mourners and musicians and followed by relations.

placed, and Tiberius, his son and heir, then made a public speech from the other, Julian Rostra, in accordance with a senatorial decree.[16]

A further novel element was that the new emperor had to be protected from the contagion of death. Tiberius needed absolution from the senate for having touched the corpse of Augustus and when he delivered the funeral oration for his son Drusus the body had to be veiled from him.[17] The Romans were puzzled by the reason for this screening of the body from the emperor. Seneca says that it was because as priest (*pontifex*) he could not look on a corpse, but Dio (liv.28.3–4; cf. liv.35.4) denies that there was any such rule concerning *pontifices*, or *censores*, and can produce no explanation of his own. In fact the *pontifices* do seem to have been barred from the sight of a corpse,[18] but the old rules were transformed with the combination of priestly and imperial office. Emphasis was laid not on the priesthood of the emperor but on his imperial power. When the funeral games for Agrippa were given, Augustus and Agrippa's sons alone did not put on black clothing.[19]

[16] Suetonius, *Augustus* 100.3; Dio lvi.34.4. So also for Augustus' sister (Dio liv.35.5) and Antoninus Pius (*Scriptores Historiae Augustae, Marcus Ant.* 7.11).

[17] Dio lvi.31.3 (cf. Tacitus, *Annals* i.62 on Germanicus). Seneca, *Consolatio ad Marciam* 15. Cf. Weber, *Princeps* i, pp. 40–3, 47*.

[18] Servius, *Commentary on Vergil's Aeneid* iii.64, vi.176; cf. *Insc. lat. sel.* (see n. 8), 6964.7.

[19] Dio lv.8.5.

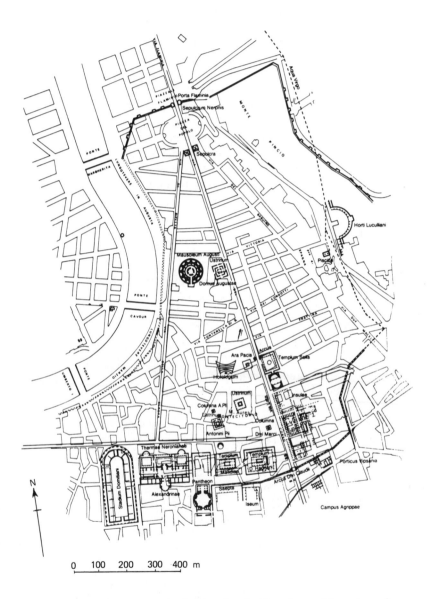

12 The Campus Martius. Note the three *ustrina*, the Mausoleum of Augustus and the two imperial temples. The forum lies to the south.

The point was surely that the emperor, as representative of the state, was not to mourn the dead nor to be in contact with death.

From the Forum the body was taken to the place of cremation and burial. While a noble was carried by his family, the imperial corpse was borne by senators or knights (an honour already granted to Sulla). Augustus, for example, was carried by the magistrates appointed for the following year.[20] As bodies had to be buried outside the boundary (*pomerium*) of Rome, the Campus Martius was ideal for imperial funerals.[21] It was still technically outside the *pomerium*, but it was also a place of great civic importance; both the census and the election of certain magistrates were carried out here. In the late Republic from Sulla onwards some people were granted the exceptional privilege of burial in the Campus Martius, but from the time of Augustus only emperors and members of their family could be cremated and buried here. One of the prominent features of the middle of the Campus, as an early imperial visitor noted, was 'the circuit wall of Augustus' place of cremation, made of marble, with an iron fence running round it and planted inside with poplars'. In the second century two other similar monuments (*ustrina*) were built on the Campus. The one which has been adequately excavated consisted of three concentric square enclosures, thirteen, twenty-three and thirty metres across; the outer square consisted of a low foundation on which stood columns joined by an iron grating. These buildings were both the monumental setting and also the memorials of imperial cremations.[22] Further emphasis on the place of cremation was given by the erection of huge columns aligned with the *ustrina*, of which that of Antoninus Pius and Faustina and that of Marcus Aurelius are still standing (though not *in situ*).

The ceremony up to the moment of cremation was rooted in the traditions of the Roman nobility: the display of the body (or effigy), the ancestral masks, the funeral oration and the cremation were all standard practices. Though they were naturally adapted and aggran-

[20] Dio lvi.34.1, 42.1. Appian, *Bellum civile* i.496–500.

[21] On this area see F. Castagnoli, 'Il Campo Marzio nell'antichità', *Atti delle Accademia nazionale dei Lincei. Memorie. Classe di Scienze morali, storiche e filologiche*, 8th ser. (1948), i, pp. 93–193.

[22] Strabo v.3.8 (p. 236). See S. B. Platner, T. Ashby, *A Topographical Dictionary of Ancient Rome* (Oxford, 1929), p. 545; E. Nash, *Pictorial Dictionary of Ancient Rome*, 2 vols. (London, 1968), ii. pp. 487–9; E. La Rocca, *La riva e mezzaluna* (Rome, 1984), pp. 87–114. C. Buzzetti, *Bull. Comm. Arch. Comunale di Roma*, lxxxix (1984), pp. 27–8.

13 Model of the Campus Martius, looking south. In the centre note two *ustrina*, and beyond them the temples to Matidia and Hadrian, with the Pantheon in the distance.

dised in various ways as appropriate for the imperial house, they did not constitute apotheosis. After the cremation the bones were gathered up and placed in an ordinary, if grand tomb; in the early empire this was the Mausoleum which Augustus had built at the northern end of the Campus Martius for himself and his family. There the inscriptions refer to the deceased simply by his or her names without adding the title *divus*.

The deceased also received the posthumous cult appropriate for those in the underworld. On the day that Lucius Caesar died there were to be annual sacrifices (*inferiae*) to his spiritis (*dii Manes*). Even extraordinary posthumous honours left the deceased in the underworld. Germanicus (died AD 19) and Drusus (AD 23), both heirs of Tiberius, were granted elaborate honours including the following: their names were entered into a special hymn, official chairs (of their magistracies) were placed where the priests of Augustus (the *sodales Augustales*) sat, ivory statues of them headed processions at circus games, images were erected in Rome and arches in Rome and elsewhere in the empire. But these posthumous honours were far from making them gods. Indeed there were annual sacrifices to their spirits on the days they died at the tomb of Augustus where they were buried.[23] These sacrifices to the spirits of the dead were part of a normal funeral cult and establish a clear opposition between the dead in the underworld and the gods in heaven. These imperial heirs were not to rival the position of Augustus. An anonymous poem, attempting to console Livia for the death in 9 BC of her son Drusus, yet another of Augustus' heirs, describes the funeral at length but makes clear that apotheosis was inappropriate for Drusus: there should be only the two new gods in heaven, Julius Caesar and (one day) Augustus.[24] But how was it possible to transform a glorified Republican funeral into the creation of a new state deity?

---

[23] *Insc. lat. sel.* (see n. 8), 139.16–26 (Lucius Caesar). Tacitus, *Annals* ii.83 and iv.9 with V. Ehrenberg, A. H. M. Jones, *Documents Illustrating the Reigns of Augustus and Tiberius*, 2nd edn (Oxford, 1955), nos. 94 a–b and J. González, *Zeitschrift für Papyrologie und Epigraphik*, henceforth *Zeit. Pap. Epig.*, lv (1984), pp. 55–100. Cf. S. Weinstock, 'The Image and the Chair of Germanicus', *Journal of Roman Studies* xlvii (1957), pp. 144–54. However, in an élite, private context the pair were shown ascending to heaven: B. Andreae, *The Art of Rome* (New York, 1977), pp. 147–8 (and fig. 57) on the Great Cameo of France.

[24] *Consolatio ad Liviam* (ed. A. Witlox, Maastricht, 1934) 213–14, 245–6. The poem is probably an exercise written a generation or so later.

APOTHEOSIS

The deification of Julius Caesar, the first Roman to receive official divine honours from the state, was a crucial development which provided a partial model for later imperial deifications.[25] Unfortunately the passing of divine honours for Caesar raises serious problems of evidence. There is some important contemporary evidence, which must be used as the basis of our account, but the two fullest extant sources wrote two hundred and more years after the events and there is a major dispute as to whether the divine honours allegedly passed in the last year of Caesar's life are historical. The dispute would matter less if we could recover at least an Augustan perspective on the cult of Caesar, but the evidence for this is largely lost. Certain key points are, however, clear.

Some divine honours were certainly passed for Caesar in his lifetime. After the decisive battle of Munda in 45 BC contemporary letters of Cicero attest that Caesar's statue was carried in festival processions along with Romulus-Quirinus and that another statue of him was placed in the temple of Quirinus.[26] These were extraordinary honours, to which Cicero was deeply hostile. Other divine honours allegedly passed in the remaining year of Caesar's life are highly disputed, but a speech by Cicero, set only six months after the death of Caesar, refers to a series of honours passed for Caesar: 'couch, image, pediment, priest'.[27] The date at which these honours were passed is impossible to know with certainty, but a date in Caesar's lifetime is easier to envisage than one in the immediate aftermath of his assassination. All four honours to which Cicero refers can be amplified from the later sources. Caesar's statue was taken by a special carriage to the Circus where it was placed on the couch of the gods. His image could be that in the temple of Quirinus. The pediment, a characteristic feature of a temple, was placed on his official residence. The priesthood, as Cicero makes clear, was modelled on the major priesthoods (*flamines*) of Jupiter, Mars and Quirinus and was to *divus Julius*; Antony was appointed as the first priest, though he was not

---

[25] Weinstock, *Divus Julius* (see n. 4), is the fundamental discussion, but see also the interpretations of H. Gesche, *Die Vergottung Caesars* (Kallmünz, 1968) and J. A. North, *Journal of Roman Studies*, lxv (1975), pp. 171–7.

[26] Cicero, *Ad Atticum* xii.45.2; xiii.28.3. xiv.14.1 and xiv.19.3 provide evidence by implication for Caesar's lifetime honours.

[27] Cicero, *Philippic* ii.110, set on 19th Sept., published end of November.

inaugurated until 40 BC. These honours either came into effect in the lifetime of Caesar, or were passed to come into effect after his death.

In either case, the status of Caesar was certainly in dispute in the aftermath of his assassination in March, 44 BC. He was accorded a grand public funeral on the traditional lines, but with some extraordinary features. The corpse was hidden by an image of wax which lay inside a gilded shrine modelled on the temple of Venus Genetrix. The use of a wax image here is peculiar, but divine descent was emphasised by the model of the temple of Venus, his ancestor. Over the bier Antony made the funeral speech, perhaps reciting earlier decrees which passed divine honours for Caesar and praising him as a god, before inciting the crowd with the display of Caesar's wounds (perhaps in part by rotating the wax image with a device to show all the wounds). The divine element in the funeral, combined with the general loyalty of the crowd to Caesar, led some to attempt to cremate and bury Caesar in the temple of Jupiter, among the gods. This plan was frustrated, but the funeral with its untraditional elements was a step towards the subsequent official deification of Caesar.

In the months after Caesar's funeral, as contemporary evidence shows, various further steps were taken. In July, at the games held in memory of Caesar, a comet appeared and was generally believed to be Caesar's soul, now in heaven. In September Antony forced the senate to add a day to the end of each official supplication of the gods, on which prayers would be made to Caesar.[28] Cicero objected that such prayers would have been better associated with the *Parentalia*, a festival in honour of the dead. Caesar's divinity was still very problematic. Finally at the beginning of 42 BC the senate passed the official consecration of Caesar, which included the building of a temple to *divus Julius*.[29] From this time on, especially with the promotion of the cult by Augustus, the cult of *divus Julius* was clearly defined and firmly established; writers of the Augustan age talk confidently of Caesar's ascension to heaven.

The deification of Caesar provided a partial model for that of Augustus and subsequent emperors. The crucial point is that at least by 42 BC there emerged the concept of an official decision recognising a new god. Prior to this there had been only the

[28] *Philippic* i.13; ii.110.
[29] Appian, *Civil War* ii.616; Dio xlvii.18.3–19.3.

establishment of cults of virtues and the introduction into Rome of foreign gods, and in neither case was there any conceptual problem. On the other hand, while Caesar's deification had been prepared to a considerable extent before his death, emperors did not receive official divine honours in their lifetime (see below, pp. 84–5) and for an emperor the events following the funeral were fundamental. Caesar's official deification came only in 42 BC; Augustus' came immediately after the funeral.

Evidence of the emperor's apotheosis was provided in the early empire by a witness, the procedure being used for the first time at the death of Augustus. After the funeral a senior senator gave sworn testimony to the senate that he had seen Augustus ascending to heaven. As a result, in the words of the official state calendar, 'on that day heavenly honours were decreed by the senate to the divine (*divus*) Augustus'.[30] The senate, which was traditionally not only the political centre of the state but also its chief religious authority, was the obvious body to take such a decision. In the Republic when bizarre events, such as the birth of a two-headed cow, occurred, they were reported to the senate, which decided whether the strange event was a sign from the gods and, if so, what the appropriate response was. Similarly the senate was traditionally responsible for introducing new deities from outside Rome. The procedure of the witness had not previously been used when deciding about the introduction of a new deity; for a deity already worshipped in another state it was hardly appropriate. But reliance on sworn testimony had a mythical precedent, as we shall see, and also considerable advantage in the circumstances. The senate was not seen to create a deity arbitrarily; like the Roman Catholic Church deliberating about a candidate for canonisation, the senate was recognising a state of affairs.[31]

The traditional models for imperial apotheosis were the ascension of Romulus and Hercules. Romulus, the founder of Rome, had risen to heaven and was in consequence worshipped as a god, under the name Quirinus. This convenient story, which goes back to at least the poet Ennius in the early second century BC, was

---

[30] Suetonius, *Augustus* 100.4, Dio lvi.46.2. *Inscriptiones Italiae* xiii.2, p. 510.

[31] P. Willems, *Le Sénat de la république romaine*, 2nd edn, 2 vols. (Paris, 1885), ii, pp. 299–327 on new cults; S. R. F. Price, 'Gods and Emperors: the Greek Language of the Roman Imperial Cult', *Journal of Hellenic Studies*, civ (1984), pp. 79–95 on canonisation. The eagle was probably not used in the early empire; below, p. 95.

greatly elaborated at the time of Caesar and Augustus. While earlier the status of Romulus had been relatively unproblematic, as the founder of Rome, considerable debate broke out in the late Republic on his precise nature. Some argued that he was killed for becoming a tyrant (an argument not unrelated to the fate of Julius Caesar), while others identified Romulus and Quirinus and established the apotheosis of Romulus as a prototype of the divinisation of Julius Caesar and Augustus. Thus Ovid in his *Calendar*, which he wrote under Augustus, after comparing Romulus and Augustus (to Augustus' advantage) gives a striking account of the apotheosis of Romulus: when he was miraculously taken up to heaven on Jupiter's chariot, the senators were suspected of having killed him.

But Julius Proculus was coming from Alba Longa; the moon was shining, and there was no need for a torch, when suddenly the hedge on his left shook and trembled. He recoiled and his hair bristled. It seemed to him that Romulus, handsome, in stature more than human, and clad in a fair robe, stood there in the middle of the road and said: 'Forbid the citizens (Quirites) to mourn, let them not profane my divinity by their tears. Bid the pious throng bring incense and propitiate the new Quirinus, and bid them cultivate the art their fathers cultivated, the art of war'. Having given these orders, from the other's eyes he vanished into thin air. Proculus called the people together and reported the words as he had been ordered. Temples were built to the god, and the hill was also named after him, and the rites established by our fathers come round on fixed days.[32]

The circulation of the story in Augustus' lifetime made the use of a witness at Augustus' death seem obvious. Though in Ovid's poem the witness saw an apparition and not the ascension, another version may have developed and our sources do compare the Augustan witness to Julius Proculus.

The second traditional model was the apotheosis of Hercules.

---

[32] *Calendar* ii 119–44, 481–512. See in general on the Romulus theme: J. Gagé, 'Romulus-Augustus', *Mélanges d'archéologie et d'histoire de l'école française de Rome*, xlvii (1930), pp. 138–81; A. Alföldi, 'Die Geburt der kaiserlichen Bildsymbolik: 2. Der neue Romulus', *Museum helveticum*, viii (1951), pp. 190–215 = *Der Vater des Vaterlandes im römischen Denken* (Darmstadt, 1971), pp. 14–39; C. J. Classen, 'Romulus in der römischen Republik', *Philologus*, cvi (1962), pp. 174–204; J.-C. Richard, 'Énée, Romulus, César et les funérailles impériales', *Mél. école fr. Rome* (see n. 32) lxxviii (1966), pp. 67–78; Weinstock, *Divus Julius* (see n. 4), pp. 176–7.

This did not provide a precedent for the witness, but it did justify the ascension to heaven from the pyre. A Greek historian of the first century BC recounted how the ailing Hercules was told by a Delphic oracle to ascend a huge pyre. When this was lighted, 'immediately lightning also fell from heaven and the pyre was wholly consumed. After this, when [they] came to gather up the bones of Hercules and found not a single bone anywhere, they assumed that, in accordance with the words of the oracle, he had passed from among mortals into the company of the gods.'[33] The mysterious disappearance of the bones of Hercules, and of Romulus, is perhaps relevant to imperial apotheosis. In Ovid's *Calendar* (iii.697–704) the goddess Vesta talks of the death of Caesar: 'he was my priest, the sacrilegious hands struck at me with the swords. I myself carried the man away, leaving only his image behind; what fell by the sword was Caesar's shade.' But even here there is no question of a total disappearance of Caesar, and it was more normal to talk of the emperor's soul going up to heaven, leaving his mortal remains behind (see below, pp. 76–7). The witness did not claim that Augustus had disappeared; after all, Livia waited in the Campus Martius for five days after the funeral, gathered up the bones and placed them in the Mausoleum.[34]

The ascent of the pyre by the living Hercules does, however, help to explain a striking peculiarity of the imperial funeral. At the funeral of Pertinax, as we saw earlier, a wax effigy of him was laid out in the forum 'and a handsome boy was keeping the flies away from it with peacock feathers, as though it were really a person sleeping' and the emperor and others kissed farewell to it only when it was on the actual pyre. Similarly Herodian (iv. 2.2–2.4) reports that, before the display of the effigy in the forum, it was placed outside the palace.

> The model lies there pale, like a sick man, and on either side of the couch people sit for most of the day ... [For seven days] the doctors arrive and go up to the couch, and each day they pretend

33 Diodorus Siculus iv.38.3–5. On this theme see D. M. Pippidi, 'Apothéoses impériales et apothéose de Pérégrinos', *Studi e materiali di storia delle religioni*, xxi (1947–8), pp. 77–103 = *Parerga* (Bucharest and Paris, 1984), pp. 89–107.

34 Bickermann, 'Der römische', (see n. 1) and D. M. Pippidi, *Recherches sur le culte impérial* (Paris and Bucharest, n.d.), pp. 149–76 make too much of the alleged disappearance of the emperor, arguing that there were two separate funerals in the second and third centuries for the body and for the wax image, which disappeared in the flames. See Richard, 'Recherches' (n. 1).

to examine the patient and make an announcement that his condition is deteriorating.[35]

Only when it appeared that he was dead, was the effigy taken down from the palace to the forum. Laying out the body was traditional practice, but in the case of the emperor it was evidently important to maintain the fiction that he had died only just before the funeral. This ensured that there was no need to give thought to the condition of the emperor's soul in the meantime (was it haunting the earth, as Gaius did before his body was properly buried?);[36] the question would otherwise have become pressing because of the dead emperor's somewhat problematic status. Though the emperor, unlike Hercules, was not supposed to mount the pyre alive, his soul could ascend from the pyre straight to heaven. Indeed the *Consolation to Livia* (255–8) explicitly compares the imperial funeral pyre to that of Hercules.

The notion of ascent to heaven was also aided by the old idea of the return of the great man to his rightful place among the stars. Cicero's treatise *The Republic* had given a classic statement of this theory. The Roman statesman Scipio was told in a dream to cultivate justice and piety. 'Such a life is the way to heaven and the company of those whose life on earth is done and who, released from the body, inhabit the region which you behold . . . and which, after the Greeks, you name the Milky Way.'[37] This philosophical doctrine gained new force from the fact that soon after the death of Caesar a comet appeared. Augustus himself noted in his auto-biography that the people believed that this star indicated that the soul of Caesar had been taken among the number of the immortal gods.[38] And Augustus in his turn was expected to return to the stars. An astronomical poem written (in part) in his lifetime includes among the heroes in the Milky Way both Julius Caesar and Augustus. The latter

> came down from heaven and will reoccupy heaven, guiding its passage through the Zodiac with the Thunderer [Jupiter] at his side; in the assembly of the gods he will behold mighty Quirinus

---

[35] For a slave fanning his master's corpse see *Codex Justinianus* vii.6.5. According to Servius, writing in the late fourth century, it used to be customary for bodies to be laid out for seven days before cremation (*Comm. on Vergil's Aeneid* v.64, vi.218).

[36] Suetonius, *Gaius* 59.   [37] vi.16; cf. vi.13 and 24.

[38] Pliny, *Hist. nat.* ii.93–4. Servius (*Comm. on Vergil's Bucolics* ix.46) shows that the interpretation of the comet was controversial.

[and Julius Caesar; the line is lost] on a higher plane than shines the belt of the Milky Way. There is the gods' abode, and here is the abode of those who are peers of the gods in excellence and attain to the nearest heights.[39]

The idea of the emperor being among the stars was even entertained by the imperial family itself. Germanicus, Tiberius' heir, included in his free translation into Latin of an earlier Greek astronomical poem a reference to Augustus' place with Capricorn, his birth sign. 'In the midst of an awestruck, quaking throng of foreigners and your own people [Capricorn], Augustus, bore to heaven your divinity (*numen*) on his body under which you were born and returned it to your mother stars.'[40] If the soul of the divinity of the emperor had returned to its rightful place in heaven, especially if this was attested by a sworn deposition, it was natural for the senate to establish a cult of the former emperor.

First, nomenclature. From the establishment of the official cult of Julius Caesar throughout the imperial period, the recipient of the cult was known as a *divus*. Thus both Augustus and Pertinax are called *divus* on the coins issued by their successors.[41] The term *divus* was originally not sharply distinguished from *deus* ('god') but from the consecration of Caesar onwards it was used almost exclusively (outside poetical texts) of properly consecrated members of the imperial family. This is not to say that *divus* and *deus* were two exclusive categories; rather, *divus* was a subcategory of *deus* and it was thus perfectly possible to refer to a consecrated emperor as *deus*. As someone who was 'translated by the senate and people of Rome into the company of the gods (*dei*)',[42] the *divus* was naturally entitled to receive the appropriate cult, or what the official calendar called 'heavenly honours'.

Secondly, therefore, the cult itself. There were three main parts of the 'heavenly honours' which could be voted singly or together to the new *divus*. Predictably, Augustus received all three: a temple, a priest (the *flamen Augustalis*) and also a priestly college (the *sodales Augustales*). Temples, of which a total of fourteen were

[39] Manilius i.799–804.

[40] Germanicus, *Arati Phaenomena* 558–60. Cf. the ascension of Theodosius to the stars in 396, Claudian vii.162–202.

[41] *The Roman Imperial Coinage*, eds. H. Mattingly, E. A. Sydenham *et al.*, 9 vols. (1923–81), i. pp. 95–6, iv.1, p. 94.

[42] *Insc. lat. sel.* (see n. 8), 72, of Julius Caesar. On *divus* and *deus* see further Price, 'Gods and Emperors' (see n. 31).

voted to the *divi* in Rome, were usually on a generous scale and in positions of considerable prominence.[43] Those to Julius Caesar, Augustus, Vespasian and Antoninus Pius were all built on the traditional Forum Romanum, while those to Vespasian and Titus, Hadrian, Matidia and Marcus Aurelius were constructed in the Campus Martius, further emphasising the crucial importance of this area for imperial apotheosis. In design they did not diverge from the standard pattern of temples to the traditional gods; the only exception is the temple to Julius Caesar which incorporated the funerary altar erected over the pyre. This is explained by the peculiar circumstances of Caesar's funeral, and the later imperial temples exclude all suggestion of mortality.

The leading personnel divides into two. The *flamen Augustalis* was to be a member of Augustus' own family, and there was a private three day festival in the palace in memory of Augustus, which continued to be celebrated by subsequent emperors for at least two hundred years. The office of *flamen* was modelled on the ancient *flamines* of the traditional gods, probably in particular on the most prestigious, the priest of Jupiter or *flamen Dialis*. The peculiar restrictions on the *flamen Dialis* cannot have been imposed on the new *flamines* (it was certainly possible to combine the new office with other priesthoods), but the prestige of the old priesthood was transferred. Like the *flamen Dialis*, the *flamen Augustalis* was probably entitled to have an official chair (the *sella curulis* to which magistrates were entitled) placed in the theatres at games in honour of Augustus.[44]

The model for the *sodales Augustales* also purported to be traditional, the ancient *sodales Titii*. This body seems originally to have been connected with the taking of omens, but from its revival by Augustus it was associated with ancient cults of Rome and Titus Tatius, king of Rome with Romulus, perhaps even performing cult to Tatius. Similarly the *sodales Augustales*, twenty-one senators plus co-opted imperial members, were to run the games in honour of Augustus and also to make funerary sacrifices in memory of

---

[43] The remains are listed in Nash, *Pictorial Dictionary* i, pp. 26–7, 164, 243–8, 304, 450, 457–61, 512–14; ii. pp. 36–7, 268–71, 501–4. See also Tacitus, *Annals* xv.23 (Poppaea), Dio lxiii.26.3 (Sabina), Platner, Ashby, *Dictionary* pp. 327 (Marcus), 153 (Divorum Aedes), and F. Coarelli, in *Città e architettura nella Roma imperiale* (Odense, 1983), pp. 41–6 on Pantheon.

[44] Dio lvi.46.5 on the festival. Weinstock, 'The Image and the Chair' (see n. 23) on the *sella curulis*.

members of the imperial family who were not deified.[45] Subsequent deifications led to modifications of the name of the *sodales* or (in the case of a new dynasty) the creation of a new body of *sodales* alongside the old. Thus in the mid-second century there were four different groups of *sodales*, the *sodales Augustales*, the *sodales Flaviales Titiales*, the *sodales Hadrianales* and the *sodales Antoniniani*. Throughout these changes the *sodales* continued to include the most prestigious members of the senatorial order.[46] Honouring former emperors was thus one of the expected roles of distinguished senators.

The cult of the *divi*, which was in part calqued on the cult of the gods, raised problems for the Romans as to the precise status of the *divi*. In a strictly religious context the *divi* were treated exactly like the traditional *dei*. For example, sacrifices performed to them by the Arval Brothers were identical to sacrifices to the *dei*, obeying the same rules for the choice of sacrificial animals. But on the boundary of a religious context the cult had problematic consequences, of which I examine just three. The image of a *divus*, unlike that of a distinguished noble, was not paraded at funerals of his descendants. Thus by senatorial decree the image of Julius Caesar was no longer to be carried in funerals, and it was in fact absent from Augustus' own funeral.[47] The status of Caesar, and later *divi*, was too ambiguous to be exposed in such a vulnerable position. By contrast, the ascension of Aeneas and Romulus was unproblematic and their images were carried at Augustus' funeral procession. Gods, but not *divi*, could be ancestors.

In addition, if the former emperor was now among the gods, a problem arose concerning the handling of offences against him. Were they to be treated like offences against the living emperor or like those against the traditional gods? The second solution was

[45] G. Wissowa, *Religion und Kultus der Römer*, 2nd edn (Munich, 1912), p. 564 on *sodales Titii*. Ehrenberg and Jones, *Documents* 94a.59–62 and *Zeit. Pap. Epig.*, lv (1984), p. 70; Tacitus, *Histories* ii.95.

[46] A. Momigliano, 'Sodales Flaviales Titiales e culto di Giove', in *Quinto contributo alla storia degli studi classici* (Rome, 1975), pp. 657–66; K. Latte, *Römische Religionsgeschichte* (Munich, 1960), pp. 317–20; H.-G. Pflaum, 'Les Sodales Antoniniani de l'époque de Marc-Aurèle', *Mémoires présentés par divers savants à l'Académie des Inscriptions*, xv.2 (1966), pp. 141–235; Pflaum, 'Les prêtres du culte impérial sous le règne d'Antonin le Pieux', *Comptes rendus de l'Académie des Inscriptions* (1967), pp. 194–208.

[47] Dio xlvii.19.2, lvi.34.2. Cf. lvi.46.4 for Augustus' own image.

adopted. Tiberius decided that a case of perjury by the divine Augustus should be treated in the same way as deceit of Jupiter: 'injury to the gods was the gods' concern'.[48] In other words heaven and not the courts would punish the perjurer. This strong line on the status of the *divi* was maintained for perjury, but actual insults to the *divi* became punishable in law. As there was no concept of a specifically religious crime, the use of the ordinary law was the normal way to handle threats to traditional religious practice. Here there was an additional reason for legal action. *Divus Augustus* was Tiberius' father and predecessor and attacks on *divus Augustus* might well be covert attacks on Tiberius.

Another problem area was that of legacies. What was to happen if the emperor or empress died between the making of a will and the death of the testator? As Roman gods could be the recipients of legacies, was the same to be true of the *divi*? In fact the second-century jurists decided that legacies should go to the new emperor, or be void in the case of a deceased empress.[49] The category of *divi*, former emperors who were now gods, was necessarily complex and ambivalent, generating a number of problems about their status. The *divi* both were and were not gods.

To modern eyes, however, the creation of the cult of the *divi* raises quite different problems; it seems deeply suspicious and scholars have often been tempted to treat it with great scepticism. Surely political considerations were paramount. As we shall see (pp. 82–91), the political context and political arguments about the merits of divinising a particular emperor were important, but so too was the expectation that the apotheosis was real. The former emperor actually did ascend to heaven and his successor established a cult because he believed in him.

To take the apotheosis of Augustus as a paradigm, in his lifetime there was the hope, as we have seen, that he would in due course become a god. The (verse) dedication of a temple in Italy to Gaius and Lucius Caesars, Augustus' heirs, includes the sentence: 'when time summons you, Caesar [Augustus], to be a god, and you return to your place in heaven from which you can rule the world, let these

---

[48] Tacitus, *Annals* i.73.5. Cf. R. A. Bauman, *Impietas in principem* (Munich, 1974), ch. 4; J. Scheid, 'Le Délit religieux dans la Rome tardo-républicaine', in *Le Délit religieux dans la cité antique* (Rome, 1981), pp. 117–71.

[49] *Digest* xxxi.56–7.

be the people who in your stead govern the earth and rule us, having their prayers to you heard'.[50]

In addition to this contemporary expectation of apotheosis, there circulated stories (at least after the event) about omens which had portended the apotheosis. Suetonius' life of Augustus included a number of these, set both at his birth and youth and also shortly before his death. For example, Cicero told his friends on the Capitol a dream which he had had the previous night: 'A boy of noble countenance was let down from heaven on a golden chain and, standing at the door of the Capitolium [temple of Jupiter], was given a whip by Jupiter'. Just then he caught sight of the then unknown Augustus and identified him as the boy of his dream (94.9). In other words, Augustus had come down from his place in heaven and was to rule with the help of Jupiter. Suetonius also says explicitly that his death and deification were indicated in advance by unmistakable signs: 'A lightning flash melted the first letter of his name [sc. Caesar] from an inscription of one of his statues; this was interpreted to mean that he would live only a hundred days from that time, the number indicated by the letter C, and that he would be numbered with the gods, since *aesar* (that is, the part of the name Caesar which was left) is the word for god in Etruscan' (97.2).[51] With heaven pointing the way by signs, how could one doubt that the emperor had ascended to the skies? Signs portending death and divinisation thus served to reinforce the reality of imperial apotheosis.

The new emperor was also expected to promote the formal consecration of his predecessor from sincere belief. A contemporary eulogy of Tiberius praises the fact that he 'consecrated his father [Augustus] not by imperial fiat but by his attitude of reverence; he did not simply call him a god, but made him one'. And Seneca, praising Augustus as a model to the young emperor Nero, says that 'we believe him to be a god, but not because we are ordered to do so'. This expectation of sincerity went together with criticism of other emperors for improper motives. A panegyric of Trajan suggested that Tiberius deified Augustus for the purpose of introducing the charge of high treason; Nero had done the same for

[50] *Insc. lat. sel.* (see n. 8), 137. See for later parallels: Lucan i.45–66 (Nero); Pliny, *Hist. nat.* ii.18 (Vespasian); Martial xiii.4 (Domitian).

[51] For other portents see: Suetonius, *Claudius* 46, *Vespasian* 23.4; *Scriptores Historiae Augustae*, *Severus* 22, *Severus Alexander* 14. Cf. Weinstock, *Divus Julius* (see n. 4), pp. 346, 357–8.

Claudius in a spirit of mockery and so on. But as for Trajan, 'you gave your father [Nerva] his place among the stars with no thought of terrorising your subjects, of bringing the gods into disrepute, or of gaining reflected glory, but simply because you thought he was a god'.[52]

The apotheosis of the emperor was thus an elaborate institution. The formal senatorial decision, based on the evidence of a witness, was central, but this decision arose from a range of prior expectations. There were the models for apotheosis, Romulus and Hercules, and the traditional idea of the return of great men to the stars; there was a general anticipation that the living emperor would ascend to heaven after his death and signs might portend his apotheosis. The establishment of a cult by the senate then generated another range of expectations. The cult of the *divus* was modelled in part on the cult of the gods, but the precise extent of the parallelism had to be carefully defined. In all this the new emperor had a leading part to play. He was supposed to be motivated by feelings of piety, but the situation was of course more complex than that. We need now to explore the changing political context of apotheosis and to discover how apotheosis relates to the roles of both emperor and senate.

THE SENATE AND PEOPLE OF ROME

In the ceremony of apotheosis the leading parts were taken by the new emperor and the Roman élite – the senators and the knights. The emperor spoke the funeral eulogy of his predecessor and sometimes had a role at the ceremony in the Campus Martius, but the overall organisation gave especial prominence to the élite. The senate made the actual arrangements and senators and knights were the chief actors in the ceremonial: at Pertinax's funeral the senators and their wives had official positions on either side of the effigy; the priests and magistrates moved the effigy down from the platform; the other senators marched in front of the effigy, which was carried by knights, to the Campus Martius; and there the ordinary senators had special stands, while the magistrates and knights took part in the military display. Finally the senate passed

---

[52] Velleius Paterculus ii.126.1. Seneca, *de clementia* i.10.3. Pliny, *Panegyric* 11.1–2. These passages of course do not imply that the emperor made his predecessor a god arbitrarily.

the formal decree recognising that the emperor had gone to heaven and establishing a cult.

The emphasis on the emperor and the senate in the organisation of the ceremony suggests that apotheosis was an aspect of the need to create and define roles, both for the emperor and for the Roman élite. For the élite one significant boundary was with the populace of Rome. Status boundaries had been very important in the late Republic and much of the political conflict of the period was between the senate and the populace of Rome. The populace had certainly played its part in the funeral of Julius Caesar, contrary indeed to the official plan. After the display of the body in the Forum it was to have been carried to the Campus Martius for cremation, but the populace rioted and the body was cremated in the Forum itself. At the place of cremation the populace built an altar and column where they sacrificed, made vows and settled disputes by an oath in the name of Caesar. This was a strictly unofficial cult (one of the consuls destroyed the altar, only for it to be rebuilt). But in the calmer atmosphere of 42 BC when the senate officially voted divine honours to Caesar these were duly put to the popular assembly for ratification and a fragment of the law passed by the assembly survives (in a Greek translation). In the words of an Italian dedication, 'the senate and people of Rome place [Julius Caesar] in the company of the gods'.[53]

The Augustan period enhanced the importance of the earlier status boundaries. Power shifted from the populace into the hands of the senate, a process which was almost complete at the death of Augustus. The following year, elections, which had continued to cause unrest under Augustus, were placed in effective senatorial control, thus eliminating the popular assembly. Tiberius also warned the populace not to attempt to have Augustus cremated in the Forum, and stationed soldiers to prevent any disturbances. Though Augustus' funeral procession is said to have included almost all the population of Rome, the populace had no official position in the consecreation of Augustus, nor, with one exception (Marcus Aurelius), of any subsequent emperor.[54] Thus at the funeral of Pertinax the subject nations and the guilds were repre-

---

[53] For the law see Price, *Rituals and Power: The Roman Imperial Cult in Asia Minor* (Cambridge, 1984), pp. 76–7. *Insc. lat. sel.* (see n. 8), 72.

[54] Tacitus, *Annals* i.8.5–6; Dio lvi. 42.1. Cf. Weinstock, *Divus Julius* (see n. 4), p. 390.

sented in the procession and funeral offerings were made by the communities of the empire and by the guilds of Rome, but the populace was not officially represented. Indeed there were not even any games held for the populace after the funeral[55] and no gifts (*congiaria*) were made to them to celebrate the apotheosis. The citizen body of Rome no longer had active political power under the empire, though it still had to be cultivated by emperor and élite, and the crucial boundary for the élite became that with the emperor.

Roman emperors were themselves members of the senatorial élite. The establishment of the imperial system derived from the struggles for prestige and primacy within the élite, and when one dynasty was overthrown, the new dynasty emerged from within the senatorial class. All emperors in the first two centuries of the empire held senatorial office, both before their accession and after assuming office. Emperors were also expected to behave like senators and had to maintain the fiction that senators were their equals. This was a matter for regular comment.

Tiberius, for example, gained good marks, treating his companions as he would have done in private life: he helped them in lawsuits, joined them at sacrifices, visited them when they were sick (without a guard) and even delivered the funeral oration. Towards the populace in Rome the emperors were expected to behave with more grandeur, but even here arrogance and excessive formality were criticised in favour of affability. Tiberius, it is said, often went to horse-racing, not only out of courtesy to those (senators) giving the races, but also to ensure that the populace was orderly and to seem to share in their holiday.[56]

The ceremonial in Rome surrounding the living emperor was therefore very restricted. In the provinces and also in Italy itself, from the reign of Augustus onwards there were cults of the living emperor, with temples, priests and sacrifices, and the most important of these were officially sanctioned by emperor and senate. Such cults were for subjects, not for the city ruling the

---

[55] Images of the *divi* were, however, paraded at subsequent games: P. N. Schulten, *Die Typologie der römischen Konsekrationsprägungen* (Frankfurt, 1979), pp. 40–1.

[56] Dio lvii.11.7 and 11.5. See the excellent article by A. Wallace-Hadrill, 'Civilis Princeps: Between Citizen and King', *Journal of Roman Studies*, lxxii (1982), pp. 32–48.

empire,[57] and emperors such as Gaius, Domitian and Commodus who attempted to introduce cults of themselves in Rome met hostility and death. In addition, the performance of acts of obeisance to the living emperor, at least in the early empire, was unacceptable for members of the Roman élite: Persians might grovel in front of their king, but senators could not do so to one another.[58] However, it was perfectly fitting for Persians or other foreigners outside the empire to do obeisance to the emperor. A knight (and senator to be) serving with the future emperor Tiberius in campaigns against the Germans reported one such incident with approbation: a distinguished barbarian made his way across the Elbe in a dug-out canoe and asked permission to land and see Tiberius.

> Permission was granted. Then he beached his canoe, and, after gazing upon Caesar [Tiberius] for a long time in silence, exclaimed: 'Our young men are insane, for though they worship you as divine when absent, when you are present they fear your armies instead of trusting to your protection. But I, by your kind permission, Caesar, have today seen the gods of whom I merely used to hear; and in my life have never hoped for or experienced a happier day.' After asking for and receiving permission to touch Caesar's hand, he again entered his canoe, and continued to gaze back upon him until he landed on his own bank.[59]

As the patronising but favourable tone of this anecdote shows, foreigners and provincials were expected to mark their subjection to Rome by obeisance and by cults of the living emperor, but the population of Rome and in particular the élite attempted to treat him as one of themselves.

So far there might seem to be no problem about the role of either emperor or senate; the emperor was to behave like a senator in his lifetime and his funeral was a grand version of the traditional senatorial funeral. But this emphasis on the emperor as a member of the senatorial élite fails to explain the sense apotheosis made to the senate, which was formally responsible for the procedure. There were of course strong, and sometimes irresistible, pressures

---

[57] Dio li. 20.7–8. For the significance of these cults to the subjects see Price, *Rituals and Power* (n. 53).

[58] Fronto, *To Appian* 3 (Loeb edn i, p. 272). Cf. Philo, *Legatio* 116.

[59] Velleius Paterculus ii.107. Cf. Dio lxii.2.4 (Tiridates and Nero), Martial v.3 (a Dacian and Domitian), *Scriptores Historiae Augustae*, *Aurelian* 41.10 (numerous nations). Jordanes, *Getica* 142–4, sets a similar story in the fourth century.

14 Gaius sacrificing before the temple of *divus Augustus*. The coin was issued to commemorate the dedication of the temple.

on the senate, at least when power was transmitted smoothly to a recognised heir. Augustus' funeral was designed by Augustus himself, who left a book of instructions to be followed by the senate. The new emperor of course also leaned on the senate to ensure that his father was duly honoured. When Tiberius died, the senate was asked by Gaius to consecrate Tiberius, but it was able to resist and Tiberius received merely a grand public funeral. Such pressures were not generally so easy to evade. At the death of Hadrian the senate procrastinated over the act of deification, but Antoninus Pius forced their hand by saying that he would not be emperor unless Hadrian were deified.[60] In addition, the cult of the deified emperor might be strongly promoted by his heir or a subsequent emperor. Gaius, having to draw a veil over the then unpopular Tiberius, went back to Augustus and was active in increasing the cult paid to *divus Augustus*.[61] But despite these pressures, the choice about whether or not to deify lay formally with the senate and not with the emperor. The senate was thus enabled to pass posthumous judgement on the emperor, symbolic-

[60] Suetonius, *Augustus* 101.4, Dio lvi.33.1 (Augustus). Dio lix.3.7–8, Suetonius, *Tiberius* 75.3, Josephus, *Ant. Jud.* xviii.236 (Tiberius); the mint at Lyons seems to have assumed prematurely that Tiberius was deified (C. H. V. Sutherland, *Coinage in Roman Imperial Policy* (London, 1951), p. 107). Dio lxix.23.3, lxx.1 (Hadrian).

[61] J. Gagé, 'Divus Augustus. L'idée dynastique chez les empereurs julio-claudiens', *Revue archéologique*, 5th ser., xxxiv (1931), pp. 11–41.

ally enacting its role of collective superiority over one of its own members.

The basis for the senatorial decision lay in the merits of the former emperor. Those who had behaved tyrannically did not receive divine honours, while the virtuous gained their due reward.[62] The use of virtue as the criterion for deification applied by extension to the wives of emperors who were deified. Imperial wives had major public roles and might wield considerable influence. Tiberius at his accession told his mother Livia to conduct herself modestly according to the same principles as he himself proposed to follow. For at the time 'she occupied a very exalted station, far above all women of former days, so that she could at any time receive the senate and such of the people as wished to greet her in her house'. And at the accession of Trajan, his wife Plotina, when she 'first entered the palace, turned round so as to face the stairway and the populace and said "I enter here such a woman as I would be when I depart". And she conducted herself during the entire reign in such a manner as to incur no censure'.[63] When Livia died apotheosis was proposed for her but Tiberius vetoed the suggestion and the ceremony was not enacted until the reign of Claudius, but by the early second century the deification of imperial wives had become standard and Plotina was consecrated at her death.

The deification of imperial children is more surprising, but it happened for the first time only in AD 63, for a four-month-old daughter of Nero, and by then the system of deifying empresses had become acceptable and could be extended even to non-powerful members of the family. Deification was not, however, extended beyond the imperial family. When Hadrian's favourite Antinous died, Hadrian arranged considerable honours outside Rome, but Antinous received no public honours at all in Rome, let alone official consecration.

Though actual records of the senatorial debates about apotheosis are lacking, we have a parody of one such debate in Seneca's *Apocolocyntosis*. This work, composed shortly after the accession of Nero, is a biting critique of the deification of Claudius. Many scholars have assumed that the critique implies scepticism about deification in general, but in fact its argument is that the particular failings of Claudius made it wholly inappropriate to deify him. The

[62] As Appian, *Bellum civile* ii.617–18, observed.   [63] Dio lvii.12; lxviii.5.5.

limping, mumbling Claudius finally died and went up to heaven, where the gods in senatorial manner had to decide whether to accept him (8–12). After some initial discussion about what sort of god he might be, Jupiter remembered that it was not proper to debate in the presence of strangers and so Claudius was led out. A formal debate followed. Janus, as consul elect, spoke first, arguing that the majesty of the gods ought not to be diminished by being given away to mortals at all. On the other hand Diespiter, also consul elect, presented the case for deification:

> Inasmuch as *divus* Claudius is akin to *divus* Augustus and also to *diva* Augusta, his grandmother, whom he ordered to be made a goddess, and whereas he far surpasses all mortal men in wisdom, and seeing that it is for the public good that there be someone able to join Romulus in devouring boiled turnips [obscure joke], I propose that from this day forth *divus* Claudius be a god, to enjoy that honour with all its appurtenances in as full a degree as any other before him, and that a note to that effect be added to Ovid's *Metamorphoses*. (9.5)

The meeting was divided between these two views, but then Augustus rose to deliver a ferocious attack on Claudius' arbitrary cruelty; someone who had chopped off heads as easily as a dog sits down should never be made a god. Augustus listed a number of murders of his relatives and proposed that Claudius be banished immediately from heaven. Augustus carried the day and Claudius was taken down to the Underworld where he stood trial for the murder of thirty-five senators and two hundred and twenty-one knights.

Much of the *Apocolocyntosis* is burlesque and includes many literary parodies, but the arguments about deification do reflect real concerns. There was a case for not demeaning the gods by adding humans to their number, and some seem to have felt this even at the consecration of Augustus.[64] But if that argument was rejected, the debate hinged on the merits of the particular emperor. There was good precedent for Claudius in Augustus and Livia, but the deciding factor was his character. His (alleged) great wisdom was weighed against his extreme savagery (Claudius had indeed executed relatives, senators and knights). In real life the pressures on the senate to deify Claudius were irresistible, but Seneca

---

[64] Tacitus, *Annals* i.10.5.

restated, in a safely frivolous genre, the argument of the élite that virtue alone entitled the emperor to a place in heaven.

The attention of the élite centred not on the specific constitutional offices held by the emperor, but on his character and behaviour. That is, they hoped to urge the emperor to exercise his supreme position for good rather than ill. For example, a philosophical treatise by Seneca addressed to the young emperor Nero (and thus contemporary with the *Apocolocyntosis*) is devoted to the emperor's *clementia*, his self-restraint in the wielding of power. It pictures Nero saying to himself:

> I am the arbiter of life and death for the nations; it rests in my power what each person's lot and state shall be; by my lips Fortune proclaims what gifts she would bestow on each human being . . . With all things thus at my disposal, I have been moved neither by anger nor youthful impulse to unjust punishment . . . nor by that vainglory which employs terror for the display of might. (*De Clementia* i.1.2–3)

That was the hope, which could be encouraged with the prospect of heaven. A contemporary writer noted that Vespasian with his two sons was progressing along the road to immortality, because of his aid to a weary world, 'and it is the oldest way of giving thanks to benefactors to enroll them among the gods'. This emphasis on benevolence and benefactions had the excellent precedent of Hercules: his labours had long been seen as in the service of the human race and as the reason for his apotheosis.[65] Like Hercules, the emperor was to labour in the service of humanity and to rise from the pyre to heaven.

The urging of virtue on a tyrannical emperor is neatly depicted in a historical drama ([Seneca's] *Octavia*) set in the reign of Nero, and written shortly afterwards. Seneca bravely argues the case for restraint to Nero, who has just ordered two cruel executions:

> It is glorious to tower aloft amongst great men, to have care for one's native land, to spare the downtrodden, to abstain from cruel bloodshed, to be slow to wrath, give quiet to the world, peace to one's time. This is virtue's crown, by this way heaven is sought. So did the first Augustus, his country's father, gain the stars, and is worshipped in temples as a god. (472–8)

---

[65] Pliny, *Hist. nat.* ii.18–19 (Vespasian). Cicero, *pro Sestio* 143, Ovid, *Metamorphoses* ix.256–8 and [Seneca], *Hercules Oetaeus* 1942–3 (Hercules).

Nero responded with a rather different analysis of how Augustus gained the stars:

> He who earned heaven by piety, the deified Augustus, how many nobles did he put to death, young men and old, scattered throughout the world, when they fled their own homes, through fear of death and the sword of the triumvirs [of whom Augustus was one] – all by the list of denunciations delivered to their destruction . . . At last the victor, now weary, sheathed his sword, blunted with savage blows, and maintained his sway by fear. Safe under the protection of his loyal guards he lived, and when he died, by the surpassing piety of his son, was made a god, hallowed and enshrined. Me, too, shall the stars await if with relentless sword I first destroy whatever is hostile to me, and on a worthy offspring found my house. (504–32)

This fictional confrontation between Seneca and Nero reveals very clearly the importance of the relationship between virtue and deification. The cool and calculating tyrant was of course not bound by moral suasion; he felt, not unreasonably, that heaven could best be reached by the path of tyranny.

Why, though, did the élite offer a reward for virtue which seems so out of keeping with the aim of restraint? Apart from the obvious desirability of deification, the answer lies in the fact that deification was a logical step on from the religious honours accorded the emperor in his lifetime. Though actual deification of the new emperor was unacceptable in Rome itself, a wide range of rituals there placed him close to the gods and emphasised the divine aspects of his nature. For example, the Arval Brothers, one of the official priestly bodies of Rome, offered annual sacrifices to Jupiter for having preserved the emperor during the previous year. Such sacrifices placed the living emperor under the protection of the gods, without implying his divinity. But the Arval Brothers also sacrificed on a wide range of occasions (imperial birthdays, consulships, arrivals etc.) to the *genius* of the emperor himself (or to the *Juno* of the empress, the female equivalent).[66] Though the sacrificial animal (*taurus*) differed from that offered to the male gods and the *divi* (*bos mas*), the context of these sacrifices emphasised the divine aspect of the emperor's nature.

Given this close association of the living emperor with the

---

[66] *Acta fratrum Arvalium*, ed. W. Henzen (Berlin, 1874), index *s.v.* 'Genius' and 'Juno'. These ceremonies cease after AD 70, for reasons which remain unclear.

heavenly powers, it would have been very difficult to remove the emperor from this context on his death and to locate him firmly in the Underworld. Banishment to the Underworld was the punishment meted out to Claudius in the *Apocolocyntosis*, and when Caracalla killed his brother Geta he abolished his memory and instituted annual sacrifices to him in the Underworld.[67] A place in the Underworld rather than among the gods was a fall from favour for which no other prize offered by the élite could compensate. Deification was the fitting end for the good emperor. Such granting of deification allowed the senate to create an honourable role for itself. While the senate had gained some political authority over the citizen body of Rome, it had at the same time lost other authority to the emperor. The ceremony of apotheosis granted the senate symbolic supremacy over both populace and emperor.

THE SYSTEM TRANSFORMED

So far the attention of this piece has been on the first century AD, extending onwards only to glance at unchanging elements in the system of imperial funerals; in particular the emphasis in the last section on the role of the senate applies primarily to the early empire. We need now to turn to changes in the system, from the shifts of emphasis in the second and third centuries to the radical transformations in the fourth century. The procedure came to focus increasingly on the pyre and from the noble tradition there evolved a peculiarly imperial funeral. This was first modified and then abandoned by the Christian emperors.

In the first century the culmination of the funeral was the report of a witness to the senate, the senatorial debate on the merits of the emperor and the senatorial decree recognising that he had ascended to heaven and establishing divine honours to him. This all changed in the second century. First, there was a change in the timing of the senatorial meeting and the passing of the decree. At least sometimes this preceded rather than followed the actual funeral. One might think this of little note, but the new order decisively altered the role of the senate. In the earlier system the senate did not take an arbitrary political decision to deify the emperor; it responded in traditional religious manner to the evidence of his ascent by voting cult to him. When the senatorial

[67] Dio lxxviii.12.6 (*enhagismos*).

decree preceded the funeral, religious tradition ceased to be relevant and the decision became more of a political formality.

So striking is this change that one leading scholar has denied that it took place, on the grounds that it would have violated all the principles of the Roman divine law,[68] but in fact one crucial piece of evidence shows that the change did occur. An official calendar, inscribed on stone at Ostia, records that on 29 August AD 112 Marciana, the sister of Trajan, died and received the title of *diva*, and that on 3rd September she was buried with a public funeral.[69] The only natural way of reading this evidence is that Marciana was granted the title of *diva* before the funeral.

A consequence of this change was that there was no place for the witness. Specific witnesses are attested only in the early empire and they clearly played no part in the procedure by the time of Dio or Herodian. In the second century only Christian writers, hostile to pagan cults, refer to the use of a witness and they notoriously tend to dredge up old information in aid of their polemics.[70] When the decision about deification did or at least could precede the funeral, the evidence of a single eyewitness that the emperor had gone up to heaven was redundant.

The senate continued to play a formal role in apotheosis through the second and third centuries into the tetrarchic period.[71] However, such minimal freedom of action as the senate had in the early empire, such as refusing to deify Tiberius, was increasingly reduced. Deification became more common and refusal to conse- crate almost impossible. Thus apotheosis could be represented as being simply the result of imperial fiat. Dio describes the cult of Pertinax as the outcome of orders by Septimius Severus, without

[68] E. J. Bickermann, '*Consecratio*', in W. den Boer (ed.), *Le culte des souverains dans l'empire romain* (Entretiens Hardt xix, Vandoeuvres, 1973), pp. 3–25 and 'Diva Augusta Marciana', *American Journal of Philology*, xcv (1974), pp. 362–76. See *contra* H. Temporini, *Die Frauen*, pp. 197–201 and H. Chantraine, ' "Dop- pelbestattungen" römischer Kaiser', *Historia*, xxix (1980), pp. 71–85.

[69] 'IIII k. Septembr. [Marciana Aug]usta excessit divaq(ue) cognominata. [Eodem die Mati]dia Augusta cognominata. III [non. Sept. Mar]ciana Augusta funere censorio [elata est ...].' *Inscriptiones Italiae* xiii.1, p. 201 = L. Vidman, *Fasti Ostienses,* 2nd edn (Prague, 1982), p. 48.

[70] Justin, *Apology* i.21, Tatian, *ad Graecos* 10.2, Tertullian, *de spectaculis* 30.3. Cf. Tertullian, *Apology* 21.23 and Minucius Felix, *Octavius* 21.9 on Romulus and Proculus.

[71] Athanasius, *contra gentes* 9.50–3 (Thomson) believes in a recent, i.e. tetrarchic, act of the senate (cf. T. D. Barnes, *The New Empire of Diocletian and Constantine* (Cambridge, Mass., 1982), p. 35).

15 The pyre of Antoninus Pius. Note the decoration on the central storeys and the chariot bearing the emperor from the top.

mentioning the senatorial decree that was passed.[72] The senatorial proceedings had lost their place as the decisive and climactic point of imperial funerals.

This diminution in the role of the senate runs parallel to its general loss of political leverage. In the second century the senate was fairly docile towards the emperors and in the third century, though it did once reassert its formal powers to confer the position of emperor against the wishes of the army, senators gradually ceased to hold positions of power. Septimius Severus put three new legions under knights rather than senators, and by the mid third century senators were excluded from military command. The administration of some provinces also passed from senators to knights. No doubt this change took place in part because senators no longer wished high and increasingly arduous office, but the result was a dramatic change from the early empire. Senators ceased to be of central importance as administrators, and some emperors had not been members of the senate before their accession. With the ending of the symbiotic relationship of emperor and senate the emperor was increasingly supreme.

At imperial funerals attention focussed more on the pyre. In the mid second century, coins commemorating imperial apotheosis started to feature the pyre, with its three, four, five or even six storeys.[73] Dio describes the three-storey pyre for the funeral of Pertinax, and Herodian a five-storey pyre, decorated with gold

---

[72] *Scriptores Historiae Augustae*, *Pertinax* 14.10–15.1; cf. *Roman Imperial Coinage* iv.1, p. 181.
[73] Schulten, *Die Typologie* (see n. 55) catalogues and analyses the coinage.

16 The apotheosis of Sabina from the pyre, watched by her husband Hadrian.

embroidered drapery, ivory carvings and a variety of paintings. The
grant of such a pyre was a great honour, as Hadrian noted in the
funeral oration he gave for Matidia, the niece of Trajan.[74] Though
the use of a pyre for cremation was traditional Roman practice,
monumental, architectural pyres were first constructed for the
emperors and were extremely impressive.[75]

The culmination of the whole funeral was now the lighting of the
pyre and the releasing of an eagle from it, which, as Herodian says,

[74] *Inscriptiones Italiae* iv.1, 77 line 34.
[75] Herodian iv.2.8, compares lighthouses.

was believed by the Romans to take the soul of the emperor to heaven. Admittedly Dio does claim that an eagle was used already at the funeral of Augustus, but he is almost certainly anachronistic in this detail; there is a telling silence in Suetonius' life of Augustus which is, as we have seen, very full on the signs associated with Augustus' death and apotheosis.[76] In the early empire on private art, particularly gems, the eagle as the bird of Jupiter is found carrying the emperor up to heaven, but this became part of the official ceremonial only in the second century when the eagle appears on the consecration coins of emperors, and the peacock, as the bird of Juno, on those of some empresses. With the release of an eagle from the pyre, instead of having a single witness who reported to the senate, now all those present became witnesses of the apotheosis.

The increased emphasis on the pyre in the second and third centuries is illustrated by the records of the Arval Brothers. In the first century they offered sacrifices to commemorate the passing of the senatorial decree, while in the second century they provided perfume for the pyre itself.[77] Two points emerge from this. The gift of perfume by the Arvals marks the increasing lavishness of the pyre. Thus at Augustus' funeral the only gifts to the pyre were the military decorations of the soldiers who were present, while according to Herodian (iv.2.8), 'every perfume and incense on earth and all the fruits and herbs and juices that are collected for their aroma are brought up and poured out in great heaps. Every people and city and prominent person of distinction vies with each other to send these last gifts in honour of the emperor.' The burning of rich gifts on the pyre was known of in Judaea, serving as a model for the funerals of leading rabbis.[78] Secondly, the Arvals in the second century use the term *consecratio*, the technical term for the passing of the senatorial decree, of the pyre itself. With the witness gone and the senatorial decree sometimes preceding the funeral, the senate had declined in importance. The pyre and the eagle were

[76] F. Vittinghoff, *Der Staatsfeind in der römischen Kaiserzeit* (Berlin, 1936), pp. 106–8 and U. Geyer, 'Der Adlerflug im römischen Konsekrationszeremoniell' (unpublished Ph.D. thesis, Bonn, 1967) for further arguments.

[77] *Acta fratrum Arvalium*, ed. Henzen, pp. 59 and 88. The importance of the pyre is argued by P. Gros, 'Rites funéraires et rites d'immortalité dans la liturgie de l'apothéose', *Annuaire de l'École Pratique des Hautes Études*, 4th section (1965–6), pp. 477–90.

[78] M. Goodman, *State and Society in Roman Galilee, AD 132–212* (Totowa, 1983), p. 112.

now central. Rather than being simply a way of disposing of the corpse, the pyre became a dramatic enactment of imperial apotheosis.

The increasing importance of the pyre becomes even more striking in the light of changing patterns of burial for the population in general. In the late Republic and early empire, cremation was the normal Roman practice for people of all classes. This is clear both from archaeology and from the comment of Tacitus on the burial of Nero's wife Poppaea: 'her body was not cremated in the normal Roman manner, but was stuffed with perfumes and embalmed as is customary with foreign kings and placed in the tomb of the Julii' (i.e. the mausoleum of Augustus). Embalming never became popular in Rome, but in the course of the second century inhumation gradually became more common. At one Roman cemetery, for example, in the early second century only cremation is found, in the mid century a mixture of cremation and inhumation, while by the end of the century inhumation was predominant. Thus the huge marble sarcophagi from Rome which now fill our museums date only from the 120s onwards.[79]

By contrast emperors continued to be cremated throughout the second and third centuries. This is obviously true of the major public ceremony; the pyre is featured on coins as late as 270 and again c. 310–13. The area of uncertainty is whether there was a regular distinction between the treatment of the actual corpse of the emperor and of his waxen image: was one inhumed and the other cremated?[80] The account of Herodian with which we started certainly states as a general rule that there was a separate funeral of the corpse and the image, but his language at the crucial point is ambiguous. The verb (*kathaptein*) for the funeral of the corpse can refer to cremation, but can equally imply inhumation. There is similar ambiguity in the other evidence; *corpus* (or *soma* in Greek) can refer either to a corpse, implying inhumation, or to the ashes after cremation. One extant sarcophagus is generally accepted as that of a third-century emperor (Balbinus, died 238), but the identification is not quite certain and the portrait on the sarcopha-

---

[79] F. Cumont, *Lux Perpetua* (Paris, 1949), pp. 387–90; G. Koch, H. Sichterman, *Römische Sarkophage* (Munich, 1982), pp. 27–30, 61. Tacitus, *Annals* xvi.6.2.

[80] *Roman Imperial Coinage* v.1, pp. 233–4, vi, p. 221. For inhumation see: R. Turcan, 'Origines et sens de l'inhumation à l'époque impériale', *Revue des études anciennes*, lx (1958), pp. 323–47; Richard, 'Recherches' (see n. 1).

gus could depict a member of the third-century aristocracy.[81] There is thus no decisive evidence that the emperor's corpse was inhumed in the second or third centuries. Why then the separation between the funerals of the corpse and the image? This was a customary practice, independent of inhumation, which was employed when someone died and was cremated outside Rome; the image was then used for a formal cremation at Rome itself (cf. p. 64). Even when an emperor died at or near Rome (as Augustus did), it was obviously convenient for the public ceremonial to use an image untainted by human mortality and corruption.

Thus imperial funerals continued to be extremely traditional in their employment of cremation, both of the corpse and of the image. The reasons for the widespread shift in burial practice towards inhumation are obscure (it is hard to relate the change to eschatology), but the implications for imperial funerals are dramatic. The emperor was buried in a way that increasingly marked him out from the élite and indeed from the rest of his subjects. Funerals of emperors, which had started from the tradition of noble funerals, had become uniquely imperial.

This disengagement of the dead emperor from the élite was followed by changes in the standing of the living emperor in the third century. Behaviour towards the emperor, even by the Roman élite, became more formal. Whereas in the early empire the emperor was in principle treated as an ordinary citizen, and obeisance seen as something foreign, by the third century obeisance before the emperor had become standard.[82] For example, Herodian (iii.11.8) reports that a pretender to the throne (Plautianus) asked one of his loyal officers to kill the reigning emperors; the officer fell in with this plan and 'prostrated himself before Plautianus as though he were already emperor'. In the third century the reigning emperor was also more closely associated with individual patron deities; this was not new (Augustus had made play of his

---

[81] Appian, *Bellum civile* i.17 (*thaptein*). Against inhumation see Temporini and Chantraine (n. 68). Dr R. R. R. Smith confirmed my doubts about the Balbinus sarcophagus (Koch, Sichterman, *Römische Sarkophage*, pp. 101–2). K. Fittschen, *Jahrbuch des deutschen arch. Inst.*, xciv (1979), pp. 578–93 rejects all other candidates for imperial sarcophagi, except 'Balbinus'.

[82] The evidence on obeisance is collected by A. Alföldi, 'Die Ausgestaltung des monarchischen Zeremoniells am römischen Kaiserhofe', *Mitt. deutschen arch. Inst., Röm. Abt.*, xlix (1934), pp. 3–118 = *Die monarchische Repräsentation im römischen Kaiserreiche* (Darmstadt, 1970), esp. pp. 45–79, but he plays down the development.

closeness to Apollo), but it is now more systematically represented. Some coin types, for example, show not just the emperor's head but also the head of a patron deity immediately behind it. This increase in divine patronage did not formally deify the living emperor, but it did emphasise that the ties of the emperor were no longer with the élite but with the gods.[83]

After the chaos of the mid third century (twenty-two emperors in the forty-nine years between 235 and 284) order and stability were restored by Diocletian. He reformed provincial administration, the collection of taxes and also the structure of power at the centre; the empire was divided between two emperors (Augusti) who each had a deputy (Caesar), an organisation known as the tetrarchy. Their power was expressed in quite different terms from that of earlier emperors, though it grew out of earlier developments. Prostration before the living emperor had become standard in the third century, but Diocletian introduced a new court ceremonial of 'kissing the purple'.[84] Similarly the earlier patron deities became formalised under the tetrarchy; the Augustus was called Jovius ('of Jupiter') and the Caesar Herculius, a pairing which reflected the rank of the two rulers.

The imagery of consecration coinage (our main evidence on tetrarchic imperial funerals) also differs from what had preceded.[85] Three *divi* were created in this period, but only one of the issues features the term *consecratio* or depicts the pyre; and novel legends appear: 'for his eternal memory' and 'rest for his most excellent deeds'. The latter legend, on the last of the tetrarchic series, is accompanied by none of the traditional types, but by the emperor sitting on a magistrate's chair, holding a sceptre. This shift away from the elaborate imagery developed in the earlier empire is at first sight inconsistent with the increase in court ceremonial; the

---

[83] R. Turcan, 'Le culte impérial au IIIe siècle', in *Aufstieg und Niedergang* ii.16.2 (see n. 1), pp. 996–1084 at 1022–8. Three third-century emperors were even called *deus* ('god') on (rare) coins, issued by one mint: W. Kubitschek, '*Deus et Dominus* als Titel des Kaisers', *Numismatische Zeitschrift*, xlviii (1915), pp. 167–78.

[84] W. T. Avery, 'The *Adoratio Purpurae* and the Importance of the Imperial Purple in the Fourth Century of the Christian Era', *Mem. American Acad. Rome*, xvii (1940), pp. 66–80.

[85] P. Bruun, 'The Consecration Coins of Constantine the Great', *Arctos* new ser., i (1954), pp. 19–31; P. Bastien, 'Aeternae Memoriae Galeri Maximiani', *Revue belge de numismatique*, cxiv (1968), pp. 15–43; S. G. MacCormack, *Art and Ceremony in Late Antiquity* (Berkeley, Los Angeles and London, 1981), pp. 93–158 is very suggestive on tetrarchic apotheosis.

tetrarchs were certainly not trying to go back to the days when emperors were expected to act like ordinary senators. But there is no inconsistency. With the focus now firmly on the person of the living emperor, who was very closely attached to and identified with the gods, death was not an important turning-point. In addition, if the emperor's descent from the gods was already emphasised by the name Jovius or Herculius, there was little that a human ceremony could achieve. Thus imperial panegyrics which touched on the apotheosis of Constantius in 306 described how 'the sun himself to take you to heaven welcomed you into his chariot which was almost visible' and how 'in truth the heavenly temples stood open before him and he was received into the divine assembly where Jupiter himself stretched out his right hand to him'.[86] The gods themselves took their own up to heaven.

The conversion of Constantine to Christianity (312) had profound consequences for imperial ceremonial.[87] Christian polemicists, as we have noted, had long expressed their hostility to the deification of Roman emperors as one element in the complex of pagan cults. Their particular objection was to the worship of dead people as gods. Taking over an earlier, Greek argument that all Greek (and Roman) gods had once been mortal kings, they extended this to the Roman consecration of their emperors. In the words of a Christian writer passed off on the Sibylline Oracle, 'they [sacrifice] in memory of kings and tyrants to the spirits of the dead as if they were in heaven'. Indeed the whole institution was absurd.

> Your tyrants and kings who, putting behind them fear of the gods, despoil and pillage temple treasuries; who, by proscription, exile and murder, deprive cities of their aristocracies; who ruin and destroy with depraved violence the honour of women and girls, you give them the name of *Indigetes* [ancestral gods] and *divi*; those whom you should pursue with the utmost hatred, you honour with processional couches, altars, temples and other cult and you celebrate their birthdays with games.[88]

Obviously a Christian emperor could not allow his own cult to

---

86 *Panegyrici Latini* vi.14.3, vii.7.3 (Budé edn). For earlier parallels see n. 50.
87 The conversion of Constantine is of course controversial. I follow N. H. Baynes, *Constantine the Great and the Christian Church*, 2nd edn (Oxford, 1972) and T. D. Barnes, *Constantine and Eusebius* (Cambridge Mass., 1981).
88 *Oracula Sibyllina* viii.392–401; Arnobius, *adversus nationes* i.64.2. Cf. Lactantius, *Divine Institutes* i.15.28–33, Tertullian, *ad nationes* i.10.29–33, *Apology* 13.8.

continue unchecked. In the last years of his reign Constantine informed a group of towns in Umbria that they might have a temple to his family but that 'it should not be polluted by the deceits of any contagious supersition', i.e. pagan sacrifice.[89]

When Constantine died (337) the ritual of a Roman apotheosis was hardly appropriate.[90] Rome itself was now rivalled in importance by Constantinople. The senate in Rome, which continued throughout the fourth century to uphold the traditional pagan values, begged permission to receive the body of Constantine and to perform his funeral in Rome, no doubt in the pagan manner, but in vain. In Constantinople, the Christian capital, there was elaborate ceremonial in the presence of the body of Constantine, but this merely perpetuated the ceremony appropriate to the living emperor and the actual funeral was decisively Christian. The first stage of the ceremony was in the palace where the body was laid out in a coffin, surrounded by candles and wearing the symbols of sovereignty (the diadem and purple robe). The officers, courtiers and magistrates 'who had been accustomed to do obeisance to their emperor before, continued to fulfil their duty without any change, entering the chamber at the appropriate time, and saluting their coffined sovereign with bended knee as if he were still alive'. This went on for some time, until Constantine's sons reached Rome. They then led a procession of soldiers and people which took the body to the Church of the Apostles.

Here the second and Christian stage began. Constantine had himself built the church with its elaborate decoration, including the mausoleum with twelve coffins of the Apostles placed on either side of his own.[91] When the new emperors and the soldiers had withdrawn from the church, the clergy and the Christian people performed the rites of divine worship with prayer. Our Christian

---

[89] *Insc. lat. sel.* (see n. 8), 705, 46–8.

[90] Our sole source is Eusebius, *Life of Constantine* iv.58–60, 65–73. See further A. Kaniuth, *Die Beisetzung Konstantins des Grossen* (Breslauer historische Forschungen xviii, 1941) and S. Calderone, 'Teologia politica, successione dinastica e consecratio in età constantiniana', in *Le culte des souverains* (see n. 68), pp. 215–61.

[91] See P. Grierson, 'The Tombs and Obits of the Byzantine Emperors (337–1042)', *Dumbarton Oaks Papers*, xvi (1962), pp. 1–63, and G. Dagron, *Naissance d'une capitale* (Paris, 1974), pp. 401–9, who argue that the church was built by Constantine, rather than Constantius II. For a recently discovered Byzantine imperial sarcophagus see C. Mango, *Annual Arch. Museums Istanbul*, xv–xvi (1969), pp. 308–9.

source, Eusebius, comments that Constantine 'continued to possess imperial power even after death, controlling, as though with renovated life, a universal dominion, and retaining in his own hands, as Victor, Maximus, Augustus, the sovereignty of the Roman world'.

The funeral ceremonial marked a radical break with the old tradition. This is so even for the first stage in the palace. There is at first sight a parallel with the attention paid to the effigy which Herodian reports (pp. 75–6), but this was designed to create the fiction of extended life, while the acts of obeisance before Constantine's body aimed to prolong his imperial powers. The second stage was even more novel. Constantine was probably the first emperor to be inhumed and the first for whom the pyre had no place. More generally the Christian service succeeded in taking over a body which had to that moment been treated with specifically imperial ritual and subsuming it permanently into a Christian context.

Constantine was commemorated by a series of coins issued by various mints throughout the empire.[92] Some coin types ('eternal piety' or 'revered memory') are found in either the western or the eastern half of the empire; only one, of low value and hence wide circulation, is found in both parts, a type showing Constantine on a chariot rising up to heaven. Eusebius in the *Life of Constantine* (iv.73) includes a description of the coin: 'the reverse showed him [Constantine] as a charioteer, drawn by four horses, with a hand stretched downwards from above to receive him up'. Was this to be seen as pagan or Christian? The chariot was a traditional pagan type, though it had not been used on coins for eighty years; the hand could be the hand of Jupiter, as in the tetrarchic panegyrics. But the chariot might evoke the chariot which bore Elijah up to heaven, where the hand could be the hand of God. Surely the imagery is neatly ambiguous, designed to be read in different ways by the pagan and Christian subjects of the empire. But despite the ambiguity the coins were not minted in Rome (or Aquileia or

---

[92] L. Koep, 'Die Konsekrationsmünzen Kaiser Konstantins und ihre religionspolitische Bedeutung', *Jahrbuch für Antike und Christentum*, i (1958), pp. 94–104 = A. Wlosok (ed.), *Römischer Kaiserkult* (Darmstadt, 1978), pp. 509–27. Ambivalence is denied by Calderone (see n. 90) and G. W. Bowersock, 'The Imperial Cult: Perceptions and Persistence', in B. F. Meyer, E. P. Sanders (eds.), *Jewish and Christian Self-Definition*, 3 vols. (London, 1980–82) iii, pp. 171–82, but on the assumption of a new symbiosis of the imperial cult and Christianity.

Siscia). The new emperor wanted to avoid antagonising the senate that had hoped to bury Constantine in Rome.

Thus the pagan ceremonial of consecration was ended, along with priesthoods and temples in the capital, and Constantine was the last emperor for whom consecration coins were struck, but the title *divus* was regularly applied to deceased emperors in the eastern half of the empire until Anastasius in 518. The birthdays of some *divi*, both pagan and Christian, were still celebrated in fourth-century Rome, and imperial images may have continued to receive veneration especially in the provinces. The procedures, if any, for granting the title of *divus* in the fourth century are obscure; the senate in Rome may have been responsible for the elevation of Theodosius (395), but no detailed evidence survives for the Roman ceremonial of imperial funerals after Constantine.[93] In any case, the title *divus* did not imply apotheosis for the Christians; Eusebius was clear that Constantine enjoyed a Christian immortality.

Christianity went increasingly onto the offensive after Constantine and we may leave the last word with the Christian Prudentius, writing in 402/3 at the time of the final struggle against paganism in Rome itself. Looking back to the pagan empire he picked out deification for criticism and ridicule. First, the deification of Saturn, Jupiter, Mercury and so on, kings deified by the credulity of their subjects (an argument we have already noticed, p. 99); then the ancestors of Rome, Mars and Venus, who were merely depraved mortals, and whose apotheosis led to the cult of numerous other mortals. The culmination of the process was the cult of Augustus, his wife Livia and of Antinous the favourite of Hadrian:

> Posterity in a tame period then followed ancestral custom; it worshipped Augustus with a month and sanctuaries, a priest and altars, it offered sacrifices of calf and lamb, prostrated itself before his couch, sought oracles from him. Inscriptions bear

[93] For birthdays: H. Stern, *Le calendrier de 354* (Paris, 1953), pp. 71, 92–3. For statues: F. M. Clover, 'Emperor Worship in Vandal Africa', in *Romanitas-Christianitas. Festschrift J. Straub* (Berlin and New York, 1982), pp. 661–74. For senate (?): *Inscriptiones Christianae urbis Romae*, ed. G. B. de Rossi (Rome, 1857–61) i. p. 338. For later Byzantine imperial funerals see Corippus, *In laudem Iustini Augusti minoris*, ed. Averil Cameron (London, 1976) iii.1–61 and the *De ceremoniis* i.60 (Bonn edn i, pp. 275–6), on which see below pp. 106–36. Imperial funerals are set in a broader context by J. Kyriakakis, 'Byzantine Burial Customs: Care of the Deceased from Death to the Prothesis', *The Greek Orthodox Theological Review*, xix (1974), pp. 37–72.

witness, as do the senatorial decrees which established a temple to Augustus on the model of the temple of Jupiter. A new act of cult made a Juno of Livia [Her infamous marriage to Augustus, who removed her when pregnant from her then husband, Prudentius criticised at length and fiercely]. This was the woman, Rome, whom you made a goddess, to whom you dedicated inscriptions and eternal honours, and whom you placed among the Floras and Venuses. But it is not surprising. What intelligent person had ever doubted that they [Flora and Venus] were of mortal stock and once alive; famous for the renown of their beauty, they sparkled in their affairs thanks to the attractions of their charms until the destruction of their reputation.[94]

The wheel comes full circle. Prudentius' moral opprobrium joins up with Robert Graves' hearty cynicism. Both fail to see the true importance of apotheosis as the central focus of imperial ideology in Rome for three hundred years.

CONCLUSIONS

Royal rituals generally spring from *rites de passage* current in a given society (Introduction, pp. 15–16). In Rome, imperial funerals were based on funerals of the Roman nobility, with a vote of a 'public funeral' by the senate, the parade of ancestral images and the funeral orations. The early stages of the funeral differed in degree, not in kind, from ordinary élite funerals, and, like any funeral, imperial funerals set the seal on a good life by stressing the virtues of the deceased and, by implication, of his successor. Emperors were supposed to behave like ordinary citizens (or at least like ordinary senators), not like kings or autocrats. But the emperor's virtues led the senate to establish a formal cult with a temple and priests for the ruler who was now among the gods. This transformation of the traditional funeral allowed imperial funerals to gain their force from the combination of two pre-existing symbolic systems, noble and divine. Thus, the modern opposition between views of the emperor either as a constitutional magistrate or as a naked autocrat misses the significance of imperial funerals.

[94] *Contra Symmachum* i.245–70. Prudentius may have been incited by reading Ovid's 'flattery' of Augustus and Livia: M. L. Ewald, 'Ovid in the Contra Orationem Symmachi of Prudentius', *Catholic University of America Patristic Studies*, lxvi (1942), pp. 55–9; I owe this reference to Dr A.-M. Palmer.

The emperor was both a virtuous noble, and, as a reward for his virtues, a god in the making.

Funerals of heads of state have an additional significance as *rites de passage* when they involve the transmission of authority to the new ruler. One of the most interesting parallels to Roman funerals is found in sixteenth-century France.[95] There an elaborate ritual surrounding an effigy of the deceased king created the fiction that he was alive until the actual funeral. The reason for this was that the transfer of sovereignty was deemed to take place not at coronation (as earlier), nor at the death of the king (as in the seventeenth century), but at the funeral ceremony. The parallels with Roman practice, which was (wrongly) claimed at the time as the origin of the French ritual, raise the question whether imperial funerals also served to legitimate a successor. But we have seen a possible eschatological explanation of the Roman attention to the imperial image, and, unlike the French case, the funeral never became the formal means of designating the new emperor. The senate remained throughout the three hundred years of the empire, and indeed beyond, the principal body whose vote turned a usurper into an emperor. Comparison between an isolated element of a funeral, such as the treatment of royal effigies, is deeply misleading. Careful examination not only of the funeral as a whole, but also of its context is essential. French royal and Roman imperial funerals constituted parts of very different systems of power.[96]

There were also significant changes in the practice of imperial funerals, which relate to changes in the imperial system as a whole. In the second and third centuries the senate played a lesser, and the pyre a greater role in the ceremonial, and the pyre itself, because of the general abandonment of cremation, became increasingly peculiar, increasingly imperial. The changes in funerary practice help to modify the standard picture of the period. The second century is normally seen as a placid and uneventful continuation of the previous century and the third century as a period of crisis which was replaced abruptly by a wholly different political system. In fact,

95 R. E. Giesey, *The Royal Funeral Ceremony in Renaissance France* (Geneva, 1960); E. A. R. Brown, 'The Ceremonial of Royal Succession in Capetian France', *Speculum*, lv (1982), pp. 266–93. For other royal funerals see R. Huntington and P. Metcalf, *Celebrations of Death* (Cambridge, 1979), pp. 121–83.

96 For a fuller analysis of the concept of power in relation to the Roman empire see Price, *Rituals and Power* (n. 53).

the funerary ceremonial implies that a major shift in the relationship between emperor and élite was beginning as early as the second century; and the establishment of a purely imperial funerary symbolism was taken further in the third century with regard to the living emperor, only to be institutionalized by Diocletian at the end of the third century. Finally, the ceremonial was transformed with the burial of the first Christian emperor, Constantine. Roman emperors were no longer Republican nobles and gods in the making, but servants of God.

3. The construction of court ritual: the *Byzantine* Book of Ceremonies

AVERIL CAMERON

Tenth-century Byzantium has left us with a remarkably detailed documentary source for royal ritual – the work known as the *Book of Ceremonies*. It seems to consist of elaborate prescriptions for court ceremony; since it was compiled by a Byzantine emperor, Constantine VII Porphyrogenitus (AD 913–59),[1] who presumably himself took part in the rituals that he describes, it is naturally a document of the highest importance for understanding royal ceremonial in Byzantium. We seem to have in it a direct record of court procedure whose accuracy is guaranteed by its authorship. It ought surely to be possible to use its evidence as a basis for wider conclusions about Byzantine society, and it has indeed usually been used by scholars in this way.

The issues I shall raise, therefore, are these: what is the real nature of this text, and what meaning can be assigned to the royal rituals which it describes? Before addressing either, it will be helpful to set out two contrasting ideas of Byzantium in modern scholarship, and in so doing to give some idea of the development of Byzantine studies to date.

THE NATURE OF BYZANTINE CULTURE

One standard view of Byzantine culture and society sees it as essentially static, dominated by a weighty concern for tradition. Most Byzantine art, for instance, and all Byzantine formal litera-

[1] Editions: I. I. Reiske, *Corpus Scriptorum Historicorum Byzantinorum*, 2 vols. (Bonn, 1829–30); A. Vogt, *Budé*, 2 vols. in 2 parts each (Paris, 1935–40), containing Greek text, commentary and French translation of i, chaps. 1–83 only. In general, see A. Toynbee, *Constantine Porphyrogennetos and his World* (Oxford, 1973), pp. 575–605; H. Hunger, *Die hochsprachliche Profanliteratur der Byzantiner*, 2 vols. (Munich, 1978), i, pp. 364–7. A similar treatise was put together in the fourteenth century and goes under the name of George Codinos (see J. Verpeaux, *Pseudo-Kodinos, Traité des offices* (Paris, 1906). Since this paper was written Michael McCormick has published an excellent introduction to

ture operated through complex and apparently rigid codes much preoccupied with the imitation of canonical models. The same theory of government had held since the fourth century AD, when the Emperor Constantine founded Constantinople and gave his support to Christianity as the imperial religion. It presented the emperor as God's special representative on earth, who was to be regarded by his subjects as the visible image of God, and whose authority thereby gained an overwhelmingly powerful heavenly sanction.[2]

These ideas (in fact a Christianised continuation of existing tendencies in the Roman Empire)[3] were given full expression in imperial art, which commonly depicted emperors and empresses in close association with Christ, the Virgin or the saints of the Christian church.[4] Moreover, the emperors themselves acted out regular rituals which frequently had religious content, and which served to display the sense of unchanging imperial majesty and to underline the link between emperor and God expressed in dozens of literary and theoretical works. One of the most highly valued imperial virtues was in fact that of impassivity, hieratic calm (Greek *galene*, cf. the earlier Latin term *tranquillitas*), whereby the unchanging face of the imperial office was thought to be revealed.[5]

Not surprisingly, many modern historians have taken these factors at face value. Byzantium has traditionally been regarded as

Byzantine imperial ceremony from a wider perspective: 'Analyzing imperial ceremonies', *Jahrbuch der österr. Byzantinistik* 35 (1985), 1–20.

[2] For Byzantine political theory see F. Dvornik, *Early Christian and Byzantine Political Philosophy*, 2 vols. (Washington D.C., 1966) and cf. also the emphasis of H. Ahrweiler, *L'idéologie politique de l'empire byzantin* (Paris, 1975), pp. 129–47.

[3] For the divinisation of Roman emperors see S. R. F. Price, chap. 2 in this volume, and his *Rituals and Power: the Roman Imperial Cult in Asia Minor* (Cambridge, 1984).

[4] A. Grabar, *L'Empereur dans l'art byzantin* (Strasburg, 1936, repr. 1971) is standard. Emperors were so depicted in the restored St Sophia of Constantine VII's day (see below). I have confined myself in this paper to the period of the *Book of Ceremonies* and earlier, but the same tendencies were continued in later Byzantine art: for a full and interesting discussion see P. Magdalino and R. Nelson, 'The Emperor in Byzantine Art of the Twelfth Century', *Byzantinische Forschungen* viii (1982), pp. 123–83.

[5] I have collected examples of this complex of ideas in my commentary on the Latin sixth-century imperial panegyric by Corippus on the Emperor Justin II (AD 565–78): Averil Cameron (ed.), *Flavius Cresconius Corippus, In laudem Iustini minoris libri quattuor* (London, 1976); for imperial calm see p. 192. The fourth-century historian Ammianus Marcellinus' description of the entry of Constantius II into Rome in AD 357 (xvi.10.2 f.) is a famous passage illustrating the value placed on this notion.

a static 'theocracy'.[6] The tone of such characterisations, moreover, has often been hostile. Take for example these words of Norman Baynes, actually one of the most sympathetic students of Byzantium:

a state which for more than a millennium continued to vegetate without originality, living on a tradition inherited from the past.[7]

But in contrast to these traditional views, some recent Byzantinists have put forward a very different kind of description. Far from being static and backward-looking, Byzantium now appears as an exceptionally fluid society unusually open in the possibility of access to office and power. Prominent among these scholars is Alexander Kazhdan, who stresses the extent of upward mobility and the instability of the imperial throne, and sees a major divide between antiquity and Byzantium – a break in the continuity of tradition – occurring in the seventh century, and closely tied to the collapse of the classical city.[8] Kazhdan also protests against the hitherto common tendency to look only for 'classical' elements in Byzantine culture and to regard them as the most important, denigrating or ignoring its other aspects (which are often categorised in extremely pejorative language).[9] On the view which he criticises, Byzantium is seen essentially as a poor and decadent imitation of Rome, as the alien 'other', locked into sterile aping of the past and doomed to develop only in the direction of 'Byzantine

6 For criticism of this view see A. Kazhdan, 'In search for the heart of Byzantium. About several recent books on Byzantine Civilization', *Byzantion* li (1981), pp. 320–32; A. Kazhdan and G. Constable, *People and Power in Byzantium* (Washington D.C., 1982), pp. 117 f. What is at stake is the correct description of Byzantine society, as realised also for instance by the French Byzantinist G. Dagron (see the preface to his collected papers, *La Romanité chrétienne en Orient* (London, 1984), pp. i–iii), where he describes Byzantium as 'un vaste champ d'expérimentation' for modern scholars, who must abandon their comfortable preconceptions and decide for themselves where they will place their emphasis and hence their definition of Byzantine culture.

7 N. H. Baynes, 'The Thought-world of East Rome', in Baynes, *Byzantine Studies and Other Essays* (London, 1955), pp. 25–46.

8 A. Kazhdan and A. Cutler, 'Continuity and Discontinuity in Byzantine History', *Byzantion* lii (1982), pp. 429–78; see too C. Mango, *Byzantium. The Empire of New Rome* (London, 1981), stressing the seventh-century collapse though laying emphasis also on the idea of the unity of the Byzantine 'thought-world'. See further P. Speck, 'Waren die Byzantiner mittelalterliche Altgriechen, oder glaubten sie es nur?', *Rechtshistorisches Journal* ii (1983), pp. 5–11.

9 An attitude which has led for example to the persistent over-valuation of the sixth-century historian Procopius for his supposedly classical approach: see my *Procopius and the Sixth Century* (London, 1985). For Kazhdan's views see also A. Kazhdan and S. Franklin, *Studies on Byzantine Literature of the Eleventh and Twelfth Centuries* (Cambridge, 1984), ch. 1.

intrigue and corruption. The elaboration of the rituals laid down in the *Book of Ceremonies* has seemed only to reinforce such a conception.

This dispute (recent in the traditionalist context of modern Byzantine studies) is really therefore about the definition of 'Byzantine'. Typically, scholars are even divided about the starting point of the period. Many make 'Byzantium' begin with Constantine the Great and the inauguration of Constantinople in AD 330, others only with the reign of Heraclius in the seventh century, when major Persian inroads into Asia Minor, followed by the loss of large areas of territory to Islam, brought important changes in the social and economic structure, including the virtual disappearance of the antique cities (though even this is subject to dispute). The former view goes with an emphasis on continuity and sameness in Byzantine civilisation.[10] The latter however is now finding more support from both historians and archaeologists, and fits the conception now current among many late Roman historians of the essential continuity of late Roman government in the east until at least the sixth century.[11] Thus the debate about terminology arises from a very real disagreement about the nature of Byzantine culture. It is currently probably too much polarised along the lines of change or continuity; we should rather recognise that there was both change and continuity at every stage, and concentrate on how and why the balance shifts at particular times instead of attacking or defending the idea of near-total breaks.

The *Book of Ceremonies* is central to any attempt to define Byzantine culture, just because it seems so well suited to reinforce the conservative view. I shall argue that its complex nature in fact demonstrates both the continuity and the change. The ceremonies which it records have their roots in the Roman Empire (as I still call the period from the fourth to the sixth centuries AD). But at the same time the book itself represents a particular set of circumstances in the tenth century, a deliberate revival of tradition

[10] See Kazhdan and Cutler, 'Continuity and Discontinuity' (n. 8); Kazhdan and Constable, *People and Power* (n. 6), pp. 117 f.

[11] For a strong statement of the continuity of the eastern empire up to the seventh century see G. E. M. de Ste Croix, *The Class Struggle in the Ancient Greek World* (London, 1981), and for a survey of recent archaeology see R. Hodges and D. Whitehouse, *Mahomed, Charlemagne and the Origins of Europe* (London, 1983). The standard view of Byzantium is synchronic to excess; there is in fact considerable change, even in ceremonial (for the twelfth century see Magdalino and Nelson, 'The Emperor' (n. 4)).

springing from a new set of circumstances. It is not possible simply to lift the mass of rituals here described from their context and regard them without further ado as indicative of the nature of Byzantine society as a whole. And yet it was the Byzantine emphasis on tradition and order that inspired the compilation of the book itself and made royal ceremonial an appropriate field for further development.

THE *BOOK OF CEREMONIES*

In the *Book of Ceremonies*, then, the Emperor Constantine VII Porphyrogenitus put together a collection of material mainly relating to imperial ceremonial as part of the large number of works either written or commissioned by him on provincial administration, imperial government, military ceremony and recent history; he also made collections of extracts on selected subjects from earlier writers, especially historians.[12] There are two main parts to the work, each conventionally known to us as a 'book', but very uneven in content, and consisting partly of earlier written material and partly of apparently contemporary description, as well as a third section, the 'Appendix' to Book i, a separate treatise on imperial expeditions and the ceremonies appropriate to them. Some of the material is not about ceremonial at all, while other parts are only loosely connected with the main theme, if such it is.[13] Since this is clearly a compilation rather than a carefully constructed unitary work, and since the manuscript tradition is still under investigation, we must be careful not to assume too readily that its original arrangement and purpose can be easily reconstructed.[14]

---

[12] For Constantine's scholarly work see Toynbee, *Constantine Porphyrogennetos* (n. 1), pp. 575 f.

[13] Toynbee, *Constantine Porphyrogennetos* (see n. 1), p. 601 describes the work as being like a file in some department of state. Cf. p. 602: '*De Administrando Imperio* and *De Caerimoniis*, in the state in which Constantine has bequeathed them to posterity, will strike most readers as being in lamentable confusion.' According to Toynbee, part at least of the reason was simply that 'a disorderly sheaf of new documents would come tumbling in, and then the work of rearrangement would have to be begun all over again'. There is at least some truth in this colourful account.

[14] Since the edition by Vogt new material has been discovered; see C. Mango and I. Ševčenko, 'A New Manuscript of the *De Cerimoniis*', *Dumbarton Oaks Papers* xiv (1960), pp. 247–9. See too I. Rochow, 'Bemerkungen zu der Leipziger Handschrift des Zeremonien buches des Konstantinos Porphyrogennetos und zu der Ausgabe von J. J. Reiske', *Klio* lviii (1976), pp. 193–7. Recent study by

Fortunately these problems need not concern us too seriously here; what matters for now is that it is clearly a tenth-century work of an official character. There may be difficulties with individual sections, but its main thrust, and the tone of Constantine's introduction, are sufficiently clear to enable us to locate it in a context and to pose questions of interpretation.

In general terms, then, book i, as far as chapter 83, is fairly clearly divided into court ritual for religious ceremonies and civil imperial ceremonies, such as prescriptions for imperial deportment at the races in the Hippodrome, or at receptions. But book ii is far less orderly: its material often overlaps with subjects already covered, without any attempt at clarifying the relation between two different accounts. Some of this raggedness may be due to revisions and additions to the text; but minor discrepancies between parallel accounts of the same ceremony may equally arise from the fluidity of the ceremonial itself and from differences in the sources available, which were both oral and written and of varying dates and quality. It would be a mistake to assume that there was one fixed form of any particular ceremony. Rather, the rituals themselves naturally changed over time, and Constantine's treatise only partially fixed a norm or harmonised differing versions.

Were we to take all this material as a direct record of the ceremonial life of Byzantine emperors in the tenth century, we would have to conclude that a very large part of their time indeed was taken up in ritually prescribed occasions. Some of the protocols would only have been needed when the specific occasion arose – those for imperial marriages, for instance, or the births of imperial offspring. Others would have arisen more often, but still irregularly, for instance the bestowal of codicils of office on ministers of state, or the appearances of the emperor at games or races. But the imperial calendar was also dictated by the liturgical year and the exact prescriptions for the days of the major Christian festivals gave a regularity to imperial ceremony which Constantine VII considered an important demonstration of order (*taxis*). However, even within the section of book i concerned with religious cere-

O. Kresten disproves the conclusions of Vogt (e.g. pp. xv f.) on possible later additions in the text. I am very grateful to John Haldon for information on this point and for other help; he should not be taken as endorsing all my arguments.

monies, we cannot tell how many of the rituals were actually carried out from year to year.

Nevertheless, exact protocols are prescribed for numerous occasions, for every great feast and saint's day and for many lesser ones. They often extend over more than one day, with prescriptions for the eve of the feast as well as the day itself. Broadly, the protocols consist of rules for imperial progresses to and from specified churches in Constantinople and the imperial palace, with fixed stopping places (stations) and rules for ritual actions or acclamations at these points from specified participants – members of the senate, ministers, the leaders of the 'Blues' and 'Greens', the groups in charge of the Hippodrome races and now the major orchestrators of imperial ritual too.[15] Not merely do Christmas, Epiphany, Palm Sunday, Good Friday, Easter, Ascension Day and so on have their own prescriptions, but also for instance the feasts of the dedication of the Nea church built by Basil I (AD 867–886), St Demetrius, St Basil, the Elevation of the Cross, the Feast of Orthodoxy and so on. The greatest concentration of ritual prescribed for the emperor relates to the Easter period, beginning with Palm Sunday and continuing until the end of the first week after Easter, but it differs only in intensity, not in kind, from that prescribed for the rest of the liturgical year.

It may be helpful to summarise the elements common to most of the prescriptions. First, movement, either real or symbolic, between sacred and profane contexts; not only the direction but also the manner is laid down, whether on foot, mounted, by boat or whatever other means. Secondly, dress: the costume of the imperial participants is strictly regulated. Thirdly, the identity of those taking part – specified officials and clergy take part at fixed points during the ritual. Fourthly, acclamation: elaborately prescribed acclamations are laid down for particular places and moments during the ceremony, to be performed by particular groups – the senate, the people, the factions. Finally, food: a

---

15 The 'Blues' and 'Greens', originally the professionals concerned with the teams in the chariot races, with their supporters, had already by the end of the sixth century acquired a recognised role in imperial ceremony in general, a natural development in view of the long-standing use of the Hippodrome and the races held there as a show-place of imperial display, and the need for experienced performers to lead the imperial rituals as they grew more complex. See Alan Cameron, *Circus Factions* (Oxford, 1976); and now G. Dagron, *Constantinople imaginaire* (Paris, 1985).

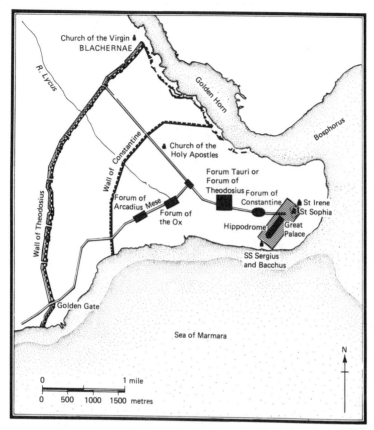

17 Constantinople. (The hatched area is shown in more detail in figure 18.)

dinner, also closely regulated and attended by specified guests, often concludes the day. In these rituals, then, sacred and profane are brought together, the emperor even coming near at times to playing the role of Christ; and the imperial palace is used as the setting for ceremonies that are undeniably religious. In the palace and the city, imperial ceremony is also religious ceremony.

Some examples will best illustrate how it worked. They are chosen not because they are special, but because they are typical.

In the first, the emperor processes on Holy Saturday to and from St Sophia, the great church next to the imperial palace:

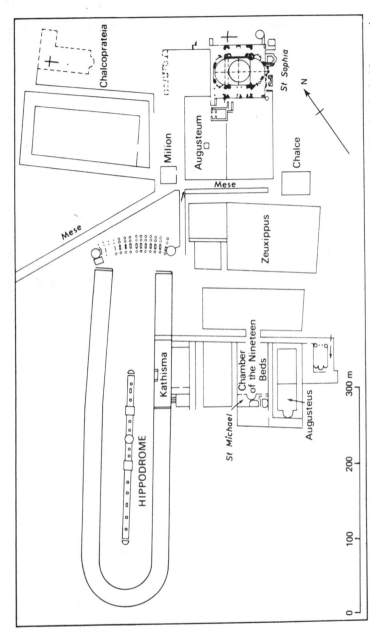

18 The palace complex, Constantinople. The Augusteum was a large open square linking the palace and the church; the Mese was the main processional thoroughfare and the Milion a large monument with formal statuary.

It should be known that the procession on Holy and Great Saturday takes place in the same manner as this procession for the Annunciation. The sovereigns dress in their robes called 'pagana' in the apartment in the Daphne part of the palace and go into the Octagonal Chamber. There they remove their ordinary cloak and leave by the Augusteus. Inside the great door of the afore-said Augusteus stands a *cubicularius* [eunuch of the bedchamber] carrying on his shoulders a bag containing a hundred pounds and walking close behind the sovereigns. The usual order for the reception is followed, as far as the procession of the Annunciation [already described]; both the notaries and the choir leaders of the factions recite iambics in their special places, as has been said in the case of the Annunication. The sovereigns pass by the Holy Well, as has been said, and enter the sanctuary, as we have said, and when the altar cloth has been spread according to ecclesiastical rite, the *praepositus* takes the bag from the *cubicularius*'s hand and gives it to the emperor, and the emperor places it on the lower part of the water bowl of the holy altar. Then the emperor censes it according to the manner laid down for the Annunciation, and they pass by the right side of the sanctuary and enter the sacristy, and there when the emperor has censed the holy vessels they sit on their golden thrones and the patriarch sits on the throne placed there.[16]

In this relatively simple ceremony the emperor processes in formal dress to the church of St Sophia, performs ritual actions there and processes back to the palace, greeted with acclamations on the way. Other more elaborate processions stopped at fixed places, where the choirs of the Blues and Greens sang greetings, while the emperor stopped and listened. Many protocols specify in detail which secular officials are to be present and take part in the ceremony. On the Wednesday after Easter and on other days the emperor invited the patriarch to the ceremonial dinner, according to a prescribed formula.[17]

[16] Vogt, i (Texte, 1935), p. 27 (or Bonn edn (n. 1), i, p. 34). Many of the technical expressions are explained by Vogt in his commentary. The Holy Well, for instance, was a relic of the well which featured in the story of Christ and the Samaritan woman. The water bowl was a basin under the altar for washing sacred vessels; it was known as 'the sea'. Note the importance attached to dress: as well as his literary scholarship, Constantine VII restored both the ceremonial apartments and the imperial vestments, crowns and diadems (Theophanes Continuatus, ed. I. Bekker, (*CSHB*, Bonn, 1838), pp. 447–8).

[17] Vogt, i (Texte, 1935), pp. 83 (or Bonn edn, i, p. 90).

Of the explicitly religious rituals, perhaps the most interesting in terms of the identification of the emperor with the Christian mythology is the ceremonial for Palm Sunday.[18] Preceded the previous night by the giving of palms with crosses of gold and silver by the emperor to the senators, patricians and officials according to rank in the church of St Demetrius, the ritual for Palm Sunday itself takes place within the palace, in the throne-room known as the Chrysotriklinos ('Golden Chamber'), where an icon of Christ stood above the imperial throne, a visual symbol of the theoretical relation between emperor and Christ.[19] The members of the government and court gather as the emperor is seated below the icon, and salute him in turn together with representatives of the church. The emperor receives crosses from certain groups as they prostrate themselves, and then leaves in procession to the singing of hymns to the churches of the Virgin and St Stephen, then back into the Chrysotriklinos, where

> the emperor goes to take up his place on the right of the Chrysotriklinos, near the arch leading to his apartments. The patricians stand on the left of the Chrysotriklinos and in front of the throne, holding their processional candles and their crosses, and the priests come to the middle of the Chrysotriklinos and stand near the throne. The deacon places the Gospels on the imperial throne and the usual litany is recited. The emperor goes with the people of his Bedchamber and the clergy to the church of the Holy Virgin in Pharos, and the patricians leave after acclaiming the emperor. Then, if the emperor so orders, they summon the patricians and they take part with the emperor in the liturgy at the church of the all-holy Virgin: if not, they celebrate the liturgy outside at the church of St Stephen in the Hippodrome. The list of those invited is read out and the signal is given, and after the ending of the divine liturgy the emperor leaves and sits at his costly table in the Iustinianos dressed in the scara-

---

[18] Vogt, i (Texte, 1935), pp. 160 f. (or Bonn edn, i, pp. 171 f.). Many details from this and other ceremonies are noted and discussed in O. Treitinger, *Die oströmische Kaiser- und Reichsidee nach ihrer Gestaltung im höfischen Zeremoniell* (Darmstadt, 1956).

[19] On this throne-room see I. Lavin, 'The House of the Lord', *Art Bulletin* xliv (1962), pp. 1–27. It was one of the apartments decorated by Constantine VII (see n. 16); see further below for its fate during the period of Iconoclasm and its subsequent restoration when the sacred images, which had been removed, were put back.

mangion like those invited; for after the procession all change their dress.[20]

It is expressly said that on this occasion the empress also receives entries and is given crosses in the same manner as the emperor.

There is therefore a complete intertwining of royal ceremony with the Christian liturgical year. The 'secular' ceremonies share in these religious overtones too. On the promotion of a *cubicularius*, for example, the emperor sits on the throne in the Chrysotriklinos and the new *cubicularius* is robed and sworn in in the oratory of St Theodore, then brought before the emperor to perform homage.[21] The installation of the leader of the senate involves the same robing in the oratory and then a move to St Sophia and a benediction from the patriarch; on the way through the Chalke vestibule the new leader is hailed by the factions with the acclamations usually given to patricians. His duties will include being at the emperor's side when he wishes to put on or take off the diadem.[22] To the extent that the spatial setting of most of the rituals combines religious and secular areas, and that movement between them is an integral part of the rituals, even ceremonies like these will tend to look partly 'religious', especially as clergy are normally present. But we find a similarly religious overtone even in more apparently secular prescriptions such as those pertaining to the emperor's appearance at the Hippodrome. Yet that is not surprising if we reflect that the Hippodrome adjoined the palace, and that the emperor's appearances there had for centuries been a major aspect of imperial display, perhaps his most impressive appearances in public.[23]

[20] Vogt, i (Texte, 1935), pp. 163–4 (in Bonn edn, i, p. 175). The scaramangion was a ceremonial tunic worn by the emperors; the Pharos chapel, perhaps dating from the reign of Constantine V (AD 741–775), became the repository for Constantinople's most holy relics, and it was here that in AD 941 Constantine VII deposited the famous 'Mandylion' of Edessa, the most celebrated of the so-called 'images not made by human hands' after its recovery from Arab control. See my article 'The History of the Image of Edessa: the Telling of a Story', in C. Mango and O. Pritsak (eds.), *Okeanos. Festschrift for I. Ševčenko, Harvard Ukrainian Studies* vii (1983), pp. 80–94.

[21] Bonn edn, i, p. 625.   [22] *Ibid.*, pp. 440 f.

[23] For instance, compare the ceremonial ordering of the figures of the emperor and court on the base of the obelisk of Theodosius; early sixth-century inaugurations actually took place in the Hippodrome, and after that of Justin II (which took place inside the palace) the emperor appeared there and received acclamations of the people (see my edition and commentary on Corippus' poem (n. 5), pp. 171 f. for discussion); further, Magdalino and Nelson, 'The Emperor in Byzantine Art of the Twelfth Century' (n. 4), pp. 164 f.; M. McCormick, *Eternal Victory* (Cambridge, 1987).

RITUAL IN TENTH-CENTURY BYZANTIUM

The prescriptions of the *Book of Ceremonies*, together with its descriptions of actual royal occasions, seem to indicate a highly developed and highly regulated court ritual, often uniting secular and religious elements within a single protocol. We would like to know just how many of these ceremonies were regularly performed. Constantine VII's introduction might seem at first sight to suggest that they had fallen into a state of decay, which he hoped to rectify.

He identifies two of the good effects that would follow in his view from the proper observance of court rituals: first, the enactment of 'the harmonious movement with which God the Creator has imbued the world ... to make the imperial power seem more awesome to its subjects and at the same time more agreeable and more impressive';[24] and second, the strictly functional aim of impressing foreigners and subjects with the splendour and dignity of the Byzantine court. He implies that not all take the rituals as seriously as he does himself: 'some who do not share our great concern for weighty affairs might think this enterprise a waste of time'. To Constantine himself, however, the imperial rituals are like 'flowers picked in the fields to decorate the imperial splendour'. So long as they are observed, and the imperial power is duly exercised with rhythm and order (*rhythmos* and *taxis*) they will display the harmony of divine and imperial dispensation. 'To us it seems very important and worthy of effort, and is closer to us than anything else, since as a result of this praiseworthy order the imperial power is revealed as more majestic and awe-inspiring and for that reason is honoured by foreigners and by our own subjects'. At least part of Constantine's purpose, then, as he wants it to be seen, is to impress foreign envoys.

But there are other aspects to it as well. To judge from the statements of its compiler, it would seem that the *Book of Ceremonies* reflected, if not the invention of tradition,[25] then certainly its conscious revival. Constantine VII took royal ritual seriously

[24] Vogt, i (Texte, 1935), p. 2 (in Bonn edn, i, p. 5).
[25] See further below, pp. 125–7, and for the idea of the 'invention of tradition', E. Hobsbawm and T. Ranger (eds.), *The Invention of Tradition* (Cambridge, 1983), especially the paper by D. Cannadine, 'The Context, Performance and Meaning of Ritual: the British Monarchy and the "Invention of Tradition", c. 1820–1977', pp. 101–64.

and was worried that others did not. He felt also that it was not always performed in the right spirit or with as much punctilio as it demanded, and his compilation is presented as a guide for future emperors and officials. It is not a straightforward record of actual ceremonies performed at any one time. Further, its compilation belongs squarely in a context of codification and antiquarianism. It is only one of several works sponsored by the emperor, in an age which saw a notable output of scholarly and encyclopaedic works. Codifying imperial ritual was seen as a task on a par with drawing up lists of imperial officials or collecting extracts from earlier works on such important political topics as diplomacy or military tactics. More importantly, it was a question of the relation of tenth-century Byzantium to its past.

It would be a mistake to assume too readily that Byzantine imperial ritual had really fallen into such a state of decay as Constantine implies. When Bishop Liutprand of Cremona visited Constantinople in AD 968 he was impressed (though not taken in) by the glories of the imperial court and the theatrical stage-management of his reception. The audience was interrupted by the start of one of the emperor's solemn processions to St Sophia, which Liutprand then describes. He reports with scorn the acclamations greeting the emperor (Nicephorus II Phocas) as the morning star and the prostrations to the ground as he enters the church.[26] Persian envoys in earlier periods had been equally carefully handled, and the *Book of Ceremonies* preserves a set of instructions for such a reception from the sixth century. Detailed rules are laid down for the escort and lodging of the ambassador on the long journey to Constantinople, and then on arrival. The high point is his reception by the emperor, for which there are elaborate regulations for the dress and positions to be adopted by the Byzantine officials and courtiers. The doors are curtained, a sign of mystery, and the envoy advances gradually, escorted by the Master

[26] Liutprand, *Legatio*, 9–10 (ed. J. Bekker, *Monumenta Germaniae Historica, Script. rerum Germanicarum*, 3rd edn (Hanover and Leipzig, 1915). Liutprand's description of his earlier reception by Constantine VII in AD 949 is even more famous: the Magnaura was fitted out with mechanical birds and beasts and a throne which could be raised or lowered at will (Liutprand, *Antapodosis*, vi.5). The banqueting hall of the Nineteen Couches, also restored by Constantine VII, (see n. 16), was equipped with a system of pulleys to get the food from the trolleys that brought it onto the tables (*ibid.*, vi.8). For such devices see G. Bret, 'The automata in the Byzantine "Throne of Solomon"', *Speculum* xxix (1954), pp. 477–87.

of Offices, making prostrations at fixed intervals, until eventually he reaches the emperor for the formal exchange of gifts – provision having been duly made in case the gifts should include horses.[27]

The development of ceremonial at Byzantium was however a living thing. It is clear from various examples that in fact innovations in ceremony were being made in the years immediately preceding the compilation of Constantine VII's book. On Easter Monday, for example, the prescription concludes with the remark that in Leo VI's time (Constantine's father) it was customary for the emperor to ride on horseback to the church of the Holy Apostles, wearing his crown, and to return the same way, but wearing a different crown and costume.[28] Constantine's grandfather, Basil I, was commemorated by his son Leo in homage paid to his image during a ceremony which he had instituted.[29] New ceremonies marked particular events such as the foundation of the Nea ('New') church in the imperial palace by Basil I: thereafter the day was celebrated annually with a formal procession with the senate and patriarch from the Chrysotriklinos throne-room to and from the Nea; inside the church the sovereigns kissed the doors, then the altar-cloths of the various altars, before lighting candles in front of the image of Basil and hearing the reading of the gospels in the adjoining oratory.[30]

Another ceremony comparatively new when Constantine wrote was that for the Feast of Orthodoxy, celebrated on the first Sunday in Lent to commemorate the return of images and the ending of the iconoclast schism in AD 843.[31] In the surviving account there are clear traces of two different ceremonies, an earlier and a later version, the latter postdating the death of patriarch Theophylact in AD 956; presumably the earlier dates from 843 or soon after. In each case, the ritual consisted of a formal progress to St Sophia, now formally recovered from Iconoclast control, and in which the famous apse mosaic of the Virgin had been set up in AD 867. Each

[27] Bonn edn, i, pp. 398ff.

[28] Vogt, i (Texte, 1935), p. 77 (in Bonn edn, i, pp. 85–6).

[29] Vogt, p. 106 (in Bonn edn, i, pp. 114 f.).

[30] Vogt, p. 109. On Basil's *Nea Ekklesia* ('New Church'), see also the *Life of Basil*, 83–4 (trans. Mango, in C. Mango, *The Art of the Byzantine Empire, 312–1453* (Englewood Cliffs, NJ, 1972), p. 194). Leo VI was also a builder: see P. Magdalino, 'The Bath of Leo the Wise', in Ann Moffatt (ed.), *Maistor. Classical, Byzantine and Renaissance Studies for Robert Browning* (Canberra, 1984), pp. 225–40.

[31] Vogt, pp. 145–48 (= Bonn edn, i, pp. 156–60).

19 Late twelfth-century roundel showing an emperor in stylised court dress against a disc evoking solar associations. The use of sun imagery for emperors began early and was also a way of assimilating emperor and Christ (the latter as the sun of justice). The elegant economy of this piece conveys much of Constantine VII's imperial ideal.

of the ceremonies was followed by the usual dinner, and the reading of the list of those invited was an important part of the formal proceedings. In book ii, finally, alongside the timeless prescriptions there are records of particular occasions, several from the reign of Heraclius (AD 610–641) as well as, for instance, contemporary rules for addressing foreign governments.

It is certain then that whereas any particular emperor (though probably not either Basil I or Leo VI, who seem to have been innovators in this regard) might have laid less stress on ceremony than Constantine VII did, the general level of royal ritual was indeed high, and that ceremonies of roughly similar kind to those envisaged in the protocols laid down by Constantine had been performed more or less regularly since at least the fifth and sixth centuries.[32] Codified or not, court ceremonial mattered at Byzantium.

THE CONTEXT OF THE *BOOK OF CEREMONIES*

I shall return later to the social context within which these rituals had developed in their early stages. We must now ask what meaning if any might be attached to the mass of ritual to which the *Book of Ceremonies* testifies. Of course we have an obvious explanation – Constantine VII's own – namely that they displayed the desired sense of divine and human order, thus that they were a symbolic enactment of the theory about the Byzantine state which had barely changed since it had first been voiced about Constantine I, according to which the emperor was the earthly representative of God.

Much of the ritual is indeed religious, just as much Byzantine imperial art is also religious art. But there were also exact prescriptions for secular occasions – imperial appearances at the races, imperial birthdays and so on. Moreover, many of the rituals were concerned with the ratification of the bureaucratic structure of the Byzantine state, in conferring promotion to particular offices.[33] Those who attended the court rituals were, if they were not clergy, office-holders appointed through the patronage of the emperor. These were not hereditary nobles, idling away a life at court. They were the members of the very class from which emperors often themselves sprang, men whose status derived from office, to which emperors have the key; their participation in the rituals was as essential as that of the emperor himself, and as minutely regulated. Thus these court rituals are as likely to tell us about the political

---

[32] See below, p. 129, and for signs of the continuity of ceremony in the seventh and eighth centuries see Averil Cameron and Judith Herrin (eds.), *Constantinople in the Eighth Century: the Parastaseis Syntomoi Chronikai* (Leiden, 1984), pp. 170, 209–10, 212.

[33] For ceremonial in relation to the official or bureaucratic structure of a state see M. Fortes, 'Ritual and Office in Tribal Society', in M. Gluckmann (ed.), *Essays on the Ritual of Social Relations* (Manchester, 1962), pp. 53–88, emphasising, among other relevant observations, the importance of prescribed dress (p. 66), and citing R. Redfield, *The Primitive World and its Transformations* (Ithaca, NY, 1953), for the technical (i.e. utilitarian) and moral (i.e. symbolic) aspects of office. For the Roman background see S. R. F. Price, above chap. 2 pp. 82–91.

relation between the emperor and the office-holding class as that between the emperor and God. It is his actual relation to the church and its living representatives, again, that is expressed here just as much as the theology of Byzantine rule. We can provide a fuller context: not long before the compilation of Constantine VII's work, the so-called *Cletorologion* of Philotheus was drawn up – a detailed list of Byzantine officials and foreign guests in strict order of precedence, and another example of the contemporary zeal for listing and codifying applied to the very real and important question of the structure of the governing class.[34]

The compilation of the *Book of Ceremonies* coincided with what has been seen as a thrust from the government towards an even greater degree of autocracy. I quote from the standard history of Ostrogorsky: 'The omnipotence of the emperor and the transformation of the state into a bureaucracy now realized their full development.'[35] That is certainly how the emperors wanted it to be seen. To that end, strict control of the official class was essential, and the *Book of Ceremonies* codified that theoretical control. The reality might be less harmonious. Skylitzes criticises Constantine VII himself for poor selection of officials, and his wife for selling offices. Similarly, the actual relations between emperor and church belied the official theory. Theoretically a layman and unable to dictate directly to the church, the emperor in fact frequently deposed patriarchs and overruled or ignored ecclesiastical opposition. The long Iconoclast controversy, beginning in the reign of Leo III in the early eighth century and lasting until the middle of the ninth, was only one of the most dramatic and long-lasting of such episodes. Constantine VII's father, Leo VI, for instance, had caused a crisis in relations between emperor and church when we went against his own recent law and took a third and then even a fourth wife; in the final stages of this crisis he defied the then patriarch and married his last wife, already the mother of his son, the future Constantine VII; when he was forbidden entry to St

[34] See J. B. Bury, *The Imperial Administrative System in the Ninth Century with a Revised Text of the Kletorologion of Philotheos* (London, 1911); the *Cletorologion* is appended at *De Caer.*, Bonn edn, pp. 702–91. For the evolution of new offices in this period see also N. Oikonomides, *Les Listes de préséance byzantine des IXe et Xe siècles* (Paris, 1972), and in general, R. Guilland, *Recherches sur les institutions byzantines*, 2 vols. (Berlin-Amsterdam, 1967).

[35] G. Ostrogorsky, *History of the Byzantine State*, trans. J. Hussey (Oxford, 1980), p. 245 (this book, of which this is a translation from the third German edition of 1963, is still the main textbook of Byzantine history).

Sophia at Christmas, AD 906 and Epiphany, 907, papal help enabled him to dethrone the patriarch and appoint a more amenable successor. This is exactly the kind of situation which the *Book of Ceremonies* entirely conceals, in its bland assumption that all is well if only the due forms are preserved.

A particular dissonance between the world of imperial ceremony and that of real life arose over the matter of imperial succession, where the theory that emperors were divinely elected and protected by God coexisted with a situation in which there was in fact no constitutional procedure for choosing an emperor. Every accession posed the threat of usurpation, and emperors were in practice frequently made by murder and intrigue. Again we can take our examples from Constantine VII's own experience. He himself was unusual in having been born in the purple – even if illegitimately. His epithet, Porphyrogenitus, literally means just that: 'Born in the Purple Bedchamber' of the imperial palace. He was raised to the title of Augustus at an early age. Yet his father, Leo VI, was actually succeeded by his brother, and Constantine was later displaced when his father-in-law, who, though not of the ruling house, had been elevated by Constantine himself to Caesar and then to Augustus, raised his own sons above Constantine and made himself senior emperor. Constantine did not assume sole power until this man had been deposed by his sons and the sons then arrested and exiled. Two generations earlier, Basil I, the founder of the dynasty and himself the son of a peasant, had seized power also after the murder of the reigning emperor.

This vulnerability, and the rapid change of dynasties, was the reality; only the political theory, emphasising the emperor's protection by God, remained stable. An emperor could be made at any time by intrigue or force; an empress could be chosen like Cinderella for her physical attributes. As for the officials invited to the ceremonial banquets and commended to take up their positions for this or that procession, they were of course the very group which might at any moment throw up a usurper. The theory, and the ceremonial round remained. It helped to legitimate a new emperor, and it effectively masked the real state of affairs.

There are many parallels for this apparent discrepancy between theory and actuality in the study of both modern and traditional societies. If it was to our eyes convenient to the Byzantines, and especially in Constantine's VII's interest, to act out an ideal harmony, that does not mean that the dissonance was equally obvious to the participants themselves. They were not cynical manipulators, however much we may be tempted to see them in that way.

Convenient, however, it certainly was. Yet neither the theory nor the ceremony was a creation of the Byzantine period itself. Both went back to the Roman Empire.

When Augustus had become effective ruler of the Roman world, after the battle of Actium in 31 BC, he had evolved an uneasy concept of himself as first citizen rather than autocrat.[36] Thus the notion of consent was retained, with the consequence that government was always vulnerable, as it was also to military coups if an emperor was unable to control the armies sufficiently tightly. Nor did imperial adoption of Christianity change the situation, as the blood bath which followed the death of Constantine I proved. It did however bring to the imperial office a whole new set of moral and religious sanctions; it could not prevent usurpation, but it could imply that it was a sin. From Constantine I on (AD 306–337), all emperors, with only one exception, were Christian, and all profited from his decision to identify himself with the institutional church and from the moral advantage it gave to their own position. Without ever fully specifying the relation between emperor and church, and without essentially altering the relations of army, emperor and governing class, a specifically Christian theory of government emerged, and with it a correspondingly impressive presentation of the emperor. It was this that Byzantium inherited and intensified.

At the same time public ceremony had also been steadily increasing. It was in some sense a replacement for the debate and competition that had characterised public life in the late Republic, before Augustus.[37] As the remaining vestiges of discussion were gradually extinguished, and the political tradition of Rome took on more and more of the appearance and associations of kingship, political life came to be dominated by the visual display of power

[36] For an interesting discussion of the implications of such a situation for imperial comportment, and the gradual change to a more monarchical, but hardly less precarious, style of rule, see A. Wallace-Hadrill, 'Civilis Princeps: between Citizen and King', *Journal of Roman Studies* lxxii (1982), pp. 32–48. See too Price, above, chap. 2, pp. 73, 78ff.

[37] On which see Mary Beard and Michael Crawford, *Rome in the Late Republic* (London, 1985).

relations. Imperial ceremony was mirrored by a lesser but equally noticeable growth of ceremonial in the cities of the empire.[38] And the patronage of Christianity by the emperors of the fourth century and later opened up a powerful new dimension for imperial ritual, since it was now also able to absorb substantial elements from Christian liturgical and processional practice. In particular, the regular round of the Christian year, observed by the imperial family and court, must have contributed to an increasingly standardised imperial ritual. In the late fourth and early fifth centuries we already find emperors and empresses taking part in religious processions. The beginnings of their formal role in the liturgy at St Sophia, so prominent in the *Book of Ceremonies*,[39] can now be clearly seen. By the sixth century, it is very clear that court ceremony had decisively increased, for it is now possible for Peter the Patrician to think of codifying it.[40] Thus the protocols in Constantine VII's book are different in scale but not in kind from the practice of the late antique period, and it was then, not later, that the ideological union of empire and church was formulated, both in political theory and in visual terms.[41]

The same sense of continuous development is suggested by another prominent feature of the Byzantine rituals, namely their

---

[38] On this see S. G. MacCormack, *Art and Ceremony in Late Antiquity* (Berkeley, 1981), and her article 'Change and Continuity in Late Antiquity: the Ceremony of *Adventus*', *Historia* xxi (1972), pp. 721–52, for a discussion of central and local ceremony in relation to one specific example.

[39] T. F. Mathews, *The Early Churches of Constantinople* (University Park, Pa, 1971), demonstrates in relation to the churches of the capital how an increase in the complexity of the liturgy went hand in hand with greater participation by the emperors in religious occasions. For an early fifth-century example, see K. Holum, *Theodosian Empresses* (Berkeley, 1982), pp. 103–4.

[40] For a brief discussion, see Averil Cameron, 'Images of Authority: Elites and Icons in Late Sixth-Century Byzantium', *Past and Present* lxxxiv (1979), pp. 6–7. Peter the Patrician was Master of Offices, and thus responsible for the organisation of the ritual: he seems to have written a book about the subject, parts of which probably survive in sections in the *Book of Ceremonies* about sixth-century inaugurations and other contemporary matter (see J. B. Bury, 'The Ceremonial Book of Constantine Porphyrogennetos', *English Historical Review* xxii (1907), pp. 209–27 and 417–39). This of course raises the important (but unanswerable) question of what effect the act of writing may have had on the ritual itself.

[41] The fully Christianised conception of imperial rule was certainly apparent long before the seventh century. See the interesting (if not very historically accurate) remarks of E. Leach, 'Melchisdech and the Emperor: Icons of Subversion and Orthodoxy', *Proc. Royal Anthropological Institute* (1972), pp. 5–14 (in E. Leach and D. A. Aycock, *Structural Approaches to Biblical Criticism* (Cambridge, 1983), pp. 67–88).

constant use of formulaic acclamation. It may seem surprising to read in the *Book of Ceremonies* that on religious as well as secular occasions the lengthy acclamations of the emperors were performed by choirs of the Blues and Greens, the old circus factions; yet these too differ only in their degree of elaboration, and indeed the professionalism of their performance from the many times repeated cries of the senate recorded in the early fifth-century Theodosian Code, or from the third-century acclamations reported by the collection of imperial biographies known as the *Historia Augusta*.[42] In the tenth century, as in the Roman Empire, acclamation on ceremonial occasions suited a society in which neither the masses nor the governing class themselves had an official political voice. In the context of court ceremony, they became increasingly elaborate and formalised. They are the complement to the endless formal panegyrics which in such a society had long been the dominant way in which one could write about an emperor.

However, while the roots of Byzantine ritual belong in the Roman empire, that prescribed by Constantine VII is undoubtedly more stylised and more complex. For this development, the sixth century seems to have been the crucial period. It was only then, for instance, that emperors began to be crowned in a fully developed inauguration ritual of a completely religious nature.[43] It was still possible under Justinian to hear the voices of the traditional élite protesting against a too elaborate court protocol.[44] But between the reign of Heraclius (AD 610–641) and that of Constantine VII, or indeed that of Basil I (AD 867–886), came a great divide, the collapse of the old urban structure and the social patterns that went with it, and a drastic reshaping of the administrative and economic organisation. The extent of this discontinuity has been much disputed. Nevertheless, the limited literary sources for the eighth century make it abundantly clear that even Constantinople was

---

[42] For the latter, see B. Baldwin, 'Acclamations in the *Historia Augusta*', *Athenaeum*, ns lxix (1981), pp. 138–49, and for a brief account of the development of acclamation in the public life of the late empire, see C. M. Roueché, 'Acclamations in the later Roman Empire: new evidence from Aphrodisias', *Journal of the Roman Studies* lxxiv (1984), pp. 181–99.

[43] For an excellent analysis of the Christianisation of inaugurations in this period see J. L. Nelson, 'Symbols in Context', *Studies in Church History* xiii (1976), pp. 97–119.

[44] So Procopius, *Secret History* xxx.21 f. John the Lydian, a civil servant under Justinian, with similarly traditional views, was also critical of contemporary developments: see Averil Cameron, *Procopius*, chapter xiv.

then in a pitiful state, its aqueduct in ruins and its population shrunken, while in the empire generally, 'it is a fact (though some historians still refuse to recognise it) that all round the Mediterranean the cities, as they had existed in Antiquity, contracted and then practically disappeared'.[45] Contemporaneous with this physical change went corresponding alterations in intellectual life; books were increasingly hard to find, or when found, to understand, and the surviving classical monuments took on a threatening and mysterious aspect.[46]

By the tenth century, however, the empire had recovered from the worst – if in changed form – and was enjoying what has often been termed the 'Macedonian renaissance'. However unsatisfactory this term, especially in the field of visual art,[47] it remains true that the Macedonian dynasty founded by Basil I and to which Constantine VII belonged saw consolidation in many spheres. The physical environment of the capital itself began to improve.[48] And at the same time there was a conscious effort to recapture learning that had been in eclipse. The emperor himself, who directed the compilation of the *Book of Ceremonies* also instigated several other major encyclopaedic works and had taken great pains to collect materials from the recent past, the reigns of his father and grandfather, as well as excerpting from major early Byzantine authors for more utilitarian purposes.[49] He was proud of his efforts, and exhorts his son Romanos to heed the precepts of his father, and to recognise the importance of knowing the examples of history,

---

[45] Mango, *Byzantium, The Empire of New Rome*, p. 69. Hodges and Whitehouse, *Mahomed, Charlemagne and the Origins of Europe*, conclude that the decline of cities, accelerated by the Persian and Arab invasions of the early seventh century, was well under way by the end of the sixth.

[46] On all of this see Averil Cameron and Judith Herrin (eds.), *Constantinople in the Eighth Century: the Parastaseis Syntomoi Chronikai* (Leiden, 1984), introduction; G. Dragon, *Constantinople imaginaire* (Paris, 1985).

[47] The notion of classicising renaissances as a means of explaining stylistic development in Byzantine art is now increasingly suspect; nevertheless, the term 'Macedonian renaissance' still has its uses (see Magdalino, 'The Bath of Leo the Wise', (see n. 30), p. 238). See also W. Treadgold, 'The revival of Byzantine learning and the revival of the Byzantine state', *American Historical Review* 81 (1979), 1245–66.

[48] See C. Mango, *Le développement urbain de Constantinople* (Paris, 1985), pp. 61–2.

[49] See Vogt, i (Commentaire, 1935), pp. xix–xx, with Constantine's own remarks (see n. 50). See P. Lemerle, *Le Premier Humanisme Byzantin* (Paris, 1971), pp. 267–300; Kazhdan and Constable, *People and Power in Byzantium* (see n. 6), p. 135.

especially those which Constantine now sets forth and which he has only been able to discover through laborious searches in the palace and in monastic libraries; even then, when he did find the record he wanted, it was badly written in barbarous Greek.[50]

So there was during this period a general enthusiasm for the revival and recording of tradition, which naturally took in the sphere of the theory and practice of imperial rule. Constantine's immediate predecessors had made some innovations in the court rituals, for they too were interested in consolidation. But even in the hard times of the seventh and eighth centuries, imperial ceremony seems to have been maintained.[51] Despite Constantine's complaints in his introduction, this was one aspect of Byzantine government which persisted in a continuous, if at times a shaky, line over many centuries.

We should not then conclude that the *Book of Ceremonies* is witness to a phenomenon peculiar only to the tenth century when it was compiled. A full explanation of these rituals would have to set them against the context of Rome as well as Byzantium. Nonetheless they were now indeed given a new emphasis in the careful compilation of Constantine VII's record. It is worth asking, then, what social function, if any, they fulfilled.

RITUALS AND MEANING

Who were the spectators of these ceremonies? Often enough it was the people of Constantinople. They could frequently see the emperors and the imperial family surrounded by officials and clergy in impressive processions from one part of the city or one church to another. The splendour of the imperial and official dress, carefully prescribed and sometimes changed even within the course of a day's ceremony, would contribute to a sense of awe, and the music and singing of the factions must have added to the effect. But it is not clear that the frequency of these occasions led to any such feelings of warmth and affection towards the emperors and their families or such fervour as often accompanies contemporary British royal occasions.[52] Was there a Byzantine Princess Diana? Conver-

---

[50] Bonn edn, i, pp. 455–7. For military precedents he begins with Constantine the Great (pp. 444ff.).
[51] See n. 32.
[52] For which see Cannadine, 'The Context, Performance and Meaning of Ritual' (n. 25).

sely, the people of Constantinople were not of much concern to their emperors, at least so long as they were giving no trouble. Political unrest of this kind was less of a worry, however, than the possibility of a palace plot and the hand of an assassin; in general, popular dissent in Byzantium took the form of heresy or religious disputes rather than political upheavals. All these considerations suggest that we must look elsewhere than to the population of the capital for the meaning of these royal ceremonies.

The retreat to the palace

In fact, their most important audience was to be found inside the palace, where most of the ritual took place. It was to be found among the officials who themselves took part, and who were at once the governing class of the empire and the people closest to the emperors. The rituals themselves were a visual sign of the hierarchy of officialdom, an order which as we have seen had recently been recorded in several handbooks, just as the ceremonies are now recorded by Constantine VII. We should remember that Constantine himself after the removal of his father-in-law and his sons had conducted a spectacular purge of their officials and other potential or actual enemies; in AD 947, in particular, their downfall had carried with it public humiliation and parades through the city, the inverse of the processions in the *Book of Ceremonies*.[53] It is not surprising, in this context, that many of the rituals prescribed concern bestowal of office or the passage from one office to another; all demonstrated publicly the relative positions of the officials in the pecking order of the court.

Dress codes too: this had doubtless always been a feature of imperial ceremony, just as levées at the British court in this century were attended by civil servants and diplomatic officials in regulation court dress – a practice which though dropped in that form still continues to be reflected in the instructions sent out on the appropriate dress for persons present at royal occasions.[54] But it had a particular significance in the tenth century, for quite apart from the dramatic reversals of Constantine's own reign, the offices

[53] See T. E. Gregory, 'The Political Program of Constantine Porphyrogenitus', *Actes du XVe Congrès international d'études byzantines*, iv (1980), pp. 124–30.

[54] For instance, that ladies should wear hats, and even on occasion gloves, both of which often entail special purchases, and are sometimes resisted, especially in academic gatherings. For the qualities of jewels acquired by the British Royal Family since Victoria's reign, see S. Meakes, *The Royal Jewels* (London, 1985).

and titles that were now codified and recognised were for the most part relatively recent, the product of a lengthy transitional period from the seventh century onwards when the state was evolving new social and administrative forms to replace the old traditional structures inherited from Rome and appropriate to the urban civilisation of antiquity. Many of the details of this development remain highly obscure for want of adequate source material from the intervening period,[55] but we can assert in general terms that by the ninth century a new bureaucratic structure had been formed.

At the same time, the collapse of the antique cities left Constantinople much more isolated than it had previously been. It became to a far greater extent than before the heart of cultural life and administrative power. From this isolation the emperors gained in personal power, in contrast to the less centralised administrative system of late antiquity, and their court ceremonial accordingly acquired a focal position that was unchallenged. In this middle Byzantine period, government went on in Constantinople and the court in Constantinople was where the ambitious needed to be.

The elaborate ceremonies of the tenth century are therefore at least in part about power, the relation between the emperors and the governing class. Since access to the throne and to office was surprisingly open, the rituals of court also helped to iron out the consequent tensions by providing a reassuring impression of stability and tradition. It was a myth which all found it convenient to believe, most particularly those who had managed, by whatever means, to advance themselves into office or onto the throne. The more centralised government became, the more the rituals themselves would need to and tend to include all the officials who mattered. Thus the ceremonial was both self-generating and self-reinforcing. Ambition engendered ceremony and ceremony made ambition respectable.

We might go further. A recent study of imperial victory celebrations[56] talks of a retreat of government from the public scene at about this time. The great public imperial occasions in the Hippodrome begin to give way to private ceremony in the imperial palace – the natural concomitant of this emphasis on the relations of emperor and officials. Power depended on that relation rather than on the relation of emperor and people; its arena was naturally the palace, and its language was ceremony.

[55] See however, Guilland, *Recherches* (n. 34).
[56] M. McCormick, *Eternal Victory* (Cambridge, 1987).

At the same time, however, elaborate ritual of this kind belongs to the general style of Byzantine high culture, which had been set in the early part of the period. It was a formal style, placing a high premium on strictly codified systems. In the case of the Greek language, for instance, the literature of high culture was very purist, preferring archaising language far removed from the forms of everyday speech.[57] Similarly Byzantine art, most of it religious, followed a set code to such an extent that modern observers, themselves usually out of sympathy with its elaborate Christian typology, have often found it hard to appreciate in aesthetic terms. That is why so many aspects of Byzantine culture, including its royal rituals, seem to pose acutely the basic ethnographic problems of rationality: how to deal with the cultural practice of a society which operates within a framework of beliefs which the ethnographer would himself classify as 'irrational'.[58] Many modern works on Byzantium have simply taken up a hostile position without debating the matter at all.

Gibbon's *Decline and Fall* has a lot to answer for in this regard, and old ideas (however inappropriate to a different age) die hard. They start from a too-ready assumption that a highly stratified bureaucracy and a highly codified élite culture indicate a generally static or immobile society. Similar thinking has affected the historiography of the late Roman period, which Gibbon, and then more particularly and for different reasons Rostovtzeff, saw as an essentially repressive regime.[59] But just as in the case of the *Book of Ceremonies*, this view mostly depended on an over-literal reading of the laws against social mobility in the Theodosian Code, until the obvious was pointed out – that laws repeated over and over again are being broken over and over again.[60] The *Theodosian Code* and the *Book of Ceremonies* alike indicate states of change.

---

[57] For a good discussion, see R. Browning, 'The Language of Byzantine Literature', in S. Vryonis Jr (ed.), *Byzantina kai Metabyzantina* i, *The Past in Medieval and Modern Greek Culture* (Malibu, 1978), pp. 103–33.

[58] On this problem see e.g. B. Wilson (ed.), *Rationality* (Oxford, 1977). In relation to Byzantine society: Kazhdan and Constable, *People and Power in Byzantium*, (see n. 6), pp. 76 f.

[59] See especially M. I. Rostovtzeff, *The Social and Economic History of the Roman Empire* (2nd edn, Oxford, 1957); the case for repression is forcefully restated by G. E. M. de Ste Croix, *Class Struggle* (n. 11).

[60] R. Macmullen, 'Social Mobility and the Theodosian Code', *Journal of Roman Studies* liv (1964), pp. 49–53. For an altogether more positive view, see Peter Brown, *The World of Late Antiquity* (London, 1971).

Religious/secular

What then of the religious aspect of these rituals and the frequent presence of patriarch and clergy? Perhaps this was a less significant element than we tend to assume. Certainly the church in Byzantium enjoyed a position of actual political power and its patriarchs were important figures in government and court; when the emperor Heraclius went off to war with Persia in the early seventh century he left Constantinople in the hands of the patriarch Sergius and the patrician Bonus, who then had to conduct the defence of the city during a near-disastrous siege. But when Constantine collected his protocols this prominence of the church had been a fact of life for many centuries. The heavily religious tone of most of the ritual in the *Book of Ceremonies* does not in itself correspond to a new development in or just before the tenth century. It was the result of a slow and steady growth since at least the fourth, and drew on the Roman imperial cult and Hellenistic ruler cult before that.[61]

On the other hand, before Constantine's grandfather Basil I came to the throne, Byzantium had seen more than a century of serious and violent religious conflict. From AD 726 to 843, Iconoclast emperors attempted to impose their will on the population and the church, resorting to the persecution of monks and deposition of clergy, manipulating church councils and – interestingly for our present subject – removing sacred images from the walls of the palace, including those in the throne-room, the Chrysotriklinos. When Iconoclasm was officially ended in 843, the images were restored. A contemporary poem celebrated their return and their juxtaposition with the portrait of the emperor who had restored them:

> Behold, once again the image of Christ shines above the imperial throne and confounds the murky heresies; while above the entrance is represented the Virgin as divine gate and guardian. The emperor [Michael III] and Bishop [Photius] are depicted close by, along with their collaborators inasmuch as they have driven away error, and all round the building, like guards [stand] angels, apostles, martyrs, priests. Hence we call the 'new' Chrysotriklinos that which aforetime had been given a golden name [='Golden Chamber'], since it contains the throne of

---

[61] See Price, above, chap. 2, pp. 73, 78ff.

Christ our Lord, the forms of Christ's Mother and Christ's heralds, and the image of Michael, whose deeds are filled with wisdom.[62]

It is important to realise the effect of the restoration of the physical setting for imperial ceremony. Not only the palace, but also the Great Church, St Sophia, scene of so many of the imperial processions, were decorated again with religious images. An eighth-century iconophile writer said of another great ceremonial church, the church of the Virgin at Blachernae on the northern edge of the city, that 'the tyrant [i.e. Constantine V] scraped down' its walls, which had been covered with religious pictures, and 'having thus suppressed all of Christ's mysteries, he converted the church into a storehouse of fruit and an aviary', that is, he replaced the holy pictures with mosaics of trees, birds and beasts.[63] In the end, the Iconophiles won the day; one of the great events of the restoration of images was the dedication of the new apse mosaic of the Virgin and Child is St Sophia in March, AD 867.

Only a few months later, Basil I had his co-emperor Michael III murdered in his bedroom in the palace and made himself the founder of the Macedonian dynasty to which Constantine VII belonged. Basil, who had come from low origins, we are told, took every opportunity to strengthen his position; we have already seen that he initiated new imperial rituals. Significantly, he also embarked on a major programme of imperial building. This included an elaborate new church and the restoration of many existing ones; imperial apartments were decorated with mosaics showing Basil and his wife and children; a particularly telling example is the ceiling decoration showing the imperial family ranged round the sign of the cross, with formal inscriptions recording the thanks of the royal parents for their children and of the children for their parents. The latter runs:

We thank Thee, O Word of God, that Thou hast raised our father from Davidic poverty and hast anointed him with the unction of Thy Holy Ghost. Guard him and our mother by Thy

---

[62] From the collection of epigrams known as the Palatine Anthology (yet another work of this period – see Alan Cameron, *The Greek Anthology. From Meleager to Planudes* (Oxford, 1987), i, 106; trans. Mango, *Art* (see n. 30), p. 184.

[63] *Life of St Stephen the Younger* (d. AD 764), in J. P. Migne, *Patrologia Graeca* c (1865), col. 1120; trans. Mango, *Art* (see n. 30), pp. 152–3.

hand, while deeming both them and ourselves worthy of Thy heavenly Kingdom.[64]

The attempts of the Iconoclast emperors to control the powerful religious forces in the state by opposing the centrifugal enthusiasm for images had failed.[65] Once more emperors claimed divine election and support, legitimising their own position by representing themselves in visual art in conjunction with divine personages; in just such a way their imperial ceremony acted out this desirable relation between secular and divine power.

Thus the reigns of Basil I and his successors marked not only a new dynasty with an interest in establishing itself by an appeal to the past, but also the restoration of unity between emperors and church on an issue more fundamental to their long-term relations than the temporary conflict over Leo VI's marriages. It was however a unity which gave power firmly into the hands of the emperor. The same year, AD 867, in which Basil disposed of his colleague and became sole emperor, also saw Constantinople in open breach with Rome; Basil took up power with different ideas, deposed the very patriarch Photius who had delivered the homily on the restored apse mosaic in St Sophia, and called a synod whose object would be to express the views of the emperor. It was not a successful move in the long term, and Photius was eventually to be reinstated. But these events show that for the Macedonians, relations with the church, especially the church as represented by the patriarch, were indeed a matter of the definition of imperial power. They inherited a situation in which the worst conflict between emperors and church seemed to have been resolved; but the resurgent church was not to be allowed to do entirely as it liked.

Ceremony, new ceremonial settings and the depiction of the imperial dynasty in symbolic harmony with God were all for very good reasons close concerns of Basil I, and when Constantine VII stressed the ideal of divine and earthly harmony, symbolically represented in imperial ceremony, he was voicing a theory which

---

[64] Trans. in Mango, *Art* (see n. 30), p. 198. For the impact of imperial building, especially within the palace complex, on the development of ceremonial, see Magdalino and Nelson, 'The Emperor' (n. 4), pp. 171ff.

[65] On which see P. Brown, 'A Dark-Age Crisis: Aspects of the Iconoclastic Controversy', *English Historical Review* lxxxviii (1973), pp. 1–34 (in *idem*, *Society and the Holy in Late Antiquity* (London, 1982), pp. 251–301).

glossed over a much tenser reality. It was a good moment for the theory to be emphasised.

CONCLUSION

Accordingly, imperial ceremonial in the tenth century had two aspects: its debt to a long and steady process of development with its roots in the Roman empire and even earlier, and its relation to the particular circumstances of recent history. It would be easier to know just how much importance to attach to the latter if we really knew the level of imperial ritual practised during the seventh to ninth centuries. But it would be surprising if there had been a major break. We may reasonably assume that during the years for which our sources are so bad the basics of court ceremony were carried on and the main traditions preserved. But for all that, by the time that Constantine VII compiled his book, a new bureaucratic structure had been formed, while in the sphere of the relations between emperor and church a new equilibrium had been reached, or was at least claimed, after a long and hard struggle. For contemporary imaginations, imperial ceremony represented one element of real continuity with the Roman past. It is reasonable then to suppose, though impossible to prove, that the compilation of the *Book of Ceremonies* also indicates a real contemporary increase in the level and formality of imperial ceremony. Both the reality and the codification spring from an actual situation.

This is why Constantine's own tastes and scholarly interests cannot provide the whole explanation for the *Book of Ceremonies*. Both the book itself and the rituals described in it testify to a need to restore a sense of order in society, to connect with the past after centuries of dislocation, and to reinforce the position of the ruling dynasty in relation to its governing class. Far from being a proof of the unchanging and timeless quality of Byzantine society, the *Book of Ceremonies* is actually an indicator of change, and a proof of the adaptability of Byzantine rule. Perhaps the claims of its compiler, Constantine VII, were not so far from the mark after all.

4. *The Lord's anointed and the people's choice: Carolingian royal ritual*

JANET L. NELSON

The main formative period for the rituals, as for the ideology, of medieval rulership lay between the mid-eighth and the late ninth century. From *c.* 750, rulers of the Carolingian dynasty and their people, the Franks, launched a series of campaigns from their heartlands in what is now north-eastern France and Belgium. Their conquests achieved the first great concentration of power in the West since the Roman Empire and imposed common patterns of thought and behaviour on most of continental Europe. Indeed it was thanks to the power of Charlemagne (768–814), the greatest of the Carolingian rulers, that the concept of Europe was first shaped.[1] The medieval kingdoms of France, Germany and Italy directly, those of England and Spain less directly, were all heirs to Carolingian institutions and traditions and ideology. European kings and emperors from the Middle Ages down to the twentieth century were inaugurated at the outset of their reigns by means of rituals which, as far as western Europe was concerned, were of Carolingian origin: anointing and coronation. Not only were the main features of these rituals directly transmitted from the Carolingian period, but there was continuity in detail: the coronation prayer pronounced over the last of the Bourbons, Charles X, in 1825 was essentially the same prayer as had been first used for his Carolingian ancestor Charles the Bald in 869.

My thanks are due to the members of the Early Medieval Seminar at the Institute of Historical Research, University of London, especially Matthew Bennett and Elizabeth Ward, for helpful criticisms of an earlier draft of this chapter. I should also like to thank the editors for patience and advice beyond the call of duty.

[1] D. Bullough, *The Age of Charlemagne* revised ed. (London, Ferndale, 1980); *idem*, '*Europae pater*. Charlemagne and his achievement in the light of recent research', *English Historical Review*, lxxxv (1970), pp. 59–105.

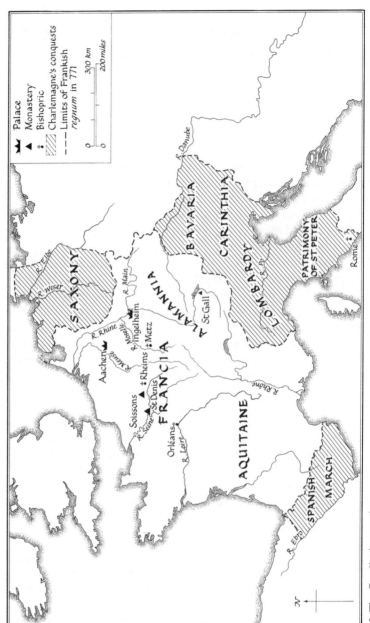

20 The Carolingian empire.

THE FRANKISH REALM

The empire of the Carolingians was of characteristically medieval type: it was a composite empire, an accumulation of kingdoms, its ruler a king over many kings.[2] When in 800 Charlemagne received the title of emperor, and when successive Carolingians used this title in the ninth century, they meant by it overlordship of many kingdoms. But those constituent kingdoms were themselves amalgams of lesser lordships. Hence people in the eighth and ninth centuries saw nothing muddled or incongruous in making do with the same word, realm (*regnum*), for total building and building-block alike. What gave the building its strength, what created it in the first place, was not only the dynasty, the Carolingians, though the leadership of successive rulers was crucial, but also the people they led, the people of the Franks, the *gens francorum*, and specifically the Frankish aristocracy. It was they, as the people in arms, who won the victories, and effected the conquests, that made the Carolingian empire. The 'leaders of the Franks' ruled it along with the Carolingians themselves.[3]

In the eighth century, the Franks were no newcomers on the European scene. They had been settled in, or dominated, the areas that are now France, Belgium and part of West Germany since the late fifth century. The first king to rule a united Frankish realm had been Clovis, descendant of the half-legendary Merovech, and founder of the so-called Merovingian dynasty. Clovis imposed his rule over what had been the Roman province of Gaul. Needing the collaboration of the still-powerful Catholic Gallo-Roman aristocrats, not least because they manned the well-endowed bishoprics of Gaul, Clovis himself became a Catholic in 508.[4] In 511, when Clovis died, and was buried in the Church of the Holy Apostles in Paris, the realm of the Franks was partitioned between his four sons, thus creating four realms in one. This division originated, 'not in tradition, but in a precise political compromise' between the interests of Clovis' widow, his sons, the Frankish aristocracy and the Gallo-Roman bishops.[5] But neither in 511, nor subsequently,

[2] J. L. Nelson, 'Kingship and Empire', in J. H. Burns (ed.), *The Cambridge History of Medieval Political Thought* (Cambridge University Press, 1987).

[3] See below, p. 148.

[4] I. N. Wood, 'Gregory of Tours and Clovis', *Revue Belge de philologie et d'histoire*, liii (1985), pp. 149–72.

[5] I. N. Wood, 'Kings, kingdoms and consent', in P. Sawyer and I. N. Wood (eds.), *Early Medieval Kingship* (Leeds, University of Leeds, 1977), pp. 6–29, at 26.

did the fact of being a king's son guarantee succession to a share of the *regnum*. In the sixth century, in the process of dynastic discarding, many king's sons were eliminated by their uncles, or even fathers. There was, naturally, a limit to the number of co-parceners the *regnum* could stand. The largest known number of sharers was four. But failures of heirs (by natural causes or elimination) usually kept the number below that. In the seventh century, a two-fold division of the *regnum* became the norm; and the two parts, Neustria and Austrasia, were not subdivided further. It was not always the eldest son(s) of the preceding king who inherited: sometimes a younger son was preferred. As magnates including leading churchmen were involved in such choices, an elective element remained within the dynastic succession system. The Merovingians patronised, and also exploited, the churches in their kingdoms. Monasteries as well as episcopal sees became great landholders, and bishops among the most important counsellors of kings. Yet the kings remained warlords, dependent on the loyalty of their warrior-retinues, and of the aristocracy, nourished on plunder and tribute from those they could dominate, as well as on the food-renders of far-flung royal estates.

How were the Merovingians inaugurated to kingship? Very little evidence exists for this or any type of Merovingian royal ritual. A chance reference in a piece of late seventh-century hagiography shows that there was by then a 'custom' governing Frankish king-makings and that nobles regarded their attendance on these occasions as essential.[6] The ritual seems to have centred on an enthronement in the presence of this assembly, and afterwards, the new king may have ritually journeyed around his realm. The enthronement has been interpreted as a ritual of household-lordship (*Hausherrschaft*) in which the king's presiding over his hall epitomised his patrimonial authority in the realm as a whole.[7] There is no evidence of any coronation ritual for the Merovingians. Was this because sacral powers were believed to reside in their long hair? Franks and foreigners alike certainly identified the Merovingians as 'the long-haired kings'.[8] But the special hairstyle may

---

[6] R. Schneider, *Königswahl und Königserhebung im Frühmittelalter* (Stuttgart, Anton Hiersemann, 1972), pp. 187–239.

[7] J. L. Nelson, 'Inauguration rituals', in Sawyer and Wood (eds.), *Early Medieval Kingship* (see n. 5), pp. 50–71, at 53.

[8] A. M. Cameron, 'How did the Merovingian kings wear their hair?', *Revue Belge de philologie et d'histoire*, xliii (1965), pp. 1203–16; *idem*, 'Agathias on the early

have been nothing but a badge of rank, denoting a 'king-worthy' member of the ruling dynasty. If Merovingian sacrality ever existed, it is very unlikely to have survived the powerful impact of Christianity on Frankish royal ideology and practice in the sixth and seventh centuries.[9] It is hard to imagine that rulers whose burials were so firmly taken in hand by the Church had been inaugurated without the participation of churchmen, or that inaugural assemblies of magnates excluded bishops, or that bishops, if present, played no active role *ex officio*.[10] On the other hand, the absence of evidence, from a period when literacy was virtually monopolised by ecclesiastics, could suggest that in rituals of king-making at least, clergy as yet played only supporting roles.

In the later seventh and early eighth centuries, a series of royal minorities, and two royal assassinations, weakened the power of the Merovingian kings. Provincial aristocrats no longer attended their assemblies and their writ no longer ran outside the Frankish heartlands.[11] From 717 onwards, the Merovingian kings became figureheads. The most powerful man in the kingdom was a magnate, Charles Martel, who held the office of senior palace official. The power he exercised in the palace was established on the battlefield. By the time of his death in 741, Martel had imposed, or reimposed, Frankish domination over a number of the peoples of the realms adjacent to Francia proper: Aquitaine, Burgundy, Alsace, Frisia. But he remained a great magnate, not a king. His two sons, succeeding to his power, divided his 'empire' as Merovingians might have done: each got a share of Francia proper plus some peripheral lands. Still they were not kings: a Merovingian continued to reign apparently because the Frankish aristocracy still regarded the Merovingians as possessing a special legitimacy, and perhaps too because they resented the ascendancy of Martel's

Merovingians', *Annali delle Scuola Normale di Pisa*, ser. II. xxxvii (1968), pp. 95–140, at 119–20.

[9] E. Ewig, 'Zum christlichen Königsgedanken im Frühmittelalter', *Vorträge und Forschungen*, 3 (1956), 7–73, reprinted in his *Spätantikes und Fränkisches Gallien* (2 vols., Munich, Artemis Verlag, 1976), pp. 3–71, esp. 19–20; P. Riché, *Education and Culture in the Barbarian West*, trans. J. J. Contreni (Columbia, South Carolina, University of South Carolina Press, 1976).

[10] E. Ewig, 'Résidence et capitale pendent le haut Moyen Age', *Revue historique*, ccxxx (1963), pp. 25–72, at 47–53, reprinted in *Spätantikes und Fränkisches Gallien*, i, pp. 362–408, at 383–9.

[11] K. F. Werner, 'Les Principautés périphériques dans le monde franc du VIIIe siècle' in his *Structures politiques du monde franc (VIe–XIIe siècle)* (London, Variorum, 1979).

family. In 750, Martel's son Pippin, whose brother had conveniently announced a monastic vocation in 746 and retired from the world, was in a strong enough position to dispense with his Merovingian prop. He consulted the Frankish aristocracy and with the support, presumably, of most of them, sent an embassy to the pope and gained his approval for the supplanting of 'him who had the title but not the reality of kingship'. The last Merovingian and his son were consigned to a monastery, and Pippin himself became the first Carolingian king.[12]

Pippin's accession in 751 was the natural occasion for innovation, as well as ancient custom, in the inauguration ritual. The innovation took the form of the anointing which preceded Pippin's enthronement. While the pope had approved the supplanting of the old dynasty, it was Frankish bishops who consecrated Pippin at Soissons with holy oil.[13] Frankish bishops certainly took part in the inaugurations of Pippin's two sons in 768, but it is unclear whether or not anointings were then performed. In the second half of the eighth century, the papacy showed a more consistent interest in anointing successive kings of the Franks: Stephen II (752–7) undertook the awesome journey across the Alps in the winter of 753 to re-anoint Pippin in person in 754 and, at the same time, to anoint Pippin's young sons. Similar papal anointings of Charlemagne's sons were performed at Rome in 781 and 800.[14]

Pope Hadrian (772–95) seems to have added yet another ritual to the inauguration process for Frankish kings: the first such occasion on which a coronation is mentioned is 781 – the consecrations at Rome of Charlemagne's son Carloman as king of the acquired realm of Italy, and of his little brother Louis as king of Aquitaine. The pope may well have borrowed the idea of coronation from Byzantium where it was the centrepiece of the imperial inauguration. Hence in 800, the pope crowned Charlemagne emperor, in an imitation of Byzantine ritual.[15] But whereas Byzantine ritual

---

12 Nelson, 'Inauguration rituals' (see n. 7), pp. 56–8; W. Affeldt, 'Untersuchungen zur Königserhebung Pippins', *Frühmittelalterliche Studien*, xiv (1980), pp. 95–187.

13 M. J. Enright, *Iona, Tara and Soissons. The Origin of the Royal Anointing Ritual* (Berlin, Walter de Gruyter, 1985), unfortunately came to my attention too late for me to take it fully into account in this chapter.

14 A. Angenendt, 'Das geistliche Bündnis der Päpste mit der Karolingern (745–796)', *Historisches Jahrbuch*, c (1980), pp. 1–94, at 40–57.

15 *Annales Regni Francorum, sub anno* (henceforth *s.a.*) 781, ed. F. Kurze, *Monumenta Germaniae Historica* (hereafter MGH), *Scriptores rerum Germani-*

featured coronation only, and not anointing, in the West the popes stressed a linkage between the two. In 816 a pope again crossed the Alps to anoint and crown as emperor Charlemagne's son Louis the Pious who had succeeded his father two years before. The idea of coronation had long since been invested with Christian connotations. In the New Testament, a heavenly crown was held out as the reward of faith for all Christians. In the liturgies of the early church, baptismal anointing was presented as a symbolic coronation, and the whole initiation-rite as a kind of king-making, complete with acclamations to the newly-raised.[16] The linking of anointing with coronation was thus in itself not really a papal innovation. The application of both to a Frankish king was. And in the ninth century, it was picked up by Frankish clergy themselves. The prayer accompanying the anointing in the earliest extant Frankish *Ordo* begins:

May the Lord crown thee with a crown of glory.[17]

But there remained one significant difference between coronation and anointing. Where anointing was in Latin Christendom by its very nature a clerical monopoly, given the central importance of oil rituals in the liturgy of the Church, coronation was not. No Frankish ruler ever anointed another, but Charlemagne did crown his son, Louis the Pious, in 813, and Louis in turn crowned his son, Charles, in 838. In 866, Charles helped in the coronation of his queen.[18] But the bishops had by then taken the pope's cue and involved themselves in Frankish coronations as well as anointings. Thus, from about the middle of the ninth century, coronation became, alongside anointing, permanently part of the ecclesiastical procedures of king-making. By about 900, clergy were also enthroning Frankish kings. In other words, some essential procedures of king-making had been 'liturgified': they took place inside a church and were stage-managed and performed by ecclesiastics. This could result in a doubling of rituals, as for instance when

carum in usum scholarum, vi (Hannover, 1895), p. 57. See C. R. Brühl, 'Fränkischer Krönungsbrauch und das Problem der Festkrönung', *Historische Zeitschrift*, cxciv (1962), pp. 205–326, at 313–14; P. E. Schramm, *Kaiser, Könige und Päpste*, 4 vols. (Stuttgart, Anton Hiersemann, 1968), i, pp. 215–63.
[16] T. Michels, 'Die Akklamation in der Taufliturgie', *Jahrbuch für Liturgiewissenschaft*, viii (1928), pp. 76–85.
[17] MGH *Capitularia Regum Francorum*, ed. A. Boretius, 2 vols. (Hannover, 1897), ii, no. 302, p. 457. See below, pp. 163–4.
[18] *Annales Bertiniani*, *s.a.* 866, F. Grat, J. Vielliard and S. Clémencet (eds.) (Paris, Société de l'histoire de France, 1964), p. 129.

an enthronement by laymen outside the church preceded the enthronement by clergy inside.[19] The former event was of course much less likely to be recorded.

PROBLEMS IN INTERPRETING FRANKISH ROYAL RITUAL

Many historians have seen these changes in rulers' inauguration rituals as symptomatic of more profound changes in the nature of royal power and its relationship to ecclesiastical authority. The influential Belgian scholar Henri Pirenne saw Pippin's consecration in 751 as a political and ideological turning-point in European history. Playing down the significance of previous changes in the fifth century and denying that the Roman Empire had then 'fallen', Pirenne regarded the Merovingian regime as still sub-Roman not only in its economic base and institutions but also in its ideology: it was, he claimed, absolutist and secular. Carolingian rulership seemed to Pirenne fundamentally different because it drew its legitimacy from Christianity and because its power was limited from its very inception by the authority of the church.[20]

Pirenne's view of the significance of Carolingian ritual innovations was largely shared, but also modified, by Walter Ullmann. He argued that the Church's take-over of Carolingian kingship was new. But he saw the roots of early medieval kingship, in Francia as elsewhere in the regions of western Europe settled by barbarians, as 'Germanic' rather than Roman. 'Germanic roots' meant persisting limitations on royal power; for, Ullmann believed, primitive Germanic kingship was rooted in the free folk who elected the king and took sanctions against royal misconduct. It was through the Carolingians' liaison with the Church, according to Ullmann, that they were elevated to a unique position of dominance over the people. The Church's very vocabulary was replete with notions of superiority and subordination: God on high had placed the king, as his deputy, over the people who were, literally, his *sub-jecti:* subjects. The prayer-texts of royal consecration-rites, the *Ordines*, Ullmann claimed, enunciated a theory of royal sovereignty which thus replaced an earlier, 'Germanic' idea of the king as merely first among equals. 'Thou shalt not touch the Lord's anointed'.

---

[19] Nelson, 'Inauguration rituals' (see n. 7), p. 54.
[20] H. Pirenne, *Mohammed and Charlemagne*, trans. B. Miall (London, G. Allen and Unwin, 1939), pp. 136, 268ff.

(Ps.105.15) But, Ullmann continued, the king's sovereignty was 'stunted' because it was mediated through ecclesiastics and hence subordinate to ecclesiastical control. The king accepted this subordination, because he was enabled thereby 'to claim effective control, that is, sovereignty over his non-ecclesiastical subjects'.[21]

Hence, for Ullmann, the ninth-century Frankish episcopally-conducted royal consecration rites marked 'the symbolic and incontrovertible ending of a long tradition' and 'the symbolic beginning of a new era in the ideology of Rulership which was to be overwhelmingly ecclesiastical in its making, theocratic in its substance, symbolic in its execution'. In king-making, a ritualised election and elevation by the people was replaced by the constitutive act of anointing performed by bishops who thus 'had removed society and Ruler to the ecclesiological precincts'. The story continued into the later Carolingian period, and beyond that into the eleventh century when a reforming papacy broke away from its alliance with the Carolingians' successors and asserted with new determination the inferiority of all secular powers to its authority. When in the twelfth century kings and emperors sought alternative legitimation for their power, their arguments could make little impact on the bastion of hierocratic theory in a world that continued to deny the secular any autonomy. Thus Ullmann saw the Carolingian period as a critical turning-point: the Church then asserted its ideological dominance, claiming that as kings and emperors were made through its ministrations, they acted also at its behest. The ritual expression of this relationship of command and executive subordination was, Ullmann thought, the clergy's handing-over of the sword to the newly-consecrated ruler at his inauguration. If the king failed in his ecclesiastically-defined task, it was for the Church to impose spiritual sanctions, or even, if necessary, to authorise resistance. The seeds of a kind of constitutionalism were to be found in ecclesiastical theory.[22]

---

[21] W. Ullmann, *The Carolingian Renaissance and the Idea of Kingship* (London, Methuen, 1969), esp. pp. 86–96; 111–13.

[22] Ibid., pp. 88, 95, 133; idem, *The Growth of Papal Government in the Middle Ages*, 2nd edn (London, Methuen, 1962), pp. 387, 445–6; idem, *Law and Politics in the Middle Ages* (London, Sources of History, 1975), pp. 246–7, 264–6. See also F. Kern, *Gottesgnadentum und Widerstandsrecht in früheren Mittelalter*, 2nd rev. edn ed. R. Buchner (Münster, Köln, Wissenschaftliche Buchgemeinschaft, 1954). For a critical appraisal of some of Ullmann's views, see F. Oakley, 'Celestial hierarchies revisited: Walter Ullmann's vision of medieval politics', *Past and Present*, no. 60 (1973), pp. 3–48, esp. 16, 29–32.

The picture of clergy in control and a merely executive lay ruler is a familiar stereotype in ecclesiastical writers of the Middle Ages. It is an idealisation, which some modern commentators have misread as a description, of the nature and distribution of power. It neglects the very real dependence of the clergy on rulers' protection and material support. And it omits a crucial dimension: the power of the aristocracy, the leading men of the kingdom. Recent research has thrown some light on both their activities and their ideas in the Carolingian period.[23] Kings relied on their support, yet were also their competitors for power. Their interests constituted the most effective restraint on rulers; at the same time, they stood to benefit, individually and collectively, from the king's patronage and acknowledged authority, and hence their regular, self-interested co-operation gave Carolingian kingship the strength it undoubtedly had. The ideology presented by historians of medieval political ideas has sometimes seemed divorced not only from the realities described by historians of medieval politics but from the ideas of most of those involved in medieval government. The divorce is an illusion, a trick of the historiographical light. Nobles, clergy and king inhabited one world. There was no power that was not religiously validated. In that very general sense, the Carolingian king was sacral, God-appointed, but the people and its leaders were also chosen by God. The king, like other Christians, was part of the Church in the widest sense of that elastic term: king and people collaborated in the Church's protection, the king leading rather than dominating. In one *Ordo* of c. 900, the king was said to have come to power 'by paternal succession': at the same time people along with clergy appeared as the king's electors.[24] Nor were ecclesiastical sources any more consistent in presenting episcopal authority as superior to royal power. Though some Carolingian bishops berated kings, others, more typically, declared the king not only their protector but their father and lord.[25] The king was the Church's strong right arm; he was also its governor. In practice, churchmen depended on the king for the promotion of ecclesiastical concerns, notably the defence of church property against lay

---

[23] See Nelson, 'Public *Histories* and private history in the work of Nithard', *Speculum*, lx (1985), pp. 251–93, esp. 256–60, 282–9 for further references.

[24] The Seven Forms *Ordo*: see C. Erdmann, *Forschungen zur politischen Ideenwelt des Frühmittelalters* (Berlin, Akademie Verlag, 1951), pp. 87, 89.

[25] MGH *Capitularia*, ii, no. 252, p. 212. See K. Leyser, *Rule and Conflict in an Early Medieval Society* (London, Edward Arnold, 1979), p. 78.

encroachments. Royal liturgy depicted the king and the bishops as sharers in the same 'service' to God: bishops 'in interior matters', king 'in exterior matters'. But another prayer in the same *Ordo* called the king 'mediator between clergy and people'.[26]

What I hope to show in this chapter is that Carolingian inauguration rituals were not designed simply to separate off the king from other laymen, though of course they defined the uniqueness of royal office, nor did they express only a hierarchy of descending power. If a crucial part of the king-making was 'clericalised', and enacted inside a church, this did not exclude the persistence of extra-ecclesiastical ritual before and after the consecration, nor did it marginalise the role of the aristocracy in the ecclesiastical ritual itself. Rather, the *Ordines*, within their stereotyped liturgical form, reflected Carolingian realities of consensus politics, and ideals of peace and solidarity within the kingdom that were shared by all participants. Hierocracy was not the only brand of Christian political thought. I hope further to reinforce this interpretation of king-making rituals by reference to other forms of royal ritual in the Carolingian period. The evidence for these other forms is mainly non-liturgical. It is to be found in a wide range of literary and historical writings of the period. Nearly all the authors were ecclesiastical, yet they do not (as liturgical texts, prescriptions for clerical actors, inevitably tend to) neglect the role of the lay aristocracy, still less imply an opposition between 'clergy' and 'people'.

At this point, it may be useful to define the Frankish aristocracy more precisely. The identity of a *gens* or people had always been rather artificial; it certainly had no ascertainable racial component, though it could be represented in terms of a fictive shared ancestry.[27] The Romans were seen as a *gens* of this kind. The groups that settled in what had been the Roman Empire were cast as *gentes* by writers trained in the classical tradition. Each could be credited, again following Roman models, and again somewhat fictitiously, with a distinct body of customary law. These laws were enshrined, between the fifth and eighth centuries, in the so-called 'barbarian' or 'Germanic' codes: the laws of the Franks, Burgundians, Visi-

26 The Seven Forms *Ordo*: Erdmann, *Forschungen* (see n. 24), pp. 88, 89.
27 S. Reynolds, 'Medieval *Origines Gentium* and the community of the Realm', *History*, lxviii (1983), pp. 375–90. For the Franks' alleged descent from Alexander the Great, or (alternatively) the Trojans, see E. James, *The Origins of France* (London, Macmillan, 1982), p. 32.

goths and so on. By the eighth century, however, law was being identified in a territorial rather than a 'gentile' way: it was becoming the law of a region rather than a group.[28] The *regnum* of the Franks, or Francia, meant primarily the Frankish heartlands where the kings of the Merovingian dynasty had their power-base in large estates. In the second half of the eighth century, Charlemagne, successor to the Merovingians' lands, 'amplified the realm of the Franks': his victories brought many *gentes subactae* (subjugated peoples) into a realm that now extended from the Ebro to the Elbe and from the Baltic to the Mediterranean.[29] A ninth-century writer explained how Charlemagne governed the conquered kingdom of another gens, the Lombards, in Italy where he made one of his infant sons king in 781:

> His royal power [*potestas*] having been thus amplified, it was necessary to put commanders [*duces*] in charge of the subdued realm and people [*regnum et gens*): they would enforce the authority of laws and cause the custom of Francia [*mos Franciae*] to be observed. Thus it came about that the palace was emptied of the leading men of the people [*populus*] and of its commanders, because [Charlemagne] gave over to his son many Franks of noble family who were to watch over and rule with him the realm he had just received.[30]

Some dozens of Frankish nobles were thus direct beneficiaries of the victories they themselves had helped win under Charlemagne's leadership. These families came to form an imperial aristocracy, with branches implanted in conquered regions, but retaining inherited lands in Francia. They intermarried with the aristocracies of the conquered peoples. It was in this way, and in this sense, that (as a contemporary put it) 'the realm of the Franks was made into a solid body out of diverse nations'.[31] In the ninth century, even after the realm of the Franks had been divided between Charlemagne's

---

28 S. Reynolds, *Kingdoms and Communities in Western Europe, 900–1300* (Oxford, Clarendon Press, 1984), p. 19, n. 21.

29 Einhard, *Vita Karoli Magni*, c. 15, G. Waitz (ed., rev. O. Holder-Egger), MGH *Scriptores rerum Germanicarum in usum scholarum*, xxv (Hannover, 1911), p. 17; *Annales Mettenses Priores*, s.a. 714, B. Simson (ed.) MGH *Scriptores rerum Germanicarum in usum scholarum*, x (Hannover, 1905), p. 19.

30 Adrevald of Fleury, *Miracula S. Benedicti*, c. 18, O. Holder-Egger (ed.), MGH *Scriptores*, xv, 1 (Hannover, 1887–8), p. 486.

31 Ibid., c. 33, p. 493. See further, K. F. Werner, 'Important noble families in the kingdom of Charlemagne', in T. Reuter (ed.), *The Medieval Nobility* (Amsterdam, North Holland Publishing House, 1979), pp. 137–202.

heirs, a single élite spanned these divisions, claiming Frankish identity, using the 'custom of Francia'. In the 880s, Notker the Stammerer, a monk of St Gall in Alemannia, said he had never visited Francia, but he identified himself with the Franks as 'the head', and celebrated their superiority over other peoples, 'its members'. He explained that by 'realm of the Franks', he meant 'all the provinces north of the Alps, since because of Charlemagne's fame and glory, Gauls, Aquitanians, Burgundians, Spaniards, Alemans and Bavarians were proud to be called the Franks' servants'.[32] Before the close of the ninth century, Carolingian writers seldom differentiated between western, eastern or middle Franks. In this chapter, I shall use the terms 'Franks' and 'Frankish' in this broader sense, to identify the dominant group in the provinces north of the Alps between *c*. 750 and *c*. 900, a group of mixed gentile origin which nevertheless presented a united front to those they ruled.

But Frankish unity was a fragile thing. In order to sustain it, the Franks needed self-identification as an imperial people. Though they were a gens that ruled over the gentes, their own unity was strained not only by traditional hostility between Neustrian (western) and Austrasian (eastern) Frankish groups, but by the consequences of imperial success. For when imperial expansion made more 'peripheral' realms available, a system of partible royal inheritance thrived, producing a plurality of kings and, hence, foci for conflict between the Franks, in each successive generation. Yet, though there were to continue to be several kings of the Franks ruling at any one time, the sources are unanimous in referring to only one *regnum* of the Franks. One Frankish gens sustained, and was sustained by, that sense of the singularity of their *regnum*. The ideal helped the Franks to live with the reality of division and conflict.

THE DEVELOPMENT OF FRANKISH ROYAL RITUAL

We must begin with 751 and the meaning for contemporaries of Pippin's royal anointing at Soissons. The Frankish consecrators were innovators in an age when all men sought legitimation by invoking the past, and when learned men used the Bible typologi-

---

[32] Notker, *Gesta Karoli Magni*, cc. 10, 24, 34, H. F. Haefele (ed.), MGH *Scriptores* NS xii (Berlin, 1962), pp. 13, 32, 47.

cally to make sense of both past and present. That is to say, characters and events were believed to have been prefigured in Biblical types, so that recent or contemporary history became, as it were, a re-run of Bible history. Thus, for instance, eighth-century writers might identify a ruler with Joshua or a battle with Jericho.[33] These were ways of understanding their world. The point in 751, however, was also to change it, by introducing a new form of ritual action. In this sense Pirenne was half-right. But he mistook the nature of the change: it was not the imposition of hierocracy. The prime authority for Pippin's consecrators came from the Old Testament where anointings of the kings of Israel by priests and prophets were described. Bible history was seen as a prototype of contemporary Frankish history. It is no coincidence that from the first half of the eighth century comes evidence of another liturgical innovation in northern Francia (specifically, in fact, the Soissons area): the anointing of the priest's hands at his ordination. Again, the Old Testament was being taken literally as a model. The papacy had never tried any such literal translations from the Israelites' liturgical practice to its own; and Charlemagne, who wished to stick to the papal line, tried strenuously to discourage them. But the Frankish clergy refused to be discouraged: they produced ever more elaborate ordination–anointings of both priests and bishops and eventually, in the tenth century, succeeded in exporting these rites to Rome itself – where they have remained ever since.[34]

Such scriptural imitation in the Frankish liturgy was a matter not just of drawing analogies, but of recognising and making concrete a symmetry that was divinely-drawn, and extended beyond priests and kings to the whole people: it was the Franks' destiny to be a new Israel. Did the *principes*, the leading men of the Franks, appreciate their new role? Presumably it was for their benefit that a new prologue added to their law-code (*Lex Salica*) late in Pippin's reign declared the Franks (in language taken directly

[33] E. Dahlhaus-Berg, *Nova antiquitas et antiqua novitas* (Cologne, Vienna, Böhlau, 1975), pp. 36–8, 76–91, 145–6, 194–6 and *passim*.

[34] *Missale Francorum*, L. C. Mohlberg (ed.), Rerum Ecclesiasticarum Documenta, Series Maior, Fontes 1 (Rome, 1957), pp. xvi, 10, 64–7; B. Kleinheyer, *Die Priesterweihe im römischen Ritus* (Trier, Paulinus Verlag, 1962), pp. 14–22; *Liber Sacramentorum Gellonensis*, A. Dumas and J. Deshusses (eds.), (Corpus Christianorum, Series Latina, 159, 159A, Turnholt, Brepols, 1981), text p. 391, introduction pp. xviii-xix.

from Deuteronomy) to be a chosen people, 'beloved of Christ'.[35] A contemporary recording Pippin's inauguration in 751 presented the 'bishops' consecration' and 'the princes' recognition' as parallel, complementary rituals, just as in the Old Testament, king-makings were depicted as the collective act of the priests and the people of Israel.[36] The bishops did not oust the lay magnates but acted alongside them. Pippin, after all, had been able to replace the last Merovingian because he could attract the support of the Frankish aristocracy. In 751, this was expressed symbolically in rituals of election: the 'recognition', involving the magnates' acclamation and perhaps kneeling or bowing before Pippin. But they acknowledged more than a single ruler: the elevation of Pippin's wife Bertrada as queen, apparently another innovation, and again carefully recorded by the contemporary source, implied the installation of a new dynasty and the prospective recognition of Pippin's sons as kings.[37] In 768, the Franks, practitioners themselves of partible inheritance, underwrote the division of the *regnum* between Pippin's heirs and, regrouped as the 'faithful men' of each resultant 'part-kingdom', participated in the ritual inaugurations of both successor kings.[38] The pattern, as we shall see, was to be repeated in the ninth century, sustaining the plurality of Carolingian *regna* along with the Carolingian dynasty's monopoly of kingship.

There is a further possible liturgical influence on the consecrators of 751: the post-baptismal or confirmation anointing prescribed for performance by the bishop in the practice of the church at Rome. In this period, as the case of priestly ordinations shows, there was as yet no ritual uniformity in the Latin Church, not even on such a fundamental as the performance of Christian initiation. The Fran-

---

[35] *Lex Salica*, prologue, ed. K. A. Eckhardt, MGH *Leges nationum germanicarum*, xv, 2 (Hannover, 1969), pp. 2, 6. Note the echoes of Deut. iv, 1–8.

[36] *Continuator of Fredegar*, c. 33, J. M. Wallace-Hadrill (ed.), *The Fourth Book of the Chronicle of Fredegar* (London, Nelson, 1960), p. 102. Cf. such Old Testament models as II Sam.ii, 4; v, 3; III Reg. i, 38–40; I Par. xi, 3; xii, 38; xxix, 22–5; II Par. xxiii, 8–11.

[37] *Continuator of Fredegar* (see n. 36), c. 33, p. 102. For a possible further consecration of Bertrada by the pope in 754, see *Codex Carolinus*, no. 11, W. Gundlach (ed.), MGH *Epistolae*, iii (Berlin, 1892), p. 505. There is no other contemporary information: see A. Stoclet, 'La "*Clausula de unctione Pippini regis*": mises au point et nouvelles hypothèses', *Francia*, viii (1980), pp. 1–42 (showing the *Clausula* to be a ninth-century work).

[38] *Continuator of Fredegar*, c. 53, p. 121; cf. *Annales Mettenses Priores*, *s.a.* 771, pp. 57–8.

kish church had evolved its own 'Gallican' rite where no episcopal post-baptismal anointing was included. But precisely in the years immediately before 751, reforming Frankish clergy had been working hard to promote the adoption of Roman practice, both because it bore the stamp of papal authority and because it enhanced the liturgical role of bishops.[39] (Hence there was no contradiction here, as in the case of ordination–anointings, between the reformers' quest for self-identification as an élite through the adoption of Old Testament ritual and their seeking of the same goal through conformity with the papacy.) The reformers included men close to Pippin: and they could have found in the post-baptismal anointing by the bishop a useful liturgical model for royal anointing, both as to form (unction of the forehead) and substance (chrism, made by adding aromatics to olive oil).

The Frankish clergy have left no direct record of their understanding of the 751 ritual. Papal views, however, are much better evidenced; and it is clear that the model of post-baptismal anointing was particularly important for a series of popes. In 754, Pope Stephen II took the opportunity of his stay in Francia not only to re-anoint Pippin, but also to anoint Pippin's two sons, first in a confirmation-rite (which they had presumably never received at their Gallican baptisms) then as kings along with their father.[40] In 781, Pope Hadrian I conferred on Charlemagne's son Carloman a post-baptismal anointing that was associated with (though liturgically distinct from) an anointing to kingship (in this case of the subkingdom of Italy).[41] Thus were forged strong personal links between pope as 'spiritual father' and prince as 'spiritual son', and also between the pope and Pippin or Charlemagne as 'spiritual co-fathers'. But the relationships between popes and individual Carolingians, though important, were not the only consequence of

---

[39] J. D. C. Fisher, *Christian Initiation in the Medieval West* (London, SPCK, 1965), pp. 52–77; A. Angenendt, '*Rex et Sacerdos.* Zur Genese der Königssalbung', in N. Kamp and J. Wollasch (eds.), *Tradition als Historische Kraft. Interdisziplinäre Forschungen zur Geschichte des früheren Mittelalters* (Berlin, Walter de Gruyter, 1982), pp. 100–18, at 106–7; *idem*, *Kaiserherrschaft und Königstaufe* (Berlin, Walter de Gruyter, 1984), pp. 75–91.

[40] Angenendt, '*Rex et Sacerdos*' (see n. 39), pp. 111–12; *idem*, 'Das geistliche Bundnis der Päpste', pp. 40–57.

[41] *Annales Regni Francorum, s.a.* 781 F. Kurze (ed.), MGH *Scriptores*, vi (Hannover, 1895), p. 57. See C. R. Brühl, 'Fränkischer Krönungsbrauch und der Problem der Festkrönungen', *Historische Zeitschrift*, cxciv (1962), pp. 205–326, at 313–14.

these papally-performed rites. In the letters sent by successive popes to the Frankish court and copied on Charlemagne's orders into a single manuscript, the *Codex Carolinus*, the royal anointings of the Frankish kings were repeatedly mentioned in terms which evoked the standard theological interpretation of the post-baptismal anointing as expounded, for instance, by Bede: the anointings of kings and priests in the Old Testament prefigured Christ, the Anointed One, who united the functions of king and priest and made all Christians, as members of his body, kingly and priestly too through their anointings.[42] This papal cross-referencing of the particular – royal anointing – with the universal – the anointing of every one of the Christian people – was apt: it was the Franks as well as their kings whom the popes addressed and whose services they hoped to enlist. The Scriptural phrase 'a chosen race, a royal priesthood' (1 Peter ii.9), interpreted by Bede and others as a typological reference to the post-baptismal anointing, was applied by Pope Stephen III (768–772) to the Frankish kings Carloman and Charlemagne, and by Pope Paul I (757–767) to the Frankish aristocracy.[43] The anointings of the kings were thus linked by the papacy with the special status of the whole Frankish gens, the new Israel. If in one sense anointing set the king apart (but he was already set apart as the enthroned one), it also exalted his people along with him affirming their common identity as *christi* (anointed ones), hence Christians.

The little we know of royal ritual in the later eighth century suggests anything but hierocracy. Royal anointings were virtually ignored by Frankish writers during Charlemagne's reign, which could well mean that, whatever message the papacy had sought to convey, Charlemagne himself and the Frankish élite (lay and clerical alike) found other ritual expressions of their relationship more congenial.[44] In the *laudes regiae*, which in the West are one of the innovations of the Carolingian Church, we have liturgical acclamations not only for the ruler but also for the royal family, the Frankish nobility and the Frankish church together. Such *laudes*

---

[42] Bede, *In Psalmorum Librum Exegesis*, Ps. 26, J.-P. Migne (ed.), *Patrologia Latina*, 217 vols. (Paris, 1841–64) (hereafter PL), vol. xciii, cols. 613–14; cf. Bede, *In Primam Epistolam Petri*, PL xciii, cols. 49–50, and Isidore of Seville, *Etymologiarum Sive Originum Libri XX*, W. M. Lindsay (ed.) (Oxford, Clarendon Press, 1911), VII, 2, ii.

[43] *Codex Carolinus*, no. 45, p. 561; no. 39, p. 522.

[44] See also Enright, *Iona, Tara and Soissons* (n. 13), pp. 119–23.

were probably sung when the whole court celebrated major liturgical feasts (Christmas, Easter and Pentecost), and were sometimes part of royal welcome rituals (*adventus*) when a Carolingian king and his entourage visited major churches.[45] The presence of Frankish judges and army in the *laudes'* list of invocations along with their king and princes is paralleled in royal blessings:

> O God, the inexpressible author of the world, . . . fill this king together with his army, with fruitful benediction by the intercession of St Martin . . . and fix [him] with firm stability on the throne of the kingdom . . . Make those peoples [*gentes illae*] keep their faith to his leadership, and this people [*gens iste*] [of the Franks] have peace.

Such a blessing was probably said over king and army as they set out for their annual campaign.[46] Victory could be celebrated in the newly-revived genre of verse panegyric. An early example, occasioned by the Franks' conquest of Bavaria in 787, began with an evocation of a Frankish assembly and the nobles' presenting of their annual gifts to Charlemagne:

> . . . the leading men of the world are seen to revere the king, carrying huge gifts of massive weight, an enormous load of silver and of gleaming gold, the holy ore thickly encrusted about the massed gems, the vestments gleaming with purple and gold thread, with a shining halter reining in the foaming horses whose necks arch high under trappings of barbarian gold – for these gifts are due annually to the exalted king . . . [47]

Otherwise, there is remarkably little evidence for royal ritual at the court of Charlemagne. In the design of the palace chapel at Aachen, liturgical purposes were paramount: altar not throne dominated the sacred space – indeed the throne was located, not to display the ruler (it is in fact invisible from the body of the church),

---

[45] E. H. Kantorowicz, *Laudes Regiae* (Berkeley, University of California, 1946); P. Willmes, *Der Herrscher-Adventus im Kloster des Frühmittelalters* (Munich, Wilhelm Fink Verlag, 1976), pp. 52–145. M. McCormick, 'The liturgy of war in the early Middle Ages', *Viator* xv (1984), unfortunately came to my notice too late to be taken account of in this paper.

[46] 'Deus inenarrabilis', in *Benedictional of Freising 'B'*, R. Amiet (ed.), Henry Bradshaw Society vol. lxxxviii for 1951 and 1952 (Maidstone, British Legion Press, 1974), p. 101. See also C. A. Bouman, *Sacring and Crowning* (Groningen, J. B. Wolters, 1957), pp. 99, 189–90.

[47] P. Godman, *Poetry of the Carolingian Renaissance* (London, Duckworth, 1985), pp. 174–7.

21 Charlemagne's palace chapel at Aachen, built *c.* 800.

but to give him a vantage point for viewing the liturgy.[48] Only on the great feast-days of the Church, says his biographer Einhard, did Charlemagne wear a crown of gold and precious stones: 'on other

[48] C. Heitz, *Recherches sur les rapports entre architecture et liturgie à l'époque carolingienne* (Ecole Pratique des Hautes Etudes, Paris, 1963), pp. 154–7. See further Bullough, *Age of Charlemagne*, pp. 150, 153, and Schramm, *Kaiser,*

days his dress differed hardly at all from that of ordinary people'.[49] Einhard stresses Charlemagne's preference for Frankish costume and his refusal to wear foreign clothes except, on the pope's persuasion, when in Rome. Where Einhard's model, Suetonius, described how the Roman emperor Titus 'lost no opportunity of gaining popularity by sometimes admitting the common people to his baths while he was bathing', Einhard presents a quite different magnanimity in Charlemagne:

> he would invite not only his sons to bathe with him, but his nobles and friends as well, and sometimes a crowd of members of his entourage and military household too, so that sometimes a hundred men or more would be in the water together.[50]

Einhard says little of any regalia other than the crown. Monastic authors say that Charlemagne gave away one sceptre to a favoured holy man for use as a staff, and laughed goodhumouredly at the suggestion he lend another to a bishop.[51] Even in court poetry, Charlemagne remains a convivial figure: the stress is on his cheerful kindliness more often than on majesty.[52] His court may have been influenced, as Donald Bullogh has pointed out, by the Franks' sharp reaction against the Byzantines' excessive veneration of icons.[53] The *Libri Carolini* commissioned by Charlemagne as a statement of doctrinal orthodoxy on this subject, promoted alongside puritanical aesthetics a cult of humility for rulers: Charle-

Könige und Päpste, i, pp. 209–12 (with the information that the chapel can hold 7,000 people). The original location of the stone throne now in the west gallery has been disputed: according to H. Beumann, 'Grab und Thron Karls des Grossen', in W. Braunfels (ed.), *Karl der Grosse. Lebenswerk und Nachleben*, 5 vols. (Düsseldorf, Schwann Verlag, 1965–8), iv, pp. 9–38, at 26–38, it was not the gallery but the courtyard outside the chapel. This hypothesis, as David Rollason kindly points out to me, would fit well with my general argument here; but it seems impossible to prove. In any case, the chapel was designed so that the ruler's indoor seat occupied the stone throne's present site: in front of it, a section of the original bronze ballustrade opens to give an uninterrupted view thence across to the altar of the Saviour in the east gallery and down to the altar of the Virgin Mary on the ground floor of the chapel's east side.

49 Einhard, *Vita Karoli Magni* (see n. 29), c. 23, p. 28.
50 Ibid., c. 22, p. 27. Compare Suetonius, *Life of Titus*, c. 8.
51 Chronicle of Moissac, MGH *Scriptores*, i, G. H. Pertz (ed.) (Berlin, 1826), p. 310; Notker the Stammerer, *Gesta Karoli Magni*, I, 17, p. 21.
52 See the poems of Angilbert, Alcuin, and even of Theodulf (whose panegyric is more conventional) in Godman, *Poetry of the Carolingian Renaissance*, pp. 112–21, 150–63.
53 D. Bullough, '*Imagines Regum* and their significance in the early medieval West', in *Studies in Memory of David Talbot Rice* (Edinburgh, Edinburgh University Press, 1975), pp. 223–76, at 253.

magne declared that he shared with other Christians the duty of protecting the Church, and attacked the arrogance of the emperors in the East: 'we do not co-rule with God, He rules in us'.[54]

By 800, as Einhard said, Charlemagne had so amplified the realm of the Franks by his wars that he almost doubled its size. On Christmas Day 800, he was crowned emperor by the pope at Rome and the Romans acclaimed the new 'Augustus and emperor of the Romans'. Einhard, writing some thirty years after the event, implied that Charlemagne's disavowal of 'the pope's plan' had something to do with Byzantium's hostile reaction to his 'Roman' title.[55] But strictly contemporary Frankish sources suggest that Charlemagne had been thinking in imperial terms, and developing Aachen as a residence to rival Constantinople, before 800.[56] His conception of empire might have been better expressed, not in a Roman coronation by the pope, but in a self-coronation in Francia.

In the last year of his life, Charlemagne staged a ritual at Aachen: the coronation of his sole surviving son and heir, Louis the Pious. The occasion was described in detail by Louis' biographer Thegan:

[Charlemagne summoned] the whole army, the bishops, the abbots, the leaders, the counts and their deputies. Royally clad and wearing a crown, he entered the church [i.e. the palatine chapel] where a golden crown lay on the altar. He asked everyone present from the greatest to the least if it pleased them that he should pass on his imperial title to his son. Father and son prayed for a while. Then Charlemagne addressed his son in the presence of the whole throng of bishops and magnates, admonishing him to love God, and to defend God's churches; to show mercy to his sisters and [half]-brothers and nephews and kinsmen; . . . not to throw anyone out of his office and lands without a reasonable cause; and to show himself blameless before God and the whole people. After offering these words to his son in the presence of all, the father asked him if he was willing to obey these precepts. Louis replied that he was. Then

[54] Ed. H. Bastgen, MGH *Concilia*, ii, Supp. (Hannover, 1924), pp. 2, 12.
[55] Einhard, *Vita Karoli* (see n. 29), c. 28, pp. 32–3.
[56] F. L. Ganshof, 'The imperial coronation of Charlemagne', in his *The Carolingians and the Frankish Monarchy*, trans. J. Sondheimer (London, Longman, 1971), pp. 45–6; Bullough, *Age of Charlemagne*, pp. 166–7. The so-called Paderborn Epic should be dated shortly after 800, however: see D. Schaller, 'Das Aachener Epos für Karl den Kaiser', *Frühmittelalterliche Studien*, x (1976), pp. 136–68.

the father ordered him to raise with his own hands the crown that was on the altar and to put it on his own head.[57]

The occasion of this ritual was a great Frankish assembly, and Thegan stresses the involvement of all those present, lay magnates and higher clergy alike. Their participation made Louis' acceptance of his father's precepts in effect a coronation oath as well as a manifesto. Here, surely, Charlemagne expressed his own ideal of Christian, Frankish rulership.

The reigns of Charlemagne's son and grandsons saw important developments in royal ritual. When a faction of dissident magnates rebelled against Louis the Pious in 833 and ousted him in favour of his son Lothar, Louis' deposition did not take the form of a ritualised application of sanctions by an assembly of noble Franks. The notion implicit in 813 was not taken up. Instead, Lothar's episcopal supporters applied canonical sanctions on Louis as an errant Christian: they imposed penance on him and thus rendered him incapable of bearing arms, hence of leading armies, a prime function of Frankish kingship.[58] The restoration and reconciliation that ensued in 834 and 835 saw Frankish bishops demonstrating Louis' recovery of power by crowning and investing him in imposing rituals, first in the church of St Denis, patron-saint of the dynasty, then at St Stephen's, Metz.[59] In 848, Frankish bishops, probably for the first time since the eighth century, and now without any sign of papal influence, anointed a Frankish king: Louis's son Charles the Bald. This was not a true inauguration-ritual, for Charles in 838 had been invested by his father with weapons and a crown and given a portion of the *regnum francorum*, and he had ruled the West Frankish kingdom since 840 when the Carolingian Empire was re-divided for that generation.[60] In 869, when Charles the Bald gained control of part of the neighbouring Carolingian kingdom of Middle Francia or Lotharingia (Lorraine), he was again consecrated king. (His consecrators cited Old Testa-

---

57 Thegan, *Vita Hludowici*, c. 6, MGH *Scriptores*, ii, p. 591. Note the influence of the Old Testament: 1 Par. xxviii, 2–10. See further W. Wendling, 'Die Erhebung Ludwigs d. Fr. zum Mitkaiser im Jahre 813', *Frühmittelalterliche Studien*, xix (1985), pp. 201–38.

58 Nelson, 'Kingship, law and liturgy in the political thought of Hincmar of Rheims', *English Historical Review*, xcii (1977), pp. 241–79, at 243–5.

59 *Annales Bertiniani*, s.a. 834, 835, pp. 12, 16. Compare *Annales Fuldenses*, s.a. 840, F. Kurze (ed.), MGH *Scriptores*, vii (Hannover, 1891), p. 31, for sceptre with crown as regal insignia.

60 Nelson, 'Inauguration Rituals' (see n. 7), pp. 61–2.

ment precedent for new inaugurations when kings acquired new kingdoms.[61] On all these ritual occasions, Frankish bishops were strikingly prominent. Their new role demands an explanation. Walter Ullmann is one of the few historians in recent years to have offered one.

ECCLESIASTICAL POWER AND FRANKISH SOLIDARITY

Ullmann drew a sharp distinction between the early Carolingian period when, he believed, the Frankish king, despite the origins of his power in election by the people, had been mighty enough to rule as a true 'sovereign', and the ninth century, when that sovereignty was 'gravely threatened' by 'the rapidly growing strength of the secular aristocracy'. It was because of this new threat, Ullmann argued, that Louis the Pious, and still more, Charles the Bald saw it as in their own interests not merely to ally with the ecclesiastical hierarchy against the secular magnates, but to sacrifice their 'unlimited sovereignty' for one that was 'limited or stunted' by being subordinated to ecclesiastical control.[62]

Though this may seem in Ullmann's hands a persuasive reading of some of the evidence, it fails to take account of the political and social context of Carolingian royal ritual in general, and of the longstanding, regular use of ritual at a division or handing-on of the *regnum Francorum* in particular. The one realm could contain, as we saw, more than one king, and conflict (real or threatened) between them often shaped the relations between kings and *fideles* (faithful men), that is, the Frankish aristocracy. The first Carolingian division between kings occurred in 768 when, according to Einhard, 'the Franks held a general assembly in a solemn way (*solemniter*) and set up for themselves Charlemagne and Carloman as kings'.[63] That *solemniter* surely implies some ritual procedure, presumably involving a formal election and recognition of the kings by the aristocracy. Charlemagne's seeking of consent to his son's succession to the imperial title in 813 has already been noted. In 817, when arrangements were made for the next generation, aristocratic consent was still more strongly in evidence in the

---

[61] MGH *Capitularia*, ii, no. 276, pp. 340–1. Compare *Annales Fuldenses, s.a.* 869, p. 70, for Charles' alleged imperial pretensions now.

[62] Ullmann, *The Carolingian Renaissance* (see n. 21), pp. 111–13.

[63] Einhard, *Vita Karoli* (see n. 29), c. 3, pp. 5–6. See above, p. 142.

official record, but a new feature preceded it. Louis the Pious related how

> we thought it necessary to gain from [God] by fastings and prayers and dispensing of alms what our weakness could not presume [to achieve]. Having solemnly celebrated these for three days, it came about by the grace of Almighty God, so we believe, that our choice and that of all our people [*populus*, that is, the aristocracy] concurred in the election of our beloved firstborn Lothar. Thus . . . it pleased us and all our people that he should be crowned by a solemn customary procedure with the imperial diadem and established by our common choice as our co-ruler and heir . . . [64]

The project of 817 was destined never to be realised. The last bout of conflict before an alternative plan was implemented in the division of 843 was described in detail by the Frankish historian Nithard. His evidence is especially valuable because he was a layman, and thus offers a rare direct glimpse of the perceptions of the Frankish aristocracy.[65] He recorded the texts of the solemn oaths sworn at Strasbourg in 842 by the Carolingian kings Charles the Bald and Louis the German, each to the aristocratic following of the other, that they would maintain their alliance against their elder brother Lothar until peace had been achieved; and Nithard also recorded the oaths of Charles' and Louis' 'people', in effect, that they would keep the kings to their promises.[66] Rather less well known than these rituals, and, perhaps more surprisingly, recorded by an author of allegedly 'firmly secular outlook',[67] is the sequel to Strasbourg. At Aachen in March 842, the same two kings decided to appeal to the bishops and priests 'most of whom were present' to legitimise the proposed exclusion of Lothar from any share in the inheritance of the Frankish realm. The clergy were to be consulted

> so that by their decision as if by divine power, a starting-point and an authority on these matters would be forthcoming.

The bishops and priests rehearsed Lothar's iniquities, and asked Charles and Louis if they would be willing to rule according to God's will. On receiving those assurances, the clergy declared:

---

[64] The so-called *Ordinatio Imperii*, MGH *Capitularia*, i, no. 136, pp. 270–1.

[65] Nelson, 'Public *Histories* and private history' (see n. 23).

[66] Nithard, *Histories*, III, 5, P. Lauer (ed.) (Paris, Les Classiques de l'histoire de France au Moyen Age, 1926), pp. 100–9.

[67] J. M. Wallace-Hadrill, *The Frankish Church* (Oxford, Clarendon Press, 1983), p. 238.

By divine authority, we advise, urge and enjoin you to receive the realm and rule it thus . . .[68]

Here, it seems to me, the clergy acted, not as would-be hierocrats, but as urgently-needed providers of reassurance to Frankish kings and aristocrats alike that God was with them and that peace could be restored to the fractured realm. If the means were different, the end was the same as that of the Strasburg oaths. The outlook of these laymen, as of Nithard himself, seems profoundly Christian. The clergy moved not against but with them, to restore the consensus on which all believed the well-being of the realm depended. But the initiative was lay, not clerical. The bishops may have been willing enough to respond. But their position was delicate: the fate of those bishops who had resisted Louis the Pious in 833 and been removed from office when Louis was restored in 834, may not have been far from anyone's mind.[69] Bishops, in the last resort, were more dependent on royal support than were lay magnates, and conflicts between kings faced bishops and magnates alike with excruciatingly hard choices. In 858, when Louis the German tried to take over Charles the Bald's kingdom, some of Charles' bishops wrote a long letter to the invader.[70] Where Ullmann heard in it the ringing tones of a 'mighty advance of the ecclesiological point of view', of the 'episcopal–hierocratic form of government and the reduction of royal–monarchic power',[71] it sounds to me like a mixture of bombast and acute embarrassment. In effect, the bishops would wait and see how the invader's cause fared before committing themselves; meanwhile, they said, they could not come to meet (and perhaps consecrate?) him because they were very busy with Christmas approaching. This was the authentic episcopal voice – of prudence, not heroism. It is hard to sound authoritative when you are afraid of losing your job. Paradoxically, it was the pope, with little to lose, who could afford to adopt an attitude of authority when intervening in Frankish politics.[72]

[68] Nithard, *Histories* (see n. 66), IV, 1, pp. 116–19.

[69] Archbishops Ebbo of Rheims and Agobard of Lyons: see *Annales Bertiniani, s.a.* 835, pp. 16–17; Flodoard, *Historia Remensis Ecclesiae*, c. 20, I. Heller and G. Waitz (eds.), MGH *Scriptores*, xiii (Hannover, 1881), pp. 471–2.

[70] The so-called Quierzy letter, masterminded by Hincmar: MGH *Capitularia*, ii, no. 297, pp. 427–41.

[71] *Carolingian Renaissance* (see n. 21), p. 86.

[72] Ullmann, *The Growth of Papal Government*, 2nd edn (London, Methuen, 1962), pp. 190–228.

This brief assessment of the position of the Frankish bishops permits a reappraisal of their role in royal inauguration rituals. The only contemporary chronicler to record Charles the Bald's consecration in 848 was himself a bishop: Prudentius of Troyes. This is what he says:

> At Orléans nearly all the high nobility along with the bishops and abbots elected Charles as their king and then solemnly consecrated him with an anointing of holy chrism and episcopal benediction.[73]

What is remarkable here is that the nobility are the main subject of the verbs 'elect' and 'consecrate'. Bishops and abbots merely accompany them. I would not press Prudentius' phrasing too literally: the anointing surely was performed by the bishops. Yet the impression of lay initiative, or at the least of a shared initiative, remains strong. Charles himself, referring to this ritual ten years later, depicted it as the outcome of the 'consent' of all his faithful men.[74] He meant the Frankish nobility: for though an upturn in Charles' fortunes in the rebellious subkingdom of Aquitaine had occasioned the 848 consecration, its placing, and the role of the archbishop of Sens as chief consecrator, show that this was a ritual of and for Franks.[75] As for its liturgical models, one was certainly the anointing of the bishop at his ordination, as practised by Frankish churchmen in the ninth century. The parallel was sometimes used by Hincmar of Rheims to invoke the authority of the archbishop as consecrator over the consecrated bishop or king.[76] But the post-baptismal anointing remained important too.

Frankish theologians of the ninth century interpreted it quite literally as a confirmation – a strengthening. Traditionally it had been linked to the preaching of the faith against the heathen. Charles the Bald's bishops insisted that the Franks needed the Holy Spirit of counsel and strength 'which we have received in the

---

73 *Annales Bertiniani, s.a.* 848, p. 55. For Prudentius' authorship here, see Nelson, 'The annals of St Bertin', in M. Gibson and J. Nelson (eds.), *Charles the Bald: Court and Kingdom* (Oxford, British Archaeological Reports, International Series ci, 1981), pp. 15–36.

74 *Libellus Proclamationis Adversus Wenilonem*, MGH *Capitularia*, ii, no. 300, p. 451.

75 That is, not just involving the kingdom of Aquitaine, as often inferred from Prudentius' account (for instance by Nelson, 'Inauguration rituals' (see n. 7), p. 61.)

76 A. Santantoni, *L'ordinazione episcopale* (Rome, Editrice Anselmiana, 1976), pp. 163–76. Cf. above, p. 152.

laying-on of the bishop's hand at confirmation' in order to 'stand manfully against our enemies and overcome them boldly'. The Franks' military failure was imputed to sin which had driven away the Holy Spirit from them. That same Spirit, summoned back through penitence, would bring victory.[77] Like the eighth-century popes, Hincmar of Rheims affirmed that all Christians became a 'royal race and a royal priesthood' through their post-baptismal anointing, and hence kings were obliged, like everyone else, to keep the laws they themselves had subscribed. Though the king might receive a further, royal, anointing, and give as a condition of that anointing a specific undertaking to keep the law, his obligation before God was not essentially different from that of other Christians.[78]

Hincmar of Rheims designed and stage-managed the consecration of Charles the Bald at Metz in 869. On this occasion there was a clear reference to a Rheims tradition and Rheims interest in Hincmar's claim to be using chrism – 'of which we still have some' – brought from heaven by a dove for a post-baptismal anointing of Clovis (the first Catholic king of the Franks) which in that case, according to Hincmar, doubled as a royal consecration.[79] The reappearance of the theme of post-baptismal anointing in this context is significant. The reality of the situation in 869 was that a substantial number of the Frankish aristocracy of Lotharingia had chosen to accept Charles as Lother II's 'legitimate heir', and had already expressed that recognition. Before consecrating Charles, Hincmar had him give an undertaking to the 'faithful people, to each in his rank' that he would keep for each his law and justice. Then Hincmar recalled the conversion of not just Clovis but the *integra gens Francorum*, 'three thousand of whom, not counting children and women, were baptised' along with their king. Hinc-

[77] *Capitulary of Pîtres*, 862, c. 1, MGH *Capitularia*, ii, no. 272, pp. 303–4.

[78] Hincmar, *De Divortio*, PL cxxv, col. 700. See Nelson, 'Kingship, law and liturgy' (see n. 58), pp. 270–1.

[79] *Electionis Karoli Capitula in Regno Hlotharii Facta*, MGH *Capitularia*, ii, no. 276, p. 340. Compare Hincmar's *Life of St Remigius*, cc. 14, 15, B. Krusch (ed.), MGH *Scriptores Rerum Merovingicarum*, iii (Hannover, 1896), pp. 296–300. For the events of 869, see W. Schlesinger, 'Zur Erhebung Karls des Kahlen zum König von Lothringen', in *Festschrift für F. Petri* (Bonn, L. Röhrscheid Verlag, 1970), pp. 454–75, at 465–71; and, for the rituals as 'a kind of ruler-presentation', N. Staubach, 'Das Herrscherbild Karls des Kahlen. Formen und Funktionen monarchischer Repräsentation im früherer Mittelalter' (unpublished dissertation, Westfalische Wilhelms-Universität, Münster, 1982), pp. 239–71, at 259.

mar's audience at Metz consisted of descendants of those Franks. Some of them could recall the ritual restoration to rulership of Charles' father Louis the Pious, crowned 'with the crown of the realm', 'by the acclamation of the faithful people' in that very same church at Metz 34 years before. Hincmar aptly concluded his speech with a request to the assembled company: 'if it pleases you that Charles should now be crowned and consecrated, say so together with your own voices'. When all had shouted their agreement, all together (*unanimiter*) sang the traditional praise-song of the Christian people, *Te Deum laudamus*. Then, and only then, did Hincmar and his episcopal colleagues proceed to anoint Charles and invest him with crown and sceptre, praying that the king receive also a heavenly crown and that clergy and people, after enjoying peace on earth under his government, would join with him the ranks of the citizens of heaven.[80] Hincmar did not fail to stress, in this liturgical context, the clergy's mediatory function. It was their job (*ministerium*) to consecrate and bless. They had been constituted, after all, as Hincmar said at another royal consecration, 'to pray first for their own sins, then for the sins of the people'.[81] But I find no suggestion here of priestly mediation as an alternative to popular election, or of the king as being less bound to his people because he was divinely-chosen and episcopally-enrolled in God's service. The people, the 'faithful people', that is, the Frankish aristocracy, were also thus enrolled. When Charles' son used the title, 'Louis, constituted king by the grace of God and by the election of the people',[82] he did not perceive (as Ullmann perceived) 'two irreconcilables':[83] he heard *vox populi* and *vox dei* as perfectly consonant, and the rituals, inside and outside the church, through which he was inaugurated to kingship, expressed unanimity, not division. His consecrator, again Hincmar of Rheims, though personally so much involved in the 'liturgification' of king-making ritual in his own part of the Carolingian world, continued both in theory and in practice to treat the older, extra-ecclesiastical forms as perfectly valid.[84]

80 *Ordo Coronationis*, MGH *Capitularia*, ii, no. 302, pp. 456–7.
81 *Coronatio Hermentrudis Reginae*, ibid., no 301, p. 454.
82 *Annales Bertiniani*, s.a. 877, p. 221. For Hincmar's authorship of these annals from 861 to 882, see Nelson, 'Annals of St Bertin' (see n. 73), pp. 24–8.
83 *Carolingian Renaissance* (see n. 21), p. 96.
84 *De Divortio*, PL cxxv, col. 758. Compare *Annales Bertiniani s.a.* 873, p. 190 (apropos the supporters of Charles the Bald's rebellious son Carloman).

In the last two years of his life, thanks to a well-timed bid for the inheritance of his nephew Louis II of Italy, Charles the Bald had the title of emperor. As such he experimented with the imperial costume of the 'Greeks', and also, perhaps, with the liturgies of eastern churches.[85] But it would be false to infer that this meant any abandonment of a traditional style of Frankish kingship in favour of Byzantine autocracy. The realities of Carolingian politics continued to demand a working partnership between king and aristocracy. As it happens, our best evidence for this comes from the last few months of Charles' life. It is the record of a dialogue that took place between Charles and his faithful men at the assembly of Quierzy in June 877, whence the king would depart for Italy on the journey from which he never returned. At Quierzy, as at Carolingian assemblies generally, the keynote was *familiaritas*: the term carried the double connotation of good-fellowship and patrimonial authority over a household (*familia*) that expanded at assembly-time to include the political realm.[86] Charles demanded of his faithful men:

> How can we be sure that when we get back [from Italy] our kingdom will not have been disturbed by anyone?

And the response came:

> As far as that's concerned, ... our answer is that there are the oaths we made to you, and the profession that all of us, clerics and laymen, gave you at Quierzy [in 858] ... We have kept these up till now, and we intend to go on keeping them. You can certainly believe we are telling the truth about that.[87]

This exchange may have been termed frank and familiar; but it was also carefully structured. Assembly proceedings generally may well have been modelled by clerical masters of ceremonies on the procedure followed at ecclesiastical synods. Such formalities shaded easily into ritual, as at Ponthion in 876 when at the final session of a long assembly Charles appeared 'clad in the Greek fashion and wearing his crown ... with the empress beside him also

---

85 *Annales Fuldenses, s.a.* 876, p. 86; Wallace-Hadrill, 'A Carolingian Renaissance prince: the Emperor Charles the Bald', *Proceedings of the British Academy*, lxiv (1978), pp. 155–84, at 165.

86 Nelson, 'Legislation and consensus in the reign of Charles the Bald', in P. Wormald (ed.), *Ideal and Reality. Studies in Frankish and Anglo-Saxon History presented to J. M. Wallace-Hadrill* (Oxford, Blackwell, 1983), pp. 202–27.

87 Capitulary of Quierzy (877), MGH *Capitularia*, ii, no. 281, pp. 356–7.

wearing a crown, and *laudes* were sung to them'.[88] The *laudes*, we recall, celebrated the Franks along with their rulers.

THE RITUALS OF THE COURT: PROCESSIONS, HUNTS AND FEASTS

Much of the foregoing discussion has centred on royal consecration rites, because that is where plentiful material can easily be found. My contention has been that this primarily liturgical evidence has been misinterpreted by some previous commentators. It is time to set my own interpretation against other forms of royal ritual in the ninth century. Here the evidence, coming from a variety of non-liturgical sources, deals with events whose ritual aspect has tended to be neglected.

For example, the assembly that was a Frankish institution was also a Frankish occasion: the theatre of 'ritually political' acts.[89] These acts included the presentation of the annual gifts, a major royal resource, to the king by his faithful men, both lay and ecclesiastical.[90] Unfortunately no full description has survived of the handing-over of these gifts: did the king sit on his throne, or wear his crown? Did he offer in exchange a small symbolic counter-gift, perhaps a ring? But three further ritual acts belong with assemblies. Firstly, the joining-in by all participants in rites of Christian worship. Secondly, the giving of a feast (or feasts) by the king. Thirdly, the hunt on which the king and his entourage went when the assembly had been disbanded. Hints of all these are provided by the chronicle sources. But it is thanks to a court poet, Ermold the Black, that we have some details. In a verse-epistle to King Pippin I of Aquitaine, Ermold describes the celebration of Easter by the court at Angeac:

> You hear the hum of various activities.
> Each in his rank hastens to obey the royal orders.
> One man runs, another stays where he is; one comes,
> another goes.

[88] *Annales Bertiniani*, *s.a.* 876, p. 205.
[89] I have borrowed the phrase, and much inspiration, from T. N. Bisson, 'Celebration and persuasion: reflections on the cultural evolution of medieval consultation', *Legislative Studies Quarterly*, vii (1982), pp. 181–204.
[90] As shown by T. Reuter in 'Plunder and tribute in the Carolingian Empire', *Transactions of the Royal Historical Society*, 5th series, xxx (1985), pp. 75–94, at 85–6.

The magnates wait: the king appears over the
threshold
And zealously goes to attend divine office.
Here the clergy advances, first senior men, then
younger ones
And with them a crowd of boys exulting.
Preceded by the older men, followed by a troop of
young men,
In the midst of great officers of state, O revered king,
you come!
. . .
As the sun illuminates the whole earth with his rays
And with his warmth puts all clouds to flight,
Signalling joy to trees, crops and sailors,
Just so does the king in his coming bring joy to his
people.[91]

In his panegyric biographical poem dedicated to Louis the Pious,
Ermold portrays the reception of the Danish prince Heriold for his
baptism in the palace-chapel at Ingelheim. First there is a detailed
description of the paintings that decorate the walls of church and
palace, showing

. . . the wondrous deeds of God and generations of
famous men.

The famous men include previous Carolingian kings, who had
linked to Rome's greatness

. . . the Franks and their marvellous achievements.[92]
Here Heriold and his family arrive and are baptised: Louis is
Heriold's godfather, Louis' wife the godmother of Heriold's wife,
Louis' son the godfather of Heriold's son, and the Frankish
magnates become the godfathers of Heriold's men. All return to
the palace where Louis loads his godson with gifts: clothing, jewels,
a sword and a crown. All proceed to mass: first Louis, clad in gold,
flanked by court clergy, and followed by his son with Heriold, the

---

[91] Ermold, *Epitres au roi Pépin*, I, lines 18–32, ed. E. Faral (Paris, Les classiques de
l'histoire de France au Moyen Age, 1932), pp. 204–5.
[92] Ermold, *Poème sur Louis le Pieux*, IV, lines 2068–2163, pp. 158–65. See
Godman, *Poetry* (see n. 47), pp. 250–5.

queen and attendant magnates. Meanwhile a great feast has been prepared. Louis takes his seat; the queen kisses his knees. All enjoy

> that day that was justly happy for Franks and for
> Danes reborn.[93]

Next day follows the hunt. Again Ermold lists the leading participants and adds that 'a crowd of magnates' attended the queen 'in honour of the pious king'. The hunt's success is celebrated on the spot by a *fête champêtre* organised by the queen. Quantities of venison and wine are consumed. Then all return to the palace-chapel where they attend the evening service 'worthily and reverently'. Later, in the palace Louis distributes the 'rewards of the chase': meat, skins, furs

> ... and a large share also fell to the clergy.

Louis presents Heriold, 'according to the ancient Frankish custom' with a horse and weapons, priests and holy books, sacred vessels and vestments:

> The quantity and quality of these gifts
> Surpass the imagination and excel my verse.[94]

This is panegryic, not reportage. Ermold was influenced by classical poetry and perhaps, too, by the contemporary imperial model of the Byzantine court; he was certainly anxious to show that the Franks now surpassed the Greeks in glory.[95] But his choice of themes was not haphazard. These were the rituals of patrimonial kingship, centring on the royal family and the palace, assimilating client-princes, noble Franks and clergy into an enlarged household.

---

[93] Ermold, *Poème*, IV, lines 2168–2361, pp. 166–81. See also Angenendt, *Kaiserherrschaft und Königstaufe* (n. 39), pp. 215–23.

[94] Ermold, *Poème*, IV, lines 2362–2503, pp. 180–91.

[95] For *imitatio imperii* in Ermold, see Nelson, 'Kingship and Empire' (n. 2, forthcoming). Similar Byzantine and late classical literary models may lie behind Ermold's references to the queen and various magnates kissing the ruler's knees or feet: *Poème*, I, 11.173, 213, 582; IV, line 2355. Compare Constantine Porphyrogenitos, *Book of Ceremonies*, II, 47, A. Vogt (ed.), 2 vols. (Paris, Société d'Edition 'Les Belles Lettres', 1935–40), ii, p. 2. There is no other evidence that this was Frankish practice (though another poet describes the defeated duke Tassilo of Bavaria kissing the knees of Charlemagne: MGH *Poetae*, i, p. 399).

The hunt was especially significant.[96] It is hardly a coincidence that the ninth-century royal annals so often mention the royal hunt following assemblies where major political crises were resolved.[97] For the hunt was an exercise in, and a demonstration of, the virtues of collaboration. The aristocracy who hunted with the king shared his favour, his sport, his military training and his largesse, and helped at the same time to provision the palace, their *magna domus*.[98] Because it also served these other vital purposes, the hunt could offer king and faithful men alike vivid experiences of collective action and reward: an apt corollary to and continuation of political and military co-operation. The author of the Life of St Trond, writing shortly before 800, described how the saint as a young man at the royal court, 'having been born into a most noble family' was urged 'as was the custom for the young men of the royal retinue, to practise together with them the rite of hunting [*ritus venandi*]'.[99] The hunt as ritual, like the processions and feasts, manifested participation as well as hierarchy, reciprocity as well as patriarchal authority. Nor were the clergy excluded: even if they obeyed the canons and did not join in the hunt itself[100] they celebrated its returns. And, as Ermold shows, liturgical and other forms of ritual were intimately interwoven. As with the procedures of king-making, these rituals were designed to incorporate, not exclude. Kingship, the clerical and lay orders, and hierarchies of ranks within those orders, all existed within the one Frankish realm.

Notker the Stammerer, writing two generations after Ermold,

---

96 J. Verdon, 'Recherches sur la chasse en Occident', *Revue Belge de philologie et d'histoire*, lvi (1978), pp. 805–29; R. Hennebicque, 'Espaces sauvages et chasses royales dans le Nord de la France', *Revue du Nord*, lxii (1980), pp. 35–57. Einhard, *Vita Karoli* (n. 29), c. 22, p. 27, notes the Franks' particular keenness on hunting.

97 E.g. *Annales Regni Francorum, s.a.* 817, p. 146; 822, p. 159; 829, p. 177; *Annales Bertiniani, s.a.* 835, p. 18; 838, p. 25; 839, p. 34; 869, p. 164; 870, p. 175; 873, p. 195. I am grateful to Stuart Airlie for drawing my attention to this point.

98 Thus called by the Frankish noblewoman Dhuoda, *Manuel pour mon fils*, III, 9, Riché (ed.), (Paris, Sources chrétiennes, 1975), p. 170. For the personal aspect of Carolingian rule, see J. Fried, 'Der Karolingische Herrschaftsverband im 9 Jh. zwischen Kirche und Königshaus', *Historische Zeitschrift*, ccxxxv (1982), pp. 1–43.

99 *Vita Trudonis*, c. 4, MGH *Scriptores Rerum Merovingicarum* vi, p. 278. Trond's refusal to join the hunt caused the other youths to despise him 'and to rate him as acting beneath his birth' (*quasi degenerem*).

100 F. Prinz, *Klerus und Krieg im früheren Mittelalter* (Stuttgart, Anton Hiersemann, 1971), pp. 23–6, 83–4.

22 The king arriving, being anointed and sitting in judgement. Frontispiece to Book
of Proverbs. See 1 Kings i.33, 38, 39–40; iii.16–28 for the Solomon stories.

again used the hunt and the dining-hall as settings for models of
rulership. Charlemagne urged his retinue to join him in the hunt:
'We must not become lazy or sluggish. We can all set out in the
clothes we're wearing!' The king in his simple sheepskin had the
laugh on the courtiers in their silken garments, which shrank and

became tattered. Meals at Charlemagne's court presented ordered hierarchy: the humblest ate last. But all ate temperately.[101] These scenes were offset by those in which Notker contrasts oriental attitudes: the ludicrous taboos that governed table-manners at the Byzantine court, and the Persian envoys' terror at the Frankish hunt.[102] Greek envoys, arrived at Aachen, found it hard to pick out Charlemagne, for instead of being raised aloft in isolated splendour, his glory was diffused among his court:

> Around him like the host of heaven stood his sons, daughters, wife, bishops and abbots, leading men and military household.[103]

Though these descriptions of the Carolingian court were produced by ecclesiastical literati for royal patrons, they may have had a wider audience among the Frankish élite. This can certainly be claimed of another work, Nithard's *Histories*; and an episode described by Nithard supplies a further dimension to our sketch of court ritual. Nithard's story is set in Francia on Easter Eve, 841, and he wrote it up six months later for men amongst whom some, at least, had witnessed the event. Just when Charles the Bald, after months of desultory conflict, seemed likely to lose both his share of the *regnum* and his life, messengers arrived in his camp from his former base, Aquitaine

> carrying a crown and all his royal gear. Who can fail to be amazed that so few men . . . were able to carry such a quantity of gold and jewels so far without coming to any harm? . . . It seemed as though this could only have happened by God's grace and with his approval. And through this [Charles] inspired wonder in all who fought along with him and encouraged them all to a confident hope that things would go well for them. And Charles and the whole joyful company applied themselves to the celebration of Easter.[104]

The story suggests the powerful reaction that royal symbols, especially the crown, could produce in Frankish observers. Nithard implies that they recognised in the arrival of the regalia a manifestation of divine approval for Charles' kingship. The sense of

---

[101] Notker, *Gesta Karoli Magni*, II, 17, pp. 86–7; I, 12, p. 16.
[102] Ibid., II, 6, pp. 54–5; II, 8, p. 60.
[103] Ibid., II, 6, p. 57.
[104] Nithard, *Histories* (see n. 66), II, 8, pp. 60–2. See also Nelson, 'Public *Histories* and private history' (n. 23), pp. 261–2.

solidarity thus evoked between them and their king was continued in their collective celebration of the Easter liturgy. This brief glimpse of royal ritual at work strengthens the impression that the literary sources' picture is not so far from reality.

MONASTERIES

The image of Carolingian kingship I have been sketching in this paper may seem an unfamiliar one. We are used to visualising the king not, as it were, in the perspective of community, but elevated in majesty. Why is this the familiar image? The answer lies in the ruler-iconography of the Carolingian Renaissance: the face that launches a thousand textbooks on medieval history is the strong, heavy-jowled, majestic face of a Carolingian king, crowned, enthroned, grasping his sceptre, touched by a symbol of the Holy Spirit from above, apparently gazing out into space or over his subjects below.[105] This serene image is much better known to us than it can ever have been to most of the Carolingians' contemporaries. For it is to be found not in monumental or public art, but only in the private art of illuminated liturgical manuscripts: in books made in, and largely for, monastic communities patronised by Carolingian kings.[106] We should be chary of inferring too much from this art about Carolingian ideology; still more chary of arguing from the image to the reality of royal insignia. We may doubt if Charles the Bald's throne was actually like the pictures of Solomon's, or if there ever was such a thing as a Carolingian orb.[107]

Yet the monasteries have their place in a survey of Carolingian royal ritual. The cults of the saints, especially monastic saints, played a central role in ninth-century religion: the translations of relics were, at least according to the monks who wrote them up, occasions for great demonstrations of popular devotion. It is therefore significant that Charles the Bald can be found present on

---

[105] Examples in Schramm, *Die deutsche Kaiser und Könige in Bildern ihrer Zeit*, rev. ed. F. Mütherich (Munich, Prestel, 1983). But see also R. Deshman, 'The exalted servant: the ruler theology of the prayer-book of Charles the Bald', *Viator*, xi (1980), pp. 385–417.

[106] Bullough, '*Imagines Regum*'; J. Wollasch, 'Kaiser und Könige als Brüder der Mönche. Zum Herrschbild im liturgischen Handschriften des 9. bis 11. Jhdts.', *Deutsches Archiv*, xl (1984), pp. 1–20.

[107] Schramm, *Kaiser, Könige und Päpste* (see n. 105), ii, pp. 109, 133.

several such occasions: as a nine-year old child witnessing the translation of the Merovingian saint-queen Balthild at Chelles, where his grandmother was abbess; as king when he attended at Hautvillers, near Rheims, an ordeal administered to the recently-acquired bones of Constantine's mother Saint Helena to test their authenticity (they passed muster); most remarkably, as a refugee during his brother's attempted invasion of his realm, when Charles found support with the community of St Germain at Auxerre, and having personally helped carry the saint's relics to a new resting-place, found his fortunes rapidly revived.[108] Such rituals offered rare opportunities for the king's piety to be made visible to a mass public outside the aristocratic milieu of palace or assembly.[109]

The great Benedictine monasteries occupied an integral position in the Carolingian regime, especially in what became, after 840, the West Frankish kingdom. Charles the Bald patronised and exploited these communities. His itinerary included many stays at such favoured houses as St Germain, Auxerre, or St Martin, Tours.[110] His reign saw a striking increase in the number of royal anniversaries commemorated liturgically, by prayers and masses, in major royal monasteries and also some cathedrals. These celebrations included ritual dinners for which the produce of specially-granted estates was earmarked.[111] Previous Carolingians arranged for one or two such commemorations. Charles the Bald instituted feasts in honour of his father and mother, grandfather and grandmother, the anniversaries of his two marriages and of his wives' births and deaths, for his sons and other close kin, and, last but not least, for

---

[108] *Translatio Balthildis*, MGH *Scriptores*, xv, pp. 284–5; *Acta Sanctorum*, J. Bolland *et al.* (eds.), 70 vols. (Venice, 1734), August iii, col. 603; *Gesta Episcoporum Autissiodorensium*, MGH *Scriptores*, xiii, pp. 403–4.

[109] Peasants did sometimes see the king in his palace: see Nelson, 'Dispute-settlement in the West Frankish kingdom', in W. Davies and P. J. Fouracre (eds.), *The Settlement of Disputes in Early Medieval Europe* (Cambridge University Press, 1986).

[110] Nelson, 'Charles the Bald and the Church in Town and Countryside', *Studies in Church History*, xvi (1979), pp. 103–18; J.-P. Devroey, 'Un monastère dans l'économie d'échanges', *Annales*, xxxix (1984), pp. 570–89, at 581–5. Compare Willmes, *Herrscher-Adventus*, pp. 75–115, esp. 83–4.

[111] For what follows, see M. Rouche, 'Les Repas de fête a l'époque carolingienne', in D. Menjot (ed.), *Manger et boire au Moyen Age*, Actes du Colloque de Nice (15–17 octobre 1982), 1: Aliments et Société (Nice, Les Belles Lettres, 1984), pp. 265–96. Against the criticisms of J.-C. Hocquet, 'Le Pain, le vin et la juste mesure', *Annales*, xl (1985), pp. 661–86, Rouche defends his methodology, ibid., pp. 687–8.

his own birth and his royal consecration on 6 June 848.[112] The geographical distribution of these commemorations coincides with the areas of the Frankish heartlands where royal estates were concentrated and the imposition of a manorial economy permitted the most intensive exploitation of peasant surpluses. Pre-eminent among the great monastic centres of royal cult was St Denis, favoured as a mausoleum by the Carolingians as by their predecessors, recipient of gifts of crowns from Charles the Bald – perhaps even used as a storehouse for his regalia.[113] To this community of some 200 monks Charles gave a charter in 862 assigning estates to provide for certain feasts and specifying the quantities of food to be consumed by each participant on each such occasion. The interpretation of such data is a risky business; but M. Rouche hazards the following guess at calories consumed per head at one of St Denis' major commemorations:[114]

bread	wine	poultry	eggs	cheese	vegetables	lard	TOTAL
4272	2015	1125	280	270	1009	256	9227

However impressionistic, such figures represent a remarkable quantification of the cost of ritual, and of the augmentation of royal resources that made possible such lavish consumption. As important is a qualitative appreciation of the piety that impelled the king to deploy resources in this way. This was a piety that involved generosity of the powerful towards the powerless – that is, towards the monks, their dependants and the poor, a number of whom participated in at least some of the commemorative feasts.[115] It was also a piety of devotion to ancestors and kin. In both respects, royalty embodied the values of Frankish society at large: Frankish aristocrats as well as kings founded family monasteries or patronised royal ones to secure commemoration of themselves and their kin, while less well-endowed Franks joined 'what they call in the vulgar, guilds or confraternities' to celebrate with *pastus et potationes* the funerals and anniversaries of their

---

[112] Rouche, 'Les Repas' (see n. 111), p. 268 and n. 26 makes a slip in dating Charles' consecration to 841: following Nithard's editor, P. Lauer (n. 66), p. 63, no. 1, he mistakes the story of the regalia, above, p. 171, for evidence of a coronation.

[113] Schramm, *Der König von Frankriech*, 2nd edn (2 vols., Weimar, Hermann Bohlaus Nachfolger, 1960), i, p. 132.

[114] Rouche, 'Les Repas', (see n. 111), p. 277.

[115] Ibid., p. 267.

dead.[116] Kings could distribute more largesse and perhaps commemorate more, and more distant, ancestors and kin than anyone else. But all such commemorations presupposed belief in 'une alchimie gastrique pieuse'[117] which transformed the bodily well-being of the living into the welfare of the souls of the dead. In the case of royalty's commemorations, as of feasts presided over by the king in person, there was a further transference between what later medieval theorists would term the king's two bodies: between the individual king or his family, and the body politic. In feasting for the king, the church feasted for the victory of the king's army and the good of the whole realm. The monk's full stomach was a form of prayer. Because laymen believed this, they provided for monastic tables. They understood, and no doubt respected, the lavish scale of the king's provision. And the king's special saintly patrons – Denis, Martin, Germain – were also the mightiest patrons of the Frankish people. If the monks' ritual services provided psychological ballast for the king, they also reassured the Franks. Through the cult of the saints, the king reached out to protect the realm.

CONCLUSIONS

'Politics isn't only a matter of parties, . . . campaigns, programmes . . . It's embedded in the depths of everyone, in their guts, as some say, or according to others, in their soul: anyway, in something far beyond all philosophies.'[118] Carolingian royal ritual, certainly, was an affair of the guts and of the soul. And it was political. If any conclusion can be drawn from this brief survey, it is that the nature of Carolingian politics, as reflected in such ritual, did not change fundamentally as between the eighth and ninth centuries. The rituals of Louis the Pious and Charles the Bald are more elaborate (and not just better documented) than those of Pippin and Charlemagne. But they convey the same perceptions of the nature of royal power and of political relationships. They express and at the same time reinforce that power and those relationships. The king ruled because God had chosen him to lead the New Israel. But the Franks

[116] Nelson, 'Les femmes et l'évangélisation', *Revue du Nord* 68 (1986), pp. 471–83, at 477–9; Hincmar, *Capitula presbyteris data*, c. 16, PL cxxv, cols. 777–8.

[117] Rouche, 'Les Repas' (see n. 111), p. 276.

[118] P.-J. Hélias, *Le Cheval d'orgueil. Mémoires d'un Breton du pays bigouden* (Paris, 1975), p. 515, quoted by Bisson, 'Celebration and persuasion' (see n. 89), p. 181. (The translation is mine.)

as the New Israel were also a chosen people. Just as Carolingian law-making was the business of 'the king, the bishops and all the noble Franks',[119] so royal ritual involved the Frankish church, the Frankish aristocracy, and, by extension, all the members of the Frankish gens that believed itself noble by definition. That bond had been forged through the creation of a Frankish empire, hence Frankish imperial kingship over many peoples. In the 820s, it was not inconceivable (though it was impracticable) that all those peoples might be united under – or subjected to – one Frankish, Christian law: a law that ennobled.[120] When some Saxons, subject-people, objected to the Franks' imposition of the practice of placing their boys as child-oblates in Frankish-dominated monasteries (a mode of forcible acculturation that other Christian empire-builders were to impose in later centuries), a leading Frankish churchman replied:

> Who does not know that the Franks came before the Saxons in the Faith and religion of Christ, and subjected them with arms to their domination, and thus becoming their superiors, drew them away from the cult of idols by the rite of masters (*ritus domino-rum*), or rather, by fatherly love converted them to the Christian faith.[121]

Carolingian royal ritual was Frankish royal ritual. In the 820s it remained, as it had been in the eighth century, part of a *ritus dominorum*.

The division of the Carolingian Empire after 840, which has seemed to modern historians inevitable, or at least irreversible, did not seem so in the ninth century: then, men spoke not of 'West' or 'East' Franks but, still, simply of Franks. Only with hindsight can we think of Charles the Bald as laying the foundations of the West Frankish kingdom, even as the first king of France.[122] Charles, like his ancestors, was an imperialist. But rather than dominating subject peoples, his eye was on acquiring, or inheriting, other Carolingians' realms: the Middle Kingdom; Italy. This made it just

---

119 Nelson, 'Legislation and consensus' (see n. 86), pp. 221–2.
120 Agobard of Lyons, *Adversus Legem Gundobadi*, MGH *Epistolae*, v, pp. 158–9.
121 Hrabanus Maurus, *Liber de Oblatione Puerorum*, PL cvii, col. 432; compare R. C. Trexler, 'From the mouth of babes. Christianization by children in 16th century New Spain', in J. Davis (ed.), *Religious Organization and Religious Experience*, Association of Social Anthropologists, Monograph 21 (London, Academic Press, 1982), pp. 115–35.
122 K. F. Werner, *Les Origines*, Histoire de France, vol. i, (Paris, Fayard, 1984), p. 417.

as necessary for him as it had been for Pippin and Charlemagne and Louis the Pious to play on sentiments of Frankish unity among élites whose members could still identify themselves as descendants of Frankish conquerors; hence, in 869, Hincmar's evocation of Clovis' followers – the *integra gens fracorum*. But the notion of the gens, part anchored in customary law, part free-floating myth, was flexible: it could expand, one gens absorbing others; or it could be accommodated in the narrower bounds of territorial kingdom.[123] In the course of Charles the Bald's long reign, frequent assemblies with their collective informal and formal decision-making, regular gift-givings, oath-takings, feasts and hunts, fostered what Susan Reynolds suggests we term 'regnal unity'.[124] The aristocracy of Charles' kingdom, Franks and non-Franks alike, were learning to think of themselves as one: Charles' men.[125] When Charles died, he left instructions for his realm to be transferred to his sole surviving son, who promised, before his consecration, 'to keep the laws and statutes for the people [*populus*] committed to me by God's grace to rule'.[126] If the coronation oath presupposed a distinction between individual king and royal office, it also presupposed a collectivity: the people of the realm.

Karl Leyser has recently made some very useful suggestions as to 'the function of the numinous face of kingship' in the tenth-century Saxon Reich that was one of the successor-states to the Carolingian Empire. The 'numinous face' helped cope with two of the Saxon kings' 'predicaments': first by marking off the king from his kin, it inhibited the rivalry of royal brothers and nephews excluded from kingship by a succession-system that maintained the indivisibility of the realm. Second, it justified royal control and exploitation of the church within the realm.[127] Neither of these 'predicaments', however, was unique to the Saxon kings. In fact the situation of the Carolingians had not been very different: the realm of the Franks was partible only to a limited extent, and hence the Carolingians too had faced the problem of disappointed brothers and nephews. Further, in their control of the church, the Saxon kings were the

---

[123] S. Reynolds, *Kingdoms and Communities* (see n. 28), pp. 254–9.
[124] Ibid., p. 254.
[125] B. Schneidmüller, *Karolingische Tradition und frühes französisches Königtum* (Wiesbaden, Steiner, 1979), pp. 101–3.
[126] *Annales Bertiniani, s.a.*, pp. 218, 221.
[127] K. F. Leyser, *Rule and Conflict in an Early Medieval Society* (London, Edward Arnold, 1979), pp. 82, 105–6.

direct heirs of the Carolingians. Yet Leyser points out that the Saxon kings, heirs though they were to Carolingian kingship, 'came to practise its rites more often and more methodically' than the Carolingians ever had.[128] The contrast is worth exploring further.

Here, two other suggestions of Leyser's in the Saxon context may be helpful. First, he argues, the endemic conflict within and between noble kindreds in Saxony produced a demand for an acknowledged arbiter who could impose settlements: 'regalis postestas [royal power] had to be hallowed because it was so desperately needed'. What Leyser (though 'not without misgivings') calls 'royal sacrality' allowed nobles 'to lose less face if they rebelled unsuccessfully'. Sacral kingship 'could not prevent risings, but it could help to restore a measure of harmony afterwards and make reconciliations . . . easier for the losers . . . It offered a higher and more objective kind of restraint to which all sides could bow'. Leyser's second suggestion is that the Saxon kings, of whom so much was demanded, lacked effective means to govern other than by their personal intervention: 'sacrality was a substitute for inadequate or failing institutions'. The Saxon kings' itineracy, imposed on them in any case by the economic backwardness of their realm and by the consequent lack of fiscal organisation, was thus also 'the most important and reliable means of communication' between the kings and the nobles who held power in the localities. The journeying itself became a 'sacral procession', the buildings on its route theatres 'to display the celestial drama of royalty'. 'The allimportance of the king's coming' highlighted the absence of any alternative to his personal intervention if his voice was to be heard in provincial affairs.[129]

On both these scores, the Carolingians, especially in the ninth-century West Frankish kingdom, present striking differences from the picture Leyser paints of Saxon kingship. The Carolingians operated from at least semi-permanent residences: Aachen, Quierzy, Compiègne. Institutions sustained their regime: they legislated; they kept archives; they taxed; they appointed agents to act for them in local courts and took steps to make those agents accountable; they summoned their leading men to attend assemblies at their palaces rather than visiting the provinces in person. They had, in short, the apparatus of government that the Saxon

---

[128] Ibid., pp. 95, 106.   [129] Ibid., pp. 90, 103–5.

kings lacked.[130] Further, though nobles sometimes rebelled, their rebellions were almost always channelled into the Carolingians' own intra-familial conflicts, rivalries between royal brothers and uncles and nephews attracting aristocratic support. Even in the reigns of Charlemagne's successors, where conflict between king and aristocracy has stolen the historiographical limelight, the humdrum everyday reality was of co-operation and collective decision-making through which tensions were, if not resolved, then made bearable. Rivalries between noble families were still brought to the court and not just fought out in the regions.[131] The centre held.

After all, the Franks, as pointed out earlier in this chapter, had been co-beneficiaries of the Carolingians' success. But this was not true of the Saxon Reich. Leyser lays great stress on the fact that the Saxon kings, because of the strength of the leading families in the gentes they ruled, had been unable to 'implant their Saxon nobles massively and systematically [outside Saxony] . . . nor could Saxon nobles monopolise all the best places in the royal entourage'. By contrast, Leyser points out, 'the creation of a nobility with lands and positions in many parts of the Frankish Empire [had been] an indispensable part of Carolingian political strategy. Its existence gave substance to the idea of the Franks as a dominant people, even if the ruling strata at Charlemagne's and Louis the Pious's courts were increasingly heterogeneous . . . '[132] It is possible to exaggerate the usefulness of the Carolingians' 'political strategy' beyond the eighth century: the export of Frankish nobles was a trick that could only be taken once even if it brought some residual benefit to Charlemagne's successors. But Leyser is surely right to contrast the Saxon kings' insecurity with the relative security of the Carolingians. And his association of the Saxon kings' political weakness with their high ritual profile is equally convincing.

In this chapter, I have argued that the Carolingians' ritual profile was relatively low. I do not think that the explanation of the contrast between them and Leyser's Saxon kings lies only in the

---

130 Werner, 'Missus-marchio-comes. Entre l'administration centrale et l'administration locale de l'empire carolingien', in W. Paravicini and K. F. Werner, *Histoire comparée de l'administration* (Beiheft der *Francia*, ix) (Munich, Artemis Verlag, 1980), pp. 191–239.

131 See *Annales Bertiniani, s.a.* 862, p. 93; 864, p. 114; 867, p. 140.

132 Leyser, *Rule and Conflict* (see n. 127), p. 110.

differing imperial experiences of the Franks and the Saxons. The differing histories of the two peoples long antedated their respective imperial phases. The Saxons had been pagan until *c*. 800, and the process of conversion in depth continued through the ninth century. Further, until the Frankish conquest, the Saxons had managed quite well without kings: they were ruled by noble *principes* who collectively made decisions (such as whether to go to war) involving the whole people.[133] The Saxons had never been part of the Roman Empire. If the Saxon kings' apparatus of government was negligible in the tenth century, the Saxons *c*. 800 had even less. By constrast, the Franks had settled in former Roman provinces, and their kings had taken over Roman institutions which, however ramshackle by the later fifth century, were still useable. The Franks had settled among (and in the case of northern Gaul borrowed the language of) Roman provincial populations long used to the exactions, and literate forms, of Roman government, and to the peace it maintained. From the late fifth century, the Franks had been ruled by a single dynasty for well over two hundred years. They had been Christian for the whole of that period, imbibing the ideology of hierarchical order, obedience and 'keeping faith' which the Church so assiduously preached. The Franks were habituated to kingship, and genuinely devoted to their kings. They were very ready, as the Carolingians found in the eighth century, to identify their kings' greatness with their own. It was this longstanding acceptance of kingship on the part of the Frankish aristocracy, quite as much as the self-interested loyalty of the church, which helped to see the French monarchy through its 'bad patch' in the tenth and eleventh centuries. Then indeed, kings had need of a 'numinous face'. They were able to design one, as the Saxon kings had done, from a Carolingian base. But this should not obscure the other 'frank and familiar' face of Carolingian kingship, nor the solidarity between the Franks and their king that was the leitmotiv of Carolingian royal ritual.

---

[133] *Vita Lebuini Antiqua*, cc. 4, 6, H. Wolfram (ed.), *Quellen zur Geschichte des 7. und 8. Jahrhunderts* (Darmstadt, Wissenschaftliche Buchgesellschaft, 1982), pp. 386, 388.

5. *Bureaucrats and cosmology: the ritual code of T'ang China*

DAVID McMULLEN

INTRODUCTION

The historical and literary sources of the T'ang period (AD 618–906) in China convey the impression that Confucian rituals were central to the life of the state. The official histories describe the emperor and members of the imperial clan performing a wide range of rites. Elaborate, specially drafted and costly rituals, some involving long journeys, marked important political developments. Rituals followed crises in dynastic rule as well as periods of stability and achievement. There was also an extensive programme of regular, annually conducted rites. Most of these involved not only the emperor and imperial clan members, but the chief ministers, general service officials and official scholars. They were often attended by onlookers from the general population, so that large numbers of people were involved. The grandest of the imperial rites had a climactic quality. One or two of the most successful performances were considered the greatest achievements of the reigns in which they took place. They strained the wealth, logistical capacities and even security of the T'ang state to near its limit.

Official scholars, on whose expertise the emperor was entirely dependent for the drafting, performance and documentation of the

I am grateful to the editors for very helpful remarks on two preliminary drafts of this article, and to my colleague Dr Anne Birrell for a series of useful observations on the first draft. In the following annotation, selected references only are supplied.

Since the completion of this article a major study of T'ang ritual has been published in the late Howard J. Wechsler's *Offerings of Jade and Silk: ritual and symbol in the legitimation of the T'ang dynasty* (New Haven, 1985). Professor Wechsler's main focus is on the role of imperial ritual in the first two reigns of the dynasty, but he provides much invaluable detail in accounts of most of the principal rituals mentioned in my article. He also analyses pre-T'ang theories of ritual and describes some of the main ritual controversies in which T'ang scholars were engaged.

rites, emphasised the importance of ritual by making it a central element in their world view. They believed that the ritual tradition extended back to the golden age of remote antiquity and that the paragon emperor Shun (reigned traditionally 2255–2205 BC) had commissioned an official to organise and direct the kingly rites. They held that later rulers had established an imperial ritual programme and set up institutions to maintain it.[1] For them the early Chou dynasty (1121–220 BC) was the source of most ideals about ritual. The late Chou and Former Han (206 BC–AD 8) were also important, for this was the age in which the Confucian canons, the authority for much medieval thinking on the state, were identified and promoted.

T'ang scholars located the sanction for the imperial ritual programme in the Confucian canonical corpus as a whole, but especially in the three rituals canons. The *Record of ritual (Li chi)*, *Rites of Chou (Chou li)* and *Observances and rites (I li)* were a heterogeneous collection, both in origin and in content. The *Record of ritual* was a group of treatises dealing with the theory and function of ritual and containing detailed directives; the *Rites of Chou* consisted of idealised institutional blueprints; and the *Observances and rites* comprised mainly idealised ritual directives.[2] Much of the material these three canons contained had little to do with the historical Confucius. But in the seventh and eighth centuries scholars accorded them enormous prestige, calling them 'inerasable authorities',[3] and they kept them and later exegesis of them in the forefront of discussion of state rituals. Scholars also frequently cited later ritual usage, especially since the Later Han (AD 23–220), when the imperial ritual programme attained approximately its medieval form, as a sanction for contemporary practice.

T'ang scholars also indicated how central they considered the Confucian state ritual programme to be by the elaborate theoretical

---

[1] For early T'ang surveys of the pre-T'ang state ritual tradition, see *Sui shu (History of the Sui)* (Peking, 1973), ch. 6 pp. 105–7; *Chin shu (History of the Chin)* (Peking, 1974), ch. 19 pp. 579–80. cf. *T'ung tien (Comprehensive compendium*, hereafter *TT*, Taipei, 1959), ch. 41 pp. 233A–C; *Chiu T'ang shu (Old T'ang history*, hereafter *CTS*, Peking, 1975), ch. 21 pp. 815–19.

[2] James Legge, *The texts of Confucianism*, Parts III–IV, *The Li Ki* (Oxford, 1885); Edouard Biot, *Le Tcheou-li*, 2 vols. (Paris, 1851); S. Couvreur, S. J. *Cérémonial, texte, chinois et traduction*, 2nd edition (Sienhsien, 1928).

[3] *CTS* ch. 21 p. 818, *CTS* ch. 8 p. 180, *CTS* ch. 27 p. 1031; Morohashi Tetsuji, *Dai Kan-Wa jiten (Great Sino-Japanese dictionary*, Tokyo, 1955), entry 19.124.

justification that they advanced for it. Again, the learning involved here derived its authority from its antiquity. For ritual had very early become conceptualised, and linked with the condition of mind that correct observance of rituals brought about. Already in the late Chou, propriety, as the term *li* is often translated in this context, had become not just one of the five cardinal virtues but a major element in theories of society. Under the influence of the New Text school of cosmology and ethics in the second century BC, it was held to be a principle of the cosmos itself.[4] Even in the vigorous and outgoing early T'ang period, in which attitudes tended to be practical rather than theoretical, official scholars endorsed, with significant variations of emphasis, this legacy of theoretical thinking on ritual, and used it to emphasise the importance of the imperial ritual programme.

Finally the official view emphasised the importance of state ritual by the stress it gave to its institutional history. Scholars traced the posts and official titles that concerned the rites back to remote antiquity and linked the ritual offices inseparably to the rites themselves. Institutional continuity reaching, with few interruptions, back into the canonical age was to the T'ang world further proof of the authority and importance of the tradition.

The great importance of Confucian sanctioned state ritual to the dynasty and the central place it occupied in the world view of scholars meant that official scholarship was particularly conscientious in documenting it. Thus the *Old T'ang history* devotes the first and longest of its eleven treatises, monographs reserved for different aspects of government, to imperial rituals. This treatise records the major changes that took place in the imperial ritual programme in the course of the dynasty.[5] State rituals occupy a significant proportion of the *Comprehensive compendium* and the *Gathering of essentials for the T'ang*, two unofficial compendia that survive from the early ninth century and that closely follow official compilations in their perspective.[6] Imperial rituals were also a major

[4] Fung Yu-lan, tr. Derk Bodde, *A History of Chinese Philosophy*, 2 vols. (Princeton, 1952–3) i, pp. 297–9; 337–57. ii, pp. 40–2; Ch'ü T'ung-tsu, *Law and society in traditional China* (Paris, 1961), pp. 230–41.

[5] *CTS* ch. 21–2 p. 815–1038. cf. *Hsin T'ang shu* (*New T'ang history*, hereafter *HTS*, Peking, 1975), ch. 11–20 pp. 307–457.

[6] *TT* ch. 41–140 pp. 233–732; *T'ang hui yao* (*Gathering of essentials for the T'ang*, hereafter *THY*) (Peking, 1955), ch. 11–23, pp. 271–448; ch. 37–8, pp. 669–99 etc.

theme in the surviving works of individual scholars of all periods in the dynasty, whether prose or verse.

More important for the present article, official scholars of the medieval period collected together their prescriptions for imperial rituals in the form of dynastic ritual codes, each of which was intended to be normative for the dynasty in which it was compiled. These successive ritual codes defined the imperial ritual programme systematically and to a remarkable degree of detail. In this respect, the sources for the Confucian state ritual of the eighth century are superior to those of earlier periods. For from this middle century of the T'ang there comes the first full state ritual code to have survived in the Chinese tradition. This code, which was completed in 732, gives a set of very exact directives for the entire Confucian sanctioned imperial ritual programme, including the rarely conducted rites as well as the annually recurrent ones. Explored fully and related to the other sources that contain information about state ritual, the code will ultimately provide an extremely detailed picture of how the imperial rites were performed and of their place in the T'ang state and in T'ang society.[7]

Enormous energy, then, on the part of emperors, chief ministers and general service officials, was expended on the state ritual programme, and enormous erudition was devoted to it by scholars who surveyed the pre-T'ang state itself. The centrality of the rites to the T'ang state is beyond contention. To those interested in assessing the varying role of royal rituals in different cultural contexts, their obvious importance to the T'ang raises a number of questions. These concern T'ang official understanding of the purpose of state ritual in relation to other purposes of government, or the official justification for the code. Behind official pronouncements lie the questions of the level of political and sectional interest in the state ritual programme, and the effect this had on the shape of the programme itself. How the official view of ritual related to unofficially or privately expressed assessments of it, and how these unofficial views changed in response to changing political realities are also aspects of the T'ang ritual tradition as a whole.

In attempting to answer these questions, comparison with other states will be helpful, for it provides a spectrum on which to place

---

[7] *Ta T'ang K'ai-yüan li* (*Ritual code of the K'ai-yüan period in the great T'ang dynasty*, hereafter *TTKYL*), photolithographic reprint of edition of 1886 published with introduction by Ikeda On as *Dai Tō Kaigen rei* (Tokyo, 1972).

the medieval Chinese tradition. At one extreme there is the case of nineteenth-century Bali, described recently in an anthropological context. Here the king's role was seen above all in terms of dramaturgical or ritual performance. 'Royal rituals enacted, in the form of pageant, the main themes of Balinese political thought', and 'statecraft [was] a thespian art'. Administration, on the other hand, was relatively unimportant and was relegated to the village level.[8] The other extreme is provided by the nineteenth-century British constitution. Here the monarchy in its ceremonial role was strictly demarcated from political activity, and was held to be secondary, a dignified rather than efficient aspect of the state.[9]

At first sight, T'ang China seems indeed to be close to the Balinese case. The time, energy and expense and the intellectual priority accorded to state ritual in the period in which the code was produced was such as to suggest that T'ang imperial ceremonials, far from being secondary, might indeed constitute the most important function of the state. Yet a more detailed account of T'ang state ritual in the early and mid-eighth century leads inevitably to the conclusion that, though any parallel with nineteenth-century Britain seems inappropriate, comparison with Bali needs qualification on several counts.

In the first place, the T'ang bureaucracy had many functions in addition to imperial rites. The very organisation of the central bureaucracy, in which ritual offices formed a proportion, perhaps one sixth only, of the total bureaucratic structure, indicates its commitment to a range of administrative operations. Official scholars accorded activities of government other than ritual a comparable importance and allowed them a comparable history and antiquity. The central government included administrative bodies concerned with education; the enforcement of criminal law; defence; taxation; and the selection and promotion of officials. These activities were the responsibility of the same officials who administered the rituals and ultimately, like the rituals, of the emperor himself. Far from being relegated to a subordinate level, these operations also commanded prestige and were not, in practi-

---

[8] Clifford Geertz, *Negara: the theater state in nineteenth century Bali* (Princeton, 1980), pp. 120–2.

[9] S.R.F. Price, *Rituals and power: the Roman imperial cult in Asia Minor* (Cambridge, 1984), pp. 239–40. Walter Bagehot, *The English Constitution*, ed. with introduction by R. H. S. Crossman M.P. (London, 1963), pp. 61–5.

cal political terms, so different in status from the regular ritual programme.[10]

Secondly, the Confucian imperial state ritual programme as it was formulated in the code did not represent the totality of the emperor's religious or ritual commitments. The wealth of rituals the code embodied were almost without exception sanctioned by the traditional Confucian outlook on the cosmos and on society. Besides this Confucian outlook however, the transcendental faiths of Buddhism and Taoism also exerted claims on the emperor's commitment, time and resources. The mid-eighth-century world did not consider these three belief systems mutually exclusive. For Buddhism and Taoism differed from the Confucian outlook to such an extent that in practice they affected an entirely different area of experience.

The Confucian tradition was above all concerned with the political and social conduct of the human hierarchy, supplying for it a comprehensive system of ethical norms. As a religious system, however, it retained some features that an important scheme for religious evolution has termed 'archaic'.[11] It had no developed sense of the transcendant; it focussed on this life rather than life after death. It involved a plurality of cosmic agents and divinities whose chief function was to affect conditions in the natural and human worlds. It posited the emperor as the main link between the people and the cosmic order, and accorded the nobility and the official classes, who also monopolised political power, a superior standing in rituals. There was no Confucian process of ordination and consequently no Confucian priesthood. Rather, rituals were performed by the emperor himself and the imperial clan, or by officials representing them, and were drafted and administered by a highly structured bureaucracy that had its range of other duties to discharge. Buddhism and Taoism on the other hand belonged to a later stage in religious evolution, one that has been called 'historic'. They promoted belief in an entirely different realm of reality. They

---

[10] Robert des Rotours, *Le traité des examens, traduit de la Nouvelle histoire des T'ang* (Paris, 1932), pp. 3–25, summarises the structure of the T'ang government. The same scholar's *Traité des fonctionnaires et traité de l'armée, traduits de la nouvelle histoire des T'ang*, 2 vols. (Leiden, 1947), provides a detailed and well-indexed translation and annotation of the *New T'ang history* monograph on the 'offices and posts' of the dynasty.

[11] Robert N. Bellah, 'Religious evolution', *American Sociological Review* xxix, 1964, pp. 358–74, and *Beyond Belief: essays on religion in a post-traditional world* (New York, 1970), pp. 20–50.

both had priestly hierarchies that existed almost completely outside the official Confucian sanctioned bureaucratic establishment. They advocated monasticism, and by the mid-eighth century, Buddhist monasteries in particular had come to be substantial holders of land and wealth. Their social outlook was, especially by the mid-eighth century, more universal than that of Confucianism and they addressed the individual and his own search for answers to questions of ultimate value. Though their clergy might be politically active, they did not, to the extent that Confucians did, provide values and traditions for the state and its administration.

The Confucian oriented official scholars who compiled the code of 732 may have been adherents of the transcendental faiths in private. But in their official capacities they regarded both Buddhism and Taoism as outside their concern. In documenting and codifying Confucian sanctioned imperial ritual, they demarcated it strictly from the Taoist and Buddhist activities of successive T'ang sovereigns. But these faiths, their clergy and their wealthy monastic institutions remained powerfully present in the mid-eighth-century T'ang state. Despite the lofty claims that official Confucian scholars made for the Confucian world view and for Confucian imperial ritual, the Confucian programme was forced to compete with the very different demands and outlays of the transcendental faiths.

In the following pages, it will be argued that Confucian sanctioned imperial ritual constituted one of the principal, but by no means the only function of the T'ang dynastic state. The ritual programme represents a unique combination of an 'archaic' belief system administered by a learned and highly structured bureaucracy. A more detailed account of the imperial ritual programme as it was embodied in the K'ai-yüan ritual code (pp. 190–204) will be followed by a brief description of the institutions within the bureaucracy that administered the code and drafted the rituals (pp. 205–14). It will be emphasised that these institutions were integrated into the bureaucracy as a whole, and that the ritual tradition was accessible to the entire official body.

Then an account of the official justification for the ritual programme will show how the officially accepted theory of ritual contained two distinct, though not mutually exclusive, emphases, the cosmic on the one hand and the social and moral on the other (pp. 214–22). In medieval China the activities and even the affirmations of support that surround a traditional operation of the state cannot always be taken simply at face value, for they very often disguise other interests. The political picture behind the state ritual programme shows scholars involved in harsh competition, in sectional conflict, factionalism and individual ambition (pp. 222–31). The very vigour and variety of this ulterior interest in the rites is essential to a full understanding of the code and its importance in the T'ang world.

Finally, it will be suggested that the unique character of Confucian state ritual, its retention of an 'archaic' belief system combined with its sophisticated bureaucratic framework, gave rise, as towards the end of the eighth century the political power of the T'ang declined, to a shift in the attitudes of some intellectuals towards the function of the rites (pp. 231–6). This change took the form of a stronger unofficial emphasis on the social and moral function of rituals, and an occasionally striking scepticism towards their traditional and publicly accepted cosmological underpinnings. An apology for royal rituals that sees their function mainly in social terms anticipates a common modern defence of royal ceremony. That scholars should have arrived at a position of this kind nearly twelve hundred years ago in China points to the vitality and sophistication of the community in which they lived.

The reign of the emperor Hsüan tsung of the T'ang (713–756), in the middle decades of which the code was produced, was traditionally a high point in the history of medieval China. The T'ang dynasty had been founded by Li Yüan (r. 618–627) in 618 and was heir to the achievement of the brief Sui dynasty (589–618) in re-unifying China after four centuries of division. The T'ang rapidly developed into politically the most stable and economically the most prosperous state that China had seen. The T'ang sovereigns governed through the mandarinate, a hierarchy of officials in nine degrees and twenty-nine classes, who numbered about 17,000, and through a substantial clerical bureaucracy below them. The T'ang empire, extending from beyond the Great Wall in the north to Hai-nan island in the south, had a registered population of nearly 50,000,000. The court resided either at Ch'ang-an, a great walled, grid-plan metropolis of some two million inhabitants and the cultural and intellectual capital of East Asia, or at Lo-yang, the smaller second capital. Up to the rebellion of An Lu-shan in late 755, there were seldom serious threats to the state's security. The empire-wide registration and taxation systems, though in decline towards the end of this period, were effective enough to supply the court and metropolis with increasing wealth. The scholarly and educational institutions established by successive T'ang rulers, benefiting from stability, were more successful than any before them. The community of scholars that supplied these academic institutions, though numerically small and concentrated on the metropolis when compared to the larger, more devolved intellectual community of the pre-modern era, was nonetheless larger than in pre-T'ang times.[12]

This long period of prosperity and institutional stability permitted the royal ritual programme inherited from the period of disunion and embodied in successive pre-T'ang ritual codes to expand and to attain new levels of sophistication and grandeur. Indeed this very expansion was an underlying reason for the production of the code of 732. For the K'ai-yüan ritual code, known even in the eighth century by the reign period in which it was compiled,[13] was the third that had been produced under T'ang rule. The first, completed in 637, and the second, finished in 658, had each in turn been considered unsatisfactory. The reasons for their rejection were complex in a way characteristic of the T'ang ritual tradition; a compound of political as well as technical ritual motives brought about their replacement. Underlying these motives, however, was a confidence resulting from unprecedented prosperity.[14]

The immediate decision to compile a new code was the indirect result of traditional veneration for, combined with practical dissatisfaction with, one of the three ritual canons. It had been suggested in 726 that the prescriptive parts of the *Record of ritual*,

---

[12] D. C. Twitchett (ed.), *The Cambridge history of China*, vol. III, *Sui and T'ang China 589–906*, Part I (Cambridge, 1979), pp. 150–463. Arthur F. Wright, 'Symbolism and function: reflections on Ch'ang-an and other great cities', *Journal of Asian Studies* xxiv.4 (1965), p. 668.

[13] *THY* ch. 37 p. 671. But cf. *TTKYL*, preface p. 4a, quoting *THY*: and *Ta T'ang liu tien* (*Administrative regulations of the great T'ang dynasty*, hereafter *TTLT*), edn of 1724 edited by Hiroike Senkurō and Uchida Tomoo, published as *Dai Tō rikuten* (Tokyo, 1973) ch. 4 p. 14a–b; and *THY* ch. 9A p. 164.

[14] For the two earlier codes, *THY* ch. 37 pp. 669–70; *TT* ch. 41 pp. 233A–C; *CTS* ch. 21 pp. 816–18; *HTS* ch. 11 pp. 305–9. Robert des Rotours, *Le traité des examens* (see n. 10), p. 149, n. 1, dates the first code to 633; this date, given in *THY* ch. 37 p. 669, probably refers to an interim set of directives only. *Tzu-chih t'ung chien* (*Comprehensive mirror for aid in good government*, hereafter *TCTC* (Peking, 1956) ch. 194 p. 6217, 637.10, and *CTS* ch. 73 p. 2595 both give date of 637.

the least homogeneous of the three ritual canons, might be systematically re-arranged to form a prescriptive authority for the imperial ritual calendar. However, one of the chief ministers of the time, Chang Yüeh (667–730), called the *Record of ritual* 'an inerasable authority over the ages', and blocked the proposal. Chang Yüeh held concurrent office as the director of the Chi-hsien yüan, an advisory scholarly college founded by the emperor under another name in 717 and the most successful institution of its kind in the dynasty. His opposition prevailed, and instead it was decided to commission a new ritual code, to 'find the mean' between those of 637 and 658.[15]

The commission appointed to draft the new code consisted of at least four scholars and was under the direction of the same Chang Yüeh. The operation took place, however, not in one of the agencies that had responsibility for running the royal ritual programme but in the Chi-hsien yüan itself. Indeed there is a hint that the emperor had originally intended that one of the main functions of this college should be the re-drafting of state ritual directives.[16] Although the commission included experienced scholars, there were difficulties and delays, frequently attendant on state initiated scholarly projects in the seventh and eighth centuries. By 730, Chang Yüeh and another senior member of the commission were dead. The emperor then brought in an outside official, Hsiao Sung, a successful general service administrator rather than a scholar, to take charge of the entire programme of the Chi-hsien yüan.[17] Hsiao Sung drafted in probably at least three other academic personnel to work on the code. In 732 it was completed, submitted, approved by the emperor and promulgated.

THE RITUAL CODE

The K'ai-yüan ritual code contains detailed directions for just over 150 rites. Many of these had well documented histories going back

---

15　*TTKYL* preface 4a–6a; *THY* ch. 37 pp. 670–71; *TT* ch. 41 p. 233C; *CTS* ch. 97 pp. 3049–57; and HTS ch. 125 pp. 4404–10, biographies of Chang Yüeh. Chang blocked another attempt to revise the *Li chi* in 726; see K. P. Kramers, 'Conservation and the transmission of the Confucian canon', *Journal of the Oriental Society* ii.1 (1955), pp. 118–32. For the Chi-hsien yüan, see Ikeda On, 'Sei Tō no Shūkenin' (The Chi-hsien yüan in the high T'ang), *Hokkaidō Daigaku Bungakubu kiyō* xix.2 (1971), 47–98.

16　*Ch'üan T'ang shih* (*Complete T'ang poems*) (Peking, 1960), ch. 3 p. 35.

17　*CTS* ch. 99 pp. 3093–5 and *HTS* ch. 101 pp. 3953–4.

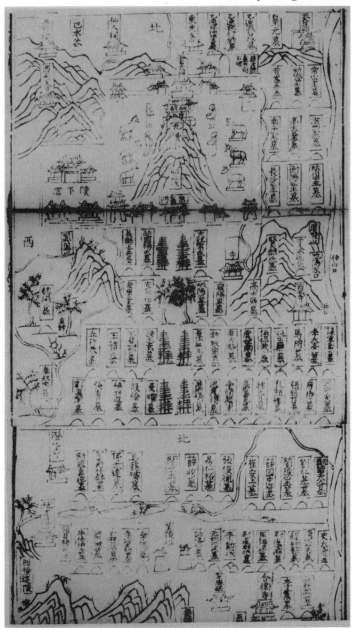

23 A traditional Chinese wood-block picture map of Chao-ling, the mausoleum of
T'ai tsung, the second T'ang emperor (reigned 627–649). From a gazetteer for
Li-ch'üan county, Shensi province, prefaced in 1535. The mound in the centre
represents T'ai tsung's mausoleum, and to its south are the tombs of the senior
civil and military officials who were given special permission to be buried near
him.

centuries. Some had been controversial in the T'ang itself. One or two were innovations, established just in time, as it were, for inclusion in the code. The rites are organised into five divisions, following, though re-arranging the order of, a scheme mentioned in the Confucian canons and believed by T'ang scholars to have existed in remote antiquity.[18] Each division contained its own category of rituals, which were distinct in terms of their subject matter or structure.

The first division was for 'propitious rituals (*chi li*)'. These concerned sacrifices (*ssu* or *chi*) to the supernatural powers or cosmological forces, which were made on the main altar sites at the capital and in the suburbs or at altars elsewhere in the empire. The recipients of these offerings were the gods of high heaven and earth, the gods of the five directions and of the harvest, the sun, moon, stars, sacred peaks, seas and great rivers. The offerings (*hsiang*) to ancestors of the emperor were also 'propitious rituals'. The imperial ancestral cult centred on the imperial mausolea, five in number at this point in the dynasty, with their tombs cut in natural rock in hills to the west of Ch'ang-an,[19] but more crucially on the dynastic ancestral temples (*tsung miao*), of which there were two, one at Ch'ang-an and a second at Lo-yang. The ancestral precincts and the rituals that took place at them stood, in a way no other rites could, for the dynasty itself, and in both ritual and political terms were extremely sensitive.[20]

A less prestigious ritual in this division was the twice yearly offering to Confucius, his immediate disciples and figures in the Confucian exegetical tradition. In the capital this ritual, the *Shih-tien*, was held at the state academy directorate, the institution responsible for the school system empire-wide.[21] A parallel offering was prescribed for the ancient teacher of military skills Ch'i T'ai

---

[18] *Shang shu chu shu (Book of documents with commentary and sub-commentary) (Ssu-pu pei-yao edn)* ch. 3 pp. 5b, 6a and 7a; *Li chi chu shu (Record of ritual with commentary and sub-commentary) (Ssu-pu pei-yao edn.)* ch. 1 p. 1b; *TT* ch. 41 p. 233A.

[19] *CTS* ch. 25 p. 973; cf. *TTLT* ch. 14 p. 27a which lists six. Hsüan tsung chose the site for his own burial late in 729; see *THY* ch. 20 p. 397.

[20] *TT* ch. 47 p. 271B; *CTS* ch. 26 p. 979; *THY* ch. 17 p. 352–5; *CTS* ch. 8 p. 177, ch. 25 p. 952.

[21] *TTKYL* ch. 53–4; *TT* ch. 53 pp. 303C–304C, 305C–306C; *THY* ch. 35 pp. 635–43; *Ta T'ang chiao-ssu lu (Record of suburban and temple offerings under the great T'ang)*, in *Dai Tō Kaigen rei*, pp. 725–820, ch. 10 pp. 5b–9b. The terms *chi, ssu, hsiang* and *Shih-tien* are officially defined in *TTLT* ch. 4 p. 33a.

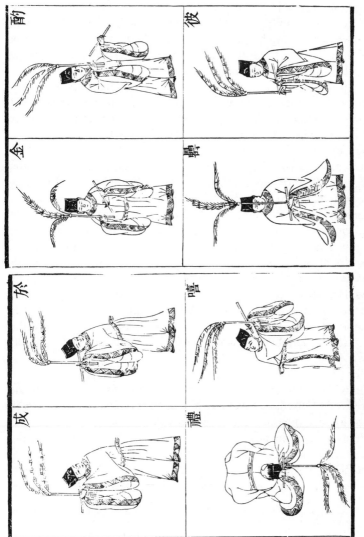

24 Representations of the positions required for dancers in a ceremony to Confucius. The final four characters read, 'Ah! We complete the ritual'. From a historical compendium on Ch'üeh-li, Confucius' birthplace, originally prefaced in 1505 and published in an amplified edition in 1870.

kung, a figure held to have lived at the start of the Chou and promoted as the military counterpart to Confucius, the exemplar of civil virtues. Though T'ai kung had had temples before, a cult at this level was a T'ang innovation, established by edict only one year before the completion of the code.[22]

This first division of the code also contained the directives for a number of rituals which were non-recurrent in the sense of not being conducted annually or at fixed intervals but rather when the emperor, ministers and ritual scholars agreed conditions to be appropriate.[23] The greatest of these, and the least frequently performed, were the Feng and Shan rites, which in T'ang tradition might be held on Mount T'ai, the sacred mountain in Shantung that was believed to link the human and spirit worlds, or on the other four sacred mountains of China. In T'ang times these rites had been performed only twice before 732, in 666 and 725 on Mount T'ai and once, early in 691, by the usurping Empress Wu, on Mount Sung, the central peak.[24] Other non-recurrent rituals concerned the reports the emperor made at the ancestral temple and at other capital altar sites on returning from journeys. In this division of the code there were also prescriptions for certain of the important rites to be conducted at local level throughout the empire, in humbler versions of their grand imperial counterparts.[25]

The programme of recurrent and non-recurrent rituals this division of the code contains was conceded to be too onerous for the emperor to discharge every year. For twenty-five of the rituals in this division the code therefore provided prescriptions for proxy celebrations in the absence of the emperor. The role of taking the place of the sovereign devolved first on the grand pacifier [t'ai wei], one of the 'three dukes [san kung]', the highest officials in the hierarchy, then, if this post was vacant, on officials of the third grade

22 *TTKYL* ch. 55; *TT* ch. 53 pp. 306C–307B; *THY* ch. 23 pp. 435–9; *Ta T'ang chiao-ssu lu* ch. 10 pp. 9b–17b.

23 *HTS* ch. 11 p. 3120 makes the distinction between recurrent (*ch'ang*) and non-recurrent (*fei ch'ang*) rites.

24 *TTKYL* ch. 63–4; *TT* ch. 54 pp. 310C–314A; *CTS* ch. 23 pp. 881–907; *HTS* ch. 14 pp. 349–53. Edouard Chavannes, *Le T'ai Chan* (Paris, 1910), pp. 169–235 translates *CTS* ch. 23. For the interest of T'ang sovereigns in celebrating the Feng and Shan rites on sacred peaks other than Mount T'ai, see my note in *T'ang studies*, ii (Winter, 1984), pp. 37–40. For the traditional position of Mount T'ai, see *Shang shu chu shu* ch. 2 p. 6b.

25 *TTKYL* ch. 56–61; 68–78.

and above. The senior officials of the agencies that ran the state ritual programme also participated.[26]

The second division of the code was the very much shorter 'rituals for guests [*pin li*]'. These were concerned with the reception of envoys from outlying territories, their procedure for their audiences, feasts, presentation with gifts and departure. It comprised only six observances. The code does not name the states involved, but refers to princes of foreign states, or 'envoys from foreign states', and these states were graded into great, medium and 'small below'. The *Administrative regulations* of 738 or 739 lists over seventy states as existing at this time, but does not grade them.[27]

The third division, only slightly longer than the second, was for 'army rituals [*chün li*]'. These included the rites the emperor was to perform at precincts at the capital, among them the dynastic ancestral temple, before he went on campaign; regulations for the proclamation of victories and the rewarding of officers. There were also prescriptions for 'rehearsals at war', to be held in the middle month of winter, for hunts and for imperial attendance at, or even participation in, archery competitions.[28]

The fourth division of the code was much longer and was more concerned with rites of passage than with cosmic or supernatural forces. The 'felicitation rituals [*chia li*]' contained prescriptions for marriage ceremonies, from those for the emperor himself, the crown prince and princesses to those for officials of the sixth grade and below. There were directives for the procedures by which the emperor and empress were to receive congratulations from the hierarchy of imperial family members and from officials. Ceremonies for the investiture of the crown prince, other princes and senior ministers and for the appointment of envoys to the provinces formed another group in this division. Yet another included coming of age ceremonies for all levels of the hierarchy to the sons of sixth grade officials and below. Finally, a number of rituals were for local performance, among them the declaration of amnesties, the announcement of the imperial will and the des-

---

[26] For the regulations for proxy celebrations, see *TTLT* ch. 4 p. 40b; *CTS* ch. 21 p. 819, ch. 43 p. 1815 and 1831, cf. also *TTLT* ch. 14 p. 12b, 156a; *TTKYL* preface 1a–4b; *HTS* ch. 11 p. 310.

[27] *TTKYL* ch. 79–80; *TTLT* ch. 4 pp. 56a–b.

[28] *TTKYL* ch. 81–90.

patch by provincial officials of memorial submissions to the court.[29]

The fifth and last division of the code was for 'rituals of ill omen [*hsiung li*]'. This contained procedures to be conducted after bad harvests, illness and mourning. The code prescribed details for those involved down to officials of the sixth grade and below. The first T'ang codification, that of 637, had included a sixth section, containing the prescriptions for imperial funerals, but this had been removed from the second code, for reasons of tact, and it was absent also from the K'ai-yüan code. This omission meant that whenever an emperor died the funeral procedures had to be drafted anew. It was not to be until 806, at a time when individual officials wrote sardonically about the sycophancy of their seventh-century predecessors over this matter, that the dynasty officially permitted directives for imperial funerals to be preserved for future use. Perhaps again because to do so would have involved 'anticipating untoward events', in the phrase used when imperial funerals were withdrawn from the code, no prescriptions for accession, or for 'proceding to the throne' were included.[30]

In a system that pre-dated the T'ang, each of the observances in the first, the 'propitious rituals' division, was ranked in one of three grades, major, medium or minor.[31] In the code as a whole, over sixty rituals specified the participation of the emperor in their titles; but he acted as principal in a considerably larger proportion than this figure implies. The titles of a further twenty-two mentioned the empress or the crown prince. Some of these royal rituals were specific to the emperor, in the sense that no ritual resembling them was performed at lower levels in the hierarchy. Others were imperial versions of rituals that were repeated, in carefully stipulated and decreasing degrees of grandeur down the mandarin scale or in the provincial administration. The main rites of the 'propitious rituals' division of the code were specific to the emperor: for

---

[29] *TTKYL* ch. 91–130. For a vivid eyewitness description of an announcement of the imperial will, at Teng-chou on the northern coast of Shantung province in 840, see Edwin O. Reischauer tr., *Ennin's diary* (New York, 1955), pp. 180–2.

[30] *TTKYL* ch. 131–50; *Lui Ho-tung chi* (*Collected works of Liu Tsüng-yuan* (773–819)) (Peking, 1958) ch. 21 p. 367–9; *THY* ch. 37 pp. 669–70. *TT*, despite this prohibition, contains directives for Tai tsung's funeral in 779

[31] *TT* ch. 45 p. 260B; *TTKYL* preface 1a–b; *TTLT* ch. 4 p. 33a; *TT* ch. 106 p. 561B; *CTS* ch. 21 p. 819 *HTS* ch. 11 p. 310. See also the article by Kaneko Shūichi, 'Tōdai no daishi, chūshi shōshi ni tsuite (Concerning the major medium and minor offerings in the T'ang)', *Kōchi Daigaku Gakujutsu kenkyū hōkoku*, 25, *Jimbun kagaku*, 1, pp. 13–19.

example the offerings at the suburban altars or the Feng and Shan rites on the sacred mountains.

The highly sensitive dynastic ancestral cult on the other hand, although its rites were held to be distinct in name and in their organisation, was in essence a grand imperial version of the ancestral cults that officials of the fifth grade and above were permitted to maintain. The T'ang ritual tradition as a whole offered varying explanations of the emperor's position before heaven, earth and man. But this provision, which was sanctioned by the canons, at least suggests that he differed in degree only from other members of the noble or official hierarchy. On the other hand to some T'ang scholars the imperial ancestral cult was different from other ancestral cults in being a 'public [*kung*]' concern, while the ancestral cults of high ranking families were 'private [*ssu*]'. This distinction was largely ethical rather than religious. Some scholars thus used the term 'public' when commenting critically on the emperor's reluctance to allow them to influence aspects of the imperial cult.[32]

One observance repeated in humbler versions through the T'ang empire-wide administrative structure was the twice yearly offering to Confucius, his disciples and the main figures of the Confucian exegetical tradition. In its grandest, metropolitan version, this ceremony, the *Shih-tien*, was conducted by the crown prince as chief celebrant, with the entire official body and the students of the state academy in attendance. In the provincial versions, the chief celebrants were the local prefects, or in the administrative subdivisions of the prefecture, the county magistrates. Their brief addresses to Confucius, stipulated in the code, were however identical, but for the declaration of their names, to that given by the crown prince. This too was a 'public' ceremony, in that private celebrations of the *Shih-tien* seem likely to have been forbidden by law. Epigraphical evidence, and the evidence of texts that were both inscribed and transmitted in literary collections, indicates that this ritual was widely conducted.[33] There were local variations

---

[32] For the laws for private ancestral temples see *TTKYL* ch. 3 p. 12a; *TTLT* ch. 4 p. 40a; also *THY* ch. 19 pp. 387–92 and *T'ang ta chao ling chi* (*Great collection of edicts and commands of the T'ang*) (Shanghai, 1959), ch. 68 p. 382. For the idea that the ancestral temple was governed by 'public' considerations, see *CTS* ch. 25 pp. 954–5; *THY* ch. 14 pp. 315–16; *TCTC* ch. 244 pp. 7876–7, 831.6.

[33] *Wen yüan ying hua* (*Flowers in the garden of letters*) (Peking, 1966) ch. 509 pp. 2b–3b; *CTS* ch. 187A p. 4874; *Liu Ho-tung chi* ch. 5 p. 74–7; *Han Ch'ang-li chi* (*Collected works of Han Yü (768–824)*) (*Kuo-hsüeh chi-pen t'sung-shu*, edn.), vol. 6, ch. 31 p. 58.

however, and accounts of how the *Shih-tien* was conducted on the remote southern coast of China caused only contemptuous amusement in the north.[34]

For the code's purposes, the lowest level in the administrative hierarchy was the village [*li*]. The code stipulates one ceremony only for village level, an offering to gods of soil and grain. This, like the *Shih-tien*, was a public ritual to be performed empire-wide. The grand, imperial version of this ritual was a medium grade observance, for which proxy directives were also supplied. Called in the code the 'sacrifice to the grand altar of the god of the soil', it involved standard offerings of cooked meat and of jade and silk to both the god of the soil and the god of the harvest in the middle month of spring and autumn. At the imperial level, elaborate equipment and the attendance of all grades of officialdom, besides the principal celebrants, were required. For the humble village version, however, the code stipulated only the participation of the head of the community and the community members, while the site of the observance was to be 'beneath a sacred tree'. As for the equipment, 'if there are no ritual vessels, other vessels are to be used as best the situation allows'. The community headmen were, however, required to celebrate in the middle month of spring and autumn, just as the emperor or his proxy were at the capital.[35]

Among other rituals that were repeated down the hierarchy were rites of passage in the fourth division of the code, like coming of age and marriage rites.[36] Such ceremonies were therefore not exclusively royal rituals, but were rather general ones, of which the imperial performance was the grandest. In their non-imperial versions at least they were considered private. In the case of rites of passage the code prescribed only to the rank of 'sixth degree (officials) and below'. In stopping its coverage at the ninth, the lowest degree of officialdom in this way, the code again underlined its concern with the apex of the T'ang social hierarchy only. Here its compilers tacitly endorsed the principle, first formulated in the

---

[34] *Ch'ün-chü chieh-i* (*Humorous stories for living in a crowd*), in *Li-tai hsiao-hua chi* (*Chronological anthology of humour*) (Shanghai, 1956), p. 59.

[35] *TTKYL* ch. 71 pp. 7a–9b; *TTLT* ch. 4 p. 39b and 51b; *Han Ch'ang-li chi* vol. 6 ch. 31 p. 58 and *HTS* ch. 164 p. 5058. For the imperial version see *TTKYL* ch. 33–4, and for confirmation of its middle grade status, *CTS* ch. 24 p. 933. Rituals involving prayers for rain were also prescribed for local level; these were by their very nature non-regular; *TTKYL* ch. 67, 70 and 73; *TTLT* ch. 4 pp. 41b–42a.

[36] *TTKYL* ch. 114–22 pp. 123–5.

Record of ritual, that 'the rules of ceremony do not go down to the common people. The penal statutes do not go up to the great officers'. The code thus bore out the hierarchical view of society that was essential to the Confucian perspective and that contrasts with the more universal outlook of the transcendental faiths. Concerning the many popular or unofficial rites and festivals that existed alongside state rituals, the code therefore supplies no information at all, just as it remains silent about the flux of religious practices among the population at large.[37]

Inevitably, within each of its five divisions rituals tended to echo one another or to have shared features. The code, rather than repeat prescriptions, acknowledged this by supplying cross-references when particular rites used procedures common to others. The internal consistency to which this feature of the code bears witness is an indication of the systematic approach of the compilers to the tradition. In the 'propitious rituals' division, rituals were treated typically under seven headings.[38] First there were directives for preliminary abstinence, for which there were two phases, 'relaxed' and 'intensive'. General regulations at the front of the code stipulate four days of 'relaxed' and three of 'intensive' abstinence for a major ritual; three days of 'relaxed' and two of 'intensive' for a medium ritual; and two days of 'relaxed' and one of 'intensive' for a minor one.[39] If these 'periods of separation', in modern anthropological terms, proved impracticably long, the code prescribed a single night of 'pure abstinence'.

During 'relaxed abstinence', business was to be done as usual, except that participation in mourning, enquiring after sickness, or deciding on or signing documents concerned with punishment or killing was not permitted, nor was the imposition of punishment on criminals or participation in 'unclean or evil activities'. 'In intensive abstinence (the participants) are permitted to attend to the business of the ritual only; the other activities are all barred'. Abstinence was not normally prescribed for the rituals whose primary purpose was social, those in the 'rituals for guests' and the 'propitious

---

[37] The orthodox view towards these was one of disapproving condescension; see *T'ang kuo shih pu (Supplement to the T'ang dynastic history)* (Shanghai, 1957), p. 65; or sometimes of harsh intervention, *CTS* ch. 89 p. 2887, ch. 156 p. 4129.

[38] Cf. *HTS* ch. 11 p. 310.

[39] *TTKYL* ch. 3 pp. 7b–8b; *TTLT* ch. 4 pp. 41a–b; cf. *Lung chin feng sui p'an (Judgements of dragon sinew and phoenix marrow)* (Hu-hai Lou ts'ung-shu edn.) ch. 4 pp. 4a–5b.

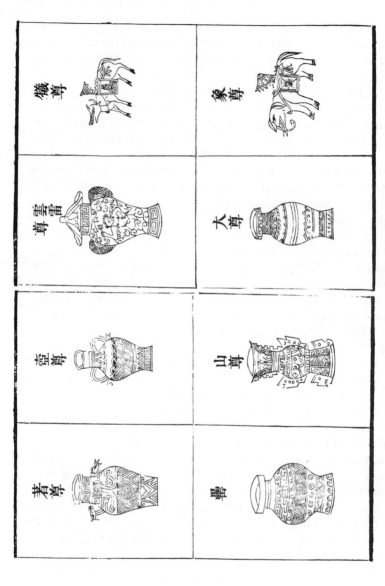

25 Drawings of traditional Chinese ritual vessels, of the sort stipulated in the code. From a historical compendium on Ch'üeh-li, Confucius' birthplace, originally

rituals' divisions. A night of 'pure abstinence' was however required of all participants in those army rituals that took place at the main capital altar precincts or in the imperial ancestral temple.[40]

The next heading concerned the deployment of the equipment to be used in the observance. Usually three days beforehand, tents (*tz'u*) would be set out where participants were to await the ritual. Two days before, appropriate musical instruments, themselves the subject of much attention and historical erudition and the responsibility of specialist offices, would be deployed. Placements (*wei*) for the ritual itself, with the position of participants and the direction they faced stipulated, would be set out. A third heading usually concerned ritual inspection of the food offerings and vessels.[41] Then there was a heading for the directives for the imperial procession as it left the palace or relevant premises and went, probably at a brisk pace, to the precinct concerned.[42] The fifth and sixth sections provided directives for the offering of the jade and silk, and the presentation of sacrificial meat and wine, by the emperor or his representative. In these, the central episodes for rituals in the first division of the code, there were again recurrent features. The code invariably prescribed three presentations or offerings to the divinity, cosmological agent, ancestor or deceased exemplar involved. For it was an accepted principle that 'ritual is perfected in threes'.[43] If the emperor participated, he made the first offering, to be followed by one of the very high ranking officials, with the president of one of the ritual agencies typically making the third presentation.

In many cases, each presentation was accompanied by the reading of a 'prayer text [*chu wen*]'. The code supplies texts in the case of some rituals; for others it gives a note stating that the text was to be composed 'near the time'. The texts the code supplies are notable for the laconic quality: they usually involved the participant stating the year, month and day, identifying himself, and then

---

[40] *TTKYL* ch. 81 p. 2a, ch. 82 p. 1a, ch. 83 p. 1a, ch. 84 p. 1a.

[41] *HTS* ch. 11 pp. 312–16.

[42] The pace may be inferred from a memorial dated 711 by the great historian–critic Liu Chih-chi (661–721); see *TT* ch. 53 p. 304C and *CTS* ch. 102 p. 3172. Han Yü implied that acolytes rushed about during ceremonies; *Han Ch'ang-li chi* vol. 4, ch. 14 p. 28 and *Shang shu chu shu* ch. 11 pp. 11b–12a.

[43] *THY* ch. 8 p. 114.

giving a very brief address in archaic and honorific language. In the case of the rite to Shen Nung, a legendary paragon emperor and originator of husbandry, for example, the emperor stated, 'I make bold to announce to Shen Nung that, at the start of the first spring month, the ploughing work begins. In accordance with the laws and precepts, reverently we attend our thousand acres.' He then used a standard formula to present the offerings: 'Diligently with a length of silk and with sacrificial grain, I reverently make replete the unvarying offering and set forth the holy oblations.'[44]

Normally even for the grandest rituals the prayer text did not involve more than a very brief report of this kind. Any 'transformative' element in modern anthropological terms, involving explicit change in the status of the performer in relation to the divinity or cosmological agent addressed was therefore missing. However, in one ritual the emperor or his proxy prayed for the grain harvest, and in times of drought or flood, a number of supplicative rituals were prescribed, down to prefectural and county levels. In these, the emperor or his local representative requested a response from the cosmic forces or from local divinities.[45] By and large, therefore, the organisation of this the central episode of the rituals in the propitious division amply bears out the this-worldly, non-transcendant or 'archaic' focus of the official Confucian religious outlook.

Another feature of the central episode of the rites in the 'propitious rituals' division of the code, again sanctioned in the *Record of ritual*, was that the recipient of the offering named in the title of the ritual was often not the only one involved. Another, 'correlative' recipient was frequently included. Sometimes this was a divinity or deceased exemplar who was loosely associated with the main recipient. Thus when the emperor made offering to Shen Nung, the code prescribed that Hou Chi, the legendary ancestor of the Chou house and superintendant of grain under the paragon emperor Yao,[46] should also receive offerings. In a number of the rituals, the correlatives were deceased members of the T'ang imperial line. In this way, the dynasty gave to its ritual programme, almost all of which was of far greater antiquity than the T'ang itself, a specifically T'ang identity. Thus in the Feng rites on Mount T'ai to high heaven, the code prescribed Kao tsu, that is Li Yüan, the

---

[44] *TTKYL* ch. 46 p. 11a.
[45] *TTKYL* ch. 6–7, 65–7, 70, 73; *TTLT* ch. 4 pp. 41b–42a.
[46] *TTKYL* ch. 46 p. 11a; *TTLT* ch. 4 p. 36b.

founder of the dynasty, as the correlative, while in the Shan rites that followed it was Jui tsung, at the time the code was compiled the most recently deceased sovereign and Hsüan tsung's own father, who was stipulated. The detailed narratives of the Feng and Shan rites on Mount T'ai in late 725 show that here the code was endorsing the precedent of the most recent celebration of this highly prestigious ritual.[47]

In some cases more than one correlative recipient was prescribed. In its version of the *Shih tien* ritual to Confucius, the code stipulated as correlatives the seventy-two Confucian disciples, and twenty-two exegetical scholars, whose lives had spanned a period of nine hundred years till the fifth century AD.[48] The counterbalancing military cult was even more accommodating, for it included, at least in middle and late eighth century times, offering to a small number of very recently deceased T'ang generals.[49] But the most immediate provision of this kind concerned the imperial ancestral temple. For a very few of the greatest officials of a reign were posthumously represented in the shrine of the deceased emperor whom they had served. To be installed as a 'correlative meritorious official' in the ancestral temple was one of the rarest of the posthumous honours the state offered.[50] The principle of the correlative recipient was thus clearly very useful, for it permitted expansion and a pluralistic approach to both divinities and past exemplars. In this way, the scope of the symbols to which the state gave approval was kept flexible, and the ability of the rites to integrate a wide range of beliefs and experiences in the interests of the dynasty was reinforced.

The sixth and final heading in the codes' directives for rituals in 'propitious rituals' division typically concerned the procedure for the return of the imperial party or the principal celebrant. This tended to be standard for a high proportion of the observances, and the code therefore simply referred to the directions given for the first ritual, that for the offering at the round altar held at the winter

[47] *TTKYL* ch. 63 p. 13a and 15a; ch. 64 p. 7b and 9b; *CTS* ch. 23 p. 889, 900 and 902; *THY* ch. 7 pp. 114, 115 and 117.

[48] *TTKYL* ch. 53 pp. 9a–10a; *TTLT* ch. 4 pp. 36b–37b; *Ta T'ang chiao-ssu lu* ch. 10 p. 7a.

[49] *TTKYL* ch. 55 p. 5a; *THY* ch. 23 pp. 435–6; *Ta T'ang chiao ssu lu* ch. 10 pp. 9b–12a.

[50] The 'correlative meritorious officials' up to Jui-tsung's reign (710–712) are listed in *TTLT* ch. 4 pp. 35b–36b and *THY* ch. 18 pp. 370–1. Neither text gives lists for the reign of the Empress Wu (690–705).

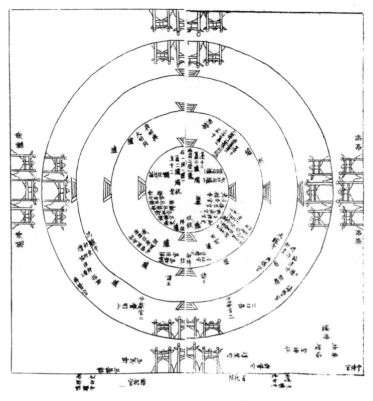

26 Eighteenth-century picture diagram of the round altar. The places for participating officials, e.g. members of the board of rites, the court of ceremonial for
foreigners, and the censors are marked, as are the positions of offering vessels,
censers, etc. From the *Chinese Encyclopaedia* of 1726.

solstice. In one or two cases the code required an assembly or feast
for the officials who had participated, to be held a day after the
ceremony concerned. The ploughing rite which followed the
emperor's offering to Shen Nung and Hou Chi was followed by a
feast in the palace of the Supreme Ultimate for all participants. The
authority for this apparently highly formal celebration came from
the *Monthly commands*, a section of the *Record of ritual*, and one
of the most important sanctions for the cosmological element in the
imperial ritual calendar.[51]

---

[51] *TTKYL* ch. 46 pp. 15b–16a; James Legge, *The Li Ki* (see n. 2), pp. 254–6. Cf.
TCTC ch. 214 p. 6810, 735.1.

THE RITUAL INSTITUTIONS

The amount of detail in the K'ai-yüan ritual code is prodigious. The Chinese text as it was copied for the imperial library in or just before 1782 runs to approximately 1000 traditional pages,[52] while the commonly available edition of 1886 approaches 1500. Rendered into English, the code's length would exceed this several fold. But T'ang official scholarly compilations tended to be highly compartmentalised. The purpose of the code was prescriptive, to provide sound directives for a programme of rituals that the compiling officials themselves had delimited. It restricted itself almost exclusively to directives for performances, not to the usages and sumptuary regulations that have also been seen as an aspect of the state ritual tradition.[53] It therefore includes little background or explanatory information. Only in the opening three chapters does it depart from its concern for specific detail and supply more general directives. This prefatory section covers matters such as divining auspicious days, imperial and official processions, the rules for dress, abstinences, definition of droughts, disposal of deficient ritual equipment, care of animals intended for sacrifice and the regulations for furnishing the tombs of officials. Modern Japanese scholarship has established that this material reflects closely contemporary statutes and ordinances governing state rituals. Its different purpose explains why it differs in tenor from the bulk of the code.[54]

This admirably tidy and disciplined approach means that other T'ang sources, mainly official histories and institutional compendia, must supply what the code refrains from giving: a more detailed description of the institutional framework that supported the ritual programme, and of its place in the bureaucracy as a whole. The implementation of the T'ang ritual programme was the responsibility of a number of special agencies in the central government, while in the provinces it normally devolved either on officials despatched from the central government or on the general prefec-

---

[52] Photolithographically reprinted in *Ssu-k'u ch'üan-shu chen-pen (Rare volumes from the complete collection in four treasuries)*, eighth series (Taipei, 1978).

[53] Etienne Balazs, 'History as a guide to bureaucratic practice', in *Chinese civilization and bureaucracy*, tr. H. M. Wright, ed. Arthur F. Wright (New Haven, 1964), pp. 136–7.

[54] Ikeda On, '*Dai Tō Kaigen rei* no kaisetsu' (Explanation of the *Ta T'ang K'ai-yüan li*), in *TTKYL* p. 823.

tural or county administrations. The ritual agencies in the central
government were, however, integral parts of the general bureaucracy. Personnel appointed to them were governed by the same laws
as officials elsewhere in the civil service. Length of tenure, regulations governing promotion and so on were therefore in no way
different. Though those in state ritual posts were often referred to
as 'ritual officials [*li kuan*]', there was no question of their being a
privileged group, still less of their having any form of special
initiation. The institutional structure to which they were appointed
was remarkably stable, more so, it could be argued, than the ritual
programme itself, for it underwent relatively little evolution in the
course of the dynasty.

The main central agencies concerned were four 'courts [*ssu*]',
all having premises in the imperial city, the great enclosed precinct in which the principal institutions of the government were
sited. The most important of the ritual courts was the court of
sacrifices. As a title at least, this went back to the Former Han
dynasty. It was headed by a president, whose grade was third
degree first class on the mandarin scale. At the time the code was
compiled, besides his role as a participant in imperial, proxy and
other rituals, he bore responsibility for administering and maintaining the great majority of the precincts in which the code's
rituals were conducted. Beneath him there were eight ancillary
bodies, whose names indicated their function. They were for the
upkeep of altar sites, for music, for 'drums and wind (instruments)', for medicine, divination, the supply of sacrificial animals,
for the numerous lesser cult shrines that the dynasty maintained,
and finally for the maintenance of the imperial mausolea. There
were also four services, concerned with keeping all equipment
used in the rituals.

The presidency of the court of sacrifices was considered a high
status position. Though it did not involve activity in the mainstream
of political life, it was sometimes used as a holding post for senior
officials. There are thus several examples from late in the eighth
or early in the ninth century of appointment to chief ministerships
following tenure of the presidency.[55] Another role that the
president of this or of the other ritual courts was occasionally given

---

[55] *CTS* ch. 119 p. 3435, Yang Wan in 777; *CTS* ch. 136 p. 3756, Ch'i K'ang in 800;
CTS ch. 147 p. 3976, Kao Ying in 803; *CTS* ch. 147 p. 3973, Tu Huang-shang in
805. Cf. *CTS* ch. 67 p. 248.7, Li Chi in 648.

was that of diplomatic commissioner to foreign states. The relations between China and its neighbouring states, this arrangement seems to imply, were conceived of as an extension of the ritual programme, of the highly regulated ceremonial framework prescribed in the 'rituals for guests' division of the code.[56]

Beneath the president there were two deputy presidents, whose grade was fifth degree third class and whose posts were also considered prestigious.[57] Below these there were two registrars and four doctors. The latter had special responsibility for drafting and revising the directives for the rituals in the code. They also had an entirely separate, and politically sensitive, function, that of proposing canonisation titles for deceased mandarins of the third degree and above. Below them again were a number of low ranking, low prestige offices bearing responsibility for minor aspects of the ritual programme. Several appear frequently in the code, having roles as heralds or ushers. In general sources they are sometimes mentioned as first appointments to junior officials. In these cases they typically led to general service appointments rather than careers specialising in state ritual.

Another, very junior role was assigned to acolytes, who might be as young as twelve and who were the sons of officials of the sixth degree or higher in the general bureaucracy. These seem to have numbered as many as 862, and were attached to the offices responsible for altar sites and to the dynastic ancestral temple. Under the influence of the usurping Empress Wu, as an aspect of her promotion of the female interest in all aspects of government, in the first decade of the eighth century there were girl acolytes. Acolytes formed one of the groups that were set facilitated examinations leading to official status. In the late eighth century there was discussion of the idea that students from the state academy might take the role of regular acolytes when the number was later insufficient, and the problem was set as an examination question. Service as an acolyte may have had its irksome aspects, for it was sometimes excused in imperial acts of grace. But the use of the ritual institutions and programme to provide sons of ranking officials with a familiarisation with the state and its procedures, though certainly a pre-T'ang practice, indicates how central the

---

[56] *CTS* ch. 196B p. 5245. cf. *CTS* ch. 196B pp. 5263–4.
[57] *P'i-ling chi (Collected works of Tu-ku Chi (725–777)) (Ssu-pu ts'ung-k'an* edn), ch. 17 p. 6b.

Confucian sanctioned ritual programme was to the official hier-archy.[58]

Of the other courts with state ritual functions, the court of imperial banquets had particular responsibility for the wine and meat used in sacrifices. Its president, with the rank of third degree second class, offered the third and final presentation in proxy imperial celebrations. Like the court of sacrifices, the court of imperial banquets ran ancillary institutions, in this case six, con-cerned with the maintenance of ritual kitchens and the preparation of ritual foods, drink and equipment.

A third court with a role in the state ritual programme, one that grew in importance in the course of Hsüan tsung's reign, was the court of the imperial family. With a structure similar to that of the court of sacrifices, its main function at the time the code was compiled was the upkeep of the records of the imperial Li family. From 737, however, five years after the completion of the code, it assumed responsibility for both the imperial mausolea and the imperial dynastic temple. In the second half of Hsüan tsung's reign its functions were substantially increased by another development. The emperor, honouring the claim that the T'ang royal house was descended from Lao tzu, one of the principal deities of Taoism, greatly promoted Taoist texts, education and examinations. He assigned to the court of the imperial family the management of the institutional aspect of this campaign to glorify the teachings of his supposed ancestor. This development represents one of the few instances when the administration of one of the rival belief systems was imported into the Confucian sanctioned institutional framework.

Finally, yet another court, that of ceremonial for foreigners, had ritual responsibilities. These concerned the reception of repre-sentatives from foreign states and the hospitality, strictly regulated, to be accorded them. This agency would seem to correlate neatly with the ceremonials prescribed in the brief 'rituals for guests' section of the code. In fact, the president of this court is not mentioned in the directives for the rituals concerned, for which the main role was taken by the president of the court of sacrifices. But

[58] *TT* ch. 15 p. 85A and *HTS* ch. 45 p. 1180 give a total of 862; *TTLT* ch. 14 pp. 2a, 3a, suggest a total of only 370, *TTLT* ch. 4 p. 7a. For girl acolytes, see *CTS* ch. 51 p. 2173; ch. 92 p. 2965; *HTS* ch. 13 p. 337; *TCTC* ch. 209 pp. 6636–7, 709.14. For the irksome nature of acolytes' duties, see *Han Ch'an-li chi* vol. 4 ch. 14 pp. 28–9; and remission of service, *T'ang ta chao-ling chi* ch. 74 p. 416.

the presidency was sometimes used as a title for diplomatic commissioners visiting foreign states.[59]

These specialist ritual courts were not, however, the only institutions with responsibility for the imperial ritual programme. In the executive ministry of the bureaucracy, the department of affairs of state, one of the six boards, the board of rites at the time the code was compiled was exclusively concerned with ritual. This body defined and administered rules of propriety and ceremonial usage covering dress, styles of address and other aspects of official life. It also received and processed reports of auspicious omens sent in from the provinces. From 735, however, it had sole responsibility for one of the most prestigious of all the scholarly operations of the dynasty, the regular examination system. But the secretary and supernumerary secretary of the board of rites, nominally at least, oversaw the whole of the ritual code. One of the dependent bodies of the board, the bureau of sacrifices (*tz'u pu*), had as part of its charge the administering of the 'propitious rituals' contained in the code. A second dependent body, the bureau for provisions for sacrificial offerings, was in charge of meat and wine used in sacrifices and offerings.

Just what functioning relationship the officials in these bureaucratic bodies had with those in the specialist ritual courts is not clear. However there was evidently some coincidence of role, for the court of sacrifices is sometimes mentioned in conjunction with the board of rites. Moreover the *Administrative regulations*, in describing the duties of the board of rites, states that regulations for certain of its operations are recorded under the entries for the court of sacrifices, the court of imperial banquets, or the court of ceremonial for foreigners.[60] But there was one difference between the senior posts in the ritual courts and those in the board of rites. For the emperor sometimes emphasised the dynastic element in the state ritual programme by appointing members of the imperial family, often in a supernumerary capacity, to the presidencies of

---

[59] *CTS* ch. 67 p. 2479, ch. 194A p. 5175, ch. 196B p. 5246 and 5251. The presidency of the court of the imperial family was also used in this way, *CTS* ch. 194A p. 5177.

[60] *TTLT* ch. 4 p. 26b and 52b, for the court of sacrifices; ch. 4 p. 52a for the court of imperial banquets; ch. 4 p. 31b and 57a for the court of ceremonial for foreigners. The board of rites and the court of sacrifices are mentioned together in *CTS* ch. 27 p. 1032. But their officials could disagree with each other; *CTS* ch. 26 p. 999.

the ritual courts.[61] The board of rites on the other hand was staffed exclusively from the regular bureaucracy. There is, however, no clear evidence, as far as appointment to high level ritual office is concerned, for a conflict of interest between the imperial Li clan and the regular bureaucracy. The senior posts in the ritual courts, especially those involving scholarly knowledge of the ritual tradition, seem to have been quite as often given to scholar officials from the general service as to imperial princes.

Nor was the drafting of rituals seen as an inaccessible or arcane activity. One of the middle ranking offices in the court of sacrifices, that of doctor, demanded scholarly expertise. But, like the senior posts, it was typically given to scholarly general service officials. Moreover its duties involved exposure to general publicity within the official community, and as a result it was much more respected than posts carrying the title of doctor elsewhere in the bureaucracy, in the state academy for example.[62] That specialisation in state ritual did occur is undeniable. Some of the great aristocratic clans of the seventh and eighth centuries preserved a family tradition of expertise in state ritual; but they did so partly because such expertise gave, and indeed was openly acknowledged as giving, general career advantages.[63] There are also a very few examples of individuals remaining in middle echelon ritual office for long periods. But these were the obsessive scholars of the subject, or the otherwise politically ineffective or unambitious, and they are reported as idiosyncratic cases, or, more likely, drop out of official biographical sources altogether.[64] Tenure of senior and middle ranking ritual office is thus to be seen as a normal feature in the careers of many scholarly general service officials, while the official scholars who staffed the metropolitan academic institutions, the state academy, the imperial library and the history office were even more often appointed to ritual office. The specialised role of the

---

[61] *CTS* ch. 86 and 95, biographies of the sons of Kao tsung, Chung tsung and Jui tsung provide over twenty examples of this. For the education of Kao tsung's son Li Hung, crown prince in the 650s, in the *Record of ritual*, see *CTS* ch. 86 p. 2828.

[62] *THY* ch. 65 p. 1136; *TT* ch. 25 p. 148A.

[63] *Liu Ho-tung chi* ch. 21 p. 369; *CTS* ch. 189B p. 4964.

[64] E.g. in the first half of the century, Wang T'ao, omitted from *CTS*, but included in *HTS* ch. 122 pp. 4354–60, for whom see also *THY* ch. 13 pp. 304 and 306 and ch. 36 p. 491. Also P'eng Ching-chih, *HTS* ch. 199 pp. 5669–70, and *THY* ch. 21 pp. 405–6. Later in the dynasty there are the examples of Wang Ching, compiler of the invaluable *Ta T'ang chiao ssu lu*, for whom see *HTS* ch. 58 p. 1493, *CTS* ch. 25 p. 956 etc. and P'ei Ch'ai *THY* ch. 65 p. 1136; cf. *HTS* ch. 58 p. 1493.

ritual posts is thus to be balanced against the fact that those appointed to them were generalists, if usually scholarly ones.

That the administration of the ritual programme was considered one of the operations of the general bureaucracy is also indicated by other bureaucratic provisions in this period. One of the conspicuous developments in the reign of Hsüan tsung was the consolidation of a system of commissionerships (*shih*) to over-ride the established bureaucracy and address specific problems. In the early eighth century there were commissioners for such widely different areas as transport, revenue, minting and the collection of books and the re-organisation of the imperial library. As early as 666 there had been a grand commissioner for the Feng and Shan rites on Mount T'ai. Probably from 710 there were commissioners for rites (*li i shih*), to manage the ever difficult drafting problems of imperial obsequies or the funerals of members of the imperial family. In 713 a ritual commissioner was appointed for a 'rehearsal at war' ceremony near the capital. Chang Yüeh was a ritual commissioner in late 723, in connection with the sacrifice to the god of the earth of that year. In 725, he was commissioner for the Feng and Shan rites. Another example was Wei Shu, a lifelong official scholar and member of several scholarly commissions, appointed in 750. Ritual commissioners are much more conspicuous in the records for the post-rebellion period than in those of Hsüan tsung's reign. But their appearance in the documentation for the first half of the eighth century indicates that the state ritual programme was subject to exactly the same evolutionary trends as other, more obviously practical areas of administration.[65]

Finally, the integration of the ritual programme in the bureaucracy as a whole is indicated by the fact that the censorate, the body that monitored the operation of the whole of the metropolitan and provincial government, also had explicit responsibility for the imperial rituals. One of its ranks, that of investigating censor, was charged with observing the rituals and maintaining their

---

[65] For ritual commissioners, see *CTS* ch. 67 p. 2487; *TCTC* ch. 206 p. 6656, 710.7; *THY* ch. 26 p. 503; *TT* ch. 43 p. 248B; *CTS* ch. 102 p. 3148; cf. *THY* ch. 37 pp. 671–2. It is possible that the use of the term ritual commissioner prior to 750 is anachronistic; but it remains certain that specific ritual tasks were often given to selected officials whose posts were not in the ritual agencies. See *CTS* ch. 189B p. 4964 for a clear example of this.

decorum.[66] This was, incidentally, a necessary function, for just as the T'ang court itself was sometimes boisterous, so ritual performances might be attended by clamour and disorder, among participants or onlookers.

No brief summary of the institutional framework supporting the imperial ritual programme can do justice to the complexity of the organisation the histories and institutional compendia describe. Other agencies in the central government, like the remaining five courts, the history office or the imperial palace services, might be involved in aspects of the ritual programme. Court diarists were required to note performances of rituals; the bureau of compositions, a department of the imperial library, produced prayer texts. Some posts in the crown prince's extensive household also had ritual functions.

A list of all officials mentioned by the code would of course extend far beyond the main ritual agencies. The attendance of such symbolically important figures as the 'three dukes', the highest ranking officials in the bureaucracy, is prescribed with great frequency. So too is that of the direct descendants of the two dynasties that had preceded the T'ang, the duke of Hsi, descendant of the Sui royal house, and the duke of Chieh, descendant of that of the Northern Chou (557–581). Their presence stood for the ideal, which had never been remotely realised, of a voluntary and non-violent transmission of power from dynasty to dynasty, in this case from the two pre-T'ang northern based dynasties to the T'ang itself.[67] Likewise the attendance at certain rituals of the lineal descendant of Confucius, at this point in the dynasty in the thirty-fifth generation, had clear symbolic value.[68] For important rites, the code required the attendance, in rows according to seniority, of all civil and military officials in the capital. For the twice yearly *Shih tien* ritual to Confucius, the entire staff and student body of the state academy were paraded, and a guard was

---

[66] *TTLT* ch. 13 p. 14b; *TT* ch. 24 p. 144C; *CTS* ch. 44 pp. 1861–3, esp. p. 1863; *Liu Ho-tung chi* ch. 26 p. 432, *Lung chin feng sui p'an* ch. 4 pp. 4a–5b.

[67] e.g. *TTKYL* ch. 4 p. 2b– ch. 46 p. 3b. For the cults to the imperial ancestors of the Northern Chou and Sui houses, see *TTLT* ch. 4 pp. 39b and 55b, *Ta T'ang chiao-ssu lu* ch. 10 p. 20a; also *CTS* ch. 43 p. 1832 for their descendants' ritual court appearances; des Rotours, *Fonctionnaires*, p. 93. From 750 to 753 however, this system was temporarily abolished; see *TCTC* ch. 216 p. 6899, 750.11, *TCTC* ch. 216 p. 6918, 753.9, *THY* ch. 24 p. 462–3.

[68] *TTKYL* ch. 16 p. 2b; *TT* ch. 53 p. 305; *Ts'e-fu yüan kuei* (*Compilation of most precious documents*) (Peking, 1960), ch. 50 p. 6a.

provided to keep onlookers in order.[69] No figures survive from T'ang times to indicate precisely the cost to the treasuries of the great imperial rituals or the numbers of those present. But the extensive distribution of imperial largesse and of tax concessions, announced in acts of grace that followed great ritual performances, involved enormous expense.[70] From the evidence of the Sung period (960–1279), it would seem that the expenditure on the principal rites could be colossal and that the total numbers of those involved might be in the order of thousands.[71]

A T'ang scholar official's career was likely to involve, in turn with general administrative tenures at the capital or in the provinces, appointment to a ritual post or an office that carried ceremonial functions. The state's ritual programme impinged on his professional life and took up his time at many points. As their surviving works demonstrate, numbers of eighth-century scholar officials submitted memorials on ritual questions in turn with proposals on other, quite practical administrative issues, for example on the reform of the taxation or registration systems or on aspects of the political or even military structure. Chang Yüeh himself, as an outstanding general service official with provincial and military experience, was also an active ritual scholar in this way; but there are many other examples from eighth-century times.[72]

This integration of the rituals into the general bureaucratic service had an important intellectual concomitant. For it meant that, officially at least, all the activities in which scholars were

---

[69] *TTKYL* ch. 54 p. 2b, ch. 55 p. 2b. Cf. *TCTC* ch. 214 p. 6810, 735.1, for the inability of the Chin-wu guard to control the clamour of onlookers after the ploughing rite of 735.

[70] E.g. following the ploughing rite of 735, see *T'ang ta chao-ling chi* ch. 74 pp. 415–16. Cf. *THY* ch. 21 p. 406 and *HTS* ch. 199 p. 5470 for a rare example of mention of the cost of an individual rite.

[71] J.T.C. Liu, 'The Sung emperors and the Ming-t'ang or Hall of Enlightenment', *Etudes Song, in memoriam Etienne Balazs* série 2, Civilization I (Paris, 1973), pp. 35–56.

[72] For Chang Yüeh, see E. G. Pulleyback, *The background to the rebellion of An Lu-shan* (London, 1955), esp. pp. 50–2. Other examples are Ts'ui Jung (643–708), *CTS* ch. 94 pp. 2996–3000, *HTS* ch. 114 pp. 4194–6; *THY* ch. 26 p. 491 (cf. *TT* ch. 40 pp. 3285A–C and *CTS* ch. 22 p. 873), and D. C. Twitchett, 'A Confucian's view of the taxation of commerce: Ts'ui Jung's memorial of 703', *Bulletin of the School of Oriental and African Studies* xxxvi (1973), pp. 429–45; Liu Chih (d.c. 759), *CTS* ch. 102 p. 317; *HTS* ch. 132 p. 4524; *CTS* ch. 25 p. 971, and ch. 27 p. 1035; and Edwin G. Pulleyback, 'Neo-Confucianism and Neo-Legalism in T'ang intellectual life, 755–805', in Arthur F. Wright ed., *The Confucian persuasion* (Stanford, California, 1960), pp. 98–9.

engaged, not merely state ritual, were to be related to the same comprehensive Confucian view of the cosmos and the state. On the other hand, the fact that the imperial ritual programme was so firmly integrated into the general bureaucratic structure may also be seen to have reinforced two developments that in effect detracted from the religious aspect of the state ritual tradition over the T'ang: the politicisation of the tradition and the growing unofficial emphasis on the social rather than cosmological function of the rites.

T'ANG CONCEPTS OF STATE RITUAL

The T'ang emperors, despite their lofty claims of descent from the deified Lao tzu, had immediate origins in the semi-sinicised milieu of the northern dynasties in the period of disunion. The early T'ang court had been less cultured, less sophisticated in its ritual tradition, and more dominated by soldierly values than the courts of the vanquished southern dynasties. Practical and out-going attitudes also coloured the court's outlook on the imperial ritual programme. There was thus almost no independent speculation on the theoretical aspects of the royal rituals that pre-T'ang tradition required the dynasty to perform. Rather, the emperor, high ministers and ritual officials had an intense and practical interest in their correct, and, from the mid-seventh century on, more grandiose performance.

An understanding of the theoretical importance of royal rituals to the T'ang state must therefore be gleaned from the documentation produced by the controversies and discussions surrounding individual rituals. The dynasty's need, again determined by practical as much as theoretical considerations, to impose its own identity on the scholarly tradition as a whole also resulted in the mid-seventh century in the re-affirmation of traditional theoretical positions with regard to ritual. Likewise the questions that examiners set, in T'ang times reflecting the general intellectual climate much more faithfully than did those of the enormous and inflexible operation of late imperial times, contained some indications of what current attitudes to state ritual were and how they changed. Much of early T'ang theorising on ritual involved repeating traditional notions. Despite their lack of fresh perceptions, however, seventh-century official scholars offered striking testimony to the sophistication of the Chinese ritual tradition.

Their first justification for ritual was cosmological. They asserted that ritual was an integral component of the universe itself. 'It forms the warp of heaven and earth and provides the structure of human conduct.' 'Its function in the good ordering of the universe is co-eval with heaven and earth.' Ritual drew its elements from the physical universe and the succession of the seasons.[73] The same early T'ang scholars who were skilled in the ritual tradition were also versed in the calendar and in cosmology. They therefore integrated the ritual programme with their view of the universe and with their numerological and calendrical systems. The official T'ang world-view was largely inherited, drawn up in the mid-seventh century by official scholars who culled as nearly a self consistent view as they could from the mass of conflicting sources they reviewed.

This was a comprehensive world-view, and it bound the human and cosmological processes together in a hierarchy of complex and highly detailed dependent relationships. As a component of the cosmos, man was governed by the same series of elements, numbers, colours, directions, tastes, musical notes and cycle of seasons. Man's own conduct, particularly that of the emperor, therefore affected this cosmic system.[74] Cosmological events, climatic irregularities, epidemics and other catastrophes, as well as good omens in this view were relevant to the ritual programme.[75] Interpretation of bad omens and of disasters might vary, and there were frequent controversies. The question, in particular, of when to schedule the major non-recurrent rituals for which the code supplied directives was seen in these cosmological terms. The frequency of requested, planned and aborted Feng and Shan rites

---

[73] *Li chi chu shu*, preface, 1a.

[74] The leading official scholar of the early T'ang who combined calendrical, numerological and ritual expertise was K'ung Ying-ta (547–648), held to be the 32nd generation descendant of Confucius. He was director of the first commission that worked on the *Wu ching cheng i* (*True meaning of the Five canons*), completed in 653; he also worked on the ritual code of 637. For key statements on the shape of the universe, see *Sui shu* ch. 19 p. 505 and *Shang shu chu shu* ch. 3 p. 3b, in both of which K'ung Ying-ta was involved. See also C. Cullen, 'A Chinese Eratosthenes of the flat earth', *Bulletin of the School of Oriental and African Studies* xxxix (1976), pp. 107–9.

[75] For the classification of good omens and their processing by the board of rites, see *TTLT* ch. 4 pp. 15a–21a. Also, Edward H. Schafer, 'The auspices of T'ang', *Journal of the American Oriental Society* lxxxiii (1963), pp. 197–225, esp. pp. 199–202; also *Lung chin feng sui p'an* ch. 2 pp. 1a–2a, suggesting a problem of falsified omen reports.

not only on Mount T'ai but also on Mount Sung and Mount Hua indicates the sense of uncertainty and dependence on cosmologically interpreted factors that might surround the principal rituals in the first division of the code.[76] The whole programme may also be assumed to have been subject to the highly developed tradition of divination as far as auspicious timing was concerned. This, the cosmological view of ritual, was part of the orthodox ideology in which serving officials were schooled. The great majority of them publicly adhered to it, out of deference to imperial power and from individual ambition.

Traditional theory, however, also permitted a more social and less cosmological emphasis in approaching the rites. This did not necessarily conflict with the cosmological view although it might sometimes coexist uneasily with it. For there was throughout the T'ang a tradition, in admonition to the emperor and in unofficial writing, of marking off the human from the supernatural and cosmological processes. But whether sceptical about the role of heaven in this way or not, in discussing the role of ritual in the state or in society T'ang scholars had certain unquestioned assumptions. An essential feature of their view of the human world was that it formed a hierarchy, a social pyramid, the strata of which were to be regulated by rules of extraordinary precision. These rules affected far more than the imperial ritual programme; but the ritual tradition, like that of criminal law, provided a context for generalising about them. T'ang scholars, reiterating a view that originated in the canons emphasised that distinctions of status were an essential feature of ritual.[77] In the state ritual programme itself and in the code, their concern was above all with the emperor, then with the imperial family and with the court and high ranking officials. The lower levels of officialdom and provincial officials were mentioned only to stipulate that ritual provisions were reduced in

---

[76] In 641 the rites planned for 642 were abandoned because of a comet; *THY* ch. 7 p. 87. In 647 those planned for 648 were stopped because of irregular tides at Ch'üan-chou on the coast of modern Fukien; *THY* ch. 7 p. 93. In 682 rites on Mount Sung were aborted because of famine, barbarian threat and the emperor's own illness; *THY* ch. 7 pp. 101–2. In 751 a fire at a temple precinct caused the rites on mount Hua to be abandoned at a late state; *THY* ch. 8 p. 138. In 725 the secretary of the board of war questioned whether it was appropriate for military manoeuvres to take place before the great celebration of that year; *CTS* ch. 194A p. 5175.

[77] E.g. *Li chi chu shu* ch. 50 p. 3b; *CTS* ch. 21 p. 815–00, ch. 86 p. 2828. Also, Ch'ü T'ung-tsu, *Law and society in traditional China*, pp. 226–41.

grandeur with descending rank on the mandarin scale and in the empire-wide administrative hierarchy.

In speaking more generally of the social function of ritual, seventh- and early eighth-century official scholars repeated the traditional view that ritual exercised a restraint on the social hierarchy and on the unruly appetites of man. It provided 'defensive dykes for the control of great floods', or 'the bit and spurs to ride a mettlesome horse'.[78] Ritual thus provided a means to control man's potential for socially disruptive behaviour. It functioned through the prescribed ceremony, which appealed to the affective side of man's nature, but channelled his emotions to make them socially and morally constructive.

This notion of ritual as a positive social value also involved understanding the concept in the broadest possible sense. For medieval scholars extended this ideal to all administrative operations. They used a traditional dichotomy, mentioned by Confucius himself, that opposed administration by 'ritual' to government by 'punishments'. Ritual government was thought of as voluntary and positive. Punishments involved coercion; and the use of the criminal law, and still more of military force, was an indication of failure. This distinction was brought up in many different contexts, including those of the major cosmically interpreted rituals themselves. For punishments, though primarily a social and political category, were also held to have cosmological implications. The greatest of the non-recurrent rites, the Feng and Shan, should therefore only be performed when 'punishments were not being applied'. Ritual occasions also enabled the emperor to affirm the benevolence of the cosmic order and of his own role in mediating between it and the human hierarchy. The great ritual celebrations were customarily followed by acts of grace (*she*). In these, the emperor might extend pardon to criminals in all categories of wrong-doing, although those guilty of the most serious crimes tended merely to have their sentences reduced.[79]

There are grounds for seeing in this frequently cited opposition between ritual and punishments one of the main themes in medieval Confucian ideology. Early T'ang Confucianism did not have, as neo-Confucianism was to develop, a generally accepted, central

---

[78] *Li chi chu shu*, preface, 1a.
[79] D. C. Lau tr., *Confucius; the Analects* (Harmondsworth, 1979), p. 63. *THY* ch. 8 p. 108; Brian E. McKnight, *The quality of mercy*, (Honolulu, 1981), pp. 64–5.

and highly analytical belief in the innate goodness of human nature. But its often repeated affirmation of the priority of ritual over punishments was a comparable expression of optimism over government and society.[80] This assertion in official and unofficial writing of the primacy of ritual was moreover characteristically medieval in another sense. For it expressed medieval concern for the state and for government, rather than for interior or psychological problems relating to the individual. In this age, when the Confucian intellectual outlook was much more court-centred than was later to be the case, it was to be expected that scholars would locate the highest good in a largely court managed activity rather than in the individual considered more universally.

The view of the rites as having a social function was also given a more down-to-earth emphasis. Emperors and ritual scholars alike saw in certain rituals a valuable and practical exemplary function. This is clearly true of the ploughing rite that might follow the offering to the paragon emperor Shen Nung, for emperors considered it a means of encouraging good husbandry throughout the empire. In performing it, moreover, they sometimes emphasised its exemplary value by setting aside the status specific aspect of the rite. Thus in 667 Kao tsung, the third T'ang emperor, rejected a decorated ploughshare, stating, 'agricultural equipment is for the use of the farmer and it depends on its functionality. How can it set value on decoration?' In the same performance, Kao tsung also deliberately exceeded the number of furrows required by canonical authority of him as emperor, in order to emphasise the importance of husbandry. In the ploughing rite of 735, Hsüan tsung also went beyond the traditional stipulations for the same reason.[81] Another, though rather seldom performed, ritual that was seen as having practical aims was the 'rehearsal at war' in the third division

---

[80] The priority of ritual over punishments is asserted in e.g. *Sui shu* ch. 25 p. 695, *T'ang lü shu-i* (*Commentarial discussions on the criminal laws of the T'ang*) (*T'sung-shu chi-ch'eng* edn) preface p. 2, in the context of criminal law; *Sui shu* ch. 74 p. 1691; *CTS* ch. 90 pp. 2913–14, in that of general administration; *Teng-k'o chi k'ao* (*An enquiry into the record of successful examination candidates* (*Nan-ching shu-yüan ts'ung-shu*, edn) ch. 1 p. 9a; *T'ang ta chao-ling chi* ch. 106 p. 542; *Po Hsiang-shan chi* (*Collected works of Po Chü-i* (772–846)) (*Kuo-hsüeh chi-pen ts'ung shu* edn) vol. 7 ch. 47 pp. 72–3, in examination questions; *Han Ch'ang-li chi* vol. 7 ch. 5 p. 84 in the context of education. See also Ch'ü T'ung-tsu, *Law and society in traditional China*, pp. 267–79.

[81] *THY* ch. 10B p. 244; *CTS* ch. 24 p. 913. Cf. also *CTS* ch. 24 pp. 913–14, for a similar move by Su tsung in 759.

of the code.[82] Again, emphasis on social or even military function did not necessarily conflict with the cosmological perspective on rituals. Both the ploughing and the military rehearsal rites were also discussed in cosmological terms, at least as far as their place in the annual cycle was concerned.[83]

But even when they reiterated high ideals about the superiority of government by ritual or endorsed the suasive function of the rites, Confucian scholars also conceded that the constraint of criminal law and the coercion of military force were necessary. The appropriate balance that the dynasty should strike between government by ritual and government by punishments was a recurrent examination question in the seventh and eighth centuries.[84] Moreover the ritual programme and the main ritual precincts were protected by some of the severest articles in the codified criminal law of the dynasty.[85] In the ritual code itself also, the preliminary announcement that a rite was to be conducted included the statement, delivered in the department of affairs of state to the participating officials that 'each is to uphold his office; if they do not provide their services, the state has unvarying punishments . . .'

Belief in the social value of state ritual nonetheless gave intellectual dignity and conviction to the approach of scholars to the great rituals in the code. Here the Confucian tradition demonstrated an ability to contain different intellectual emphases, religious and social or ethical, that was one of the reasons for its durability. Emphasis on the social function of rites is apparent in one or two of the controversies of the reign in which the code was promulgated.[86] Later, however, in the post-rebellion period, it combined with a new scepticism about the role of 'heaven', and became the predominant emphasis among those scholars who reassessed the function of state rituals.

---

[82] *THY* ch. 26 pp. 501–4; *CTS* ch. 8 p. 171; *Chen-kuan cheng yao* (*Essentials of the good government of the Chen-kuan period*) edn prepared by Harada Taneshige and published as *Jōkan seiyō teihon* (Tokyo, 1962), ch. 9, p. 266. Neither *CTS* ch. 21–2 nor *TT* ch. 76–8 documents this ritual; cf. below at n. 103.

[83] *TT* ch. 46 p. 236C and *THY* ch. 10B p. 243, ch. 10B p. 347, ch. 26 pp. 502–3 and *Li chi chu shu* ch. 14 p. 14b; *THY* ch. 26 pp. 403–4.

[84] See above, n. 80 and n. 87 below.

[85] In the dynastic criminal code, of the most serious crimes, the 'ten abominations', the second, 'plotting great sedition' and the sixth 'great irreverence', had specific reference to ritual precincts and equipment; see *The T'ang code*, tr. with an introduction by Wallace Johnson (Princeton, 1979), i, pp. 17–23, 63–5, 69–70.

[86] *CTS* ch. 25 pp. 965–73; *THY* ch. 37 pp. 680–4; *CTS* ch. 27 pp. 1032–6.

A final and central feature of the official view of state rituals in the eighth century was that the programme it involved, though ultimately sanctioned by the 'inerasable authority' of the Confucian canons, was far from being unchanging. Again, this view of ritual as an evolving tradition was amply outlined in canonical literature, by Confucius himself,[87] and in the exegetical tradition. The idea of historical change in ritual was basic to the activity of revising and re-drafting rituals, in which so many eighth-century scholars were engaged. Early T'ang official scholars had documented the evolution that had taken place in individual rituals over the Chin dynasty (AD 265–420) and the period of disunion. The changes that occurred then and in the Sui and early T'ang may prove to be small when compared to the changes between the Former and Later Han. Yet the admissibility of ongoing change was a vital aspect of the medieval tradition. The T'ang emperors T'ai tsung, Chung tsung and Hsüan tsung all committed themselves explicitly to a view of state ritual as evolving. When T'ai tsung rejected the suggestion that the ploughing rite should take place in the southern rather than the eastern suburb and endorsed the sanction of the *Book of documents* (*Shang shu*) rather than that of the *Record of ritual* which conflicted with it, he stated, 'Ritual follows the feelings of man; what question is there of it being unvarying?'[88]

Likewise the great majority in the scholarly community, though always apt to adduce canonical sanction in re-drafting rituals, supported the idea of evolution.[89] They advocated change not least because as individuals they often stood to gain by identifying themselves with the innovation that they knew the sovereign wanted. Scholars had therefore to reconcile the bookish element in the tradition, their instinct to condemn what was 'not ancient' in ritual and their ideal of a 'clear text' in the canons or a 'canonical basis' as a sanction for particular rites on the one hand with the expanding resources of the dynasty and the ambition of its sover-

---

[87] D. C. Lau, *Confucius: the Analects* (see n. 79), p. 66.
[88] *CTS* ch. 24 p. 912; *HTS* ch. 199 p. 5670; *T'ang ta chao-ling chi* ch. 74 p. 416; *CTS* ch. 25 p. 9531; *Ch'üan T'ang shih* ch. 3 p. 35.
[89] *CTS* ch. 26 p. 1024–6 and 1030; *TT* ch. 53 p. 304C; *CTS* ch. 102 p. 3172; *THY* ch. 12 p. 298; cf. *Teng k'o chi k'ao* ch. 5 pp. 10a–b and *Po Hsiang-shan chi* vol. 7 ch. 48 pp. 79–80.

eigns on the other. The result was the casuistry that is so apparent in records of ritual discussions.[90]

The pragmatic attitude of the T'ang scholarly community to the ritual programme combined with the recognition of evolution to make T'ang attitudes to individual rites strikingly flexible. A ceremony that might have lapsed for many centuries might be revived for reasons that seem little more than fortuitous. A case in point is a local ritual to the god of the earth associated with the great emperor Wu ti of the Former Han (reigned 140–87 BC) at Fen-yin in modern Shansi. In 722 Hsüan tsung passed through Fen-yin and, at Chang Yüeh's suggestion, revived it. From a note in the *Comprehensive compendium* of 801, it seems likely that he commandeered and adapted an existing temple for the purpose.[91] Another example is a cult to the 'precious spirits of the nine palaces (*chiu kung kuei shen*)', the justification for which was cosmological. This cult had originally been established in AD 134, but had long since lapsed. In 744 Hsüan tsung, responding to a memorial from a magician, re-established it and it lasted well into the following century.[92]

The divinities or correlatives that received sacrifices in well-established rituals might also be changed as the result of argument. Thus in the case of the ritual for husbandry that preceded the ploughing rite, there had been from 685 to 705 different positions with regard to which gods were to be the recipients of sacrifices. From 705, the gods of the soil and of grain had been prescribed, with Kou-lung shih, a divinity associated with the earth as correlative. But in 731, a year before the completion of the code, the paragon emperor and first teacher of husbandry, Shen Nung, was substituted, with the Hou Chi as correlative. Accordingly it was to these two exemplars that the code of 732 prescribed offering. The arguments involved in this change of practice imply that for T'ang

---

[90] For condemnation of what was 'not ancient', see *Ta T'ang chiao-ssu lu* ch. 5 pp. 3b–4a, *TT* ch. 70 pp. a385A–386A, *THY* ch. 12 p. 249. For the need for a 'clear text (*ming wen*)' *THY* ch. 11 p. 273 (*CTS* ch. 22 p. 853 reads only 'without a text'); *CTS* ch. 21 p. 826, ch. 20 p. 980, 27 p. 1036. For the desirability of a 'canonical basis (*ching chü*)', *CTS* ch. 25 pp. 953 and 968; *THY* ch. 6 p. 69.

[91] *Shih chi* (*Historical records*) (Peking, 1959), ch. 12 pp. 464–5 and ch. 28 p. 1392; *TT* ch. 45 pp. 260B–C; *TTLT* ch. 4 p. 34b. *CTS* ch. 8 p. 185, ch. 24 p. 928, ch. 97 p. 3054 and *TCTC* ch. 212 p. 6755, 723.3. This cult was mentioned in a decree examination answer of 726; see *Teng k'o chi k'ao* ch. 8 p. 20a.

[92] *THY* ch. 10B pp. 256–60; *Ta T'ang chiao-ssu lu* ch. 6 pp. 1a–6b; *CTS* ch. 24 pp. 929–34.

ritual scholars it was the context provided by existing altars and a ploughing site and by a place in the ritual calendar that provided premises for the debates. The problem of which divinities might be involved resulted from these practical administrative considerations. This flexibility over the selection of cult figures was again demonstrated in 735, three years after the promulgation of the code. The ploughing rite was redrafted and yet another divinity, Chu-mang, a god associated with spring and the element wood, was substituted for Hou Chi. In 759, however, Hou Chi was restored as correlative.[93]

Belief in change and adaptation was, therefore, an inbuilt feature of the state ritual tradition. In the course of the eighth century this feature was to combine with unofficially expressed scepticism about the cosmological aspects of state ritual, and was indirectly to reinforce the market shift that took place towards understanding the rites principally in terms of their social and moral function.

POLITICAL DIMENSIONS

A certain blandness in the traditional justification for the state ritual programme that T'ang scholars reiterated, and the fact that their ritual institutions were not original to the dynasty, should not give the impression that eighth-century ritual practice was uneventful or placid. On the contrary, accessible as ritual issues were to the scholarly bureaucracy at large, they elicited fierce competition. They were also fought over by other competing interests, religious, political and even military. The political vitality of the early and mid-eighth century was thus expressed in the ritual tradition, and this political dimension added to the importance of imperial rituals in the T'ang state.

A major source of tension for the Confucian ritual tradition concerned the relation of the rites contained in the code, for Confucians the orthodox programme, with the other principal belief systems and the wealth of lesser cults that existed. The most obvious threat to the regular implementation of the rituals in the code, particularly those in its first division, came from the transcendental teachings of Buddhism and Taoism. The Confucian rituals as they are prescribed in the code, with their laconic prayer

---

[93] *Ta T'ang chiao-ssu lu* ch. 10 pp. 1a–b, summary only; *TT* ch. 45 pp. 262B–C; *THY* ch. 10B p. 245, ch. 42 pp. 421–4; *CTS* ch. 24 pp. 913–14.

texts, can have done little to satisfy deeper religious instincts. At best they might move the individual to reverence for the unseen cosmological powers or for past exemplars, or to pride in the dynasty. Or they might stir the emperor to compassion for deceased members of his family, as Hsüan tsung was said to have been stirred when making offering in the ancestral temple to Jui tsung, his father in 717.[94] The Buddhist and Taoist traditions on the other hand provided copiously for the religious imagination, and in particular promised abundantly for the afterlife.

Successive T'ang sovereigns encouraged the idea of the fundamental compatability of Confucianism, Buddhism and Taoism. But, in fact, representatives of the three teachings at court competed against each other for the patronage of the emperor, the imperial family and the court. Individual clerics urged the requirements of their own faiths, sometimes openly deriding Confucian religious traditions.[95] They were often successful, for despite the protest of Confucian orientated officials, under Hsüan tsung's immediate predecessors, resources that might have gone into the upkeep of ritual precincts or buildings were used on a lavish scale for Buddhist and Taoist temples.[96] In the second half of Hsüan tsung's reign, the emperor's promotion of Taoism and establishment of Taoist schools and temples, to be managed by the court of the imperial family, again must have been to the detriment of the programme prescribed by the Confucian ritual code. Emperors were also liable to take up and develop their own religious interests, perhaps new or dubiously canonical cults, on the margins of orthodoxy. They were often supported in this by the ambitious or opportunistic, from within the bureaucracy or outside it. Such cults might also result in ritual obligations that competed with the orthodox programme.

In this situation, the almost complete precision with which the compilers of the K'ai-yüan code resisted the intrusion of rituals from the other teachings and from other cults is both striking and historically important. Only one of the cults introduced in the decades prior to the code and included in it was clearly unsanctioned by the canons or the exegetical tradition. This, the 'cult of

[94] *CTS* ch. 25 p. 952; cf. *CTS* ch. 25 p. 973.
[95] Lo Hsiang-lin, 'T'ang tai san chiao chiang-hua k'ao (An examination of the debates between the three teachings in the T'ang age)', *Journal of Oriental Studies* i (1954), pp. 85–97; *CTS* ch. 192 p. 4128.
[96] *CTS* ch. 89 pp. 2893–4, ch. 101 pp. 3155–61, ch. 88 pp. 2870–1.

the five dragons', was promoted by Hsüan tsung himself, and celebrated the favour he believed the supernatural powers had shown him as crown prince.[97] The code's compilers were largely successful also in excluding the syncretic approach towards Taoism and Confucianism that Hsüan tsung developed in the second, fervently Taoist half of his reign. The enforcement of rigid classificatory lines like this was, of course, a feature of the medieval Chinese official approach to any scholarly activity; but the compilers of the code may also have been helped in maintaining its discrete Confucian character by a bureaucratic factor, by the institutional framework in which they operated. For the main institution concerned with implementing the code, the court of sacrifices, had a long tradition of providing administrative support for Confucian rituals. There were, at least at the time when the code was compiled, separate institutional provisions for the other teachings. Only the board of sacrifices (*tz'u pu*), a department of the board of rites, was administratively concerned with all three teachings. And it is not clear how much, in practice, the officials of the board of sacrifices were active in the imperial ritual programme the code prescribed. Even though the compilers of the code formed an *ad hoc* commission that worked not in the court of sacrifices but in Hsüan tsung's own advisory college, the Chi-hsien yüan, they observed the lines of demarcation that these separate institutions provided.

The code's compilers also set aside their own religious beliefs, for it is very probable that as individuals and in private they were adherents of one or other of the transcendant faiths. For them to have promoted the rival teaching of Buddhism, or indeed to have expressed their own personal belief in Buddhism, in the context of the code, however, would have been both to have disregarded traditional lines of demarcation and to have offered help to forces within the bureaucracy or outside it with whom they were in competition for the emperor's interest and patronage. The lines of demarcation between the Confucian outlook and Taoism were never so clear, for Confucian orientated scholar officials were also scholars of classical Taoist texts. But in their official capacities they

---

[97] *TTKYL* ch. 51 pp. 5b–8a; *THY* ch. 22 pp. 433–4; *Ta T'ang chiao-ssu lu* ch. 7 pp. 6b–9b; Robert des Rotours, 'Le culte des cinq dragons sous la dynastie des T'ang (618–907)', *Mélanges de sinologie offerts à Monsieur Paul Demieville* (Paris, 1966), pp. 261–80.

generally stopped short of promoting religious Taoism, and they certainly did not permit it to intrude into the imperial ritual code. Again this was both because they were observing traditional distinctions and institutional lines of demarcation and because they did not wish to lend support to rivals of whose attitudes and motives they were suspicious. Hsüan tsung's promotion of Taoism through the court of the imperial family came after the promulgation of the code. But there is relatively little evidence that it intruded into the imperial ritual programme embodied in the code.[98]

A scarcely less important expression of the broad sectional interest of the compilers of the code concerned their attitude to the military element in it, to the 'army rituals' and related ceremonies. The scholars who staffed the academic agencies stood above all for civil virtues. The military element in the T'ang state, on the other hand, was enormous. In the mid-K'ai-yüan period, the *Old T'ang history* records, the dynasty could call on at least 120,000 men at the capital, who served 20,000 at a time for two months of the year. The armies at the frontiers numbered in excess of 400,000. The generals or commissioners who controlled these armies were often drawn from the general service of the bureaucracy.[99] Chang Yüeh himself had military experience in three high-ranking frontier posts. But the scholars who staffed the Chi-hsien yüan and those who compiled the ritual code were typically metropolitan academic officials whose careers had not involved military appointments. They were 'book men [*shu sheng*]' and 'Confucians [*ju sheng*]'. Highly selected and identified as the intellectual and scholarly élite, they had great confidence in their own value system. They and many Confucian orientated general service officials, like Chang Yüeh himself, had a political interest in controlling the power of the armies. They were also strongly opposed to imperial military adventurism beyond the frontiers, for they saw in this historically one of the most disruptive forces of internal political and economic stability that unwise imperial conduct might unleash. Though they might occasionally

---

[98] One indication that most Confucian orientated scholars may have been willing to accept the classical Taoist element in the Taoist programme Hsüan tsung promoted may be seen in the fact that aspects of the Taoist cult to Lao tzu were documented in some official and unofficial surveys of the Confucian ritual programme, eg. *CTS* ch. 24 pp. 925–8; but especially *TT* ch. 53 p. 305B.

[99] *CTS* ch. 97 p. 3049. cf. E. G. Pulleybank, *The background to the rebellion of An Lu-shan*, pp. 65–6, and 'The An Lu-shan rebellion and the origins of chronic militarism in late T'ang China', in John Curtis Perry and Bardwell L. Smith (eds.), *Essays on T'ang society* (Leiden, 1976), pp. 33–60.

come forward with ideas on strategy, they did not generally have good relations with professional soldiers or even with some of the officials in the general service who had practical military experience.[100]

The fact that the drafting of the state ritual programme was dominated by these Confucian orientated academic officials, with their civil ideals, may explain why the military element in the state was as little represented in the code as it was. The Confucian canons themselves supported two notions as far as the proportion of military and civil in the state was concerned. One was that of a symmetry or balance between the military (*wu*) and the civil (*wen*). The second was that of three seasons given to agriculture against one for war. Neither ideal was fully realised in the code, though scholars brought up both in the course of ritual debates. Thus the 'army rituals' divison of the code was the second shortest, exceeded in brevity only by the section prescribing ceremonies for foreigners. Moreover although most of the army rituals involved offerings at altar sites and in the ancestral temple, the preliminary abstinences the code prescribed for them were much shorter than for rituals involving the same precincts in the first, the 'propitious rituals' division of the code.

The hostility or at best indifference of the Confucian orientated scholar community generally towards the military is also seen in the relative failure of the military cult to Ch'i T'ai kung. This had been reconstituted in 731 on a scale to balance the expanding civil cult to Confucius. Some scholars at least believed that a cult for T'ai kung had the sanction of the *Monthly commands* section of the *Record or ritual*.[101] But in the aftermath of the An Lu-shan rebellion it provoked opposition. It was re-established and expanded in 760, lapsed, to be revived and expanded yet again in the early and mid-780s. Surviving memorials concerning the cult at this later stage show that opposition, expressed in terms of the priority of 'ritual' over 'expedient action [*ch'üan*]', was by now highly articulate.[102] Another ritual, the 'rehearsal at war', scheduled for the

---

[100] For this distinction between official scholar and general service official see e.g. *CTS* ch. 102 pp. 3164 and 3177. Cf. also *CTS* ch. 157 p. 4158. For the scholar's contempt of professional soldiers, *TCTC* ch. 214 p. 6822, 736.16. The T'ang tradition of admonition against military adventurism is represented in *TT* ch. 200 pp. 1085B–1087B and *Cheng-kuan cheng-yao* ch. 9 pp. 271–81.

[101] *Ta T'ang chiao-ssu lu* ch. 10 p. 14b.

[102] *Ta T'ang chiao-ssu lu* ch. 10 pp. 12b–15b.

winter and designed to express the canonical ideal of three seasons for agriculture and one for war, although it had its advocates, the Emperor's T'ai tsung and Hsüan tsung and the Empress Wu among them, is poorly documented. It too lapsed after the An Lu-shan rebellion.[103] The conclusion must be that the scholars who drafted and managed the ritual programme were opposed for reasons of sectional interest to giving more than minimal recognition to the military aspect of the state.

Official scholars were, however, less successful, and certainly less united in resisting another of the forces that helped shape the ritual programme the code embodied. The growing wealth of the dynasty in the seventh and early eighth centuries fostered in at least the longer reigning sovereigns the ambition to celebrate the great traditional rituals in ever more grandiose ways. And again their motives were less than straightforward. By performing her own versions of the greatest non-recurrent rituals, the usurping Empress Wu claimed the support of the cosmological and supernatural powers and asserted the legitimacy of her own regime.[104] Hsüan tsung's celebration of the southern suburban rite in 723, although the emperor described it in self-deprecating language, was intended to mark twelve years of stable and successful rule.[105]

The increase in the scale of the major imperial rituals from the seventh century to the mid-eighth, however, ran through the reigns of successive sovereigns and is sometimes clearly recorded in the official histories as doing so. Describing a grandiose offering to the river Lo made by the Empress Wu in 688, the *Old T'ang history* relates, 'The imperial sons all followed; all officials, civil and military, the headmen of the barbarian (states), all stood according to their positions. Rare birds and beasts were all deployed before the altar. Since the start of the T'ang, decorated items and processional equipment has never been so resplendent'.[106] The celebrated Hall of Light (*Ming t'ang*) that the Empress Wu constructed at Lo-yang in 688, and then, after a disastrous fire, rebuilt on the same site was envisaged as a central ritual precinct. The edifice was on a scale and used materials and furnishings far more

[103] *Chen-kuan cheng-yao* ch. 9 p. 266, *THY* ch. 26 pp. 501–4, *CTS* ch. 89 p. 2900.
[104] *CTS* ch. 6 p. 119 – ch. 24 p. 922. cf. *TCTC* ch. 204 p. 6454, 688.14; R. W. L. Guisso, *Wu Tse-t'ien and the politics of legitimation in T'ang China* (Western Washington University, 1978), p. 65.
[105] *CTS* ch. 8 p. 186, *T'ang ta chao-ling chi* ch. 68 pp. 380–1.
[106] *CTS* ch. 24 p. 922; *CTS* ch. 6 p. 119.

lavish than those envisaged by the more cautious ritual scholars who had discussed it in the reign of T'ai tsung. Descriptions of the Hall of Light imply that it surpassed all previous buildings in the use of architectural techniques and resources.[107] Under Hsüan tsung, expansion was also the theme in the dynastic ancestral temple. Canonical authority required that the temple contain not more than seven shrines, representing seven generations of deceased ancestors of the imperial line. In 722, however, it was expanded to nine.[108] In 734, after a debate in which at least five scholars from outside the ritual agencies, and one from the board of rites, disagreed with the president of the court of sacrifices, the provisioning of offerings in the ancestral temple was also expanded.[109]

The amounts involved in imperial largesse to participants after major ritual celebrations and the range of the pardons included in acts of grace also increased in the course of the first half of the dynasty. The celebration of the Feng and Shang rites on Mount T'ai by Hsüan tsung in late 725 was particularly lavish. It was called at the time 'an event in a thousand years'. The 'whole state' made the journey east to the mountain, and the procession included representatives of foreign states, recorded in more detail than on any previous occasion.[110] The performance thus invited favourable comparison not only with Kao tsung's celebration of 666, but also with those by past emperors extending back to the great Wu ti of the Han in 110 BC. Under Hsüan tsung expansion of the Confucian shrine, too reached a high point: Confucius and his immediate disciples were represented by statues, while pictures of the larger circle of his followers, numbering over seventy, were drawn on the temple walls. The dynasty also honoured all these figures with grandiose posthumous titles.[111]

This expansion of the state ritual programme and of its precincts was sustained till towards the end of Hsüan tsung's reign. Some scholars asked for restraint, and their submissions were carefully preserved by official scholars of the post-rebellion period. But by

---

[107] *TT* ch. 44 pp. 251A–45B; *THY* ch. 11–12 pp. 271–92; *CTS* ch. 22 pp. 849–79; R. W. L. Guisso, *Wu Tsu-t'ien*, pp. 35, 46, 65, 129.

[108] *TT* ch. 47 p. 270C; *THY* ch. 12 p. 298; *CTS* ch. 8 pp. 183 and 185; *TCTC* ch. 212 pp. 6750, 722.10 and 6756, 723.11.

[109] *CTS* ch. 25 pp. 969–72; *THY* ch. 17 pp. 349–52.

[110] *CTS* ch. 99 p. 3098; *T'ang shih chi shih* (*Record of events relating to T'ang poems*) (Peking, 1965), ch. 3 p. 35; *CTS* ch. 194A p. 5175.

[111] *Ta T'ang chiao-ssu lu* ch. 10 pp. 6b–8b; *TT* ch. 53 pp. 306A–C; *THY* ch. 35 pp. 637–8; *CTS* ch. 24 pp. 919–21.

and large only after the rebellion of An Lu-shan had drastically reduced the resources and political power of the dynasty did scholars more generally condemn the period as one in which the classical virtue of austerity had been set aside. By late eighth-century times, however, this post-rebellion condemnation of the excesses of the second half of Hsüan tsung's reign became an aspect of a radical reassessment by certain intellectuals of the function of imperial rituals in the state.

The flourishing ritual tradition of the first half of the eighth century provided a medium for competition among officials and a means to gain access to officialdom for those as yet commoners. For the dynasty exploited in several distinct ways the enormous prestige of the official career in its service and that of the great state rituals. The major non-recurrent ritual events, held in celebration of propitious conditions, good harvests and general peace, became focal points for support for the dynasty. They were used to hold special examinations for recruiting to the public service, known as 'great ritual candidatures (*ta li chü*)'.[112] The Feng and Shan rites were thus accompanied by special decree examinations or intakes into the bureaucracy. These were sometimes announced in antici-pation of performances that in the event did not take place. This happened in 647, while examinations were held in connection with the successful performances of 666 and 725.[113]

The major rituals, or aspects of them, were also made the topics for composition in the annually held *chin-shih* examination, the most prestigious of all examinations. The requirement here was for a highly wrought and high-flown panegyric style in praise of the dynasty. In 713, for example, candidates were required to compose a prose-poem on the ploughing rite. They would have been aware that they were treating a topic on which Kao tsung, the third T'ang emperor, had composed a prose-poem, and for which the great scholar-emperor Wu ti of the Liang (r. AD 502–550) had written a poem.[114]

The dynasty also encouraged open and competitive discussion of

[112] *CTS* ch. 100 p. 3116.
[113] *T'ang ta chao-ling chi* ch. 66 pp. 368–9; *Teng k'o chi k'ao* ch. 2 pp. 12b–14a; ch. 7 pp. 16a–17a. A special intake was also announced after the ploughing rite of 735; see *T'ang ta chao-ling chi* ch. 74 p. 415 and *Teng k'o chi k'ao* ch. 8 pp. 11a–b.
[114] *Teng-k'o chi k'ao* ch. 5 pp. 12b–14b; *THY* ch. 10B p. 245; *I wen lei-chü* (*Literary encyclopaedia*) (Peking, 1965), ch. 39 pp. 702–5; *Ch'u hsüeh chi* (*Record for early learning*) (Peking, 1962), ch. 14 pp. 339–41.

specific ritual issues. If a scholar risked imperial irritation by offering criticism in terms of unwelcome Confucian austerity, he was normally protected from drastic punishment by the prestige attached to the tradition of frank admonition. But in fact the emperor could assume that all contributions to the resulting debates would fall within acceptable limits. No radical dissent would be voiced by a scholar community the lower ranks of which were dominated by the hope of promotion and the higher levels of which might be, as Chang Yüeh was, reluctant to allow change. Irregularities or sharp departures from conventional practice were, therefore, more likely to come at the wish of emperors themselves or their sycophants than from the regular academic establishment. Typically a ritual problem was discussed initially on imperial order by the 'ritual officials'. But, as in the case of the debate on the provisioning of the imperial ancestral rites in 734, others whose posts had nothing to do with the ritual agencies might participate. Even a commoner might make a submission.[115] Difficult decisions, however, were sometimes taken, after general discussion, by the chief ministers.[116] Here again was an indication that the ritual tradition, though represented by specialist bodies, was the concern of the bureaucracy as a whole.

The state ritual tradition, therefore, was a vehicle not only for the display of scholarly erudition and judgement by ritual specialists, general service officials and aspirants to office; it was also at the same time a camouflage for general political ambition. Not surprisingly it also became a medium for factional activity. It is no coincidence that in the course of the 'event in a thousand years' on Mount T'ai in 725, the scholarly chief minister Chang Yüeh, by allowing very few officials to accompany the emperor up the mountain, and by showing anti-military bias in the distribution of largesse that followed, first incurred the enmity of his aristocratic rival for power Yü-wen Jung. In doing so he helped draw for the first time the deep factional lines that were to dominate political life for the remainder of Hsüan tsung's reign.[117] But this celebrated rite on the eastern peak provides one instance only of a ritual event acquiring a factional dimension or calling forth a response from the

[115] *TT* ch. 47 p. 271A; *THY* ch. 17 pp. 353–5; *CTS* ch. 24 pp. 952–3.
[116] *CTS* ch. 25 pp. 948–9; *THY* ch. 17 pp. 349–52; *CTS* ch. 25 pp. 969–72, ch. 27 p. 1030.
[117] *CTS* ch. 97 pp. 3054–5; E. G. Pulleyblank, *The background to the rebellion of An Lu-shan*, p. 50.

scholarly bureaucracy at large. Indeed, the K'ai-yüan code itself, like other medieval official scholarly compilations, may be understood on several levels. A set of highly detailed, practical directives, it was also the result of the vigorous sectional and political forces that gave it the shape it has.

THE LATER HISTORY OF THE CODE

From its promulgation in 732 until the end of the dynasty, the code held an unchallenged official position. Its high standing is to be seen in the frequency with which, from about 780, extant sources show scholars appealing to it or citing it in debates on ritual issues.[118] On both official and unofficial initiative, a number of supplements to the code were produced; these too paid homage to it either in their titles or in the memorials with which their compilers presented them.[119] Scholars thus never compiled another complete code under T'ang rule. In 789, moreover, the dynasty established a regular annual examination in the code. This made it, remarkably, the only T'ang official compilation to be accepted as an official syllabus in this way. The examination lacked the standing of the *chin-shih*, the most prestigious of the regular examinations, and is poorly documented in consequence. But it continued into the Five Dynasties period (906–960). No questions or answers survive, though the names of a handful of successful candidates are known.[120]

The continued high standing of the code, however, did not mean that the full range of its directives was in any sense mandatory in the imperial ritual programme. From almost immediately after the code's promulgation, ritual officials were again involved, sometimes at the emperor's behest, in re-drafting individual rites.[121] It is thus abundantly clear that the K'ai-yüan code, like its predecessor codes drawn up under the T'ang, was never conceived as providing permanent or definitive answers for all the problems that arose, or as preventing continued evolution. Even in the period after the An Lu-shan rebellion of 755, when the political and economic power of the T'ang was drastically reduced, there were long-running ritual

---

[118] E.g. *CTS* ch. 21 pp. 843–4; *TT* ch. 41 p. 233C; *Teng-k'o chi k'ao* ch. 16 p. 2b.

[119] *THY* ch. 83 pp. 1529–30 and *CTS* ch. 150 p. 4046; *Liu Ho-tung chi* ch. 4 p. 44; *CTS* ch. 171 p. 4454, ch. 157 p. 4155.

[120] *TT* ch. 15 p. 84B; *THY* ch. 76 pp. 1396–7; des Rotours, *Le traité des examens*, (see n. 10), pp. 148–9.

[121] E.g. *THY* ch. 36 p. 658, ch. 20 p. 403.

controversies, and continual readjustment in the ritual programme took place.

The public deference of scholars towards the K'ai-yüan code in the post-rebellion period is thus to be understood largely as a public expression of reverence and nostalgia for the politically prosperous, stable and expansionist era in which it had been produced. For by the closing decades of the eighth century the intellectual world recognised that the remarkable security and wealth the court had enjoyed in the reign of Hsüan tsung were beyond recovery. To scholars writing in an official context and to examination candidates, the code, like the great celebration on Mount T'ai in the winter of 725, had come to stand for the highest point in the history of the dynasty.

These public affirmations of dynastic loyalty and of nostalgia were, however, accompanied by a change in the unofficial attitudes of at least an element in the scholar community towards the ritual programme. This shift may be understood in part as a natural result of what this article has attempted to establish as a central and unique combination of features in the T'ang imperial ritual tradition: the Confucian sanctioned belief system the code embodied retained 'archaic' characteristics. Its focus was this worldly; despite its maintenance of the plurality of divinities and cosmic agents, it had no developed sense of the transcendant and no priesthood. At the same time those who drafted and administered the rites were members of a highly structured and increasingly sophisticated bureaucracy. The interaction of these disparate features was bound in the course of time to produce a change of attitude towards the rituals. In the post-rebellion period moreover, precisely because of the deterioration in the political and economic situation, scholars were less bound by conventional or official attitudes than at any earlier period in the dynasty, and more aware of the relative and perishable nature of many of the traditions surrounding the state.

In this intellectually vigorous climate, a few radical reformist thinkers, writing unofficially, came to apply to the imperial ritual programme and to the belief system it represented the same demands for practicality, austerity and effectiveness that they had applied to the range of problems they encountered in their general administrative roles. Their urgent priority was now, not the ritual celebration of unprecedented success, but the restoration of effective government, or, in the metaphor used in this period, the curing of the state's illness.

The resulting critique of imperial ritual developed the idea that the activities of heaven or of the cosmos and of man were separate. It led one or two intellectuals at the end of the eighth century to a strikingly agnostic view of the Confucian sanctioned ritual programme. Liu Tsung-yüan (773–819), though at least in his later life a committed lay Buddhist, was the most determined of these sceptics. In effect he queried the 'inerasable authority' of the ritual canons. For he even went so far as to criticise parts of the *Monthly commands* section of the *Record of ritual*. This was the canonical authority that most clearly integrated the cosmological view of ritual with the annual ritual programme, and it had been of particular concern to T'ang emperors and to official scholars.[122] Liu Tsung-yüan charged that the functioning correlations between man and the cosmos that the *Monthly commands* posited were baseless, and insisted that 'it is not necessary to regard as supernatural' the activity of making offering to divinities or to the spirits of deceased exemplars. Rather, he maintained, rituals had a moral function, that of increasing the respect and admiration of society for good conduct and elevating the position of the emperor.[123] A modified form of this agnostic or sceptical view of Confucian sanctioned ritual was probably widely accepted in the late eighth and early ninth centuries. The celebrated verse writer Po Chü-i rehearsed it in a specimen examination answer he drafted in 806. Tu Yu, the compiler of the *Comprehensive compendium* of 801, referred indirectly to it.[124] Such an outlook might involve its advocates in re-assessing and down-grading particular rites in the code on the grounds of their extravagance or pointlessness. Liu Tsung-yüan, again the most extreme proponent of this outlook, even went so as to suggest that the Feng and Shan rites were meaningless.[125] But these criticisms never resulted in rejection of the idea of a dynastic ritual code. For even in this period of radical reassessment, the

---

[122] *Chen-kuan cheng-yao*, ch. 1 pp. 29–31; *THY* ch. 26 pp. 291–2, ch. 75 p. 1374, ch. 77 pp. 1410–11; *CTS* ch. 22 pp. 867–73, ch. 24 p. 914; *TT* ch. 70 p. 385C; *THY* ch. 26 p. 492 ch. 35 p. 645,, ch. 77 p. 1411; *T'ang yü lin* (*Anthology of T'ang remarks*) (Shanghai, 1957), ch. 2 pp. 48–9.

[123] *Liu Ho-tung chi* ch. 3 pp. 52–6; ch. 16 pp. 296–7, ch. 26 pp. 432–4, ch. 31 pp. 503–4, ch. 45 p. 787.

[124] *Po Hsiang-shan chi* vol. 7 ch. 47 pp. 72–3, ch. 48 pp. 81–2; *TT* ch. 41 p. 233C.

[125] *Liu Ho-tung chi* ch. 1 p. 18; cf. *T'ang chien* (*Mirror for the T'ang*) (*Ts'ung shu chi-ch'eng* edn) ch. 4 p. 29.

most sceptical thinkers did not attack the code as a whole. Liu Tsung-yüan indicated that he did not want to see the imperial ritual programme lapse. He also expressed gratification when in 811, after a long interval, the ploughing rite was scheduled.[126] Po Chü-i and Tu Yu were among those who, in an official or semi-official context, praised the K'ai-yüan code most fulsomely, and their knowledge of the state ritual tradition was not in doubt.

In terms of the cultural spectrum suggested at the start of this article, these late eighth-and early ninth-century scholars had moved significantly further than their predecessors in the K'ai-yüan period from the Balinese position, in which royal rituals were accorded a place as the dominant activity of the state. Their outlook might even be thought to have approached that of nineteenth-century Britain, in which royal ceremonial was allocated a dignified and secondary rather than an efficient role in the constitution. But such an interpretation would be misleading; these figures remained firmly Confucian. They never surrendered the idea that an imperial ritual programme expressed canonically sanctioned and essential social and moral priorities and therefore performed a vital function for the state. In Liu Tsung-yüan's words, those parts of the programme that related to 'the surburban and ancestral temples and the hundred divinities are the transmitted records of antiquity and should not be set aside'.

Despite the development of these critical attitudes towards state ritual in the second half of the T'ang, the influence of the K'ai-yüan ritual code extended far beyond the dynasty. For the re-establishment of strong dynastic power tended to be accompanied by the re-assertion of the traditional view of the emperor, the state and the cosmos. All later dynasties of any duration, therefore, followed the T'ang in producing one or more ritual codes. The Sung did so not only in the period 968–75,[127] but again in 1111.[128] Even the non-Chinese Jurched dynasty, the Chin (1115–1234) approved a

---

[126] *Liu Ho-tung chi* ch. 43 p. 736; *THY* ch. 10B p. 255; *HTS* vol. 14 ch. 359 p. 60. The performance was eventually cancelled and Liu expressed regret, *Liu Ho-tung chi* ch. 43 p. 533.

[127] *Sung shih (History of the Sung)* (K'ai-ming shu-tien ed., Taipei, 1961) ch. 95 pp. 4731C–D; Ikeda On, 'Dai Tō Kaigen rei no kaisetsu', p. 827.

[128] *Cheng-ho wu li hsin i (New ritual directives for the five divisions of ritual of the Cheng-ho period)*, reprinted in *Ssu-k'u ch'üan shu chen-pen*, first series (Shanghai, 1934).

code in 1195.[129] The Ming code, the *Collected rituals of the great Ming (Ta Ming chi li)*, was completed in 1370 and re-published in 1530.[130] The Manchu Ch'ing dynasty commissioned a code in 1736, which was completed in 1756.[131] These Sung, Jurched, Ming and Ch'ing codifications are merely the extant examples of a tradition that lived through until the end of the imperial era. The extant codes may be assumed to bear the same sort of relation to the many other prescriptive treatises, compendia and the background documentation produced in the dynasties concerned that the K'ai-yüan code had to the abundant documentation of the T'ang. In the same way, the imperial ritual programme of later dynasties was administered by ritual institutions that perpetuated the T'ang nomenclature.

There seems, on superficial inspection, to be considerable continuity in the content of these extant later imperial ritual codes. With the exception of the Jurched code of 1195, they are all organised in the same five divisions that the T'ang scholars had used, though later compilations placed the five divisions in a different order. Many of the rituals contained in the K'ai-yüan code recur down to Ch'ing times. The compilers of the Ch'ing code acknowledged this continuity, for in their preface they cited the K'ai-yüan code as the first extant authority of its kind.

These continuities should not however preclude an understanding of the K'ai-yüan code and of the milieu in which it was produced as essentially medieval. For the great change in the Confucian tradition that has enabled intellectual historians to characterise a neo-Confucian era in Chinese thought from Sung times resulted in changed attitudes to the imperial ritual programme. The principal social trend here was towards a much larger, less court-centred and more devolved intellectual community. As a result, perspectives on man in society became more universal. Where analysis of ethical and social questions was concerned the level of generalisation became higher. Neo-Confucianism also developed a theme that had been present in early, pre-medieval Confucianism. Self-

---

129 *Ta Chin chi li (Collected rituals of the great Chin dynasty)*, reprinted in *Ssu-k'u ch'üan shu chen pen*, eighth series, (Taipei, 1978).

130 *Ming chi li (Collected rituals of the Ming)*, reprinted in *Ssu-k'u ch'üan shu chen-pen*, eighth series, (Taipei, 1978).

131 *Chin-ting ta Ch'ing t'ung li (Imperially commissioned comprehensive rituals of the great Ch'ing dynasty)*, reprinted in *Ssu-k'u ch'üan shu chen pen*, eighth series (Taipei, 1978).

cultivation and contemplation, the individual's quest for sage-hood and enlightenment now assumed major importance in the teaching of neo-Confucian masters. There was also a more agnostic spirit, and less interest in the supernatural or cosmological justification for the state.

The effect of these changes on the creative mainstream of the Confucian tradition was that the great majority of individual philosophers had much more distanced attitudes as far as the detailed ceremonial and ritual traditions surrounding the apex of the state were concerned. The shift was, moreover, a general one, for it affected the official scholarly milieu as well as the now much larger unofficial intellectual world. Expressed in terms of proportion, it meant that royal rituals took up a smaller part of the total official documentation that the history office and other official academic agencies generated.[132]

The sense of immediacy and of involvement in state ritual by a large proportion of the intellectual élite that the T'ang sources so strikingly convey had receded. The balance between belief in cosmological and supernatural elements in government on the one hand and more sceptical and society orientated attitudes on the other, had already, in the second half of the T'ang, the age of Liu Tsung-yüan and Tu Yu, begun to change. In the neo-Confucian era it shifted still further towards the ethical and social. The K'ai-yüan ritual code, longer and more detailed than almost all its extant successors, strikes a characteristically medieval balance between traditional religious beliefs and bureaucratic attitudes. As late eighth-century scholars themselves had already suggested, it stands for an epoch in the long history of imperial China.

[132] Etienne Balazs, 'History as a guide to bureaucratic practice' (see n. 53), pp. 135–42.

6. Gifts to the gods: power, property and ceremonial in Nepal

RICHARD BURGHART

At the turn of the nineteenth century the King of Nepal saw himself as a divine actor in his realm. He considered himself to be an embodiment of the universal god Vishnu and his palace was known as a temple. His divinity, however, was not a singular phenomenon, for he acted in a universe which was populated by a proverbial thirty-three million gods. Moreover, the king was not even the sole human god. Other mortals took themselves to be earthly replicas of celestial deities. Brahmans claimed to be embodiments of Brahma; and Saivite and Vaishnavite ascetics thought themselves to be 'walking temples' of Siva and Vishnu. Thus the implication of the king's divinity in Hindu society was rather different from those societies in which an absolute distinction is posited between the one true god and humankind. In the Hindu universe the mere fact of royal divinity was not so important as the relations which the king formed with other gods and men, and the contexts in which he was able to assert his divinity.

These contexts, which were ritually constituted, framed the encounters between the king and other human gods. Brahmans conceived of the universe on organic terms. The four main castes, comprising the priests, warriors, producers and exchangers of wealth and the servants and artisans, sprang from different parts of the celestial Brahma's body and each was endowed with the qualities to perform a particular function so that the social universe might survive as a whole. In this functionally inderdependent world Brahmans were the first-born and they performed the most excellent function. Hence they enjoyed the highest rank. Seen in these terms, the terrestrial authority of the king was secondary to

Many of the ideas presented in this paper were clarified in discussion with Audrey Cantlie, Chris Fuller, Ronald Inden and Jonathan Parry. I am grateful to them for their helpful comments and criticisms. Thanks are also due to Michael Aris for his help with the illustrations.

and derivative of the spiritual authority of Brahmans. By contrast, ascetics saw the universe in temporal terms. Renouncing their families, they sought reunion with the ever present Brahma and release from the endless cycle of rebirths. The king was a house-holder who lived, died and was reborn in the transient world. By realising the state of eternal bliss, ascetics claimed that they transcended the entire temporal universe; thus their authority exceeded that of kings. Meanwhile, the terrestrial king saw himself as the divine protector of his subjects. In the form of the universal monarch Vishnu, he sat upon his throne in the centre of the kingdom; in the form of a self-existent person, he roamed at will throughout his realm. The functions of government and the four main castes (including that of the Brahman) were ritually integra-ted within his mysterious body as aspects of his universal person.

The different claims of superiority made by Brahmans, ascetics and kings did not necessarily conflict, for they were advanced in separate contexts – that of the Brahman in the organic universe, the ascetic in the temporal universe and the king in the terrestrial universe. Hence the contexts were incongruent. Once the context had been agreed, each was ready to accept the other's relative superiority. The point of their complex hierarchical claims was not so much to settle scores about who was *really* the supreme person in the universe as it was to assert the existence of a domain in which each person was an autonomous actor. These domains, of course, intersected. In Nepal the king saw himself as an autonomous person, both with regard to his encompassment of the body politic as well as his apical position in controlling the political economy. Yet the king recognised that his autonomy was constrained by other gods, both celestial and human, whose authority he drew upon in authenticating and empowering his own rulership. In brief, the discourse on hierarchy among kings, Brahmans and ascetics was a discourse on autonomy in which each person asserted his power of agency in a particular universal context and yet also drew upon the powers of others.[1]

[1] I have condensed here an extremely complex and contentious problem. The present argument has been elaborated in my 'Hierarchical Models of the Hindu Social System', *Man* (NS) xiii (1978), pp. 519–36; 'For a Sociology of Indias: the Intracultural Approach to "Hindu" Society', *Contributions to Indian Sociology* xvii (1983); and 'Renunciation in the Religious Traditions of South Asia', *Man* (NS) xviii (1983), pp. 635–53. I have used the term autonomy as a gloss on a variety of native terms, such as absolute isolation (*kaivalya*), mover-at-will

The assertion of agency was a constant problem, if not a preoccupation, of the king. It was built into the structure of the political economy; and it mattered – regardless of how 'dynamic' any particular royal incumbent might or might not have been. With regard to home affairs there were always some courtiers and regional lords who were subverting, or suspected of subverting, the king's exercise of power. With regard to foreign affairs it must be born in mind that throughout this period, labour, not land, was the scarce resource. The king increased his income not by investing at home but by conquering the cultivated land of neighbours or by encouraging the immigration of cultivators and soldiers. Even if the king was not personally ambitious (and the ideal king was), he had to be on his guard that rival kings neither seized his lands nor won over his subjects.

Such was the case at the turn of the nineteenth century. At that time the modern kingdom of Nepal had not yet been formed, and the southern flank of the Himalayas was fragmented into five political configurations. Of central importance was the Nepal valley in which were situated the capital cities of Katmandu, Patan, and Bhadgaon. To the east of this valley were the hill kingdoms of Makwanpur and Vijayapur which extended up to the frontier with Sikkim. To the west of the Nepal valley lay the League of Twenty-four kingdoms and the League of Twenty-two kingdoms, which adjoined Kumaon in present-day Uttar Pradesh, India. The present-day kingdom of Nepal was founded by Prithvi Narayan Shah and his successors who ruled Gorkha, a petty kingdom in the League of Twenty-four Kingdoms. Upon ascending the throne of Gorkha in 1743, Prithvi Narayan conceived the ambition of bringing all these mountain kingdoms within his sway; and throughout the next seventy years he and his descendants fulfilled that ambition. By battle, diplomacy and marriage all five major political configurations on the southern flank of the Himalayas were annexed to Gorkha.

There can be no doubt that Prithvi Narayan Shah was a shrewd, resourceful and ambitious person; in a word, he was powerful. Moreover, his army, while perhaps a rough lot, fought with a determination and courage that the East India Company – and later

(*kāmacārin*), and self-government (*svatantratā*). These terms have slightly different meanings and fields of reference, the elucidation of which is beyond the scope of the present paper.

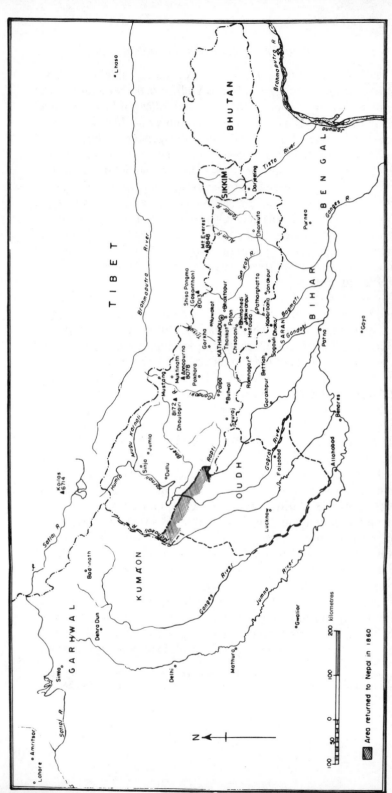

27 Nepal and neighbouring regions in 1850. At the turn of the eighteenth century the dominance of Nepal extended into Sikkim in the east and across Kumaon and into Garhwal in the west.

the British government – came to respect. Yet in seeking to fulfil his territorial ambition (and at the same time avoid being engulfed by the Chinese army or the Company) his personal power was not always sufficient to the task. Whenever the king's life or possessions were under threat, or he was about to launch a new campaign or his lines of military communication and supply were overstretched, he sought the favour of celestial and human gods in order that his aims be furthered. Divine support, and the rituals to gain that support, were an integral part of state policy. Of particular importance were royal gifts, for it was by offering gifts that beneficial alliances with gods were formed. Gifts of land were critical here: not only because bestowing land upon Brahmans, ascetics and celestial gods was a way by which the king gained or retained land but also because the king ruled the land, hence only he could give it away. In brief, royal gifts of land to the gods were an important act of statesmanship in which royal agency was asserted and the limits on that agency acknowledged. They offer an insight into the relation between pomp and power in Hindu royal ritual.

My account of these royal gifts begins with a consideration of the types of gift offered by the king and the different relationships which they structured between donor and recipient. Only one type of gift, namely religious gift (*dān*), is considered here. These were gifts by which relations of reciprocity were created by human and celestial gods; they were also the most important in furthering the aims of state. No discursive descriptions of these rituals are available, for that kind of information was not thought worth recording by Nepalese chroniclers of the time. From the Brahmanical codes, however, there is information on the procedures followed in the ritual and in the royal archives at Kathmandu may be found the land grants which note that these procedures were followed by the king in his gift-giving. These sources reveal that both the procedures and the entitlement to make gifts of land were a royal privilege; and in making such gifts, the king acknowledged his dependence upon the divine recipient. These status implications are analysed in detail; as are the reasons which led the king to offer religious gifts. From the perspective of the present-day rulers of Nepal the gifts of land appear to have been acts of piety by their forbears, but an analysis of contemporary documents reveals that they were also fundamental to the organisation of the pre-modern Hindu state. They were as much a means of furthering the aims of state as they were constituent of authoritative relations within the realm.

THE REDISTRIBUTIVE AND RECIPROCAL STRUCTURE OF ROYAL GIFTS

In common parlance the Nepali term religious gift (*dān*) is used to designate any offering in which the donor, acting with a religious intention, relinquishes his possession over an object so that it might be accepted by the recipient. This common usage (which is not as nuanced as that found in Brahmanical texts)[2] glosses over a further differentiation between two types of religious gift offered by the king: those which the king offered by virtue of his divine status as donor and those which he offered in consideration of the divine status of the recipient. Both of these were commonly referred to as religious gifts, and in both cases the act of their donation was a state event. They had, however, different hierarchical implications and they occurred in the context of different social relationships, the former in a relation of redistribution and the latter in a relation of reciprocity.

Gifts which were offered by virtue of the ritual status of the king comprise those royal donations which the king offered to the subjects under his protection. For example, in the course of his coronation the king offers gifts (*dān, bhikṣā*) to the poor. Also on other auspicious occasions in the life of the royal family, such as the birth of a prince or the marriage of a princess, a member of the royal family distributes food and clothing to needy recipients at the palace gate. On such occasions the gods were invited to look down upon the royal family and bless them from their respective heavens. It was important, therefore, that the king be seen at such times to fulfil his sacred duty of providing for the welfare of any of his

---

[2] The Brahmanical codes of conduct distinguish between a 'gift' in which the donor irrevocably alienates his possession of an object and the recipient accepts it; and 'offerings', such as sacrificial oblations, in which the donor can only intend the recipient to accept the offering. For the importance of this distinction in the emergence of classical Hinduism see M. Biardeau and C. Malamoud, *La Sacrifice dans l'Inde Ancienne* (Paris, 1976); and for its importance in changing patterns of political legitimation in Hindu society see N. Dirks, 'Political Authority and Structural Change in Early South Indian History', *The Indian Economic and Social History Review* xiii (1976), pp. 125–58; and R. Inden, 'The Ceremony of the Great Gift (Mahādāna): Structure and Historical Context in Indian Ritual and Society', in *Asie du sud, traditions et changements* (Paris, 1979), pp. 131–6.

subjects who might be in distress. Such gifts were not rendered effective by Brahmanical ritual, nor were they offered to particular named recipients. Nor can it be said that those needy subjects who came to the palace gate were fulfilling a sacred purpose by virtue of their acceptance of the gift. The sacred purpose was that of the king who cast himself in the image of the 'all-providing universal man'. If comparable situations from present-day Nepal are a reliable guide for understanding the past then the king would have been hailed as a divine lord in this situation.

According to this conception of the monarch, the king's subjects would have been incorporated within the kingship as constituent parts or extensions of this universal person. Thus the king, in making such gifts to his subjects, did not create any relationships; rather he fulfilled his royal duties stemming from pre-existing relationships. Moreover, as constituent parts, the otherness of the recipient was not recognised in offering the gift. Given the ritual superiority of the donor in this context, it is unlikely that the king received a blessing from the recipients; indeed, the king was expecting to be blessed by the heavenly witnesses of his giving. From the point of view of the compilers of the Brahmanical codes of conduct such gifts were not 'religious gifts', for the needy recipient was not necessarily entitled to reciprocate the gift with a blessing. Instead the structure was one of redistribution whereby the ruler fulfilled his moral obligation to protect his subjects by redistributing the wealth he had received from them in revenue payments.[3]

The other type of royal gift is the one in which the recipient accepts the gift in order to fulfil a sacred purpose. This sacred purpose could be his enjoyment and well-being as a human or celestial god; or it could be the enabling of the recipient to perform his religious duties, as in the case of a marriage when a man offers his daughter as a religious gift to his prospective son-in-law. In this context the groom has a sacred duty to beget sons who will nourish

[3] For the distinction between 'gift' and 'religious gift' see P. V. Kane, *History of Dharmasastra*, 2nd edn, 5 vols. (Poona, 1974), vol. 2, pt 2, p. 842. For the use of the term *dān* and *bhikṣā* in referring to redistributive gifts see, for example, A. C. Rajbhandari, The Coronation Book of their Majesties of Nepal (Kathmandu, 1956), p. 29. There is a popular notion among Hindus that beggars bear the image of god and that for this reason it is meritorious to give to the poor. I doubt, however, that this idea was salient in the royal distibution of gifts at the palace gate; and certainly in the context of the coronation it was the royal donor, not the recipient, who was the god.

his ancestors, for which purpose he requires a wife. Ordinarily the recipient blesses the donor for offering the gift, and the donor receives merit for his generosity. Thus the kind of gift links donor and recipient in a relationship of reciprocity.[4] Unlike the redistributive gift, the reciprocated gift recognises the otherness of the recipient with whom the donor creates a relationship. It is only this reciprocated gift which conforms to the criteria of a 'religious gift' in the Brahmanical literature. Although I shall return to the topic of redistributive gifts in conclusion, the body of this essay is concerned only with those gifts in which donor and recipient are bound together in a relationship of reciprocity.

THE RITUAL AUTONOMY OF THE ROYAL DONOR

A royal gift of land in favour of a deity was usually enacted on an auspicious day and the ceremony, which involved the entire court, took place at the residence of the king. The Brahmanical codes of ritual practice stipulated four stages in the ritual: first, the donor's avowal of his pious intention in making the gift; second, the donor's offering of a sacrifice in the name of the divine recipient; third, the donor's declaration that the gift has been made in the name of the divine recipient; and fourth, the donor's offering of a sacrificial fee to the Brahman priest who rendered effective the first three stages of the ritual.[5] These Brahmanical procedures were not specifically

[4] There is a common belief among Hindus that the 'ideal gift' is the one which is given without any thought of personal gain. Yet a gift is classified as a 'religious gift' by virtue of its being reciprocated with a blessing. It unavoidably follows that the donor acquires merit. Thus all religious gifts have some element of personal gain, regardless of the donor's intentions. This conflict between intention and outcome does not appear, however, in the material on Nepalese kingship. One reason may be that gift-giving for the king was not made the object of ascetic interpretation. The ideal king was the ambitious ruler who sought not to deny gain, but to increase his lordship over territory and men.

[5] This account is a summary of the procedures explained in the ninth and tenth edicts of Ram Shah as found in T. Riccardi, 'The Royal Edicts of King Ram Shah of Gorkhɔ', *Kailash* v (1975), pp. 46–8. These procedures conform with the indications in the Brahmanical codes of conduct (see Kane, *History* (n.3), pp. 855–6). The documents concerning gifts to both human gods (see nn.12 and 13) and to celestial gods (see n.15) confirm that these procedures were used in Nepal at the turn of the nineteenth century. There are also a few remarks in S. Lévi, *Le Népal*, 3 vols. (Paris, 1905), i, p. 301. Gifts of land were sometimes offered outside the capital by royal agents on tours of inspection; in such cases other members of the court took on the role of the prince. See, for example, 'lāl mohar rājā gīrvāṇ yuddha vikram śāh ko kāji amar siṃha thāpālāī samvat 1864 vaisākh sudi 14' in D. Laṃsāl and R. Bhattarāī, 'Janakpur añcalako purātātvik

royal; instead they were followed by any Hindu who was entitled to offer a sacrifice and for whom a Brahman would serve as priest. There was, however, one significant aspect of the royal enactment of this ritual which made a royal gift unlike that of a commoner. In offering land for religious purposes, the king himself did not actively participate in the ceremony. Rather, the officers at his court took the active role in giving the gift while the king 'co-ordinated' their movements. The significance of this procedure was that unlike commoners who offered religious gifts as individuals, gifts from the king were in a sense a gift from the entire kingdom as constituted within the body politic of the king.

In the first part of the ritual the royal priest situated the impending act by noting the time and place of the ritual and then informed the divine recipient of the intention of the donor, such as to please a particular deity or to bring peace to the king's deceased father in the ancestral world. Ordinarily a donor made this vow in response to the priest's instructions in the course of the ritual. The royal inscriptions imply, however, that the royal priest recited the entire vow, including the part of the donor. This, at least, is the meaning of the typical phrase found in the documents: '[such-and-such a] priest recited the words in making the vow'. The second stage of the ritual was carried out by an agnate of the king; this person was ordinarily one of the king's brothers who held the title of Cautariyā, or prince, at the court. A clod of earth from the gifted tract was brought to the palace and the prince took on the role of sacrificer, offering water, sesame, barley, and grass (*kuśa*) to the earth in the name of the divine recipient. These offerings were in a sense consumed by the deity. Since the sacrifice only took place by virtue of the grace of the deity, the fact that the deity allowed the sacrifice to come to its conclusion (rather than to stop it by mystical means, such as the breaking of the sacrificial implements) was a sign that the ritual gift would be acceptable to the deity. Having been reassured of the acceptability of the gift, the third stage of the ritual then followed in which the ministers at the court declared that a specific tract of land was now gifted to the deity. An auspicious group of five ministers participated in this declaration (which was

sarvekṣaṇ samvat 2028', *Prācin Nepāl*, xxvi (1974), pp. 26–7. In all cases, however, the donor was the king *in absentia* and the different stages of the ritual were carried out by different persons; hence the mode of enactment remained that of the king, not of the commoner.

also witnessed by the everwatchful Sun and Moon) and they were followed by five more persons who served as witnesses of the boundary. The boundary witnesses were ordinarily a group of 'five good men' who were leaders of local lineages, but officers of the royal household were also known to take on this role. The fourth stage of the ritual was the offering of the sacrificial fee by the sacrificer to the royal priest. Strictly speaking, the fee was the gift by which the sacrificer discharged the obligations which he had undertaken with the priest at the time of stating his vow. Unfortunately, the Nepalese documents do not divulge the identity of the donor of the sacrificial fee, but since it was the prince who entered into the sacrificial relation with the priest, it would have probably also been the prince who submitted the sacrificial fee to the priest at the conclusion of the ceremony.

The most important feature of this specifically royal enactment of a Brahmanical ritual is that the king did not actively participate in the ceremony; rather the ritual was carried out by others on the king's behalf. The ruler provided the gift of earth, but the people through whom he ruled did the actual giving. A brief explanation of this procedure may be found in the edicts of King Ram Shah (1606-c.1636), the extant version of which was compiled at the turn of the nineteenth century. The tenth edict states:[6]

> In endowing land for a god or pilgrims hostel or in gifting land to a Brahman, the purpose of the water jug [used for pouring water in the sacrifice] of the prince is this: the prince is one's own brother. A brother is one's principal limb. If one makes one's limbs strong and gives gifts, one receives the fruits according to what has been said [in the Brahmanical codes of conduct]. This is the reason for the water jug of the prince. The meaning of the declaration of the minister is this: the minister beseeches the king without partiality for what is right and what is not right. This is the meaning of the minister's declaration. The meaning of the 'five good men' of the boundary is this: members of the six clans [from which most officers of the court were recruited] and respectable men from other families, having witnessed the extent of the valley land and the hillside land and having determined the entrance way, exit, and thoroughfare between fields, sink four pegs thereby giving the borders. This is the meaning of the 'five good men' of the boundary.

[6] T. Riccardi, 'The Royal Edicts', p. 48 (with some rewording of his translation).

The key notion in this passage is the idea of the 'body politic' in which the functions of government are royal limbs co-ordinated by the king. The tenth edict notes that the prince is the king's main limb and implies that the ministers and 'five good men' were also his limbs. The Brahman priest, however, does not figure in the passage. Given the crucial position of the Brahman in authenticating the king's rulership, the Brahman's absence from the tenth edict deserves some scrutiny.

The notion that different aspects of rulership are limbs of the ruler may be found in the Brahmanical codes of conduct, the codes of ritual procedure, and the codes of political economy. These diverse sources, however, do not agree on the number of limbs, their names, or their functions. In considering these inconsistencies, one may note a general pattern: there are lists of limbs in which the Brahman is absent and there are lists of limbs in which the king is absent. In both cases the person who is absent is superior to those who are present. In the Brahmanical codes of conduct (e.g. *Manu* ix.295) and the codes of political economy (e.g. *Arthasastra* vi.1) the seven limbs of state comprise in descending order of importance: the king, minister, country, fortified capital, treasury, army and allies. Here the Brahman is absent, for the list contains the basic elements of political economy which are encompassed by the dharmic preoccupations of the Brahman. In the Brahmanical codes of ritual procedure (e.g. *Satapatha Brahmana* v.3.1–2), however, the royal limbs comprise the four royal consorts, the four main castes, and the four charioteers. In this list the king is absent, but the Brahman caste is present as one of the twelve powers of kingship. These powers are aspects of dominion which the king integrates within his person; otherwise they would leave him, placing his rulership in peril.[7]

It is interesting to note that Dumont, who saw in Hindu society a disjunction between ritual status and temporal power, claimed that the Brahman priest secularised the kingship and supported his claim with reference to the first set of limbs in which the absent Brahman with his dharmic duty encompasses the king's politico-economic domain. By contrast Gonda, who described the religious character of ancient Indian kingship, focussed on the second set of

[7] See J. C. Heesterman, *The Ancient Indian Royal Consecration* ('S-Gravenhage, 1957), pp. 49–57.

limbs in which the absent king co-ordinates the powers of rulership within his body politic.[8] Given the presence of both lists it is obvious that a consideration of Hindu kingship which focusses on only one list to the exclusion of the other will give a rather misleading impression of the nature of royal authority.

Returning to the Nepalese material, it is now clear that the tenth edict is ambiguous, for *both* king *and* priest are absent from the passage. Assuming that one is not dealing here with a third type of list, my conjecture is that in the context of the royal gift of land the priest figures as a limb of the king. My reasons for this are twofold. First, the royal priest is the spokesman of the king's vow. Therefore he takes an active part in the ritual whereas the king's role is unambiguously that of the passive co-ordinator of his limbs. Second, in the politico-economic domain Brahmanical status is superior to that of the king, but in the context of certain royal rituals the king integrates the power of Brahman within the body politic. Since the present context is clearly that of royal ritual, it would appear that in offering land to a deity, the royal priest serves as a limb of the king.

Regardless of this conjecture, one can nonetheless state with certainty that in giving land to a deity, the king did not take on the role of sacrificer. Since so many descriptions and analyses of royal authority in Hindu society focus on the relation between Brahman priest and royal sacrificer, the importance of this fact cannot be overemphasised. In offering land to a deity, the king of Nepal placed his brother in the inferior position of sacrificer and reserved for himself a superhuman stature which encompasses the relationship between Brahman priest and sacrificer. The persons who acted on his behalf throughout the four stages of the ritual were instruments of his rule; and by integrating these instruments within his body, the king constituted the kingdom as an encompassment hierarchy which possessed only one will. In this sense the king was everyone and therefore the only one. There were no other legitimate autonomous actors in his kingdom and in this ritual form the king, as body politic, offered his own land as a gift to the deity.

---

[8] L. Dumont, 'The Conception of Kingship in Ancient India', *Contributions to Indian Sociology*, vi (1962), pp. 48–77; J. Gonda, *Ancient Indian Kingship from the Religious Point of View* (Leiden, 1969).

THE TENURIAL AUTONOMY OF THE ROYAL DONOR

Although all Hindus could offer ritual gifts for religious purposes, the king reserved for himself the prerogative of giving land. The reason for this lay in the king's claim of tenurial autonomy. At the turn of the nineteenth century the king of Nepal saw himself as the autonomous lord or master of his territorial possessions and of the people who lived upon his land. Although his subjects may have tilled the soil or practised a trade in the kingdom since time immemorial – and hence enjoyed a customary right to pursue their livelihood – still the king asserted his own proprietary authority by annually entitling his subjects to pursue their livelihood upon his possessions. The tenurial entitlements which the king assigned to his subjects differed with respect to the specific rights and duties toward the king (the submission of rents, levies, duties and fees) and the different powers (e.g. inheritability, transferability, irrevocability and divisibility) in the enjoyment of those rights.[9]

The king of Nepal derived his income, largely assessed in cash rather than kind, from the agricultural rents on the cultivation of crown land; from the duties on the exploitation of other primary resources, such as fishing, grazing, mining and logging; and from the duties on trade. The administration of his possessions was financed not by drawing on his income which accumulated in the treasury but by assigning his source of income in land to intermediary revenue-collecting officers. In the southern lowlands of the kingdom revenue was collected by civil administrators who were remunerated with rent-free land (*nankar* tenure) or by the profits of tax-farmers who bid for the revenue collection rights in auction. In the hill regions certain districts were administered by military officers who were maintained by annual assignments of rent-free (*jāgir* tenure). Other hill districts were administered by civil administrators or by tributary kings who submitted annually a fee of obeisance to the king.

This revenue collecting structure had important hierarchical implications, for a revenue officer was superior to those persons to whom he assigned a tenurial status and from whom he collected revenue. Revenue collection, however, was not the sole function of

---

[9] This summary of the tenurial system at the turn of the nineteenth century is taken from M. Regmi, *Land Tenure and Taxation in Nepal*, 4 vols. (Berkeley and Los Angeles, 1963–8) and *Landownership in Nepal* (Berkeley and Los Angeles, 1976).

the tenurial administration; revenue collectors also served as judges, militia commanders, executive officers of the king, and ritual representatives of the king.[10] In other words, these intermediary officers acted like kings in a pyramidal state system defined with reference to tenurial status, each revenue officer claiming lordship over the revenue officers and subjects from whom he received revenue. For the most part, the administrative system was differentiated territorially, but not functionally. Each rank within the pyramid of authority was a kingship over an administrative unit which was defined territorially. The territorial jurisdiction of each successively higher rank incorporated the territorial jurisdiction of the ranks below. At the highest rank was the king who ruled the largest territorial unit, the kingdom. The absolute superiority of the king in this control hierarchy was signified by the fact that he assigned the district officers to their posts and he received revenue from them, but he, in turn, depended upon no one for his rights over his possessions and he submitted revenue from that land to no one. In brief, the king was autonomous and by virtue of his tenurial autonomy he ruled his possessions and claimed his independence of neighbouring rulers.

Royal gifts of land entailed the bestowal of a tenurial status, called *kusa birtā*, upon the divine recipient. The rights, duties and powers of this status will be described in the next section. For the present it shall only be emphasised that *kusa birtā* status was unlike other tenurial statuses which the king assigned to his subjects. This may be inferred from the fact that the king annually reviewed his appointments in the tenurial administration, but in making a ritual gift, the king irrevocably alienated his pre-eminent right to enjoy and repossess the land. This was symbolised by the appearance of an actual clod of earth in the transfer of rights. The earth did not figure in any other tenurial assignment, all of which were revocable and many of which were annually renewable. It is for this reason that the king did not entitle anyone but himself to gift land for religious purposes; for such a gift, even by others, would have curtailed the king's privilege of revoking or renewing the tenurial arrangements on his possessions. Hence out of the ten classic religious gifts offered by Hindus, commoners were entitled to offer

---

[10] My main sources on district administration at this time are F. Hamilton, *An Account of the Kingdom of Nepal* (Edinburgh, 1819) and M. Regmi, *A Study in Nepali Economic History: 1768–1846* (New Delhi, 1971).

nine: gold, cows, sesame, ghee, clothes, rice, molasses, silver, and salt. Only the king, or the agent of the king, could offer the tenth gift of land. In brief, the tenurial implications of offering land as a religious gift were such that only a tenurially autonomous person could do it. Thus a ritual gift of land was by implication a gift of the king.

Although the king reserved for himself the privilege of offering land to deities, there were occasions when the king did permit commoners to make such gifts. For example, King Rana Bahadur Shah assigned *kusa birtā* rights to the wife of a Brahman astrologer so that she might endow a pilgrims' hostel. The inscription reads:[11]

Among all astrologers Sri Kulanand Sarma was illustrious. His son, Mamu Sharma, possessed all good qualities and carried out the pious duties appropriate to his station in life. His daughter-in-law Vasundhara, being pious, alert, and intelligent, caused a hostel to be built in the middle of her village so that travellers might find repose. In Sakasamvat 1707 AD [1785] on the third day of the month of Vaisakha [April–May] Vasundhara worshipped cows and Brahmans and then in a great spirit of devotion caused the hostel to be consecrated so that contentment might be brought to the lame, deaf, blind, orphans, widows, and others. Full of faith I grant 40 *muri* [approximately 1¼ acres] of fields on the banks of the Tandring stream to provide for the hostel. If anyone, acting out of greed, causes loss to this endowment, these mean men will be treated as criminals and their actions will be equivalent to the murder of Brahmans and others.

Another example concerns the gift of land from King Rajendra Vikram Shah in 1843 to Girija Datt Misra, the District Officer of Mahottari, to endow a temple, pilgrims' hostel, and pond at Dhanusa, where lay a piece of the Bow of Siva which Lord Rom broke at the time of his marriage with Sita.[12]

Because the right to give land for religious purposes was a royal prerogative, gifts of land by commoners implied that the com-

---

[11] 'Boriāṅko raṇa bahādur śāhako pālāko abhilekh samvat 1842 vaisākh sudi 3 (no.43)', in D. Vajrācārya and T. Śreṣṭa (eds.), *Śāhakālakā Abhilekh* [*Inscriptions from the Shah Period*] (Kathmandu, V.S.2037, 1980, pp. 161–3. (Hereafter cited as *Śāhakālakā Abhilekha*.)

[12] 'Lāl mohar rājendra vir vikram sāhako sūbā girijā datt miśralāī samvat 1900 śrāvan vadi 15'. The document is in the possession of the heirs of Suba Girija Datt Misra at Pipra village, Mahottari district, Nepal.

moner was like a king.[13] Being aware of this implication and ever mindful that gifts of land diminished his income, it would seem that the king did not readily grant such permission except in cases of personal respect (Vasundhara's father-in-law, Sri Kulanand 'Jyotisi' Sharma, foresaw King Prithvi Narayan Shah's conquest of the Nepal valley, see below p. 263) or duress (Girija Datt Misra refused to submit the revenue from Mahottari district until King Rajendra acceded to his request). In spite of such king-like behaviour from commoners, the king reserved for himself his royal mode of enacting the ritual. Commoner donors stated their own vow to the priest, offered the sacrifice, made the declaration, and submitted the sacrificial fee. In other words, they enacted the ritual as an individual rather than as a co-ordinator of the powers of rule. These 'little kings' did not constitute ritually a body politic. Even though the king ceded his tenurial autonomy in order to enable a petitioner to make a religious gift, the king still retained for himself his ritual autonomy within the realm.

THE RITUAL SUPERIORITY AND TENURIAL AUTONOMY OF THE DIVINE RECIPIENT

According to the Brahmanical codes of conduct an offering was considered a religious gift when two conditions were met: first, the gift was given for a sacred purpose; and second, the donor irrevocably transferred all of his rights and duties over the gifted object in favour of the recipient. A royal gift of land to a deity was an especially significant act, for in meeting the first condition the highest temporal authority in the land acknowledged the ritual superiority of another person, and in meeting the second condition the king alienated the very basis of his proprietary authority. In this section I shall describe the ritual and tenurial status of the recipient and consider the implications of this status for the authority of the king.

With regard to the first condition of a religious gift – namely its sacred purpose – land appears to have been gifted for one of two different reasons: either the king was enjoined in the Brahmanical

---

[13] This implication appears to have been especially important in medieval South India. See Dirks, 'Political Authority' (see n.2); A. Appadurai, 'Kings, Sects, and Temples in South India, 1350–1700 A.D.', *The Indian Economic and Social History Review*, xiv (1977), pp. 47–74; and B. Stein, *Peasant State and Society in Medieval India*, (Delhi, 1980).

codes of conduct to offer gifts at certain times or on account of doing certain acts (or what is known in the Brahmanical codes as the *naimittika* category of ritual act) or the king sought to obtain an object of his desire by means of such gifts (the *kāmya* category of ritual act). A purview of the published inscriptions suggests that Brahmans usually received gifts at certain times or on account of the king performing certain ritual acts; and celestial deities usually received gifts motivated by royal desire. Finally one should mention that Hindu ascetics did not receive gifts of land at all from the king.

A case in which gifts were offered at certain times concerns the land offered to Brahmans at the time of a lunar or solar eclipse. A lunar eclipse is thought to occur when the celestial demon Rahu 'eats' the moon goddess Candra, the gradual disappearance of the moon behind the earth's shadow being understood by Hindus as the otherwise invisible demon consuming the Moon. During the several minutes in which Rahu ingests the Moon the cosmic order is inverted. Untouchables claim the right to receive alms, and everyone – both gods and men – becomes temporarily poi...d. Eventually Rahu is warded off, and the Moon is released from danger. Pious persons purify themselves; and temples are similarly purified. Upon restoration of order Brahmans are given gifts, as was the case of the Brahmanical healer Nanda Misra Vaidya to whom land was given by Queen Regent Rajarajesvari following the lunar eclipse of 1803. The Queen offered the gift with the simple declaration: 'Our family has wished you well; may you and your descendants take this land to be *kusa birtā* and enjoy it'.[14] An example of land being ᵍ...ed to a Brahman in the fulfilment of certain ritual acts may be found in the gift of King Girvan Yuddha Vikram Shah on the death of his father Rana Bahadur Shah in 1806. Upon completion of the mortuary rituals the chief mourner, now in a state of purity, offers gifts to Brahmans. In this connection Girvan Yuddha offered a gift of land to the Brahman Bhakta Ram Upadhyaya so that the deceased Rana Bahadur Shah might 'rest in peace'. One year later on the anniversary of his father's death Girvan Yuddha gave a further gift of land to two other Brahmans.[15]

[14] 'Lāl mohar rājā gīrvāṇ yuddha vikram śāhako nanda miśra vaidyalāī samvat 1858 jyeṣṭha sudi 8 (no. 94)', in *Śāhakālakā Abhilekha*, pp. 330–2.

[15] 'Lāl mohar rājā gīrvāṇ yuddha vikram śāhako bhaktarām pādhyālāī samvat 1866 māgh vadi 9 (no.139)'; 'lāl mohar rājā gīrvāṇ yuddha vikram śāhako dāmodar pādhyā arjyāllāī samvat 1866 māgh vadi 9 (no.140)'; 'lāl mohar rājā gīrvāṇ

In sum, in the case of these religious gifts a Brahman was taken to be an auspicious icon of Brahma from whose subtle body materialised the universe at the dawn of time. The enjoyment of land by this icon was the religious purpose of the gift and the context was the restoration of order after a period of cosmic chaos (e.g. the eclipse) or personal liminality (e.g. the stage of being a disembodied ghost). In acknowledging this purpose the king respected the ritual pre-eminence of the Brahman. Thus even though in the act of giving the gift the royal priest may have been co-ordinated by the king within the body politic, this was not the case for the other Brahman in the ceremony, namely the icon of Brahma who received the gift. In the context of the ritual that other Brahman was separate from and superior to the king.[16]

Many religious gifts of land appear to have been occasioned by the second of the above-mentioned reasons: namely the king's desire for prosperity, health and victory. For example, during the reign of the infant king Girvan Yuddha, the Queen Regent Kantavati gifted land to the deities Kali, Cangu Narayan, Adhisthatrdevata, Daksinakali and Taleju. The religious intention of these gifts was to bring about the deity's pleasure by providing for their worship, but this intention was, in turn, motivated by desire. At the time of offering these tracts of land to various deities the Queen Regent was gravely ill, and her gifts were the means by which she appealed to the gods to restore her to health.[17] Gifts of

yuddha vikram śāhako harikṛṣṇa vajhālāī samvat 1866 bhādra vadi 5 (no.136)' in *Śāhakālakā Abhilekha*, pp. 477–8; 479–81; 466–8.

[16] It must be born in mind that although Brahmans did receive numerous grants of land from the king, most of these grants were not religious gifts but merely tenurial assignments in connection with the Brahman's non-religious duties as an officer at the court. The grants were revocable and entailed the submission of a fee of obeisance and crown levies indicating the dependence of the Brahman upon the king. Because the language of description of Hindu society by western scholars is the language of caste the literature sometimes confounds the tenurial dependence of the Brahman courtier upon the king and the ritual autonomy of the Brahman *vis-à-vis* the king.

[17] 'Lāl mohar rājā gīrvāṇ yuddha vikram śāhako gorkhā darvār kālisthānlāī samvat 1853 āśvin śukla 8 (no.77)'; 'lāl mohar rājā gīrvāṇ yuddha vikram śāhako cāmgunārāyansthānlāī samvat 1853 āśvin śukla 8 (no.78)'; 'lāl mohar rājā gīrvāṇ yuddha vikram śāhako kāthmāḍaum talejulāī samvat 1853 āśvin śukla 8 (no.79)'; 'lāl mohar rājā gīrvāṇ yuddha vikram śāhako śāntipur adhiṣṭhātṛdevatalāī samvat 1853 āśvin śukla 8 (no.81)'; 'lāl mohar rājā gīrvāṇ yuddha vikram śāhako dakṣiṇakālīsthānlāī samvat 1853 āśvin śukla 8 (no.83)' in *Śāhakālakā Abhilekha*, pp. 277–80; 281–4; 285–8; 293–6; 301–5. The background on Queen Regent Kantavati's illness is found in pp. 304–5.

land were also made at times of war when the king, desirous of victory, sought to obtain the grace of a deity. During an uncertain moment in the military campaign against the East India Company, Kaji Amar Sinha Thapa urged the king to gift land to Brahmans so that victory might be theirs. Also many of the Vaishnavite and Saivite temples situated along the southern frontier of the kingdom were endowed with land on the occasion of wars fought between hill kings and the kings of the Ganges basin. It was thought that the blessings of these gods, and the ascetics who served them, would favour the hill kings in battle. The importance of such gods in warfare was also noted by Father Guiseppe who observed that the Newar king of Kathmandu did not bother to defend the strategic hill of Syambhunath from Gorkhali attack, for the people believed it to be 'protected by their idols'.[18]

In reviewing these land grants, it is significant that Hindu ascetics, unlike celestial gods and Brahmans, do not appear to have been gifted land. Instead the king assigned to prominent ascetics an income by entitling them to claim cash and kind in alms from householders and to receive the income from judicial fines pronounced upon the members of their sect. Prithvi Narayan Shah offered this privilege to his ascetic guru Bhagavantanath with respect of the Gorakhnathi Jogis throughout the entire kingdom. For the Muslim fakirs this privilege was assigned within the Nepal valley to Fakir Ghasi of Kathmandu; and for the Vaishnavite ascetics the privilege was assigned outside the Nepal valley to the Venerable Abbot of Matihani and his descendants.[19] The original documents concerning the bestowal of these privileges have not yet been published, but it would appear that these privileges were a royal assignment, not a ritual gift. The 'levy on alms' of Bhagavan-

[18] See 'Letter from Amar Sinha Thapa at Rajgarh to the King of Nepal, dated 2nd March 1815' in East India Company, *Papers Respecting the Nepaul War*, (London, 1824), pp. 553–6; R. Burghart, 'The Disappearance and Reappearance of Janakpur *Kailash*', vi (1978), pp. 257–84; Father Giuseppe, 'An Account of the Kingdom of Nepaul', *Asiaticke Researches*, ii (1790), p. 314.

[19] 'Lāl mohar rājā raṇa bahādur śāhako śrī gosāĩn bhagavantanāthlāī samvat 1843 phālgun sudi 2 (no.511)' in *Itihāsa Prakāśa*, ii (V.S. 2013, 1956 AD), p. 289; 'Royal order from King Jay Prakasa Malla to Fakir Ghāsi, 1738 AD' in M. Gaborieau, *Minorités Musulmanes dans le Royaume Hindou du Népal*, (Nanterre, 1977), pp. 36–7; 'Letter from Prime Minister Jang Bahadur Rana to Venerable Abbot Lalit Das of the Matihani Monastery, 1877' in R. Burghart, 'Regional Circles and the Central Overseer of the Vaishnavite Sect in the Kingdom of Nepal', in K. Ballhatchet and D. Taylor (eds.), *Changing South Asia: Religion and Society*, (Hong Kong, 1984), pp. 165–79.

tanath was not a source of income appropriate for a king; he could respectfully offer it up to an ascetic but not give it, for it was not something previously enjoyed by him. As for the land, ascetics saw themselves as being unattached to the things of this world; hence for their public image, if not for the fate of their soul, they were reluctant to hold property rights in the kingdom. In other words, one way in which the ascetic claimed his autonomy of the king was in not accepting gifts of land from him.

A search among Nepalese inscriptions has brought to light only one instance in which a ritual gift of land was offered in the name of an ascetic. The recipient of the gift in this case was the legendary Gorakhnathi saint Ratannath; the land comprised several villages at the locality of Caughera in Dang; and the beneficiaries were the Gorakhnathi Jogi followers of Ratannath.[20] At the time the gift had been made, however, the historical Ratannath had long since given way to a legendary figure who transcended the mortal boundaries of time. The purpose of the gift was to provide a campsite where Jogis could bathe and build their smouldering fires. The religious purpose of the gift lay in the fact that Jogis bathe in water in order to purify their material bodies and they 'bathe' in ashes from their smouldering fires in order to purify their subtle bodies. The consequence of this double purification is their release from the chains of rebirth. Hence the land grant served a religious purpose.

In spite of the fact that ascetics appear not to have received gifts of land in their own name, still they did enjoy usufructuary rights over land which had been gifted in the name of a celestial god. Numerous temples along the southern frontier of Nepal and in the western Himalayas were managed by Vaishnavite and Saivite ascetics who enjoyed the usufruct of the deity's income after the religious conditions of the endowment (e.g. worshipping the deity and feeding pilgrims) had been fulfilled.[21] The enjoyment of this

---

20 'Lāl mohar rājā rājendra vikram śāhako śrī ratannāthlāī samvat 1883 vaisākh sudi 11 (no.544)', in *Itihās Prakāśa*, ii (V.S. 2013, 1956 AD), pp. 310–11.

21 See, for example, the royal orders to the abbots of the Janki monastery, Ram monastery, Laksman monastery, and Hanuman Nagar monastery in D. Laṁsāl and R. Bhaṭṭarāī, 'Janakpur añcalako purātātvik sarvekṣaṇ samvat 2028', *Prācin Nepāl*, xxvi (1974), pp. 23–35. The enjoyment of the usufruct did not necessarily follow from the authority to manage the shrine. If the published inscriptions are representative of all the royal endowments of temples it would appear that the king favoured Brahmans by gifting them land in their own name, but to ascetics he assigned the usufruct of the land gifted to their tutelary deity. Brahman managers of temples were not necessarily entitled to the usufruct, although it

remaining income by the ascetic still served a religious purpose in that the ascetic was also a deity whose blessing was sought by the king. In sum, the gifts of land to Brahmans and celestial gods and the usufructuary rights to ascetics served a religious purpose. These land grants met the first condition of a ritual gift and the king, in offering the gift, acknowledged his personal dependence upon a pre-eminent deity.

The second condition of a ritual gift was that the donor irrevocably alienate all of his rights and duties over the gifted object in favour of the recipient. In the case of a royal gift of land this meant that the king transferred all of the ways by which he 'enjoyed' the land to the divine recipient. The tenurial status of the gifted tract was variously known as 'personal means of livelihood [gifted ritually] with *kuśa* grass' (*kusa birtā*), 'personal means of livelihood [in which] all sources of revenue (*sarb aṅk birtā*) [are waived]', or [land managed by an] association (*guṭhi*) [for religious purposes]'

Royal gifts of land in the hill districts of Nepal merely note the tenurial status of the gifted tract; the inscriptions from the temples in the border regions of southern Nepal are more informative in that they detail the specific revenue sources which were waived.[22] First, the king waived his right to a share of the income from those persons who derived their livelihood from the king's land. The king's intermediary revenue officers were not entitled to collect from the divine recipient's tract of land the rent on the cultivation of crops, the use of communal supplies of firewood and water the taking of fish from ponds and watercourses by net, trap, or hook, the felling of timber from the forests, and the grazing of buffalo and

seems that they claimed it *de facto* until the mid-nineteenth century. In 1852, Chief Minister Jang Bahadur Rana, seeking funds to prepare for war against Tibet, scrutinised the temple endowments and claimed on behalf of the army the surplus income of those temples in which the manager had not been assigned the usufruct. This policy seems to have affected Brahmans more than ascetics. See M. Regmi, *Land Tenure and Taxation in Nepal* (Berkeley and Los Angeles, 1968), iv, pp. 73–4.

[22] This summary of tenurial privileges has been taken from the following land grants: 'Lāl mohar rājā gīrvāṇ yuddha vikram śāhako mahant amar girilāī samvat 1867 phālgun sudi 1'; 'lāl mohar rājā gīrvāṇ yuddha vikram śāhako mahant prtam dāslāī samvat 1867 bhādra sudi 5'; 'lāl mohar rājā gīrvāṇ yuddha vikram śāhako mahant pati rām dāslāī samvat 1867 bhādra sudi 5'; and 'lāl mohar rājā gīrvāṇ yuddha vikram śāhako mahant visambhar dāslāī samvat 1867 phālgun sudi 10' in Laṁsāl and Bhaṭṭarāī, 'Janakpur' (see n.21). The meaning of some of the revenue terms is obscure. The authority in this matter is M. Regmi, *Land Tenure*, (see n.21), but I have followed my local informants in the Tarai with regard to *sagārḥā, siṅgār,* and *cumāvan.*

goats on pastures. Administrative fees in connection with the registration of these modes of livelihood were also waived. These included the fees on land transactions received by the district revenue officer, the divisional revenue officer and the divisional records keeper; and the fee on land surveys, which was presumably claimed by the chief clerk at the district revenue office.

Second, the king's revenue officers were not entitled to claim any duties on the monopoly trade of hides and skins, bones, birds, catechu, and so forth nor on goods transported by land and by water across the boundaries of revenue districts. They could not collect the levy on trade conducted in the bazaar held twice a week, nor on tradesmen, such as barbers, blacksmiths, and curd vendors, who provided services within the tract of land. Also waived were the local levies on primary marriage and on secondary marriage. Third, proceeds from judicial fines and the fine on adultery which had been pronounced by the king's revenue officers upon subjects living on the gifted tract were remitted by the revenue officers to the divine recipient of the gift, not to the king. Fourth, neither the king nor any of his administrators claimed from the recipient any goods, money, or services in connection with the management of their personal estates or the sustenance of their person. Hence the local civil and military administrators and the members of the royal family on tour in the region were not entitled to collect miscellaneous levies from the king's subjects on the gifted tract, nor could they appropriate goods for their travelling expenses, nor labour for agricultural services or porterage services; nor food for their entertainment expenses, or funds for the celebration of a festival. Finally the levy on alms for the benefit of the royal priest was not collected from persons on the gifted tract nor could the revenue officers claim any special crown levies for the royal family. These included: the levy at the time of the sacred thread investiture of the prince; two levies on the occasion of the marriage of a princess – the first being the ceremonial washing of her feet by her relatives and the second being the worship of the groom upon his arrival at the palace; and finally the levy on the occasion of the coronation of the king.

In sum, with regard to the income from the *kusa birtā, sarb aṅk birtā*, or *guṭhi* tracts of land, the recipients were completely outside the revenue system of Nepal.[23] Since the king administered his

---

[23] The only exceptions to this were the abbots of certain Dasnami monasteries endowed by the Sen kings of Makwanpur and Vijayapur who were obliged to

territorial possessions through his tenurial system, the consequence of not 'eating the fruits of the land which has been gifted to others' was that the king transferred his tenurial autonomy to the divine recipient. By enjoying for themselves this tenurial autonomy, the deities became like kings.[24]

Having alienated these rights in favour of the recipient, the king also waived his right of escheat in order to ensure that the gifted tract would never revert to him. Should the Brahman householder's line of inheritance become defunct, the *kusa birtā* rights escheated to the temples of Pasupatinath and Cangu Narayan. Should the ascetic's line of pupillary succession become defunct, the king assigned the right of escheat to the ascetic who was the central overseer of the recipient's sect within the kingdom.[25] Thus the gifted tract never reverted to the king.

The king then undertook to protect these rights by setting himself up as the protector of the deity's right of enjoyment. A typical expression of this protective role may be found in King Girvan Yuddha Vikram Shah's gift to Daksinakali:[26]

If the manager or any wicked person, acting out of greed, interferes with the daily and occasional worship at this shrine then his deeds are equivalent to the 'five great sins'. Sri Daksinakali will also cast a terrible gaze upon him. Having considered the crime and caste of the criminal, if according to the code and regulations loss of life is necessary then the criminal shall be executed. As for his family, his sons and daughters will be cast into slavery. If the offender is a Brahman or of some other caste whose life cannot be taken then his head shall be shaved. If it is

submit the crown levies at the palace gate. See 'lāl mohar rājā gīrvāṇ yuddha vikram śāhako mahant bahādur bhārthīlāī samvat 1869 vaisākh sudi 8' in *Purātattva Patra Saṁgrah*, iii (1963), p. 37 and 'lāl mohar rājā gīrvāṇ yuddha vikram śāhako mahant anup girilāī samvat 1869 jyeṣṭha sudi 9', in *Śāhakālakā Abhilekha*, pp. 547–50.

24 In addition to receiving the gift, the recipient also takes on certain personal qualities of the donor. These qualities may be detrimental to the status of the recipient. For example, funeral priests take on the sins of the deceased and celebate ascetics are urged not to accept certain kinds of gifts in order to avoid the desires of the donor. Of all donors the king is the most dangerous, for he passes on not only his personal qualities but also those of the entire realm.

25 For the escheat of Brahman householders see Hamilton, *An Account of the Kingdom of Nepal*, p. 218; and for that of ascetics see Burghart, 'Regional circles' (see n.19).

26 'Lāl mohar rājā gīrvāṇ yuddha vikram śāhako dakṣiṇakālīsthānlāī samvat 1853 āśvin śukla 8 (no. 83)' in *Śāhakālakā Abhilekha*, pp. 301–5.

necessary to impose a fine then he will be deprived of his property. If it is necessary to banish the criminal from the realm then he will be banished.

This, of course, applied to everyone but the king. What would happen if the protector himself became greedy and resumed the gift? Here the king could only undertake a solemn vow of his own personal misfortune. The land grants usually end with the formulaic curse: 'Whoever confiscates land which has been gifted by himself or by others shall be reborn as a worm living in excrement for 60,000 years.'

By alienating in this manner all of his tenurial privileges upon a tract of land, the king enabled a deity to enjoy a relationship with the land and people which was equivalent to that of the king. In so far as 'sovereignty' was defined with reference to tenurial autonomy then the possessors of these gifted tracts were superior to and separate from the king. The superiority derived from the fact that the king had gifted the land in a ritual act; and the separation derived from the tenurial autonomy of the recipient. There were, however, two restrictions on this gift relationship which indicate the limits beyond which the king was not willing to compromise his royal authority. First, it would appear from the published inscriptions that the king gifted the land in a ritual context only in the case of the divine recipient being someone who 'respected Brahmans and cows'. There were instances in which the king assigned *kusa birtā* land to Buddhist monks and *sarb aṅk bitalab phakirānā* land to Muslim fakirs, but the documents do not mention any ritual context in which these rights were assigned.[27] It cannot be certain whether the avoidance of the ritual was due to the religious beliefs of the king or the reluctance of the royal priest to participate in any ritual involving persons who did not respect Brahmanical authority. One can only note that the king acknowledged his own inferiority with regard to human and celestial gods who respected Brahmans and cows; that is to say, Hindu deities.

The second restriction concerned the relinquishment of the king's moral authority. Ultimately the king was the protector of the

---

[27] 'Lāl mohar rājā narbhūpāl śāhako hlupā lāmālāī samvat 1798 phālgun vadi 5 (no. 11)' in *Śāhakālakā Abhilekha*, pp. 43–4; 'Sarba anka bitlab fakirana grant from King Rana Bahadur Shah to Rahman Khan Samvat 1843 vaisakh sudi 1' in *Regmi Research Series*, vii (1975), p. 121. See also the land grants to Buddhist Lamas in G. E. Clarke, 'A Helambu History', *Journal of the Nepal Research Centre*, 1980, iv, pp. 1–38.

moral order of the universe. This entailed the punishment of any subject who desecrated the realm by slaughtering cows and by causing confusion in the caste system (through inappropriate commensal and connubial relations). The punishments for such criminals were five in number: execution, bodily mutilation, banishment, expropriation, and enslavement (some lists also include degradation of caste). It was part of the king's duty to protect his realm through the exercise of these 'five punishments'. The king was the sole person in the kingdom who could pronounce these punishments; and in alienating his proprietary authority the king did not relinquish this moral authority. The human deities who received gifts of land were not entitled to pronounce the 'five punishments' on the king's behalf and if they themselves committed a crime meriting such punishment, then they were not exempt from the king's justice. The implication of this was that even though the king recognised in proprietary terms the separation of the divine recipient from the donor, still the recipients did not stand completely outside the bounds of royal authority. The king retained his moral responsibility as protector of the realm.

ROYAL DESIRE, DIVINE GRACE, AND THE POLITICS OF GIFT-GIVING

Of the many religious gifts of land given by Himalayan rulers at the turn of the nineteenth century it would appear that gifts prompted by the desire for victory and prosperity were especially numerous. In order to understand why this was so, it is necessary to focus not only on the activities of kings in defending or aggrandising their territory but also on the way in which they saw their territorial possessions to be abodes of one or more gods. For example, the Nepal valley was an abode of 5,600 Bhairavas and Bhairavis (the terrible forms of Siva and his consort); the goddess Kali dwelled at Vijayapur; and Jvala Mai at Dailekh. Other deities were linked to a place by virtue of their being a tutelary deity of the king; as was the case of Taleju who was brought from Ayodhya and worshipped by the Malla kings of the Nepal valley. As an abode of a deity, the territory over which the king ruled was also an enduring field of that deity's grace. Everything which happened upon that territory, happened by the grace of god. The focal point of that field was the deity's temple which was likened to a celestial palace. The regalia

28 Prithvi Narayan Shah, founder of modern Nepal, from a contemporary picture in the Old Palace, Kathmandu.

and ritual at these palace-like temples were roughly equivalent to the regalia and ritual at the king's temple-like palace. In making himself an object of that deity's grace, the king took on the role of a devoted servant offering gifts to the deity at the deity's court.

The clearest statement of the relation between the king's desire for land and the territorial god's grace in bestowing it may be found in the *Divya Updeśa* (Celestial Teaching) of King Prithvi Narayan Shah. In this text, compiled in 1775, the founder of the modern kingdom of Nepal recounts the time when he, accompanied by his astrologers, contemplated the conquest of the Nepal valley while standing on a mountain ridge overlooking the capital cities of Kathmandu, Patan, and Bhadgaon:[28]

> The thought came to my heart that if I might be king of these three cities, why, let it be so. At this same time these two astrologers [Bhanu Jyotisi and Kulanand Jyotisi] said to me, 'O King, your heart is melting with desire.' I was struck with wonder. How did they know my inmost thoughts and so speak to me? 'At the moment your gaze rested on Nepal you stroked your moustache and in your heart you longed to be king of Nepal, as it seemed to us.' 'Will this come to pass?' I asked. 'You, O Prince, have held at all times great respect for cows, Brahmans, guests, holy men, the gods, and goddesses. Also, in our hands lies the blessing of Sarasvati. You will one day be king of Nepal.'

After devising his diplomatic strategy and forming an army, Prithvi Narayan visited the goddess at Salyankot in the western hill districts. He was not allowed to behold the image of the goddess in the temple (for that was the privilege of the king and chief priest of Salyan) but he was allowed to sit at the temple gate and concentrate his thoughts day and night on the goddess:[29]

> One night I had a dream. A seven or eight-year old maiden came to me, bearing a sword in either hand. She covered her head with a pale rose-coloured cloth and came close to me. I asked her who her father was. She answered that she was the daughter of the Rana (Magar) priest of the temple. Saying this, she placed the swords in my hands. Then she took from her bosom a small object shaped like the *arasi* [an insignia of the goddess Sarasvati] and placed it on my lips, saying: 'This also you must swallow.

[28] L. Stiller, *Prithwinarayan Shah in the Light of Dibya Upadesh* (Ranchi (Bihar), 1968), p. 39.

[29] Ibid., 40–1.

29 The temple complex of Pasupatinath, a form of Siva, lies at the spiritual centre of
the Nepal valley. Both the Shah dynasty, as well as the Malla rulers before them,
sought the protection of Lord Pasupatinath by richly endowing the main temple
(positioned in front of the bull Nanda who is Siva's vehicle) and the outerlying
temples and monasteries of the complex.
    The photograph, taken by Landon in 1924, of the main temple precinct is
unique in that untouchables, such as Englishmen, were not permitted to behold
Pasupatinath. Landon's presence presumably disturbed the priests. The temple,
which is usually thronged with itinerant holy men, pilgrims and local devotees, is
curiously deserted.

Then whatever you wish for, you will receive. I also have a
request', she added. 'Receive this and go.' And so saying, she
took steps and vanished. At this I awoke, I called for Bhanu
Jyotisi and Kulananda Jyotisi as well as the Rana priest, and I
asked them to explain this to me. The astrologers and the priest
said that this was the goddess and that I had received a vision. At
this moment I presented incense, lights, flags, and a feast. For
the permanent worship I added seven buffaloes and seven goats
and income from Borlang Ghat and the ridge near the Ghat.
    In order to abide in the grace of the deity it was not only land
which the Nepalese kings gifted. They also embellished the temples

of their realm so that the deity's terrestrial abode was appropriate to his or her celestial status. Where a temple door had been wooden, the king ordered that a golden door be installed; where a temple had been a mere thatched hut, a brick building with a tiled or brass roof was constructed. Temples without bells were given bells; and temples with bells were given even bigger and louder sounding bells. In all this there was some element of competition between donors, as in the rivalry between the Shah kings and the Malla kings over the endowment of the loudest sounding bell in the Himalayas; yet it was not simply rivalry over prestige which provoked these endowments.[30] Instead these gifts were a means by which rulers obtained the grace of a deity in the pursuit of their political aims. For example, three days before the Gorkhali attack on Kathmandu, Prithvi Narayan Shah's younger brother offered a bell to the goddess Bhairavi at Nuvakot. The inscription on the bell reads: 'Salutations to Sri Bhairavi. On Samvat 1825 [AD 1768] on the fifth day of the month of Bhadra [August-September] Mahoddam Kriti Shah, full of affection for Bhairavi, offered a bell to the goddess with a view to weakening the enemy'.[31] Some years later, when Chinese troops stormed down from the Tibetan plateau and threatened to overrun the Gorkhali position at Nuvakot, Rana Bahadur Shah further offered to the Bhairavi temple a golden door and roof.[32]

By virtue of a place being an abode of a deity, the deity was thought to possess a pre-eminent claim upon the territory. The respect by the king of this claim is evident in the policy of the Shah dynasty in their conquest of the kingdoms on the southern flank of the Himalayas. The rulers of the Himalayan kingdoms had seen themselves as devoted servants of the territorial or ancestral deities whose claim to the territory pre-dated and transcended the transient claims of kings. In conquering a rival kingdom the Shah rulers confiscated the land grants of the defeated nobles and military officers but they confirmed the tenurial rights which the deposed king had gifted to the gods. The reason for this was not simply the legalistic one that the king ought not to confiscate that which has

---

[30] D. Vajrācārya and T. Śreṣṭha comment on this in *Śāhakālakā Abhilekha*, pp. 90–2.

[31] 'Abhilekha mahoddām kīrti śāhako nuvākoṭ bhairavalāī samvat 1825 (no.22)' in *Śāhakālakā Abhilekha*, pp. 89–92.

[32] 'Lāl mohar rājā raṇa bahādur śāhako nuvākoṭ bhairavīlāī samvat 1850 jyeṣṭha kṛṣṇa 14 (no.54)' in *Śāhakālakā Abhilekha*, pp. 201–6.

been gifted by others; rather it would appear that the main reason was the belief that by the grace of these gods the Shah rulers had gained victory.[33] Thus upon conquering Kathmandu, Prithvi Narayan Shah made certain to receive the blessings of Taleju, the tutelary deity of the Malla king whom Prithvi Narayan had put to flight.[34] After the conquest of Vijayapur, Girvan Yudda Vikram Shah confirmed the land rights of the goddess Kali at Vijayapur and of Narayan at Varahakshetra, both of whom had been supported by the Sen kings of Vijayapur; also the temples of Ram, Sita, Laksman, and Hanuman at Janakpur and the Saivite temple at Jalesvar, which had been places of worship for the Sen kings of Makwanpur, were similarly confirmed.[35]

The confirmation of the tenurial status of these gods – both Vaishnavite and Saivite, devotional and Tantric, vegetarian and carnivorous – was not a case of religious tolerance, but of territorial relativism. The territorial god possessed a pre-eminent claim to the territory and the king integrated the kingdoms of his realm by forming an unmediated personal relation with the deities of the lands he conquered. In doing this, he made certain to deprive the vanquished king of his status as principal devotee at the temple. After victory it was the Shah king who became the principal devotee at the temple, claiming the right of precedence in the worship at the shrine.[36] In sum, the religious gifts offered by the Nepalese kings were a means of securing certain political ends; and the right to offer certain kinds of gifts to territorial deities served to

---

[33] I doubt the force of the legal norm, for there were instances in which the king was alleged to have resumed religious gifts; these resumptions, however, seem to have been directed against Brahmans. See Regmi, *Land Tenure and Taxation in Nepal* (see n.9), iv, pp. 68–9; East India Company, *Papers* (see n.18).

[34] B. Ācārya, 'Śrī Baṛāmahārājādhirāja, Pṛthvinārāyaṇ Śāha', 4 vols. (Kathmandu, 1968), iii, pp. 503–4.

[35] The inscriptions have been cited in nn. 22 and 23.

[36] The best description of the role of the king in the worship at these shrines is A. Vergati-Stahl, 'Taleju, Sovereign Deity of Bhaktapur' in *Asie du Sud, traditions et changements* (Paris, 1979). The displacement of the vanquished king from the worship at his royal shrine appears, however, only to have occurred in the kingdoms conquerd by the Gorkhalis. Those other kings who accepted Gorkhali suzerainty and paid tribute to Gorkha were entitled by the Shah rulers to gift land to the gods. The one royal privilege which the tributary kings could not exercise (and which therefore served as a marker of Gorkhali overlordship) was to administer the 'five punishments'. See on this K. K. Adhikari, 'The Status, Powers, and Functions of Rajas and Rajautas during Nineteenth Century Nepal in the Light of Contemporary Documents', *Contributions to Nepalese Studies*, viii (1980), p. 151.

structure the authoritative relations between king and commoner in the Kingdom of Nepal.

CONCLUSION: THE RELATION BETWEEN ROYAL RITUAL AND POLITICAL ECONOMY

So far, royal gifts of land have been described as a sign of status and as a means to an end. Yet it seems that more can be said about these rituals than their being both an expressive and a technical act. At the turn of the nineteenth century the royal ritual of gift-giving was powerful in its own right as a way of constituting authoritative relations in the realm. Of particular importance here was the representation of the political system as a body politic. The auspicious body of state, which was formed at the time of coronation, had two important ideological implications. First, the king subjectified the entire polity by conceiving of all persons who derived their livelihood upon his land as being members of a single body politic. Second, the king objectified his agents of rule together with the ruled as the limbs of his body which the king, as mind, co-ordinated and commanded. In objectifying the polity, the divine king honoured his existing social relationships with human commoners by offering gifts in a structure of redistribution; and in subjectifying the polity, the divine king created personal relationships with other gods by offering them gifts in a structure of reciprocity.

This ritual representation of authoritative relations was not an empirical description of events, for the agents of rule had their own strategies of local dominance and, as Regmi has shown, there were numerous instances in which the king was frustrated in his attempt to administer the provinces.[37] It would be inappropriate, however, to assess the representation with regard to its referential accuracy, for that would overlook the more compelling fact that the body politic not only represented authoritative relations but it was also influential in its own right as a way in which power was constituted and distributed in the collectivity.

That this representation served as an unreflected basis for action may be seen in the battles led by 'limbs of state' in the Gorkhali conquest of the Himalayas. In the invasion of the Nepal Valley, Sur Pratap Shah, the brother and chief limb of Prithvi

[37] Regmi, *A Study in Nepali Economic History: 1768–1846* (see n.10), pp. 124–41.

Narayan Shah, led the 1764 attack on the fortified town of Kirtipur. The battle raged on until Sur Pratap was struck in the eye by an enemy arrow at which moment the Gorkhali troops fled from the battle in panic.[38] One year later the Gorkhali troops returned to the Nepal valley and by intrigue managed to breach the defences of Kirtipur and then, renewing their campaign against Kathmandu, put the Newar King Jay Prakasa Malla to flight. Jay Prakasa sought refuge at the court of Bhadgaon, but subsequently Gorkhali troops advanced on Bhadgaon and broke into the palace. A fight ensured which lasted one and a half hours until Jay Prakasa was wounded in the foot, causing the entire defence of Bhadgaon to collapse.[39] Four decades later Gorkhali troops, led by their commander Amar Sinha Thapa, pushed across the western Himalayas, conquering Kumaon and Garwhal and advancing on Kangra. In the military campaign in Kangra the Gorkhali soldiers tried to dislodge the troops of the East India Company from the ridge they were defending at Deothul. Throughout the several hours of battle Amar Sinha Thapa encouraged his troops in combat by standing immobile on the hillside just within the range of musket fire from the Company position.[40]

From these few instances it would seem that the ritual representation of the body politic not only signified royal autonomy, it was also highly persuasive in its own right, spreading fear and panic in soldiers when injured and inspiring them to bravery when seeming inviolable. The force of this representation is difficult to understand from a modern perspective yet it seems comparable to the fear and panic which seizes Europeans when a crowd is transformed into a mob. In the European case there is the implicit belief that collective order is maintained by individual, rational men. When men 'lose control of their reason' and become 'subject to their passions' then fear of public disorder ensues. In the Nepalese case there was a collective, rather than individual, basis of the collective order and this basis was represented by the body politic. Injury to the royal person caused immediate fear and confusion in the government. Disorder in the royal body entailed disorder in the realm.

It still remains to consider why the body of the king was such a

---

[38] Father Giuseppe, *Account* (see n.18), p. 318.
[39] D. Wright, *History of Nepal* (Cambridge, 1877), p. 255.
[40] T. Smith, *Narrative of a Five Year Residence at Nepaul*, 2 vols. (London, 1852), ii, p. 11.

persuasive symbol in eighteenth-century Nepal. One possible explanation lies with the ritual enactments of the king. In the course of the royal consecration all powers and qualities of the universe were drawn within the monarch so that he became a cosmic person. The powers of the gods of the eight directions and the qualities of the four main social orders were invested in him. His ministers, army and other functions of rule were likened to his limbs, such that the realm was seen to lie within his body. Thus to say in Nepal, 'Hail the realm, hail the king' (*jay deśa jay nareśa*) was, in a way, saying the same thing twice over. The ritual procedures of gift-giving, in which the king co-ordinated his limbs of state, affirmed this notion of the body politic.

Such an argument, couched in terms of the ritual and symbolism of the time, has plausibility, for it is based on native belief. It only fails to convince when one bears in mind that the present king of Nepal, Birendra Bir Bikram Shah, underwent a similar consecration in 1975 at which time the realm, was ritually constituted within his auspicious body. As for 'Hail the realm, hail the king', it can be seen stencilled across the windscreen of every bus and lorry that plies the perilous mountain roads of the kingdom. Gorkha soldiers, however, are not known any more for becoming panic-stricken in battle when their leader is wounded or killed. Nor are they necessarily inspired into action by their commander deliberately putting himself in a situation of danger but in which no harm comes. In sum, the ritual symbolism of the auspicious body of the king and the identity of king and realm still persist in native belief, but have lost their power to influence the believers. The pomp goes on, but there was a time when the pomp was also powerful.

Since the idea of the body politic as an encompassment hierarchy has remained unchanged, the change in the force of the idea cannot be explained with reference to the idea itself. Indeed the explanation would seem to lie outside any analysis cast in terms of the meaning of events. In considering other differences between eighteenth- and twentieth-century Nepal, the transformation of the political economy appears significant. During the reign of Prithvi Narayan Shah the king exercised proprietary authority over his subjects; by contrast in the twentieth century, land and labour were increasingly allocated by 'market forces', not by the force of royal command. In administrating the kingdom by means of a control hierarchy, it would appear that this control hierarchy in the eighteenth century and the encompassment hierarchy of the body politic mutually reinforced one another so that the king's ritual status appeared powerful in its own right.

By the late nineteenth century, however, the political economy in Nepal underwent formal differentiation into a polity and an economy. Royal ritual, which hitherto had been significant for the polity (it specified the internal order) and the economy (it specified the prosperity) became important for neither. Meanwhile the government of Nepal became increasingly bound up with its citizens rather than its gods. Gifts of land by the king remained an integral part of statesmanship, but by the early twentieth century, religious gifts of land had already lost their *raison d'être*. Instead the king gave land to the 'public', by endowing schools and hospitals. Although celestial and human gods no longer received gifts of land, the memory of such gifts in the past was kept alive as living testimony of the piety and religious tolerance of the Nepalese rulers. These attitudes, so characteristic in the definition of modern Hinduism, are used to mark and legitimate the regional autonomy of modern Nepal as a Hindu kingdom. Throughout this period of transition the Nepalese state as a body politic has remained an important idea, but in the course of its perpetuation it seems to have become merely an idea.

7. The ritual of the royal bath in Madagascar: the dissolution of death, birth and fertility into authority

MAURICE BLOCH

The study of royal rituals is beset by a tension between pointless particularism and platitudinous generalisation. On the one hand anthropologists have argued that royal rituals serve to maintain the social and political; perhaps the best presentation of this functionalist case is Gluckman's analysis of the Swazi *Incwala*, an annual ceremony centred on the king which reaffirmed the relationship between the king, the powers of nature and the well-being of the nation. But this approach is open to the charge of reductionism. By attributing a single social function to the performance, it not only explains the indubitable by the unknowable, it also ignores most of the specific details of the ceremonial.[1] Such criticisms of functionalism have led to more careful studies of royal rituals, but the danger is the transformation of anthropologists into Orientalists, or Islamicists or whatever, who have lost the original generalising vocation of the subject. With the abandonment of cross-cultural concepts in favour of particularism, generalisation becomes impossible. In fact, we do not have to choose between the polarities of particularism and generalisation. This chapter is an attempt to study particular meaning and general significance simultaneously.

Royal symbolism is, I believe, constructed out of non-royal symbolism, both logically and probably also historically. This hypothesis forms part of a larger theory, that all symbolic construc-

I would like to thank the participants in the intercollegiate seminar 'The problem of Order' organised by Mark Hobart in the University of London for giving me the opportunity to present a very early draft of this paper. Since then I have benefited from many useful comments especially from C. Fuller, M. Esoavelomandroso and J. Parry.

[1] H. Kuper, *An African Aristocracy, Rank among the Swazi* (London, 1947); M. Gluckman, 'Rituals of Rebellion in South-East Africa' in *Order and Rebellion in Tribal Africa* (London, 1963), pp. 110–36. Criticised by T. O. Beidelman, 'Swazi Royal Ritual', *Africa* xxxvi (1966), pp. 373–405.

tions of authority involve the same elements.[2] The first step is the creation of an order which transcends mere human experience and action. This construction can only be achieved by the symbolical devaluation of human mutability: i.e. birth, death, and exchange, because an alternative unchanging order which is beyond experience can only be created through dramatic contrast with what is experienced seen in a special light. Once the transcendent order has been created, human authority then becomes represented as the delegation of order in this life; it is a claim to regulate human existence by reference to the transcendental model. However, this construction inevitably implies a problem. Human life cannot systematically renounce movement and exchange. Yet the construction of authority means that ideal existence is represented as the attempt to follow an anti-life. This is because the transcending order has been created in antithesis to life by means of symbolical drama. The symbolism of authority must therefore not be just a matter of following a transcendental model, but also of compromising with this model to make it relevant to this life. It must involve a contradiction which allows for the reintroduction of real existence into what still remains the ideal.

The significance of this view of the construction of symbolism is twofold. First, in order to understand royal symbolism it is necessary to stress the relationship of the practices and concepts governing royal life and those governing the life of ordinary people; only in this way will we be able to understand the emotional and political power of these rituals for those who witness them. Secondly, it is necessary to bear in mind that the relationship which exists between ruler and ruled is first and foremost political and economic, and so the circumstances and reasons governing borrowings and transformations are not to be explained by the ritual itself, but by such factors as the need to establish new political legitimacies in a very short time. This was the case for eighteenth- and nineteenth-century Madagascar, though for reasons of space this point cannot be properly discussed here.[3]

Thus the royal rituals of the Merina state of Madagascar are best understood in a dual fashion. They share universal characteristics

---

[2] This view has been outlined jointly by J. Parry and myself in *Death and the Regeneration of Life* (Cambridge, 1982), pp. 1–44.

[3] For a full discussion see Bloch, *From Blessing to Violence: History and Ideology in the Circumcision Ritual of the Merina of Madagascar* (Cambridge, 1986).

From a Sketch by W Ellis

ANTANANARIVO.

P. 82.

30 Antananarivo, the capital of Madagascar, with the procession of Prince and
Princess Royal passing along the eastern side of the city.

of the symbolical construction of authority and also gain specific meaning through their adoption and adaptation of symbolic forms which organised non-royal life in Merina culture. The first section of this chapter describes and analyses the ritual of the royal bath, and the second investigates the background of contemporary non-royal rituals of death, birth and fertility; the final section emphasises the unity of meaning and function in royal rituals.

THE ROYAL BATH

The Merina, sometimes called the Hova, are a people who live in central Madagascar and one of their kingdoms began to expand rapidly towards the end of the eighteenth century, so that by approximately 1860, the Merina had conquered a great part of Madagascar and ruled over perhaps rather more than two million people. The causes of this expansion are complex but they have much to do with the capture of trade routes and a tacit and uncertain alliance with the British in Mauritius.[4]

Throughout this period, the rulers of the Merina yearly practised the ritual of the royal bath. This is a ritual which we know surprisingly well from a number of descriptions by European travellers, officials and missionaries. The earliest account dates back to 1817 and there are numerous descriptions of the ritual until the time of the French conquest in 1895.[5] There are also a few

[4] Among discussions of the historical causes of the growth of the Merina kingdom see H. Isnard, 'Les bases géographiques de la monarchie hova', in *Eventail de l'historie vivante. Hommage a Lucien Febvre*, 2 vols. (Paris, 1953), i, pp. 195–206. M. Bloch, 'The Disconnection between Power and Rank as a Process: an Outline of Development in Kingdoms in Central Madagascar', in J. Friedman and M. Rowlands (eds.), *The Evolution of Social Systems* (London, 1977), pp. 303–40.

Work in preparation by historians such as F. Raison, S. E. K. Ellis, G. Berg and S. Ayache will show the critical importance of the slave trade to the rise of the Merina monarchy, (personal communication).

[5] The earliest account is found in the Journal of J. Hastie of 1817. This has been published in a French translation in the *Bulletin de l'Académie Malgache*, ii (1903), pp. 91–114, 173–92, 241–69. The main accounts on which I have relied for the summary analysis here are in descending order of importance:

The account from Malagasy manuscripts in the collection of R. P. Callet, *Tantara ny Andriana eto Madagascar*, 2nd edn, 2 vols. (Tananarive, 1908), i, pp. 157–73.

The account by R. P. Abinal found in a manuscript in the archives of the Society of Jesus in Toulouse as 'Lettre de Vals' (November, 1867), pp. 25–33, and also published as R. P. Abinal, 'Le "Fandroana" en Imérina en 1867', *Bulletin de l'Académie Malgache*, n.s. xxix (1949–50), pp. 20–5.

The article by J. Sibree, 'The Fandroana, a New Year's Festival of the Malagasy',

accounts by Merina written either directly or indirectly.[6] This wealth of sources presents a problem for a description in a chapter such as this. It is obviously impossible to discuss all these accounts and I shall have to use only a very simple and general summary of what happened, based on the features which most sources agree on. Even so, I shall deal only with the basic outline of the ritual, ignoring certain aspects, either because of restrictions of space,[7] or because, as in the case of the notion of *hasina* (the mystical sanctity of authority) or the ranking system of traditional Merina society, I have discussed them elsewhere.[8] Similarly I cannot consider here transformations which have taken place in the ritual, during the main period for which my description of the ritual applies: 1820–70.[9]

This ritual has already been discussed by a number of historians and anthropologists; particularly important is the work of a Malagasy theology student Razafimino who wrote a study of the royal bath in 1924 pointing out some of the connections between the ritual and funerary ceremonies,[10] as well as a few extremely perceptive pages in a recent work by the historian A. Délivré, who stresses the significance of the convergence of social and cosmic order.[11] I have incorporated several ideas from both these writers in what follows. Other important studies include those of Molet and Raharijaona.[12] In fact rituals which are more or less distant variants

Antananarivo Annual, xxiv (Christmas, 1900), pp. 489–96.
There are also a great many other sources which can be used, as nearly every foreigner in Tananarive had to attend the ritual and a surprising number of them have left some sort of description.

6 The most important accounts are to be found in the various writings of Raombana who refers to the ritual in very many places. The significance of this work has been discussed in S. Ayache, *Raombana l'historien* (Fianarantsoa, 1976) and the first volume of Raombana's History has appeared, edited by S. Ayache: Raombana, *Histoire* (Fianarantsoa, 1980), i, pp. 71–3.

7 For example I have not discussed the killing of a cock early in the ritual as a means of purification. This act is separate from the main action and satisfactorily interpreted by all our sources.

8 Bloch, 'The Disconnection between Power and Rank', pp. 318–29.

9 These dates correspond roughly to the period from the beginning of our documentation to the time when the Merina monarch became Christian. This led to changes which cannot be discussed here.

10 C. Razafimino, *La Signification du Fandroana* (Tananarive, 1924).

11 A. Délivré, *L'Histoire des rois d'Imèrina* (Paris, 1974).

12 L. Molet, *Le Bain Royal à Madagascar* (Tananarive, 1956). This book caused a furore by suggesting on no real evidence that the ritual of the royal bath originated in the practice of necrophagy. It develops some of the ideas of Razafimino (*La Signification*, see n. 10). It however suffers from looking at a

of the Merina ritual of the royal bath occur among many other peoples in Madagascar and beyond; this has led to many discussions which take in, at one time, these numerous variants. This has not made for clarity.[13]

The ritual of the royal bath should occur both at the beginning of the agricultural year, before the coming of the rain which will enable the transplanting of rice to begin, and at the beginning of the calendrical year at the time of passage from the arabic lunar month of *Alohotsy* to that of *Alahamady*. The combination of the lunar year and the solar year of course caused a problem, as they need not occur at the same time.[14] This problem is reflected in the sources, which seem to have great difficulty in agreeing when the ritual should have occurred, and it perhaps explains the rather arbitrary dates on which it actually did occur. There is no doubt however that the ritual is associated with the idea of the new year, even if it is not clear which year is in question. People greeted each other at the time of the royal bath with a phrase which meant: we congratulate you on the coming of the new year.[15]

The contrast between the two arabic months which should occur on either side of the ritual is of great significance. The month of *Alohostsy*, which precedes the ritual, is a weak month, but *Alahamady*, which follows it, is associated with all the most important Merina values, especially the direction north east, which in turn is associated with the ancestors, the king and growth in general.[16] Passing the boundary marked by the ritual was, therefore, a matter

whole range of related rituals throughout Madagascar without separating the specific logic of any particular one. Molet's more recent work, *La Conception Malgache du monde, du surnatural et de l'homme en Imèrina* (Paris, 1979), does not suffer from the same problem in its discussion of the royal bath and the analysis is quite compatible with that carried out here. The study by S. Raharijaona, 'Ny Fandroana Heviny sy tantarany' appears in *Hiratra*, ii (1980), pp. 95–172, iii (1981), pp. 153–244. This study stresses strongly the calendrical aspect of the rite and its link-up with the cycle of the seasons without making clear how this squares with the lunar month. It attempts a history going very far back by using material from outside Imèrina, an always risky procedure. These articles nevertheless represent a thorough examination of many useful sources.

[13] Molet, *Le bain royal* (see n. 12), Raharijaona 'Ny Fandroana' (see n. 12).

[14] There are reasons for believing that the attempt to correlate the feast of the royal bath and the lunar year occurred shortly before the period under consideration and the problems this raised were never fully sorted out.

[15] Subsequently, aspects of the ritual became partly associated with national days, such as 14 July during the colonial period, and with Christmas and to a certain extent New Year.

[16] Callet, *Tantara* (see n. 5), i, p. 27.

of passing from a period of decline to a period of growing strength and sanctity. Similarly, certain parts of the ritual, especially after the bath itself, were concerned with the growth of the new moon which was represented as a young chick which is being encouraged to come out of its shell. This was done by people throwing dried cattle dung, itself a symbol of wealth and strength, to it.[17] In other words, as with so many other royal rituals, the royal bath linked directly the processes of kingship with the cycles of time and renewal. By the ritual, the authority of the king was naturalised, in that it was merged with cycles existing beyond human action and therefore human challenge. This aspect is, however, only a small part of a much more complex picture which must now be examined. See figure 32 (p. 293) for a depiction of the sequence of events and the significance of the order in which they occur.

The beginning of the ritual period was marked by a formal announcement, some two weeks before the actual bath. This announcement was made from a stone associated with both coronation and circumcision rituals. From that moment on, certain restrictions marked the period of the ritual. First, all incomplete tasks, such as weaving, had to be finished; ensuring that no activity spilled over from one year to the next and so negated the clarity of point of departure of the new cycle. Secondly, a series of restrictions concerning death was enforced. Until the ritual of the bath actually took place, no animal could be killed. The most important such rule was that, during this period, no funeral could occur. If someone died, which in any case was considered extremely unfortunate, the matter had to be hushed up, the corpse could not be taken into the family tomb, none of the normal mourning or burial procedures were allowed to take place and the body had to be, as far as possible, hidden. A number of other activities also could not take place. The holding of markets was forbidden; this was because Merina markets implied week-long cycles, since one day of the week was allocated to each market place by the king, and all cyclic activity, overlapping with the division marked by the ritual, was unacceptable. Complete bathing, that is involving washing higher than the upper lip, was also forbidden until the day of the actual bath. This was so that the clarity of the newness and importance of the action of bathing the head, which was an essential part of the ritual for the king's subjects, should not be obscured.

17 Callet, *Tantara* (see n. 5), i, pp. 68–70.

The ritual, like all occasions having to do with the king or the state, was marked at various stages by the paying of taxes. Of these, only those which are specific to the royal bath ritual concern us. The first of these was called the *vidy aina*, the price of life. This was paid to the sovereign in recognition of his part in a ritual which renews life. The second was called the *jaka*, a word which is often translated as 'new year present', a rendering which does not convey its great significance. Indeed, although all subjects had to give this present to the monarch, this was only a small part of a more general pattern of the giving of the *jaka* by inferiors to superiors. The Catholic missionary Abinal, who witnessed the royal bath in 1867, gives the following account:

> The days preceding the feast are almost entirely taken up with visiting. Kinsmen visit kinsmen, friends visit friends, inferiors visit superiors ... In the context of the feast of the *fandroana* these gifts are called *jaka* (new year presents). The visitor presents his piece of money as politely as he can saying the following formula 'Blessed be God. As we are beginning a new year and the season of fragrance is here, we offer you this *jaka* ... '[18]

Abinal goes on to explain that, in the past, meat instead of money was given. This was still so at the height of the ritual when preserved beef, called *jaka*, was consumed. From the start, the ritual required society to be *in order* and this order was marked by the giving of presents. People aligned themselves along the lines of social linkages, especially along the lines of authority marked by the unequally reciprocated gift of the *jaka*. Furthermore, because of the calendrical nature of the ritual, this social order became part of temporal and astrological order. This theme of social order is repeated again and again during the ritual.

After the gift giving the ritual proper began. On the hillsides, torchlight processions took place and bonfires were lit to mark the beginning of this happy time. However, the night before the night of the actual bath women had to weep together inside every house. This weeping was mourning for all those who had died and was similar to the weeping that took place at funerals. But unlike weeping at funerals it was orchestrated state wide, as if the individual events of each family had been brought together and synchronised. Abinal gives a theatrical description of this night in

[18] Abinal, 'Le "Fandroana" en Imèrina', p. 21 (my translation).

Tananarive: 'From the little bank in front of my house listen, if you will, to the sounds and noises of the town. Everywhere you will hear weeping and groaning, howling almost.'[19] After this night of sorrow, women took everything out of the house in the morning and washed it as they did after any funeral.

The next day followed the same theme. People dressed in clothes reminiscent of shrouds for the dead, and then went to the family tombs to invoke the dead in a number of ways. In particular, they might take some of the soil from the tomb to add to the water of the bath. The king did likewise, and went to the tombs of his predecessors, to make physical contact with their remains, in a way that is not clear from our sources, who probably did not attend this part of the ritual. In any case everyone called on their ancestors to bless them and their family.[20] From that moment, the tombs of the dead stayed open until after the ritual meal, which followed the bath. The night of the royal bath itself, which is the centre of the ceremony, followed this day at the tombs. Here, our sources are again somewhat unclear, especially over one point. On the one hand, they stress how everybody should be in their place: children at the house of their parents, slaves in the house of their masters, and above all wives in the house of their husbands. This last point is often mentioned, as separated couples had to return together for that night. On the other hand in constrast to all that order, the night is also said to be a night without sanctions. What this seems to have involved is a relatively discreet orgy. Everyone could have sexual relations with anyone, irrespective of the various rules normally restricting such contact.[21] The details of what happened remain unclear, partly because of the nature of our sources, but the central contradiction between order and disorder can be sorted out. The obligation to be at the right place at the right time applied, above all, to the ritual meal which followed immediately after the bath, while the orgy of sexual disorder preceded it in the earlier part of the night.

[19] Abinal, 'Le "Fandroana" en Imèrina', p. 22.
[20] Abinal, in the manuscript version of his account, gives most details saying the tombs were cleaned and decorated and the corpse of the dead king wrapped in cloth, in one case by the queen herself. This is however unsupported in the other accounts and Abinal is inconsistent in that he suggests that only the houses built on top of royal tombs were open. If this were so there would not be access to the royal bodies.
[21] Callet, *Tantara*, see n. 5, i, pp. 167–8.

Then, in the middle of the night, came the bath itself at the very moment of the turn of the year. For the royal bath, youths whose father and mother are still living (that is their name, as well as the criteria by which they are chosen) went to fetch water from certain special streams and lakes. These streams and lakes are associated with creatures called Vazimbas. Vazimbas are represented as rather vague indigenous inhabitants of Imerina who were defeated by the Merina and especially by the ancestors of the royal line who took away their land and in some cases married their women. However, because of their original ownership of the land, their spirits still control certain aspects of its fertility and have thus to be worshipped rather as nature spirits. This non-human fertility is symbolised in most Merina rituals by water. The Vazimbas possess a kind of wild uncontrolled vitality which normally contrasts with the life-giving power derived from the blessing of ancestors. The Vazimbas are associated with women and it is particularly significant that the principal source of water for the ritual of the royal bath is lakes in which Vazimba queens, defeated rulers but matrilateral ancestors of the Merina kings, are believed to have been buried. The symbolic role of the youths whose father and mother are still living is complex, and also found in other rituals. We may simply note that they are associated with the continuity of descent between generations.[22]

Once this water had been obtained, it was brought back to the palace and warmed. The monarch, at the very moment of the turn of the year, took off the old clothes in which he had been dressed, and stepped into and then out of the bath. He then put on particularly fine *new* clothes. The ruler then took some of the water from the bath and sprayed his assembled subjects with it. This is the blessing of the bath. The London Missionary Society missionary Sibree described the event when it took place under Queen Rasoaherina, who was then already strongly influenced by British and French customs.

Meanwhile other attendants of the Queen had been preparing the bath for her Majesty. This was of silver, and was placed in the north-east angle of the apartment, and screened off from view by scarlet lambas held up by ladies of the court. The Queen was then conducted behind the screen to bathe, at the conclusion of which

---

[22] Their role is particularly prominent in the circumcision ceremonies. See Bloch, *From Blessing to Violence* (n. 3).

31 Audience at the Palace, Antananarivo.

ceremony all the cannon were again fired to announce to the people the completion of this most important part of the festival. After a few minutes' interval, her Majesty reappeared, with her hair and face wet from the bath. On making her entry she repeated the usual form of thanksgiving: 'samba samba Andria-manitra, Andriananahary, ho arivo tratry ny taona anie tsy hisara-mianakavy!' i.e., Blessed, blessed by God, may we reach a thousand years of unseparated family! To this all present replied by explaining: 'Tarantitra', i.e. Reach old age. Holding in her hand the horn filled with warm water, and attended by the higher officers, the Queen passed through the people, sprinkling them on either hand, and then the soldiers and officers on guard in the verandah. (In more recent times, Ranavalona III, who knew us all very well, would roguishly give some of us a splash in the face as she passed through the crowd, evidently enjoying the fun.)[23]

Receiving this water was a sign of filiation, either political or kinship, (in fact the two are merged) and so if any slave received the blessing of the water of the bath he was automatically freed.

The same ritual was repeated in every house in the land when the head of the family bathed after a signal had been given from the palace. Ordinary people however did not take a complete bath but bathed only the upper part of their head, the part which it had been forbidden to bathe after the announcement of the ritual. As it had been for the water of the king's bath, this water was then used to bless junior members of the family and dependants.

The ritual meal which followed the bathing was almost as important. The rice for this meal was prepared in special antique pots, immediately before the bath, and was eaten immediately afterwards. Before being eaten the rice was mixed with two ingredients, milk and honey, and the mixture was called *tatao*, a word stressing superiority. In addition, *jaka* was eaten. This was a mixture of recently slaughtered beef and preserved beef from the previous year.

At the palace, where the preparation of this meal was highly elaborate, a little mixed *tatao* and *jaka* was placed on the king's head before he began to eat. The same was done in the houses of subjects after the signal had been given from the palace that the ruler had performed his part. Similarly, following the royal meal,

[23] Sibree, 'The Fandroana' (see n. 5), p. 493.

every household sat down to a meal, in which everybody participated. The next day, or a little later, the meal was repeated by
children who served food to each other during what most sources
describe as a picnic. The meal following the bath completed the
night of the bath. The next day was marked by a distribution of
cattle from superiors to inferiors and especially from the monarch
to his subjects. This was because the feast commemorated the
discovery by the Royal ancestor of the edibility of cattle (see below
p. 290). The cattle given and eaten for this feast were of two kinds,
one, particularly fattened, was called famous cattle (*malaza*), the
other, associated with the sovereign, was called *volavita*, which I
believe, (although this is nowhere confirmed) is a contraction of
volana vita, completed moon, and referred to the circular white
mark which defined this cattle. This would fit well with the
astronomical aspect of the ritual. The slaughtering of this cattle had
to be done in a special way. The rump or royal part was cut off, and
this was then placed over the head of the ruler, who licked it.

The distribution and killing of cattle marked the high point of the
rituals of the day following the actual bath. After that the ritual
acts, which continued for a number of days, seem to have been less
important; they involved such things as the paying of yet further
taxes, and various thanksgivings.

THE CONSTRUCTION OF RITUAL

Clearly this royal ritual is of great complexity and the next part of
this chapter will consider how it can be understood, at least in its
main features. The first point to note, as I have already emphasised
in several places already, is the alignment of society, royalty and
astronomy which the whole ritual implies. That royal rituals often
do this has been a commonplace of anthropology. The political
significance of this has also been evident; it represents royal
authority as a thing beyond challenge, since it is then an aspect of a
whole which is beyond the mere creation of man. The ritual of the
royal bath presents at its highest point an image of the world where
everything is in its place: the heavenly bodies, the kingdom, the
kinship system. Hence, the absolute necessity that all social ties be
manifested by proper locality; that husbands and wives, parents
and children, masters and slaves be together and, further, that they
mark their relation by presents which express the lines of depend-

ency. The way in which the royal bath links the cosmic and the political order and in this way legitimates the latter is clear. This has been well analysed by Délivré (see n. 11), but the linkages go even further. The ritual links the cosmic order with the emotions aroused by death and rebirth, but with these emotions ordered and synchronised. Internal and external order are made to go together.

The next point to note is equally fundamental but requires more specific knowledge of Merina ethnography. The royal bath, like a number of other rituals, some of which will be mentioned below, is primarily a ritual of blessing. The word blessing is here a translation of the Malagasy word *tsodrano* which literally means to blow on water, since the most ordinary blessing, from a father to his child, as well as the most elaborate, as here, involves the scattering of water onto those blessed.

The ordinary ritual of blessing can be carried out by any superior for an inferior, any father for his son, any elder for his dependants, on a very great number of occasions, almost whenever such a blessing is requested. It always involves the same elements: first, an invocation to the dead ancestors, often at the family tomb, by the superior who will give the blessing. Second, the person who will do the blessing must obtain specially holy water and place it in a container – often with other powerful and pure objects. He then recites a prayer asking God, the ancestors and other supernatural beings to bless the child. Third, the person blessing will then blow the water on to the person to be blessed, at the same time wishing blessings which are enumerated (many children, power, fertility, wealth, strength, good fortune etc . . .). The central concern is how to pass on blessing, to transmit it, from ascendant to descendant. The elder is only acting as a transmitter of the blessing from preceding generations, the ancestors in the tomb, as well as other less important supernaturals. The blessing therefore implies the following line of transmission:

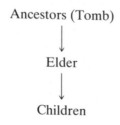

Ancestors (Tomb)

↓

Elder

↓

Children

There is however another element. Blessing involves the transferral of the power of ancestors down the line of generations, down to those who are being blessed, but this ancestral fertility is also supplemented and added to by wild, uncontrolled, unsocialised, Vazimba fertility, represented by water. The association of the wild fertility of the Vazimba with water is complex, but it is particularly clear in cases such as the royal bath, when the water is taken from locations believed to be burial places of Vazimbas.

The significance of this natural fertility, associated as it is with strength, virility, life, women, sexuality and the biological processes of birth and death, is central to Merina thought.[24] Fundamentally this strength is ambiguous. This is demonstrated in the relation of the Vazimbas to the ancestors. The ancestors drove out the Vazimbas in the remote past. The ancestors are dead, in the tomb, dry, as the Merina stress, they have got rid of their vitality, their strength, their sexuality, their feminine side (linked with wet and warmth), which are all symbols of the Vazimba. The elaborate Merina funerary rituals, which in many ways are a matter of drying the corpse and which make ancestors, are therefore also a driving out of the Vazimba aspect of the person.[25] The ancestors are therefore doubly anti-Vazimba both historically and ritually.

However it is as if the moral purity of the ancestors, who have abandoned this life, its softness, wetness and pleasures, were not enough for the living. The blessing which the ancestors transmit is the blessing of the dry dead, but it also needs to be supplemented, to be rendered vital. This is what is acted out in the blessing. The power of the Vazimba who were once beaten and driven out is used, in the form of water, to *add* to that from the ancestors. This contradiction is a source of endless paradoxes in Merina mythology and ritual, yet it is this which lies at the centre of blessing. Merina blessing is the transfer of the power of the ancestors, but to it is added the power of vitality, the power of the Vazimba who in another guise must be expelled. Here is the first example of the paradox of the general symbolism of authority, referred to above. The ideal which transcendence requires to legitimate authority is by definition impossible for the living and so it must be represented as compromised in the life at least. The same pattern underlies the

24 Bloch and Parry, (n. 2) *Death and the Regeneration of Life*.
25 M. Bloch, 'Death, Women and Power', in Bloch and Parry, *Death and the Regeneration of Life* (see n. 2), pp. 211–30.

nation-wide ritual of the royal bath, which is also said to be a ritual of *Tsodrano* or blessing.

The king, having associated himself with his ancestors by his visit to the royal tombs, then blesses his children/subjects by spraying them with water which has come into contact with his body. Again this ancestral blessing has to be fortified by Vazimba vitality, but in this case, as befits the occasion, these are royal Vazimbas: Vazimba queens.

The differences between this royal blessing and lesser blessings are, at first sight, insignificant. Instead of the water being contained internally by the mouth of the elder, it comes externally in contact with the body of the ruler in the bath. As a result, instead of blowing out the water, the ruler scatters it with his hand. This pattern is also repeated by the head of every family, but with the difference that ordinary people do not immerse themselves in the bath, but only wash the top part of their head. I return to the significance of this difference between ruler and subject below.

The sociological and political significance of the equation of the blessing and the royal bath is, however, more complex. In the ritual the king is acting as the father or elder to his subjects, and he actually says so during the ceremony. The whole population of the kingdom is represented in the ritual of the bath as the king's juniors, that is as his children or his younger siblings. The fertility he confers through the royal bath is the same as the fertility which an elder would transfer from the ancestors to his descendants. There is, however, a hidden problem in this equation of descent group blessing and royal blessing. In the descent group case the ancestors, the source of the blessing, are the equivalent, in a different generation, to the blessed. Those who are blessed will one day (in theory at least) become ancestors. In the case of the royal blessing the children/subjects will never become royal ancestors. This difference shows the ideological significance of the merging of the two types of blessing. The transferring of fertility between generations, which lies at the very heart of all Merina religion and kinship, absorbs and obscures a very different relation by placing royalty within its idiom.

Another aspect of this difference needs stressing. At the back of the notion of descent group blessing is a static representation of time where every new generation replaces the next, as if the descent group never changes. This is transferred to the royal ritual in that the succession of monarchs is represented as this regular succession of incumbents. This does not create the classical anthropological distinction between incumbents and office but leads to a parthenogenetic representation of royal descent, kings become depersonalised replacements for one another, each other's children, simply by coming into contact with the bodies of their predecessors, irrespective of kinship connections.

In fact the history of the Merina, like that of most other similar peoples, shows no such continuity. Merina royal succession is a matter of who wins by intrigue or on the battlefield. The ritual obliterates the disreputable way in which Merina rulers gain power and replaces it by an ahistorical cycle of succession. In this way the consideration of the ritual of the bath brings us back to the idea of order. Not only does the ritual show the social, emotional and political processes to be continuous with the astronomical ones, but also the social processes themselves are revealed as implying a continuity which outflanks mere human time. It is the continuity of smooth replacement, of generation after generation, of king after king, who transfer to each other their power which therefore endures unchanging.

This point draws our attention to certain aspects of the ritual which at first sight seem contradictory with it. If the royal bath implies total order, why the disruption of the sexual orgy and why the emphasis on death and mourning which comes to the fore at certain points? The answer to both these questions is similar and is to be found in the nature of the ritual itself. Rituals, as many anthropologists have pointed out, are a little like theatre. They create images by dramatic means, and especially by contrast. The demonstration of the sweetness of order requires the acting out of disorder so that order can appear triumphant. This is what is involved in the sexual orgy. It precedes the extreme social order of the bath and the meal, and thereby partly creates the image of orderly antithesis. This is also emphasised by the day–night contrast which occurs in other Merina rituals and myths. In this case, however, the symbolism is compressed into one night, and what is contrasted is the period when the night is increasing, until about two o'clock in the morning, and the period when it is moving towards morning. The bath marks the break between the two. Before the bath, in the first part of the night, there is chaos; after the bath, in the second part of the night, there is royal order.

The same pattern clearly holds between the night of mourning and the next day of the visit to the tomb. This depends on one of the key concepts of Merina symbolism – the idea that the tomb represents a victory over death. Such symbolism is possible by means of the very type of antithetical creation we have just discussed. For the Merina, death has two sides. First it has a polluting, sad side, which is associated with the house and the first temporary burial. The corpse is kept in the house after a death, surrounded by weeping women, in some cases for a considerable time. It is then buried temporarily to dry. After a considerable time, it will be placed in the family tomb. For this it is exhumed, taken back to the house, to be surrounded again by women. Finally, on the day of the entry to the tomb, it makes a journey from the house to the tomb. This is a joyful journey because the, by now, dry corpse has left the polluting world of women, houses, softness and flesh to become an unchanging eternal ancestor. The Merina do not stress the continuity of the individual but the permanence of the tomb, a solid stone structure which symbolises the permanence of the undivided descent group. The journey to spiritual, eternal life, is therefore the journey from the house of weeping to the tomb of rejoicing.[26] That is the victory over death. The tomb symbolically becomes the source of future blessing for future generations.

With this background we can see how the sequence of mourning at night, followed the next day by a visit to the tomb, re-enacts the contrast between the two funerals and the journey which separates them. The night of mourning is replaced by the day of ancestral rejoicing and order. It also follows that the two should be separated by a ritual of purification, the washing of the clothes, so that nothing of the world of decomposition and sorrow is carried over to the next day of blessing at the tomb. The image of the permanent order of the ancestors is, therefore, created by the contrast between the two images of death, and these are linked to the calendrical aspects, since the ritual of the bath emphasises the cycles of the moon, the cycle of the year, and the cyclic alternation of day and night. The effect of this emphasis on cycles is not to stress mutability, but rather to suggest that beyond evident and immediate change there is, like the tomb, an underlying order which makes these fluctuations meaningless.

26 Ibid.

There is, however, another aspect of the bath as both a double funeral and as a blessing which becomes apparent when we put the two elements together. To do this it is essential to remember the order in which the two parts of the ritual occur. First we have the night of mourning by women associated with houses, flesh, decay, women; then this element is vanquished by the visit to the tomb, the symbol of the permanent and unchanging social order of the ancestors. This visit is also the beginning of the blessing which will culminate in the royal bath. All blessing must begin, as this one does, with an invocation at the tomb of the ancestors. After the episode of sexual disorder, the full blessing takes place but, again as for all blessings, this has required the addition of the vitality of the water of the Vazimba because only through this water, and the power it brings, is it possible for elders and kings to bless their descendants.

This brings us back to the fundamental contradiction which is found in Merina ritual and mythology. On the one hand, vitality linked with femininity, houses, Vazimbas, is represented as negative, something to be expelled. This comes to the fore in the first funeral where women mourn inside the house associated with decay. This association is confirmed in many other ways. The house is also associated with birth in many rituals, but this does not have the implications we might imagine. Natural birth, seen as purely a concern of women, is demonstrated in the circumcision ritual, the other main Merina ritual, to be impure and polluting by contrast with circumcision itself, which marks the child coming *out of the house* towards the tomb.[27] Death, birth and sexuality are all linked in the symbolism and all stand in opposition to the tomb. The natural, feminine, domestic, Vazimba world should therefore be shunned. This is the message of the first stages of the ritual. But then, through the symbol of the water, this very element is reintroduced to vivify the blessing of the ancestors through the water from the Vazimbas. It is as if what was being said was that the ancestral purity of the dry dead in the tomb, although ideal, is impossible for the living who must reintroduce in a positive form what they have expelled in a negative form.

The ambiguity of the vital Vazimba element is well brought out

27 Ibid.

in the myth of origin of the ceremony of the royal bath.[28] The myth is very well known to every Merina. The king Ralambo, the founder of the royal dynasty, was wandering around the countryside when he noticed fat cattle left by Vazimbas whom he had just driven out. Until that time nobody knew the cattle were edible. They just died and their dead bodies were left to rot making an awful stink. Ralambo however had the idea that they might be eaten, and after many precautions had their flesh roasted. As a result a wonderful smell of roasting meat developed. He had succeeded in transforming decay into a source of strength. Indeed he was so pleased with this feat that he changed the name of the animal and furthermore he instituted, in memory of this discovery, the feast of the royal bath.

This myth is revealing in a number of ways. First it shows how the sources of strength and of sexuality, with which cattle and the Vazimba are also associated, are highly ambivalent and dangerous; one moment they are the source of the pollution of the decomposition of death, at another they are the source of the strength which makes for a successful life. The two are very close and the danger of this proximity is most revealing of the ambiguity of non-ancestral fertility. The myth, however, shows us much more than this; it shows the role of royalty. This royal role explains the parts of the ritual not so far examined and the symbolic construction of royalty.

In the myth, Ralambo, the king, is represented as the person who makes the eating of cattle safe by killing them and then conquering them in much the same way as he had just beaten the Vazimba then used their vitality and fertility. This is significant because of the continuing association of cattle with royalty which is acted out in the ritual in the dramatic distribution of cattle from the king to his subjects. These cattle are like the cattle cooked by Ralambo, particularly fat, particularly strength-giving.

In the ritual, this royal victory over corruption is symbolised by the *jaka*, the meat of cattle which has been preserved from the previous year and which is consumed at the ceremony of the bath, mixed with fresh meat killed for this year's ritual. This is a most telling symbol. It denies the finality of time and corruption which it replaces by cyclicity, one of the themes which we have already seen

---

[28] For a full discussion of this myth and the Merina symbolism of food see 'Almost eating the ancestors', *Man* NS xx (1985), pp. 631–46. The text of the myth appears in Callet, *Tantara* (see n. 5), i, pp. 145–7.

as central to the ritual as a whole. Above all, it demonstrates the overcoming of death, as putrefaction, which Ralambo had succeeded in achieving in the time of the myth by initial royal violence and then by daring to eat meat.

When we move from a consideration of the blessing and funeral aspects of the bath to the symbol of the *jaka*, we therefore move from general symbolism found in non-royal rituals to the specifically royal part of the ritual which dominates the final stages, that is, ritual which marks out the king as an exceptional being who has resolved all contradictions.[29] It is this which explains the major aspects of the ritual, not so far discussed. It underlies the climax of the whole performance.

Specifically royal representations in Imerina express the idea that royalty not only abolishes the opposition between the negative and positive side of vitality, but that it even abolishes or overcomes the opposition between vitality and descent, that is between Vazimba and Merina. First of all the king negates the opposition between Vazimba and ancestors in himself because, unlike his subjects, he is always represented as half Vazimba. The founding kings of the Merina ancestors are all believed to have Vazimba mothers. These mothers were the queens whom the Merina defeated and are the very Vazimba queens from whose aquatic graves the water for the royal bath is taken. Through his ancestry, the monarch therefore, after his initial conquest, is able to rejoin the Vazimba and the ancestors. This is what he does again, dramatically, when he enters the bath and plunges into the water of his Vazimba ancestresses. We can now understand why the king totally immerses himself in the water, while his subjects bathe only a small part of their bodies. For them the Vazimba element remains dangerous, the opposition cannot be fully resolved. The king, however, is triumphant; he has

---

[29] This representation of royalty also occurs in other contexts. Probably one of the most striking examples of this representation of royalty as resolving the contradiction created by ideology concerns the symbolism of tombs and houses. The opposition tomb/house is fundamental, the one being associated with wild uncontrolled fertility, the other being concerned with the ancestors. For ordinary people tombs and houses should be as far away from each other as possible. However for kinsmen of the ruler the tombs are placed next to the houses inside the village walls. For very close kinsmen of the ruler however there are model houses on top of the tombs. Finally for the ruler himself the tomb is at the very centre of his house in his courtyard. This is another example of the symbolism discussed here, where the opposition between vitality and descent are represented as abolished by royalty.

totally defeated the Vazimba and he can therefore incorporate them with impunity, he is both ancestor and Vazimba; he therefore plunges completely into Vazimba water.

The final manifestation of the royal resolution of opposition concerns rice and cattle which is again a manifestation of the ancestor/Vazimba dichotomy.[30] Eating rice is linked with the ancestors. As such it is a pure but austere activity. In normal circumstances nothing, not even salt, may be added to rice when it is cooking or when it is served. The rich food that one adds, and which gives one strength, vitality and even sexuality, is served separately and is ideally beef and especially beef fat. Unlike rice, and like the Vazimbas with which it is associated, beef is highly ambivalent, as we have already seen in the Ralambo myth.

All this explains the symbolic meal, whose central importance is clear in all accounts; there the separation of cattle and rice is triumphantly abolished. Since royalty has overcome the dangerous potential of cattle, that is, that it can decompose, royal cattle is no longer a threat to the life-transcending and permanent elements of descent and tomb. As a result, while ordinary people enjoy, but also keep at a distance, the vitality of cattle, the king totally identifies with it, coming close to *being* cattle himself. This is shown by the way that the rump cut off from the *volavita* bull is placed over the king's head and is then licked by the king: for the Merina, licking constitutes extremely close identification.

This is done similarly with rice; the king, and after him all his subjects, put the rice that they are about to eat on their heads. The rice of the royal bath, however, is special. Normally rice is represented as an austere food which should not be mixed with rich ingredients. At the time of the royal bath, however, this is precisely what is done in the ritual. The rice is mixed with milk and honey, supremely rich foods which have associations with the vitality of the Vazimbas in a number of ways.[31] Finally the beef, which mixes meat of the past and present, and the rice which has been mixed with rich relish, are themselves mixed together and placed on the

[30] This is in an article on the symbolism of food, Bloch, 'Almost eating the ancestors' (see n. 28).

[31] The honey used for this ritual is said to be 'of a living mother'. This means that it was taken without killing the bees. Things said to be 'of living mother' are always symbols of Vazimbas. They stress the matrilateral aspect of supposed Vazimba kinship.

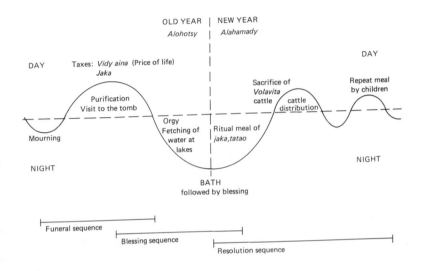

32 Simplified diagram of the royal bath.

king's head. There can be no clearer demonstration that in him all oppositions have been resolved.

The royal meal is as much the highlight of the ceremony as the bath, and like the bath it reconciles and makes safe the joining of rice and cattle, the ancestors and the defeated Vazimba. This is the typical action of kings who combine in themselves all contradictory aspects through their valour. Of course, once the king has brought about this union it can then be reproduced safely by the rest of the population, his children as they are represented in the ritual, and even his children's children. This explains the final act of the ritual, the children's meal, which imitates and repeats the meal of the adults on the night of the bath.

The whole structure of this complex ritual reveals itself to be both simple and subtle. First the opposition between vitality and the tomb is played out. Vitality in its negative appearance is driven out by the victory of the tomb over mourning. This is the mourning sequence (see fig. 32). Then vitality is brought back in its positive aspect in the form of the water from the Vazimba queens used in the bath. This is the blessing sequence (see fig. 32). So far, the ritual parallels the structure of all other Merina rituals; but then on the night of the bath a different element, not found in non-royal rituals, intervenes: the reconciliation of oppositions by the half ancestral, half Vazimba king. This takes place in the bath itself and in the royal meal and is echoed by the domestic meals and the children's meal. This is the resolution sequence.

CONCLUSIONS

The first point to be made in conclusion is a simple functionalist one. The ritual clearly demonstrates the legitimation of authority, making royal power an essential aspect of a cosmic social and emotional order which is unitary and unquestionable. To say this, however, does not mean that this function explains the ritual. It does not. To go some way towards this, it has been necessary to consider both specific Merina formulations and what can be called the necessary logic of the construction of authority.

The ritual of the royal bath is posited on other symbolism which it repeats and advances. This is particularly clear if we look at the overall pattern, the movement from the funeral sequence, to the blessing sequence, to the resolution sequence. This demonstrates well a point made in one of the most recent and perceptive contributions to the *Incwala* debate in an article by Pierre Smith where he stresses the need to look at such rituals as wholes, and to understand them in an organic sequence.[32] When we follow the various acts of the ritual through we see not only how the ritual parallels others but also how it uses the symbolism of other rituals to create the uniqueness of the royal construction.

The succession of sequences has relevance for the theoretical position outlined by Geertz in his discussion of Balinese royal rituals.[33] Geertz argues that these rituals cannot be explained in terms of their social or political functions, but for all that, he does not offer the usual benefit which follows such criticism: a detailed analysis of the actual rituals. In a sense, Geertz, in spite of his

[32] P. Smith, 'Aspects de l'organisation des rites', in M. Izard and P. Smith (eds.), *La fonction symbolique* (Paris, 1979), pp. 139–70.

[33] C. Geertz, *Negara: the Theatre State in Nineteenth-Century Bali* (Princeton, 1980).

protestations, evacuates both poles of the generalist–particularist controversy. This is a result of his central theoretical point; that the Balinese state existed as a theatre, reflecting an order which was superhuman. As a result, the representation of the state is not to be understood either in terms of the ways it maintained itself as a politico-economic entity, or in terms of symbolic systems which organise the life of lesser mortals. No doubt this is how Balinese autocrats represented their policy, and the general result is that the book considers the political side of Balinese royalty and the ritual side without any relation of the one to the other, but whether we are to accept this view for our analysis is a totally different matter.

The ritual of the royal bath, like the Balinese ritual, reveals the king as an exemplary centre, the point where the order of the heavens comes down to earth. This however is achieved not by receiving from above, but by the elaboration of the below. Perhaps the difference with Bali is an ethnographic one, but I doubt it. The connection between royal and non-royal ritual will by now, I hope, appear convincing to the reader, but that does not mean that it would necessarily have been obvious at first glance and the kind of analysis of the symbolism of royal rituals carried out here is singularly absent in *Negara*.

The connection between royal and non-royal rituals in fact explains two problems which arise both in Madagascar and in Bali. First, why does the royal ritual have emotional and ideological power to move and organise the participants? Splendour, which is Geertz's answer, does not seem to me a satisfactory explanation; it is not *any* splendour, but a particular splendour which in the terms used by Althusser in his discussion of ideology calls out and addresses the participant so that he feels that what is being presented is true for him.[34] Surely it is in this connection between the royal ritual and the non-royal ritual that the source of the power of the royal ritual to move is to be found. Indeed in Madagascar the connection between the rituals of the court and that of ordinary people goes two ways since the court ritual is the signal for the repetition of the royal ritual actions, on a smaller scale and somewhat differently within every home in the kingdom. In the ritual of the royal bath the actions of the court were not just a spectacle which others watched but also an event of which all were a

[34] L. Althusser, *Lenin and Philosophy* (London, 1971).

part. This shows how misleading the idea of the theatre state can be.

The political significance of this fact cannot be over-stressed. On the one hand the ritual of the royal bath is the same as the ordinary rituals of blessing by which each and every Merina assures and represents the reproduction of his family and himself. As such the royal ritual is a large scale descent group ritual and the whole kingdom appears as one large family. On the other hand the ritual of the royal bath is a ritual of the pre-eminence of the king, represented in the ritual as the violent conqueror and absorber of cattle and the Vazimba. Within this idiom the king is by implication a violent being whose violence, whether directed towards outsiders or subjects, is justified. These two sides of the representation are in the ritual quite inseparable and as a result subjects can celebrate their own subordination as though it were their own reproduction. It is by this inseparable merging of what are analytically two opposed facts that a royal ritual such as this performs its sociological and political function. This cannot be understood unless we refuse to separate the two sides as Geertz does.

Secondly, Geertz's theoretical position presents us, and him, with a historical problem. Because Geertz insists that royal rituals can be explained only in terms of themselves, he is unable to link their content with the politico-economic side of Balinese kingdoms, which he therefore has to discuss quite separately. However, in the end the ritual must have been created by circumstances and human action in social context. How this can have occurred is quite incomprehensible from Geertz's perspective but when we see royal rituals as transformation of others then the process becomes possible to imagine.

The royal representation is built out of the symbolism of such things as funerals and initiation ceremonies. This is so logically but of course this does not mean that it is so historically. To demonstrate this a history of the ritual of the royal bath would be necessary and none has been carried out here. However, in parallel to this study I have carried out a much lengthier historical study of the other great royal Merina ritual, the ritual of circumcision (see n. 3). This shows that in that case, at least, the royal construction is historically subsequent to the non-royal elements and that the royal construction is built out of these pre-existing elements. It seems highly probable that the same thing happened for the royal bath.

The success of the royal ritual is only possible because it resolves the contradiction which had been set up by the construction of authority elsewhere. Contradictions are inescapable results of legitimation by reference to a transcendental order. This 'resolution' however seems to present a problem for the theoretical starting point which identified the necessary contradiction in the symbolism of authority as being an inevitable result of the impossibility of transcendence. Has the royal ritual achieved the impossible? This is certainly what it declares.

However, if we step right out of the enchanted world of the unending hermeneutic circles within which rituals contain both participants and analysts it will become clear that this resolution is as illusory as other attempts to escape human nature. The problem is that the royal resolution can exist only in terms of the contradiction it recognises and which is created by rituals such as this. It cannot therefore obliterate these contradictions since if that was so the reason for the ritual and the demonstration of royal authority would become unnecessary. Instead the ritual can only restate the contradiction and its resolution again and again but never progress. The royal solution can therefore only be a thing of moment when the king steps into the bath. He must however come out again.

8. The person of the king: ritual and power in a Ghanaian state

MICHELLE GILBERT

Man *is* not a microcosm; he has to be *made* one in order that he may control the universe for prosperity. The ritual establishes an equivalence that was not there.

A. M. Hocart

That kings are sacred is an anthropological and historical truism, but they are not born so, and must be made sacred by those over whom they reign.[1] It is difficult to know how a king is made because today most kingships seem to be little more than weakened shells of their former selves, and the rites surrounding them are either no longer performed or at best performed without substance, sometimes merely as entertainment to please the people. When this happens it is a sign that the meaning of kingship for them has faded. Beliefs in the mystical forces underlying the rites of kingship seem the first elements to become irrelevant and forgotten, even when the superficial pomp is still carried out. Yet it is precisely these beliefs that are critical for understanding the sacred and crucial quality of kingship.

This paper is about the making of a king in Akuapem, a small Akan kingdom in south-eastern Ghana. To describe the king's installation, or enstoolment as it is called, one must discuss both the secular and sacred elements of the process of transformation of a man into a king, and also the source, the acquisition and the loss of political and ritual power by destoolment.[2] (One could well argue that to make this complete one need also describe a king's death and burial.) The key operative notion is the indigenous concept of

[1] See A. N. Hocart, *Kingship* (Oxford, 1927), and *Kings and Councillors* (Chicago, 1970). The quotation above is from the latter book, p. 69.

[2] Meyer Fortes, 'Of Installation Ceremonies', *Proceedings of the Royal Anthropological Institute for 1967* (1968), pp. 5–20, asks why 'entry into . . . high office tends to take a ceremonial form, in which submission to some sanctioning authority is acknowledged?' (p. 5), and notes that 'deposition from office often mirrors inauguration' (p. 6).

power and its relation to cosmology, not that of power in its form of legitimated and responsible authority. For this reason, structural features of succession, organisation or political power and authority and reciprocity between ruler and subject will be mentioned but not elaborated. It follows that it is necessary first to examine the source of the king's authority and power in its symbolic representation as a Black Stool, an object which is both a shrine and symbol of the ancestors, because the ancestors both legitimise the king's authority after the electors have selected and indeed share with him their power itself. Therefore two rites will be described: first the creation of a Black Stool, and second the enstoolment of a new king. Care shall be taken not to make the elusive notion of power more concrete than do the people of Akuapem themselves.

THE KINGSHIP OF AKUAPEM

Rites of enstoolment have been described for the Asante, the best known and largest of the Akan kingdoms.[3] Rites in Akuapem and a number of the ritual officials are similar but not the same, reflecting different structures and historical events. Much of the literature on the Akan blurs or ignores such local differences, many accounts being generalised for all the Akan and thereby being accurate for no one of the twelve or so Akan states. This paper draws on material solely from the town of Akuropon, the capital of Akuapem.

The following description is based on accounts by reliable palace elders, not on my own observation. Although I resided in Akuropon for nearly two years (1976–8), I arrived just after the installation ceremonies of the present king, Nana Addo Dankwa III, and so could not witness them. In any case, certain phases of these rites are so secret that it is highly unlikely that an outside observer would be permitted to view them directly. As for the creation of a new Black Stool, this has probably not occurred since the end of the nineteenth or early twentieth century, yet even today people are wary and fearful of discussing it. My emphasis on the mystical

---

[3] Meyer Fortes, 'Of Installation Ceremonies', *Proceedings of the Royal Anthropological Institute for 1967*, (1968), pp. 5–20; and *Kinship and the Social Order: The Legacy of Lewis Henry Morgan* (Chicago, 1969; London, 1970), ch. 9; R. S. Rattray, *Ashanti Law and Constitution* (Oxford, 1929); and *Ashanti* (Oxford, 1923); Lucy Mair, *African Kingdoms* (Oxford, 1977); Jack Goody (ed.), *Succession to High Office* (Cambridge, 1966), introduction.

33 The King of Akuapem, Nana Addo Dankwa III, being carried in a brocade-covered palanquin through the streets of Akuropon beneath a royal umbrella. Seated before him, wearing a gold and feather headdress, is his 'soul child', *okra*, who symbolically shares the King's destiny.

power that explicitly underlies the authority of the king necessitates the spelling out of certain issues which in the past have been rather delicately avoided, in particular, human sacrifice and certain events pertaining to stool disputes.[4]

The kingdom of Akuapem lies in the hills twenty-five miles northeast of Accra, the national capital of Ghana. Its seventeen towns, varying in size from several hundred to six or seven

[4] I sincerely hope I have not offended anyone in discussing these issues. To protect their anonymity I have purposely omitted naming specific informants who generously gave of their time, knowledge and trust and to whom I am deeply grateful. The research itself would not have been possible without the measured wisdom, tact and enthusiasm of Mr B. E. Ofori and the assistance, approval and encouragement of Nana Addo Dankwa III, Okuapehene, and Nana Boafo Ansah II, Kurontihene of Akuropon. Mr D. K. Abbiw of the Legon Herbarium, University of Ghana, identified the plants. I should like to thank the School of Oriental and African Studies for a Governing Body Post Graduate Exhibition for financial assistance and the University of Cape Coast, Ghana for sponsorship. I wish to thank the National Endowment for the Humanities for an independent study and research fellowship and T. O. Beidelman, Barbara Bianco and John Middleton for their help with this paper.

thousand people, are set along two high parallel ridges some 1500 feet above sea level. Ethnically the most heterogeneous of all the Akan states, it includes members of two main linguistic groups, with marked variations in modes of inheritance, succession and custom. Only Akuropon and one other town are composed of Akan or Twi-speaking matrilineal people of Akyem Abuakwa origin; three other towns are also Twi-speaking and matrilineal, but of Akwamu origin; and the other towns are composed of patrilineal Guan-speakers, although some now speak Twi. Due largely to these internal variations, Akuapem towns are not linked to each other and the capital by means of a kinship idiom as are towns in other Akan kingdoms; some of the political functions of royal rituals differ from those found elsewhere as well. A brief summary of the rather turbulent history of the state may clarify the nature of its persistent problems of identity and cohesion.

The Guan were loosely organised and settled in most of the modern-day towns by the early seventeenth century. They were conquered by the Akwamu in 1681, and in the early eighteenth century invited members of the Asona clan from the Akan kingdom of Akyem Abuakwa to the west to help overthrow their oppressors. Most of the Akwamu fled east of the Volta River and the Akyem leaders remained, to establish a dynasty in 1733. In the mid-eighteenth century the region came under the hegemony of the Asante but was finally liberated by the Akuapem in alliance with the Ga, Fante, Akyem, British and Danes in the Akantamansu War of 1826.[5]

The Basel Mission arrived in Akuropon in 1835 and gradually built a complex of churches and schools, introduced cash crops, including cocoa, and helped develop commerce in local commodities and European goods. Akuapem lay on the sphere of influence of the Danes at Accra from 1781 until the British formally took over in 1850 and slowly established a centralised administration for the then Gold Coast. This brought Akuapem into a wider economic

[5] The only comprehensive history of Akuapem is fortunately a modern and excellent one, by M. A. Kwamena-Poh, *Government and Politics in the Akuapem State 1730–1850* (Evanston, 1973). See also C. C. Reindorf, *The History of the Gold Coast and Asante, Based on Traditional and Historical Facts from about 1500–1860*, 2nd edn (Basel-Accra, 1951); Ivor Wilks, 'The Growth of the Akwapim State: A Study in the Control of Evidence', in J. Vansina, R. Mauny, L. V. Thomas (eds.), *The Historian in Tropical Africa* (London, 1964), pp. 390–411.

and political system and led in time to the stripping of much jural and military power from the king and his chiefs, a process that has continued during this century both before and after Independence. None the less, loyalty to the kingdom and to its ruler is extremely important in the lives of the people. The king may have lost much of his former judicial authority and can certainly no longer declare war, own slaves or condemn people to death, yet he remains the undoubted religious and political head of the kingdom.

Today the resident population of Akuapem numbers about 70,000 and that of Akuropon about 5,000; there are perhaps four times these numbers from the state and town who reside elsewhere.[6] Most residents are food-crop and cocoa farmers and there is a sizeable number of wage-earners, largely teachers. The state is fairly rich and most of its population is highly educated and Christian. The people of the capital recognise that historically they are immigrants and a minority of the kingdom's population. Thus the royal rituals performed in the town may be seen both to link a disparate people together under the king's central authority, and also to maintain the ritual and political hegemony of the capital town's inhabitants.

The events, processes and beliefs described in this paper are those of today or the relatively recent past, not myths of a vanished age. Of course, political and social conditions have changed, as have aspects of many ritual performances since the turn of the century: most notable, certainly, is the cessation of human sacrifice. There is, nevertheless, a believed necessity for ritual to be immaculate and unchanging, both in the literal sense of resistance to altering the location of a rite in order to accommodate larger numbers of spectators, but also in a more subtle sense; when, for example, a castrated ram is substituted for a man in a rite, the people still recognise it as a human sacrifice and gasp in fear and awe, even though they see that it is not really a man. There is both an actual continuity of tradition, changes being in detail and not in essentials, and also a strongly held belief that this should be and in fact is so. For the palace elders and ritual specialists such ritual expresses the cosmic order on earth; and on that account, to the people of Akuropon the performance of rituals pertaining to

---

[6] See David Brokensha (ed.), *Akwapim Handbook* (Accra, 1971); John Middleton, 'Home-town. A Study of an Urban Center in Southern Ghana', *Africa* xlix (1979), pp. 246–57.

kingship must be seen to be unchanging and so conform to their sense of ethnic identity and history, the past that validates the present.

THE NOTION OF THE PERSON; DEITIES AND ANCESTORS

It is useful to examine the characteristics thought to compose a person, for the person of the king is both that of an ordinary man writ large and also a representation of the 'person' of the entire state both at the moment and over historical and future time. The person, in this sense, is seen to result from the conjunction of his matrilineage and his father's line of affiliation. The people of Akuropon are divided into eight named and exogamous matri-clans, *abusua*, whose membership is recognised across all Akan kingdoms. These clans are divided into named lineages, each of which is the core of a 'house', in the sense both of a building and of a residential group. In Akuropon non-royal clans typically have only two or three lineages, but the Asona clan has eight, seven being non-royal and one containing three named 'houses' from which the king and Queen Mother are selected by rotation. A person's primary social identity, conceived of in terms of 'blood', comes from these groups. An individual also receives 'moral' character from his or her father through the affiliation known as *agyabosom* ('father's deity'). There are nine such named lines. These two elements, 'blood' and 'character', together with that known as *kra* (soul) which is given to everybody by God, make up a 'person'; and it is the first two that are basically relevant in the selection of a new king.

Traditional Akuropon beliefs in gods and ancestors resemble those described for other Akan kingdoms,[7] and indeed a good many of the gods were brought to Akuropon from elsewhere. At the head of the pantheon is the Supreme Being, Onyame, the giver of rain and sunshine, and Asase Yaa, the Goddess of the earth; both are too remote to be approached directly. Beneath them are the deities, *abosom*, sometimes said to be the children of the skies or messengers of God since they act as intermediaries between God and man and are responsive to direct prayer and supplication. They

---

[7] See Helaine Minkus, 'The Philosophy of the Akwapim Akan of Southern Ghana' (Northwestern University Ph.D. thesis, 1975), and for comparison, M. D. McLeod, *The Asante* (London, 1981); and R. S. Rattray, *Ashanti* (Oxford, 1923).

number hundreds and may be invoked individually or as a collectivity; many are associated with rivers, streams, mountains and rocks. Most are benign and provide guidance and aid, but some have destructive powers and can be called upon to punish wrongdoers. They may be called upon anywhere, although those that are worshipped regularly are built shrines or spirit-houses for periodic offerings. In addition, there are smaller deities, man-made objects called *asuman*, which may be protective or destructive; generally their power is narrower and more specific than that of *abosom*. Allegiance to particular deities has always fluctuated over time; however the influence of Christianity has weakened much of the active participation in *abosom* and *asuman* cults and many of the older practitioners have died without being replaced.

There are also the ancestors, known as *asamanfo* or *asaman*. They are said to live somewhere together in a place called Asaman. It is said that in going there one must ascend a high mountain or cross a river; either way there is a boundary. The world of the ancestors is said to look like places on earth; and just as there are kings and commoners on earth, so too are there in Asaman. Thus if a chief has died he will live like a chief there and will need attendants to serve him. An elder explained:

We do not conceive of all the chiefs there together – that is, all the former ones together. Rather, the deceased was a chief here, therefore he will be a chief there. He had a stool here, therefore he will have a respectable position there.

Ancestors, it is said, can see what the living do on earth, and they may like or dislike what they see and may send help to the living or punish infractions of custom.

If the ancestors dislike what is happening on earth, they may ask you to come to them and explain your conduct. So you may fall sick and if a . . . [ritual specialist] is able to notice the illness is caused by ancestral spirits because of one or two things you did, he will tell you what to do to recover. In the old days, the ancestors prophesied die or live – and you did.

A day cannot go by in Akuropon when someone does not pour a libation to the ancestors and deities informing them of what is about to occur and begging that the coming event be peaceful. When on formal occasions a long libation is poured, all the known deities are mentioned, preceded by Onyame and Asese Yaa; only respectable and 'good' ancestors are called, and not solely those of one's own clan or lineage.

We do not pour libation for people who lived bad lives on earth; only for those who led respectable lives, important and honourable men – for these we pour libation. If there is a special activity in the 'house' or an important question ... we can call ... their names to come witness and drink. They are regarded as having some power, or as people who should be made to know what is happening in the 'house'.

In contrast to the cults of the deities, Christianity has affected that of the ancestors in Akuropon remarkably little.

THE POWER OF THE BLACK STOOLS

Upon entering the palace one day in early 1977, I noticed some grafitti on a door in the outer courtyard. It consisted of a drawing of a Black Stool; above it was written *tumi* (the Twi word for 'power'), and below it the word *pawa* (the English 'power'). The rites of enstoolment and destoolment centre on this complex notion of power, as do the periodical rites known as *adae* and *Odwira*.[8]

Black Stools both symbolise and contain power. The royal ones are kept in the palace in a special stool room set within a complex called the stool-house.[9] Both areas are normally closed to outsiders. Here oblations are made to them and libations poured for health, strength, money, long life and prosperity. 'Everyone comes to beg for these in this house. Extraordinary things happen here.' It is said that a person who enters the royal stool-house without ritual preparation and authority will be dazzled or even blinded by the sight. It should be noted that most people do not know in detail what occurs in the palace, especially in the stool-room, and the fact that palace rites are unknown and unknowable to ordinary people arouses immense awe and even terror.

The stool-house is symbolically the centre of the palace, of the

[8] *Adae* is a periodic rite held every forty-two days which combines secular functions with honouring and feeding the ancestors and asking for their blessing. *Odwira* is the great annual purification rite of the kingship. See Michelle V. Gilbert, 'Rituals of Kingship in a Ghanaian State' (University of London Ph.D. thesis, 1981).

[9] A photograph of the royal Black Stools of Akuropon *in situ* may be seen in E. O. Ayesi, 'The Basis of Political Authority of the Akwapem Tribes' (University of London Ph.D. thesis, 1965).

town of Akuropon, and of the state of Akuapem. Akuropon elders say of it,

> This is Akuropon here: this house is Akuropon.
> All Akuapem, their heads are here.

In other words, from Apirede to Berekusu, from the northernmost to the southernmost town of Akuapem, 'it is their house, where they all serve: this is where the ultimate power of the state rests'. While this is literally a reference to the head-pad for carrying loads in the case of serving a master, it would appear to be an elliptical allusion to the heads of those formerly sacrificed to the stools, for sacrifices renew ancestral power, and the latter is dependent upon those who 'serve' in the sense of being killed.[10]

Black Stools are similar in shape to ordinary wooden stools, but are never used for seating. Kept in special rooms when in use, and in boxes or trunks when not, they are anointed with blood, spider's web, eggs and other matter,[11] the resulting shiny black surface providing their name. In Akuropon all lineages of importance have Black Stools, generally only one. The royal Asona lineage has six Black Stools which commemorate and represent certain former kings of Akuapem.[12] The Black Stools of the king's lineage are different neither in appearance nor in principle from other Black Stools, but, as the following proverb, spoken on the talking drum, illustrates, the kingly line is considered more sacred and so more powerful than any other:

---

[10] The revenging spirits of those killed in sacrifice to the royal stools are pacified during part of the Akuropon *Odwira* rite.

[11] Eggs are delicate (a reminder to handle the Black Stools with care) and also boneless thus 'peaceful', alluding to the peaceful nature of the stools. The use of spider's web may refer to the wisdom of Ananse the trickster spider, and by analogy to the wisdom of the dead rulers and of those who come afterwards to 'sit on their stools', as Peter Sarpong, *The Sacred Stools of the Akan* (Tema, 1971), p. 43 suggests. Since the spider's web comes generally from the kitchen, blackened by smoke from the fire, it is likely to be a reference to the wisdom (about matters to do with genealogical relationships) that the old women (*mmerewatia*) of the matrilineage are thought to possess.

[12] Formerly there were seven royal Black Stools in Akuropon, but one was stolen. They are still referred to as if there were seven, which is a number considered to be symbolically propitious. In some other Akan kingdoms Black Stools are carved for every 'good' king or chief and thus there may be many; in Akuapem this is not so. In any case, a stool is never blackened for a destooled king, nor for one who dies a 'bad death' through sudden accident or unusual disease; a bad king should not be remembered.

> A mouse differs from another mouse
> It differs from a striped mouse
> It differs from a good mouse
> But only one mouse is holy.

That is to say, there are chiefs, and chiefs among chiefs, but there is only one true king.

Many Black Stools in Akuropon, other than the royal ones, were either brought to Akuropon by the earliest settlers who were then given permission by the king to keep them, or were created in Akuropon in recognition of unusual services rendered to the state or prowess in war. The king could refuse to recognise non-royal Black Stools or even have them destroyed.[13] Black Stools have also been captured in wars. Until the middle of the nineteenth century, they and other precious belongings were carried to war, their spiritual power giving the warriors courage and incentive to fight and win.

Some stools were captured in war, and if they were carried to war and we returned with them (i.e., captured them) we were given honour. So we have stools and swords, and so on, which we got from war. In the old days, we would take everything to war because we did not know what would happen behind us.

There have been no wars for over a century, but there have been times of general chaos throughout the state, usually deriving from succession disputes. On some of these occasions, Black Stools, along with other valuable ritual paraphernalia, have been hidden for 'safe-keeping' until peaceful conditions resumed and the factional disputes were calmed, if not resolved. On a few such occasions, Black Stools of a king threatened with destoolment were actually stolen by his ritual elders who then refused to hand them over to the new king-elect because they believed it was not his turn to be king (the elders themselves went into exile). This type of momentous event resulted in a king ruling without his ancestral stools, that is, without the key symbols which are the visible loci of his power and the source of his authority. It was a rare occurrence, fraught with dissention, turmoil, and the weakening of the kingship. In the past it led to the succeeding king's eventual destoolment and the now oft-repeated expression: 'We don't serve men, we serve the stools.'

13 Three Black Stools for certain *Ankobea* 'houses' were made unofficially in the early twentieth century in Akuropon and were destroyed (burnt) by (King) *Nana* Kwadade in 1941.

The rituals performed in the creation of a Black Stool help us better to understand the source of their power. Until this century, it is said, a stool to be blackened for the royal Asona line might be the one used by the deceased king to sit on, but usually a new stool was carved to order. A stool was blackened traditionally with the blood of a human being.

The Black Stool has power, but you must get that power from a relative who is important to you. You do not just take any man from anywhere to make a Black Stool. It must be a fellow lineage member. His head is cut off to make the stool ... You use gun powder and spider's web and mix it with the blood ... You use an executioner's knife to pierce the neck and the blood comes out and is poured onto the stool. You put the head on the stool, and the heart and sex organs, you put them on the stool for a while. Then power [*tumi*] has come into the stool. The head will be taken later and buried; the power is already in the stool. The heart will lie on the stool for some time; then it will also be buried.

I asked if a fellow lineage member was used in order to identify the Black Stool with the group and if this were true in other rites as well:

It is only when making a new stool that an important lineage member is used. Someone who is associated with the king for many years who the king trusted and loved ... Something which is valuable is used, not something useless.[14] It is not merely 'to identify' and therefore a lineage member; but rather someone from the family is more valuable than anyone else. The most precious blood is blood from the lineage ... Also you must make sure the blood is clean. It must be blood of someone whom you know and someone whose blood will not defile.

On subsequent occasions, such as during *Odwira* or the periodic rite known as *adae kese*, when the Black Stools are anointed afresh, formerly a man was killed and his blood used to anoint them. This man was rarely, if ever, a lineage member. When I inquired about this, I was told shortly that if lineage members were used for all such sacrifices there would be none left! The implication of this

---

[14] On another occasion I was told that to make an *Omanhene*'s Black Stool, formerly a very important chief should be used, such as a Divisional Chief; and I was referred to the case of the *Apagyahene* at Kyebi in Akyem Abuakwa who was sacrificed to make a stool for *Nana* Ofori Atta I (1912–43).

seems to be that generally a slave was used.[15] Albinos were also used in the creation of Black Stools, regardless of their particular lineage; they were also buried under the hearth in the stool-house in the palace when it was built. Albinos are regarded as having immense mystical power in themselves: 'everything unusual has special power'; many regard albinos as being children of deities.

Human sacrifice has not been performed since the turn of the century, and castrated rams, which are considered to be symbolically clean and peaceful, are used instead. It is probable that a few so-called recent stools in Akuropon were created with the blood of sheep. Some Akuropon elders say that

New stools are not regarded as good stools because they are not strong enough; no good blood was poured on them.

'Good' here is clearly a euphemism for 'human';

Later kings did not have Black Stools in their name because the British stopped human sacrifice. You cannot make stools without the blood of human beings.

Writing about the Asante, Kyerematan states that the Black Stool belongs to the matrilineage, but when sacrifices are made and the names of the matrilineal ancestors are called what is addressed is the spirit derived from the patriline of the deceased stool occupant, and it is this which occupies the stool. So, 'the Black Stool may . . . be seen as a substitute for the physical body . . . of the dead person, and like it houses the spirit . . . inherited from the father; both body and stool, however, belong to the matri-lineage'.[16] This statement applies equally to Akuropon and allows us to see how the Black Stool physically symbolises the two elements ('blood' and 'character', matriline and patriline) which are among the necessary and complementary components of a 'person', and also the two elements that compose a king.

THE KINGMAKERS AND THE SELECTION OF THE KING

Rites of enstoolment, like others that take place in the palace, are not performed personally by the king but by various officials. These

---

[15] For sacrifices on the stools, women were never used, nor were circumcised men, i.e. northerners: the blood of both would be thought to defile the stools. They could be ritually killed on other occasions however. Royals (*odehye*), on the other hand, were considered to be persons 'who were never touched with a knife'.

[16] A. Kyerematen, 'The Royal Stools of Ashanti', *Africa* xxxix (1969), pp. 1–2.

34 Nana Addo Dankwa III, the King of Akuapem, seated in the palace at Akuropon, surrounded by his palace officials. To his right is the Asonahene, a senior member of the royal family. The child attendant seated in front carries the cushion for the King's chair.

latter have titles which can in most cases be translated into English, but the translations are superficial and often misleading, just as would be translations into Twi of English titles such as Chamberlain, Groom, Knight, and so on. A brief account of them must be given here so as to provide the context for the rites to be described.

Most Akuropon people rather simplistically categorise palace officials into three main groups, *Ankobea*, *Okoman* and *Akyaeme*; the relations between them and the king are represented spatially in the palace seating patterns. Those known as *Ankobea* ('they do not go anywhere') comprise trusted advisors and powerful ritual specialists; they are sons and grandsons of former kings and are closely and personally identified with the king and his ancestors. They are seated to the left of the king. Those known as *Okoman* ('defenders of the state') include the heads of the seven non-royal Asona lineages whose members originally came from Akyem Abuakwa, as well as the *Kurontihene*, who is the head of the *Okoman*, the Senior Divisional Chief of the state and the regent when the king is absent from the capital; this group may be said to represent 'the state'. Its members are seated to the right of the king.

35 Palace official, *Okra*, traditionally chosen from people born on the same day of the week as the King, thus sharing his soul (*kra*) or destiny. He takes part in rites to purify the King's soul. The large gold disc worn around his neck formerly meant he would accompany the King to his grave.

There is thus represented a dichotomy between the basically mystical or religious and the political realms: the *Okoman* represent the concept of matriline (or political), the *Ankobea* that of the patriline (or mystical); and the king refers to the *Ankobea* as his 'sons' and to the *Okoman* as his 'mothers' brothers'. This may be represented:

Right	King	Left
Okoman		*Ankobea*
'political' realm		'religious' realm
living		ancestors
matriline (*abusua*)		patriline (*agyabosom*)
'blood'		'character'

There are also less important officials, called *gyaasefo* ('people of the household'), who look after the king's physical body and the palace itself, and belong collectively to the *Ankobea*.

Immediately in front of the king are seated the extensions of his own inner spiritual nature. Nearest him sit the *akrafo* ('souls'), who are chosen when children and whose beauty represents that of the king himself; they share the destiny of the king (in the past they would die when he did), and prevent dangers from coming close to him. Beyond them are the *akyeame* (usually translated as 'linguists'), spokesmen and mediators for the king in all verbal exchanges between the people and the king; they also act as counsellors in legal affairs. Also in front is the *esen* ('herald') who keeps order in the palace. He wears a hat made of the fur of the colobus monkey who in the animal kingdom is said to 'supervise the assembly'. The *esen* is generally deformed in body and forms a symbolic bridge between society and the wild and uncontrolled powers of nature. Beyond, again, stand the drummers, who are able to communicate directly with the ancestors and the king by using drum language; and the *abrafo* ('executioners') who guard the doorway to the stool-house. The last two are the only palace officials privileged to trace the ancestry of the king.[17]

In Akuapem there are eleven electors of the king: all are of the Asona clan. They include eight from inside Akuropon: the chiefs of the original seven non-royal Asona lineages in Akuropon, (the *Okoman*, sometimes called the 'seven stool people') and the Queen Mother (who is a senior woman in the royal lineage and not literally the king's mother); and three from outside Akuropon: the chiefs of the towns of Aburi, Ahwerease and Amanokrom, chosen for various historical reasons. Selection of a new king is made without delay, as it is inconceivable for the state to exist without a king. It

[17] These positions are described more fully in Michelle V. Gilbert, 'Rituals of Kingship in a Ghanaian State' (University of London Ph.D. thesis, 1981).

should be noted that today the final authorisation of the king's enstoolment is by notice in the official government gazette. Installation papers are sent to the House of Chiefs at Dodowa and Kumase and the Eastern Regional Commission has the final authority to accept or reject the candidate.

The election of a new king assures the populace that he is legitimate (by belonging to the correct kingly 'house' in the cycle of rotation); that his physical body is complete or whole; and that his moral character is good. The basis for selection thus is two-fold: the physical or 'blood' (i.e., membership in the royal 'house', determined matrilineally) and the moral or 'character' (which derives from the patriline). There is no adherence to the rule of primogeniture; the eldest son of the senior woman of the royal family may or may not succeed. Formerly, there was a member of the royal family, the *Asonkohene*, who was leader of the young men and heir-apparent; even his succession was not automatic however, but depended upon the choice of the elders or kingmakers.[18]

When the king's stool is vacant, the *Ankobea* tell the *Kurontihene* that the state needs a king and that he should ask the Queen Mother whom she will present as candidate. The Queen Mother replies that she will give them the answer in two or three days' time, while in private she asks the *Ankobea* whom they consider would take up the kingship. She then formally meets with the elder women (*mmerewatia*) of the seven non-royal Asona lineages composing the original *Okoman* (the eldest women of a 'house' or lineage are believed to possess specialised knowledge about succession and inheritance). At this meeting of women the representative from Kodumase lineage (the *Kodumasehene*) is, for historical reasons, the only man in the group;[19] he advises them as they examine the question of who should be the next king and acts as spokesman for the Asona.

---

[18] The hereditary nature of the position was abolished in 1948 in an attempt to contain the continuous succession intrigues and disputes. More precisely, because the king was being undermined by the incumbent of the Asonkohene stool, the latter's position was changed from that of heir to the king (i.e., an Asona royal) to that of a non-Asona and thus no longer an heir. See the general discussion of this problem by Jack Goody (ed.), *Succession to High Office* (Cambridge, 1966), introduction.

[19] The history of *Kodumasehene*'s stool will be discussed in a forthcoming publication.

Now the Queen Mother and *Asonahene* (Chief of the Asona clan)[20] set a date for the kingmakers to meet in the palace; on that day she is the only woman present. The *Ankobea*, *Akyeame* and members of the seven original *Okoman* assemble in the large courtyard of the palace, the location signifying an occasion affecting the whole state. The spokesman for the *Ankobea* asks the Queen Mother whom she nominates. She may nominate three candidates; formerly the Asonkohene as heir-apparent was named first, whether good or bad. If her nominees are rejected then theoretically the *Ankobea* could now propose their own candidate. I do not know whether or not this has ever happened, but it is important that it is believed that it could happen, for it shows the complementarity of the *Ankobea* and *Okoman*.

When agreement is reached, and it is supposed to be by a majority, the *Ankobeahene* (Chief of the *Ankobea*) summons the palace attendants to bring the person nominated by the Queen Mother. The king-elect is not informed in words but is 'captured': he must claim not to wish to hold this onerous office, and should hide and try to escape. It would appear that the hiding and capture are almost always simulated, but the symbolic expression of fear to become the holder of this mystical and dangerous office is important: the king should seek neither political nor ritual power. The *Kodumasehene* brings the nominee and the *Ankobea* examine him to see that he is 'whole' and 'unblemished'; he is inspected by the *Kodumasehene* as well, representing the *Okoman*. His physical body must be 'complete' for as king the well-being of his body is a symbol of that of the state. Circumcision or any bodily defect would disqualify him as it is thought to pollute or defile the ancestral stools; so-called 'hidden illnesses' such as leprosy or epilepsy are similarly taboo. It is the purity of his moral character that is the essential factor; purity not being visible, the body stands for his inner quality.

If he qualifies, his right arm is smeared with white clay and he is brought to the palace courtyard: 'He has come out in white.' This is

---

[20] The history of the *Asonahene*'s position is complex and need not concern us here. He is presently the head of all the Asona lineages, a position that cannot be held by the king, for as in Asante, the king 'belongs to the whole people'. See Meyer Fortes, *Kinship and the Social Order: The Legacy of Lewis Henry Morgan* (Chicago, 1969; London, 1970), p. 163.

a sign that he is victorious, and has achieved a morally unambiguous status.[21]

During the week, while the king-makers decide on a candidate, the Divisional Chiefs of Akuapem[22] must be consulted. If anyone has a complaint it must be stated, and if serious enough for the nominee to be refused then a new candidate should be found.

The nominee is then taken to the *Kurontihene* by the *Kodumasehene*, who swears the state oath of Wukuda-Sokodee[23] that the Asona electors have selected this man and confirms this by paying a small sum of money; he also swears that the nominee is 'perfect'. The *Kurontihene* accepts him and inspects him to confirm whether what they say is correct. (It is incumbent on the *Kurontihene* to accept only someone brought by the *Kodumasehene*.) Then the *Kurontihene* hands him over to the *Ankobea* for what is called 'safe-keeping', a period of seclusion. The *Kurontihene* instructs the *Gyaasehene* ('head of the royal household') to beat the palace drums to announce that on the following day the Akuropon elders will meet at Santewase, a site near the palace where formerly grew a large shady tree frequented by the young men of the town. This is a public place representing the area of ordinary citizens.

In the morning at Santewase, the *Ankobeahene* brings the nominee and stands before him. He informs the *Kurontihene*: 'This man was inspected and found perfect'. The *Adumhene*[24] kills a sheep and the blood is poured over the nominee's feet; this is to 'cleanse' him and is the first sign of separation from his former status as an ordinary person. He is handed over to the *Ankobea*

---

[21] In other contexts it is a sign of success in a court case and recovery from illness. It is also smeared on a baby when after eight days it is 'out-doored' or named, signifying that it has permanently joined the living from the realm of the ancestors; and on deity priests when they are ritually in contact with the deities.

[22] In Akuapem, as in other Akan kingdoms, the state is organised into a military formation of Divisions or Wings. The internal structure of these Divisions differs from that in Asante. There should properly be five Divisions.

[23] There are several types of oath in Akuapem. Most refer to terrible calamities or losses too painful to be properly mentioned; frequently the exact histories of an oath have been forgotten. Wukuda-Sokodee, the Great Oath for all Akuapem, 'belongs' to the king, which means when it is sworn, the person is brought to the king for resolution of his or her case.

[24] The *Adumhene* is an *Ankobea* elder. In former times of human sacrifice, the *Adumhene*, Chief of the *Adumfo*, was said to be the first to handle the person. 'He pierces with the knife' and then the 'executioners' (*abrafo*) did the final killing. I was told, 'The *adumfo* have the sword for killing. The *Adumhene* is told by the stool-carriers that we need blood for the stool – we need a person.' The wider duties of the *Adumhene* include assisting in the burial of the king.

who confine him, usually for one week,[25] and a date is fixed for the installation. During this period of ritual seclusion he is seated for most of the time on the skin of a white sheep and his face and arms are covered with white clay. The Divisional Chiefs of Akuapem, who represent the state as a polity, visit at this time to settle any previous disputes they may have had with him in his former role. By this they extinguish the social and political characteristics he had as an ordinary man. The Divisional Chiefs visit at night because settlement of important family matters always take place under cover of darkness, 'hidden', and outside ordinary secular time, so that each family group appears flawless or factionless to the outside.

THE ACQUISITION OF SACREDNESS

Now that his existing public and legal status has been jurally extinguished, the next phase concerns his internal moral status and identity. On an appointed date the king-elect is taken at night to the ancestral stool-house in the palace. First his outer cloth and the loin cloth that he wore as an ordinary man are removed and handed to the *Asonahene*: then his sandals are handed to the *Kodumasehene*: these things will be kept by them so long as he is king.[26] The cloth that is taken from him is called 'sacred' or 'holy' because it is 'separated from him and kept hidden'. He is given a small cloth to cover himself temporarily, and a new cloth is sent for to replace this: the cloth has no ritual significance and is merely something to cover his nudity.[27] He is now without clothes, without signs of his former social person. He is outside all social life; his previous jural persona as an ordinary man has been removed and he is placed symbolically in the state of being newly born.

The king-elect is then blindfolded and led by the *Kodumesehene* to the stool-room. The *Nkonguasoafohene, Banmuhene, Adum-*

---

[25] Some say the seclusion should be for forty-two days, the period from one *adae* to the next.

[26] The choice of these two officials is not accidental: both represent lineages which once were intimately related to the royal Asona lineage. This is an example of the ritualisation of history, and will be developed in a future publication.

[27] Following Sir Kenneth Clark's contrast between 'nude' and 'naked' in *The Nude* (London, 1956), T. O. Beidelman in 'Some Nuer Notions of Nakedness, Nudity and Sexuality', *Africa* xxxviii (1968), pp. 113–31 refers to the unclothed liminal state as 'nudity' when a person passes from one social status to another and 'becomes a kind of human *tabula rasa* . . . ' (pp. 114–15).

hene and their attendants accompany him.[28] Other *Ankobea* officals remain in the open courtyard adjoining the stool-room, the doorway of which is shielded by a woollen blanket made by the Fulani of Mali far to the north. A libation is poured to inform the ancestors of the coming events. Inside the stool-room the blindfolded king-elect is told to choose a stool. No lamp is lit. In the darkened room are only the six Black Stools. Made for former kings, some of them represent reigns of peace, some represent war, some disputes and some 'disorder in the state'. The new king gropes for one of the stools. If he touches that of a warrior, then it is thought that his own reign will have wars; if that of a peaceful king, his will be a peaceful reign. The choice of the stool is said to be guided by power beyond the control of the king or the royal ancestors. In fact, the official known as *esen* ('herald') guides the king to the stool considered by the palace elders to be 'good' for the state. He has been sent to the stool-room first and is hidden behind the stools. When the new king enters, the *esen* shouts 'listen, listen' thereby leading the king to the chosen stool.

Then a large brass oil lamp is lit, using (instead of matches) the outer leaves of maize touched to the hearth, and the *Nkonguasoafohene* goes to see which stool the king has touched. Having chosen a stool which signals the character of his reign, the new king is told 'You have touched [e.g.] Kwadade's stool, therefore give him drink'. The new king then pours a libation on the stool. Those in the outer room of the stool-house are informed of the king's choice and they sing war songs. Some say these songs are sung at this time because traditionally the *esen* was beheaded after he performed his duty.

Another libation is poured by the *Nkonguasoafohene*. Then the *Adumhene* enters carrying a sheep on the back of his neck. Formerly, the stool handled by the new king was anointed with the blood of a slave killed for that purpose; today a sheep is substituted. The king now leaves the stool-room. The head of the animal and

[28] These officials work together: all are *Ankobea*. The *Nkonguasoafohene* is the chief of those who look after the king's Black Stools, and of those who carry the king's stools. The *Banmuhene* (Chief of the Banmu) is in charge of the first place where a deceased king is buried, the Banmu, and where certain very powerful *asuman* are kept. His assistants carry the body of a deceased king for burial and in the old days supervised the execution of people killed for such a burial. The *Banmuhene* had the power to pardon anyone about to be killed; he is senior to the *Adumhene*.

other parts are cut in small pieces and thrown in the courtyard because, it is said, 'many ancestors are gathered there and all can have a share'. Some of the blood is used to anoint the stool and the covering of fat from the lower intestines of the sheep is smeared on the four corners of the stool. I was told: 'People think the ancestors eat that, but the idea is the fat keeps the wood strong, makes it cool.' On this day, only this one stool is anointed. Blood from the stool is used to mark the head of the king – then he is identified with it and its power comes into him. A fire is then lit in the small courtyard of the stool-house and the meat of another sheep is cooked there for the elders to eat.

It is said that on this day 'He is now a king'. One may note that the acquisition of ancestral identity is analogous to the trans-formation of an infant. A newly born baby is not a social being until the eighth day after his birth when he is 'out-doored', given a name, clothed and decorated with beads. The king-elect is at first nude and temporarily without social status; he then touches the royal stool and thereby receives a name and ancestral identity. But he does not yet have the full accoutrements of a kingly person, nor full kingly authority.

The Black Stool chosen by the new king is now carried to the Banmu, a house and compound opposite the palace on the street called Mogyawee, 'Where blood runs'. The Banmu is still today so fearful a place, shrouded in secrecy, fear and danger, that the elders were reluctant even to speak of the following events. The new king is carried, as though a baby, on the back of a palace attendant through a small side door in the palace. In the Banmu, the ancestral stool selected by the new king is placed on top of the special stone, an *oserebo*, formerly used it seems for sharpening knives for the execution of sacrificial slaves. Placed beneath the stool is a piece of very old elephant hide that is normally kept in the stool-room under the oldest of the ancestral stools. (Elephants are thought to be the most powerful animals of the bush or forest and are thus identified with the king; the stool, being so sacred, cannot touch the earth.) The ritual specialists who are responsible for a king's funeral surround the stool: *Banmuhene*, *Adumhene*, and others. The new king is lowered onto the stool three times: this is the central act of the enstoolment process. When the king's buttocks touch the stool it is the ultimate conjunction of his bodies 'natural' and 'politic':[29] he has now been given the power and sacredness of his ancestors. In addition, the place, the use of the ritual sharpening stone called *oserebo*, the identity of the particular ritual officials who surround the stool, the 'nudity' of the king-elect, and even the reluctance of informants to discuss it, suggest that the former 'person' has symbolically been killed and is now dead. Those assembled sing war songs, appropriate for funerals of stool-elders:

If someone is dead, it is from war. Death is a serious matter. Therefore we sing songs indicating a serious thing has happened in the 'house'.

A sheep is sacrificed and libation is poured. The king is then carried back to the palace, again on an attendant's back: he is still like a baby. This time, however, they pass through the main entrance of the palace where near the doorway a libation is poured to inform the ancestors. They then return to the stool-house, where again a libation is poured and there they remain awake all night. 'No one sleeps the whole night: they keep watch, drink, sing and talk.' This, then, is like the wake-keeping of an ordinary funeral, a sign that the king's former status is now extinguished; on a more subtle level he is himself dead and has symbolically joined the ancestors. From now on, he is identified with the royal ancestors in general and also specifically with a previous ruler. Thus the present king, called Addo Dankwa III, and previously, Addo Dankwa II (1927–31), are both named after Addo Dankwa I (1815–36) whose stool they touched.

The new king is now considered to be transformed both physically and morally. It is said: 'He has been made complete, the king'. The verb used to express this (*abeye*) refers to the process of making oil from palm nuts; thus he has been transformed. The analogy may be taken a step further, for palm nuts are transformed from a wild plant into a domestically consumable material, one that because of its transformation has a new meaning for living men.

Because he now has the moral status of a king, he enters the palace through the main door as a king for the first time. He now has everything except the public recognition of his new status as

---

[29] Ernst H. Kantorowicz, *The King's Two Bodies: A Study in Mediaeval Political Theology* (Princeton, 1957).

king. He has the internal body of the king, but not yet the external body: he has not yet been clothed as a king.

In the past a subsidiary rite occurred at this point which gave extra protection to the new king. The more powerful an individual or chief, the more protection he requires, for he is increasingly vulnerable to dangers from both ordinary people and non-ancestral powers. Old men and chiefs, while hardly affected by witches, do fear people poisoning their drink and food; because of this they need the protection of *asuman*. The king cannot be affected by witches, but he too needs extra protection. Ancestors are thought to be more immediately powerful than deities and deities in turn more powerful than *asuman*, but *asuman* provide specific kinds of protection.

In the old days, we worshipped God through *asuman*, small fetishes. They were closer to us than God.

Until the early twentieth century, there was a special room in the palace reserved for *asuman* brought from many places which were used to protect the king. The palace elders swore an oath to the new king promising to show him all the 'secrets' in the palace and on a selected day he was taken to the *asuman* and 'they made him strong [*koben no*]'. This expression literally means putting food on fire to roast it, though there is also the implication of becoming clever and knowledgeable. The king is thus protected by the *asuman* but also, by being shown the secrets of mystical external powers, he is given strength by being given knowledge. He is now symbolically 'cooked'.

THE PUBLIC INSTALLATION OF THE KING

The final phase of the enstoolment process occurs on a later date when all the Divisional and Town Chiefs of Akuapem have been called by the *Kurontihene* to assemble with the Akuropon elders in the large courtyard of the palace to recognise the new king as head of state. A special sword that has been used in war is handed by the *Gyaasehene* ('head of the royal household') to each of the Divisional Chiefs and the Senior Divisional Chief in turn. No one speaks, indicating that the period of seclusion is not quite ended (although this occurs in daytime, the occasion is still a liminal one). The *Kuronthihene*, who has been acting as regent and as a non-Asona and Senior Divisional Chief represents the people at large, tells the king that he is 'handing over the power of Akuapem' to him and tells him the offences he should not commit, which centre on ignoring the wishes and advice of his people or abusing them by calling them 'fools' or 'slaves'. The king is then carried, hidden by cloth, in a palanquin to the boundary of the town. At the end of the town, the cloth is removed, he is raised high above the heads of all and carried beneath a state umbrella through the main street of Akuropon for all the populace to see. The period of seclusion is finally ended. He enters the town from its outside boundary and is now dressed in the finest cloth and surrounded by the most beautiful of kingly regalia. Silence is broken: drums are beaten, horns blown and guns fired. The people see him now as a king for the first time and they praise his beauty and majesty.

Before the Mpeni tree in front of the palace, the king now swears an oath to the Queen Mother saying,

You are my mother and you have made me king. I swear Wukuda-Sokodee that I shall always obey you. Any advice you give me I shall accept and I will serve you. If I do not, then I break this oath.

and then he swears to all the chiefs in turn, saying,

You have made me king. I will stay with you. I will be one with you.

And they, in turn, all swear their loyalty to him, saying,

I swear by Wukuda-Sokodee, today you have been made *Omanhene* ['king']. If I ever tell a lie or hide anything from you, if you call me day or night and I fail to come, I break the oath.

Money and drink are distributed equally among them. This money is called the 'head-pad for service', for these people will serve the new king and support or carry him as they would a load for which they are responsible; they will serve the king, but he will always remain dependent on them for support. From this time onwards, he is 'King of Akuapem' (*Okuapenhene*). The king now leaves the custody of the *Ankobea* and prepares to go to the palace. He rises (which means those assembled may do likewise) and the talking drum announces:

Great One, gently, gently. Grandfather, walk softly.

Sometime after the king's installation (it may be as much as a year later) he is given another name, which is an appellation. His first name, that of his former ancestor, was chosen in the seclusion of the stool-room; his second name, more in the nature of a public or praise name, is associated with the loyalty of the town and state and is given to him, therefore, by the living, and reveals the people's view of the king's political power and authority. Those considered for the present king included:

> One to whom you are always grateful
> He says it and that is the end of it
> Owner of the land
> Powerful One
> Delivered from war
> He does what he says

While only one is chosen officially, any of these appellations could be used informally as terms of reference or praise.

At the moment, the *Asantehene* uses *Otumfo* (Powerful One) for himself officially, therefore we allow him to and we do not use it for ... our king. But in general, we can refer to the King of Akyem or to our own king or any chief as *Otumfo*. *Otumfo* derives from *tumi*, power, so we also refer to Onyame, God, as *Otumfo* ...

THE REMOVAL OF A KING

Rites of destoolment must be discussed because they are really the reversal of mirror image of rites of enstoolment; both are performed by the same officials and both throw light on the nature of the kingship. Destoolment (getting rid of an undesirable king) is related to abdication (getting rid of a sick king); both often imply an element of compulsion and both are related to problems of litigation and regicide. Akan kingdoms are as a whole plagued by litigation mainly over land-rights and rights to chiefship at various levels and by destoolment procedures;[30] whereas regicide, while institutionalised in many divine kingships throughout Africa, is not documented for any Akan society. There are, however, suggestions that certain types of regicide may have occurred, albeit very infrequently, in the distant Akuapem past. Perhaps more pertinent

---

[30] A. F. Robertson, 'Ousting the Chief: Deposition Charges in Ashanti', *Man* new series, ii (1976), pp. 410–27 discusses the wide range of charges – traditional and modern – simultaneously included in destoolment cases.

is the possibility that in Akan societies destoolment seems to function symbolically as regicide does elsewhere.[31]

The formal causes invoked for the destoolment of a king refer to defects in the person of the king and the abuse of his power. They include his drinking in the streets, seducing other men's wives, offending his elders or calling them 'sons of slaves', bringing a deity-priest into the palace without the knowledge of the elders, walking alone at night without an attendant, travelling outside the palace without his elders' knowing where he has gone, asking for loans of money, driving the children of a former king from the palace without cause, going alone to the stool-room to pour a libation to his ancestors, failing to abdicate if he has a 'contagious' disease or if he has not begotten a child after three years. While any of these factors may be used as grounds for destoolment, they may be ignored until such time as there is enough general political support to pursue these highly disruptive procedures. For example, if he is in other respects favoured by his people and his court officials, it may be overlooked if he has committed incest, or has a minor deformity (such as a missing toe), factors that under normal circumstances would be thought to defile the ancestral stools and thus disqualify him from office. Wider government interests really only seem to have prevailed after Independence, during the period of the Convention People's Party. Offences committed by a king before his enstoolment are forgotten once he is made king: 'No one mentions them'; but if he repeats the offence once he is king, it can be made a charge for destoolment.

The rite of destoolment is the reverse of the rite of enstoolment in that the effect is to desacralise what was formerly made sacred. The destoolment of a king is brought about mainly by the *Gyaasefo*, the lesser attendants, who have this responsibility as members of the royal household. They inform the elders:

They (the *Gyaasefo*) are close to the king and know his weaknesses and secrets. They can tell the elders, before the elders get

---

[31] J. G. Frazer, *The Golden Bough: A Study in Magic and Religion* (London, 1890 and later editions) argued that regicide was central to divine kingship. See also E. E. Evans-Pritchard, *The Divine Kingship of the Shilluk of the Nilotic Sudan* (Cambridge), 1948, *Essays in Social Anthropology* (London, 1962), ch. 4; R. G. Lienhardt, *Divinity and Experience: The Religion of the Dinka* (Oxford, 1961) ch. 8; M. W. Young, 'The Divine Kingship of the Jukun: A Re-valuation of Some Theories', *Africa* xxxvi (1966), pp. 135–53 for differing perspectives on this and Gillian Feeley-Harnik's comprehensive survey of the issues in 'Issues in Divine Kingship', *Annual Review of Anthropology* xiv (1985).

reasons for removing him and then the elders bring charges against the king.

An Akan proverb asserts: 'When an insect bites you it is from your own cloth'.

First the *Ankobea* submit a report to the Queen Mother, who in turn invites the kingmakers to examine the charges. These elders go to the king in private and ask him whether what they have heard is true or not. If he denies the charge then they inform him that the Queen Mother will invite him to answer the specified charges in public. The place of assembly is the Mpeniase, the public plaza beneath a large shady tree whose roots stretch, proverbially, under every house in Akuropon. This change of place (the Santewase as the place for enstoolment, the Mpeniase for destoolment) marks the change in the king's status. As king-elect he was an ordinary man; as king he is symbolically related to the whole town.[32]

The king goes to the assembly with only a few attendants, as he is in trouble. When he arrives the *Akyeame* rise, and the *Ankobeahene* reads the charges in public. If the king can answer the charges he does so, but if he is guilty they hoot at him three times, thereby insulting him as an ordinary man, an act otherwise inconceivable towards a king. It is of utmost importance that while a king on destoolment may be personally abused, no one may curse his ancestors,[33] for it is the king, not the kingship, that is in question. The king is then told by the *Akyeamehene* ('chief of the linguists'):

> Because you are not able to defend yourself satisfactorily, therefore ... I ... am instructed to tell you that from today onwards you are no longer king. If you call yourself king, you break our great oath of Wukuda-Sokodee and you shall be killed by Gyamfi, Manteasa, Akonedi and Kofi-A-Onni-Somanka [the powerful deities of Akuapem].

Then they fire two shots from a gun.

The former king is now given an ordinary stool made of wood to sit on, not a proper chief's stool, and the elders remove the royal

---

[32] As in Asante, shady trees are associated with the concept of kingship and with the spiritual 'coolness' or peace of the whole town. The tree was 'part of the town's moral state'; See M. D. McLeod, *The Asante* (London, 1981), pp. 29–30. 'A large tree has fallen' is a common euphemism used to refer to the death of a king; similarly 'to cut a fresh leaf of the shade tree' or 'to cut a leaf from the Mpeni tree' are indirect ways of cursing the king. In Akuapem, as in Asante, the shade of a king's state umbrella is likened to the shade these trees give to the people.

[33] R. S. Rattray, *Ashanti Law and Constitution* (Oxford, 1929), p. 146.

sandals from his feet and his royal cloth. The articles of clothing worn by the king before his enstoolment are now returned to him by those *Okoman* elders (the *Asonahene* and *Kodumasehene*) who had them in safe-keeping throughout his reign. He is told, 'Now you are an ordinary person; take these and go', and his head is hit three times with the sandals.

One of his wives and one attendant are called and he is told, 'These two people are your attendants, go with them.' He is then given a knife for tapping palm wine and a pot used to collect the palm wine sap and told 'Go to the village and tap palm wine and drink.' He is not permitted to remain in the town, though he may choose to live in any village belonging to the town. He is instructed to go and 'stay quietly, without making any trouble'. Palm-wine tapping implies an isolated life in the bush, outside the town. It should be noted that they do not suggest he become a hunter: according to tradition it is the hunter who first acquires land, then founds a new town as others join him, and who then becomes the first chief or king (*ohene*).

The final phase of this rite is performed by the priest of the major town deity, Ntoa, who swears an oath against the ex-king and curses him in the names of the gods of Akuapem and elsewhere. He tells the deities to kill the destooled king if he ever acts like a king again:

Because you offended the state, if you call yourself a king or act like a king, Ntoa and other deities shall kill you.

Note that here, as in other curses, it is the deities that are called upon to kill, not the ancestors. There is thus a change from ancestral protection to the destructive force of the deities who can punish without mercy.

When the king is finally destooled, all the office bearers collect the regalia in their possession (swords, horns, drums, and so on) and hand them to the *Gyaasehene* of Akuropon who takes charge of them until a new king is enstooled.

It has happened that the people may later decide to bring back a formerly destooled king. If this occurs, all the chiefs in the state must be consulted and any former troubles between them must be smoothed out. They meet at the Mpeniase and a cleansing rite is performed. This rite is really the reversal of an oath, the priest of the deity Ntoa removing the curse placed on the former king during his destoolment. Water is brought in a large brass pan with a number of ritually significant leaves and sheep's blood, and he is cleansed. Then he is king again and he is carried in a palanquin from one end of the town to the other so that all the state knows he has been brought back. Brief mention of regicide and abdication must be made. As in most, if not all kingships, the well-being of the king symbolises the well-being of the state. If a king becomes ill, it is believed that the annual purification celebration of *Odwira* cannot be performed, and if this occurs it is thought that grave misfortune will follow, in the shape of famine, pestilence, defeat in war, and the like. Should the king become ill and should the illness persist, something must be done. Among the Shilluk and Yoruba, the sick king would be killed to save the kingship. In Akuropon, the solution is voluntary abdication, the ill king becoming again an ordinary citizen. (Two cases are known in this century of abdication due to illness.) If he becomes ill, but recovers, it is thought comparable to a king who has been to war and has then succeeded: for example, King Kwame Fori I (1880–94) who recovered from smallpox.[34] If, however, he fails to agree to abdicate, he can be removed by destoolment procedures.

While it seems very likely that there have been several cases of poisoning and what I suppose might be called assassination by believed mystical means during the twentieth century as part of dynastic intrigues,[35] I do not believe these can be considered institutionalised regicide. Nor perhaps can the traditional war-time custom of beheading one's own king in order to prevent the enemy from so doing, an event of incredible terror and power.[36]

CONCLUSION: THE PERSON OF THE KING

I have described the use of ancestral power by the living to make a king. There is not the space here to show how after his installation the king remains in continual contact with his ancestors (he feeds

---

[34] B. S. Akuffo, *Ahemfi Adesua* (Palace Teachings), 2 vols. (Exeter, 1950), i, p. 147.

[35] E. Samson, *A Short History of Akuapim and Akropong (Gold Coast). An Autobiography* (Accra, 1908) cites earlier examples of this.

[36] Beheading is never good, under any circumstances. In former days of war, the body of a slain chief was cut up and divided by the enemy, in the same way as an animal shot by a hunter, or a sacrificial beast. The head was then given to the most superior person involved – in this case to the army commander – somewhat like a trophy or souvenir. The head would then be attached to one of the king's

them and talks to them daily in the stool-house) and how at the great annual *Odwira* ritual the conjunction between his body and the ancestors is renewed by his being anointed with ancestral grave-dust. However, two questions still need to be asked: once he is transformed into a king, a sacred person, what kind of person is he and what kind of power does he have? The answers to these questions are interlinked and cannot be artificially separated.

Just as ritual performance can be dangerous because it brings together domains normally kept apart, so the king, who combines attributes of the living as well as of his ancestors, is considered dangerous as well as beneficent. Symbolically he is separated and different in quality from ordinary men, but he also partakes of all human features rather than the limited few possessed by ordinary people. In this ambiguity lies what is usually referred to as the 'sacredness' of a king.

The king is distinguished from ordinary people in many ways. One is that symbolically he does not share their limitations of time. He straddles the spheres of the living and the dead, and is given a symbolic immortality: as such he does not die.[37]

> We do not say the king has died, rather that he goes to his village. We say 'something has happened', quietly; and when you hear this, you know it is the king. When this happens the whole town becomes quiet . . .

> Ordinary people die and are dead. But the king is never dead. He is still alive. We do not talk of the death of the king. We never say that.

> We do not say the king has died. We say his *okyeame* is sick. If we say he is dead, it is almost like . . . a curse, a sacrilege.

Another difference is that the king does not occupy ordinary space in the sense that he is neither of the earth nor of the sky, the domains of people and of deities: he neither steps barefoot on the ground, nor walks without an umbrella over his head.

fontomfrom drums. When these drums are beaten, dancers grimace, mocking those whose skulls are attached to the drum. Formerly only the king danced to such drums.

[37] It is recognised that at death the king's body 'goes into the earth', but his spirit is thought to be 'still living'. This is seen in the fact that salt (which is eaten by the living) is not included in offerings to the common dead nor to deities, but is included in small amounts in offerings to the king's ancestors since they are regarded as in some ways still living and not as dead. Apparently, the spirits of the royal ancestors are somehow less remote than those of ordinary ancestors.

The king is distinguished from ordinary mortals in other ways as well. He appears neither to eat nor drink since he does these two things only in the seclusion of his private quarters in the palace. He appears neither to speak nor to hear. Because he speaks with the power of his ancestors, his words are dangerous and therefore when in public, an *okyeame* interprets his murmured words to the people and repeats their words to the king. His used bath water is thrown away by reliable attendants; were they to bathe in it afterwards it is said that it would make them too powerful to control. Finally he is distinct from ordinary people even when asleep. He is awakened by a special attendant because his ancestors are more powerful than those of ordinary people:

To wake him up, you knock at his pillow, then you turn away. You cannot make him look at your face. If he is to talk to you it must be while you are turned away. If he looks at you and you see the power in his eyes, it may hurt you, because he has been asleep with his ancestors.

Because of his sacred qualities, the king is hedged about with taboos and prohibitions of many kinds. Some of these prohibitions separate him from the polluting power of others, especially those who themselves are anomalous or ambiguous such as menstruating women, the dying and the recently dead. Others, such as the fact that a king cannot swear a fetish oath, may reflect the separation of ancestors and deities, though it is said to be because the king should be tolerant and forebearing, not harsh and intolerant. In general, the king must keep himself in a state of physical perfection, as an outward sign of his moral perfection and of the proper conjunction of his two bodies, the 'natural' and the 'politic'.

At the same time that he is given symbolic attributes that are different from those of ordinary people, the king becomes the only person who is given the characteristics of all men. The talking drum says

King, part of you is *odum* (a hard tree; *Chlorophora excelsa* or *C. regia*)
part of you is *ɔnyaa* (a soft tree; *Ceiba pentandra*)
part of you is *ɔfetefrɛ* (a strong tree; *Bussea occidentalia*)
part of you is *akakapenpen* (a brittle tree; *Voacanaa africana*)

That is to say, that part of him is angry, part forgiving, part tactful, and part aggressive. The king is said to be able to do the impossible: 'He can remove a ring through his shoulder.'

However great his power, expressed in his unique differences from ordinary people, he can exercise it only in the form of authority. This is defined and legitimated by the various rites of enstoolment. But its abuse is limited and indeed prevented in several ways. He cannot rule alone, he is surrounded by ritual prohibitions that he cannot break, and finally he can be destooled. No matter how respected and feared, the king should continually consult his elders; if he reigns arrogantly and dictatorially, he will lose support and there may be plots to destool him. To prevent this and to gain supporters, he may create new positions or give added favours, such as allowing lesser officials to ride in palanquins. He may also attempt to destool or cancel the power of the stools of elders who oppose him.

> In the old days he could do that. He could even execute a stool occupant. These days, each step must be well thought out, otherwise the others' lawyers may get hold of him and he will find his action is of no use, and then he would be disgraced . . .

The people have a number of ways to show their lack of support, but the simplest is by the withdrawal of services. Someone offered a vacant post may fail to take up the duties, and the 'stool will be left vacant'. Or an elder may show his opposition by not attending the ritual and political functions at the palace. Each ritual official is conscious of the fact that without his services the palace rites could not be held properly. Much public opposition today and probably in the past is shown by non-verbal manipulation of royal and ritual symbols, such as provocative and disrespectful gestures and proverbs expressed in dances, public processions or the display of particular regalia in the capital which should properly only be shown in the lesser towns. There is also, always, an enormous amount of gossip and telling of moralistic folk-tales.

A final question is that of the relationship between the king's qualities and office and the cohesion of the entire kingdom. I mentioned above that Akuapem is an extremely heterogeneous state, formed after conquest by an immigrant minority. The effectiveness of the 'system' is shown by the facts that secession attempts have always been unsuccessful, and that despite disputes over land and office between towns of Guan- and Twi-speakers, it is never seriously questioned that the king of Akuapem is king as of right, and that he reigns because of the mystical powers vested in his office. The royal Black Stools hold the power and the incumbent ancestors bestow it on particular kings and thereby legitimate them. The Black Stools were carried to war as the loci of the mystical power of the nation (the *abosom*, deities, did not go to war), and so it is through them that the Akyem came to Akuapem, defeated the Akwamu, and established the kingship over the Guan. The facts that the control of royal ritual and so of the expression of royal ancestral power is basically in the hands of the *Ankobea* in the capital town and that belief in the necessity for royal rites to be performed immaculately are important. By these means both the continuity and legitimacy of royal ancestral power vested in the king and also the sense of identity and continuity of the ruling group are legitimated. By the believed immaculateness of rites which, even if they may in actuality change in detail over time, are accepted as being the same as those of the early eighteenth century as well as of an immemorial Akan tradition, the kingship is seen as standing above continual local disputes and intrigues. These rites are the contemporary expression of a timeless myth. The importance of destoolment and symbolic regicide lies here also. Any threat to the state that could come from the loss of moral purity on the part of the king can be dealt with immediately and within the bounds of tradition; even though stool disputes are endemic, there is a traditional means to resolve them that is effective and allows for the continuity of the reign. It is never forgotten that it is because of the state that the king is powerful, without the state he is nothing: as the talking drum says, 'It is the river that makes the fish proud.'

Index

Page numbers in *italics* refer to illustrations or their captions

331

bishops, Frankish, *see* Frankish clergy
Black Stools of Akuapem, Ghana, 12,
16, 299; anointing of, 306, 308,
317–18; choosing of stool by
king-elect, 317; creation of, 299,
307, 308–9; lowering of king onto,
318–19; removal of, in times of
chaos, 307; as reservoir of power,
299, 305–9, 318, 319, 330; sacrifice
to, 306, 308–9; stool-house, 305–6,
309, 312, 316–17, 319, 323, 327; *see
also* enstoolment
blessing, 34, 38, 154; *see also* bath,
royal ritual of
'Blues' and 'Greens', Byzantine ritual
performers, 112, 114, 127
board of rites, T'ang, 209–10; bureau
of sacrifices, 209, 224
body, imagery of, 237–8, 246, 247–8,
267–9; 'two bodies of king', 5, 11,
175, 318–19, 328
body politic, *see* Nepalese kings
Bonus, Byzantine patrician, 133
Book of Ceremonies, Byzantine, 9,
106, 109, 110–19, 130, 132, 133, 136;
chronological context, 122–9;
structure, 110–12
Book of Documents, T'ang, 220
Borsippa, Babylonia, 28, 33
boundary witnesses, Nepalese, 246
Brahma, Hindu deity, 237, 238, 254
Brahmanical codes of conduct, 241,
242 n.2, 243, 244, 246, 247, 252–3
Brahmans, 245, 247–8, 251;
relationship between Nepalese king
and, 237–8, 247–8, 254, 257; royal
gifts of land to, 241, 246, 253–4, 255,
257
Britain, British, 5, 241, 274, 301, 309;
monarchy, 7, 14, 16, 17 n.20, 129,
130, 185, 234; *see also* England
Buddhism, Buddhists, 186–7, 222, 223,
224, 233, 260
building programmes, royal, 10, 37,
46, 47, 49, 50–1, 134, 227–8
bull, sacrificial, 33, 52, 90
Bullough, Donald, 156
bureaucracy, 122–3, 131, 132, 136; *see
also* palace officials; T'ang
bureaucracy
Burgundians, 141, 147, 149
burial, *see* cremation; inhumation;
mausolea; tombs

Byzantine court ritual, 106–36 *passim*,
142–3; aim of impressing foreigners,
118, 119–20; continuity of, 109,
121–2, 129, 136; development and
innovation, 120, 125–6, 127, 129,
136; level of, in 10th century,
118–22; and legitimation of imperial
power, 118, 124, 135; and
reinforcement of official hierarchy,
122–3, 130; religious aspect, 111–17,
133–5; as representation of divine
and imperial harmony, 118, 122,
135–6; roots in Roman ritual, 107,
109, 125, 127, 133, 136; union of
secular and religious elements, 113,
117, 118; *see also* acclamation; *Book
of Ceremonies*
Byzantine emperors: claims of divine
election and protection, 107, 122,
124, 135; coronation, 127; depiction
in art and literature, 107, 133, 134–5;
power of, 123, 131, 135, 165;
relations with church, 123–4, 125,
126, 133–5, 136; relations with
office-holding class, 123, 125, 130,
131, 136; relations with populace,
129–30; role in liturgical ritual,
111–17, 126
Byzantium, 9, 106–36, 156, 157, 168,
171; aristocracy, 116, 117; art and
literature, 106–7, 122, 128, 132, 133,
134–5; collapse of urban structure,
127–8, 131; dynamic or static
society?, 13, 106–9, 132, 136;
Macedonian dynasty, 128, 134, 135;
and Rome, 100, 108, 131, 135; zeal
for codification, 119, 123, 126, 130,
132, 136; *see also* Byzantine court
ritual; Byzantine emperors

Caesar, Gaius, 63, 80
Caesar, Julius, 57, 75; deification, 8,
70, 71–3, 74, 76, 77, 79, 83; funeral,
64, 72, 78, 83; temple to, 78
Caesar, Lucius, 63, 70, 80
Caesar, title, 98, 124
calm, imperial, notion of, 107
Cambyses, king of Persia and Babylon,
51
Campus Martius, Rome, 67, 69, 70,
75; role in imperial funerals, 59, 60,
61, 68, 78, 82, 83
Candra, Hindu moon goddess, 253

Past and Present Publications

General Editor: PAUL SLACK, *Exeter College, Oxford*

Family and Inheritance: Rural Society in Western Europe 1200–1800, edited
  by Jack Goody, Joan Thirsk and E. P. Thompson*
French Society and the Revolution, edited by Douglas Johnson
Peasants, Knights and Heretics: Studies in Medieval English Social History,
  edited by R. H. Hilton*
Towns in Societies: Essays in Economic History and Historical Sociology,
  edited by Philip Abrams and E. A. Wrigley*
*Desolation of a City: Coventry and the Urban Crisis of the Late Middle
  Ages*, Charles Phythian-Adams
*Puritanism and Theatre: Thomas Middleton and Opposition Drama under
  the Early Stuarts*, Margot Heinemann*
*Lords and Peasants in a Changing Society: The Estates of the Bishopric of
  Worcester 680–1540*, Christopher Dyer
*Life, Marriage and Death in a Medieval Parish: Economy, Society and
  Demography in Halesowen 1270–1500*, Zvi Razi
Biology, Medicine and Society 1840–1940, edited by Charles Webster
The Invention of Tradition, edited by Eric Hobsbawm and Terence
  Ranger*
*Industrialization before Industrialization: Rural Industry and the Genesis of
  Capitalism*, Peter Kriedte, Hans Medick and Jürgen Schlumbohm†*
*The Republic in the Village: The People of the Var from the French
  Revolution to the Second Republic*, Maurice Agulhon†
Social Relations and Ideas: Essays in Honour of R. H. Hilton, edited by
  T. H. Aston, P. R. Coss, Christopher Dyer and Joan Thirsk
*A Medieval Society: The West Midlands at the End of the Thirteenth
  Century*, R. H. Hilton
Winstanley: 'The Law of Freedom' and Other Writings, edited by Christo-
  pher Hill
Crime in Seventeenth-Century England: A County Study, J. A. Sharpe†
*The Crisis of Feudalism: Economy and Society in Eastern Normandy c.
  1300–1500*, Guy Bois†
The Development of the Family and Marriage in Europe, Jack Goody
Disputes and Settlements: Law and Human Relations in the West, edited by
  John Bossy
Rebellion, Popular Protest and the Social Order in Early Modern England,
  edited by Paul Slack
Studies on Byzantine Literature of the Eleventh and Twelfth Centuries,
  Alexander Kazhdan in collaboration with Simon Franklin†
The English Rising of 1381, edited by R. H. Hilton and T. H. Aston*

Praise and Paradox: Merchants and Craftsmen in Elizabethan Popular Literature, Laura Caroline Stevenson
The Brenner Debate: Agrarian Class Structure and Economic Development in Pre-Industrtial Europe, edited by T. H. Aston and C. H. E. Philpin*
Eternal Victory: Triumphal Rulership in Late Antiquity, Byzantium, and the Early Medieval West, Michael McCormick†
East-Central Europe in Transition: From the Fourteenth to the Seventeenth Century, edited by Antoni Mączak, Henryk Samsonowicz and Peter Burke†
Small Books and Pleasant Histories: Popular Fiction and its Readership in Seventeenth-Century England, Margaret Spufford**
Society, Politics and Culture: Studies in Early Modern England, Mervyn James
Horses, Oxen and Technological Innovation: The Use of Draught Animals in English Farming 1066–1500, John Langdon
Nationalism and Popular Protest in Ireland, edited by C. H. E. Philpin
Rituals of Royalty: Power and Ceremonial in Traditional Societies, edited by David Cannadine and Simon Price
The Margins of Society in Late Medieval Paris, Bronisław Geremek†
Landlords, Peasants and Politics in Medieval England, edited by T. H. Aston

* Published also as a paperback
** Published only as a paperback
† Co-published with the Maison des Sciences de l'Homme, Paris